Innovation and Change in School:
History, Politics and Agency

Book 3 of the T
Anatomy of Educatɪ
A Mid to Lor.
Re-study and Rɛ

Explorations in Ethnography Series

Series Editors: Stephen J. Ball (King's College, London) and Ivor Goodson (University of Western Ontario).

During the past ten years ethnographic research has begun to flourish in studies of education and schooling. On the basis of a handful of classic British and American investigations a broad and diverse field has been established. The primary concern with describing social events and processes in detail has won acceptance for ethnography from policy-makers and practitioners. The methods and analytical techniques of ethnographic research are now established on a more rigorous basis. A set of firm methodological principles are being established which allow for the evaluation and comparison of ethnographies.

In this series we shall be attempting to collect together high quality ethnographies, which blend descriptive clarity with analytical insight. While drawing upon a variety of specialist areas within and outside of mainstream education we shall aim to reflect issues and topics of major contemporary concern. Australian, British, European and North American work will be represented.

Book 1   Educational Innovators: Then and Now

Book 2   The Fate of an Innovative School. The History and Present Status of the Kensington School

Book 3   Innovation and Change in Schooling: History, Politics and Agency

A trilogy Written by Louis M. Smith, Paul F. Kleine, John J. Prunty, and David C. Dwyer.

Explorations in Ethnography Series

Innovation and Change in Schooling: History, Politics, and Agency

Louis M. Smith
Washington University

David C. Dwyer
Apple Computer Company

John J. Prunty
Maritz Communications Company

Paul F. Kleine
University of Oklahoma

 The Falmer Press

(A Member of the Taylor & Francis Group)
New York, Philadelphia and London

UK	The Falmer Press, Falmer House, Barcombe, Lewes, East Sussex, BN8 5DL
USA	The Falmer Press, Taylor & Francis Inc., 242 Cherry Street, Philadelphia, PA 19106-1906

Copyright © L. M. Smith, P. E. Kleine, J. J. Prunty and D. C. Dwyer 1988

First published 1988

Library of Congress Cataloging in Publication Data

Innovation and change in schooling: history, politics, and
    agency/Louis M. Smith . . . [et al.].
        p. cm. — (Explorations in ethnography series: 3)

    Bibliography: p.
    Includes index.
    1. School districts—United States—Administration. 2. School
management and organization—United States. 3. Educational
innovations—United States. I. Smith, Louis M. (Louis Milde).
II. Series: Exploration in ethnography series: v. 3.
LB2817.156 1987 379.1′535′0973—dc 19 87-33036
ISBN 1-85000-360-2
ISBN 1-85000-361-0 (pbk.)

Jacket design by Caroline Archer

Typeset in 10/12 Bembo by
Imago Publishing Ltd, Thame, Oxon

Printed in Great Britain by Taylor & Francis (Printers) Ltd, Basingstoke

Contents

Contents

Figures

Preface

Now in the final stages of our study of school innovation, we find ourselves, once more stating our intentions as afterthoughts of what we have wrought. This book, *Innovation and Change in Schooling: History, Politics, and Agency*, is intended for school policy makers: administrators, board members, teachers, patrons, and citizens. And it is intended for those of us in the Universities who train teachers and administrators and who do research and theorizing on the nature of schooling.

Our focus on the anatomy of educational innovation and change is clarified by the early admonition of C. Wright Mills (1959) that no social study is ever completed until it deals with history, biography, and social structure. We present here a sixty-five year history of Milford, a particular school district. In the course of our presentation we place one Superintendent, Steven Spanman, and one major innovation, the creation of the innovative Kensington Elementary School, in the context of the four other superintendents of schools who preceded and succeeded him, and the array of changes that have occurred over the sixty-five years in the Milford School District. We believe that this is a unique and potent view of innovation and change in schooling.

A further try for uniqueness and potency comes from the fact that this is the third book of a series. The first, *Educational Innovators: Then and Now* is a biographical and life history account of the original faculty and administration of the Kensington School and the Milford School District. We described and analyzed their early history before they arrived in Milford, and then we traced their subsequent careers and life histories over the fifteen years after they opened the Kensington School in 1964–65. The second book in the series, we called *The Fate of an Innovative School: The History and Present Status of the Kensington School*. The tenure of its four principals was anchored by an ethnography of its first year, 1964–65, and of the fifteenth year, 1979–80. Interviews and documents spoke to the intervening years. Each book stands alone and each book presents alternative perspectives on the anatomy of innovation and change in schooling.

The *Trilogy* is a 'thicker description' of the phenomenon of educational innovation that began with our first study of the Kensington School which we called, *Anatomy of Educational Innovation: An Organizational Analysis of an Elementary*

School (Smith and Keith, 1971). As we argue throughout, it is not as though we had it 'wrong' in the earlier account, but that there was more to tell, both descriptively and analytically. We have now done that. Hopefully it will be as instructive to others as it has been to us.

Among the many people who contributed to our work we can mention only a few. First and foremost are the teachers, administrators, and patrons of the Milford Schools. Their cooperation and their tolerance were unbounded. In the development of this volume, Superintendent Ronald George, a social studies teacher and historian by training, stands as a paramount supportive figure and symbolizes the best of the relationships between outside inquirers and busy school personnel. In an earlier era, Superintendent Steven Spanman played a similar role. As different as each is, they transcended their immediate role and seemed to enjoy the intellectual thrust of our attempts for understanding. We are very grateful to them and their colleagues.

At Washington University's Department of Education, where the project was located, we have consistently received support from our colleagues, who listened to us and who read drafts of papers and chapters, and from the several deans, directors, and chairs who were caught in the multitude of administrative problems and details of a large, long term project. It has been almost ten years since we first began to think about 'Kensington Revisited,' our early label for the project.

Our project officer at NIE, Fritz Mulhauser, saw what we were trying to do and helped in so many ways. He remains our image of the best of public service — intelligent, caring, and resourceful. In recent years, as the final report became a trilogy of books, our thanks goes to Ivor Goodson and Malcolm Clarkson of Falmer Press, who also saw what we were trying to do and who were willing to gamble on the publication of three books. Our two secretaries, Sandi Stritzel early and John Pingree later, can realize our indebtedness in a way no one else can. The steps from original drafts, to a myriad of colloquium and symposium presentations, to long and overdue final reports, to three books is a long litter-strewn road. A final perspective is shared by our wives, Marilyn, Becky, Joni, and Eilene. They, too, managed to survive it all.

As the exhaustion of that final survival begins to fade, the joys of being on to socially important and difficult intellectual problems, with colleagues of many years, in a context of intellectual and academic freedom rise up. Among the many ways one might choose to live we find this to be among the best.

LMS
DCD
JJP
PFK

Prologue, Problem, and Method: A Perspective

Chapter 1

The Drama of School Change

The Vagaries of Research Problems

Some years ago we had the opportunity to study the first year in the life of the innovative Kensington Elementary School[1]. This turned out to be an exciting intellectual experience which we called, *Anatomy of Educational Innovation* (Smith and Keith, 1971). We played out, from intensive ethnographic observation, a descriptive and analytical account of that first year of its life. Now, after fifteen years we have 'revisited,' gone back to this school, to see the mid to long term consequences of the Kensington experiment and to determine how the school had fared, over this decade and a half. This book is an outgrowth of that project, 'Kensington Revisited: A Fifteen Year Follow Up of an Innovative School and Its Faculty.'

In the course of that study, from conversations and interviews with current members of the staff and district patrons and from reading various accounts of the District, we were puzzled by the anomaly of an ultra modern, radical school being built in what seemed like a very conservative community and school district. Why was the Kensington School built in the Milford School District? At the time of that puzzlement another fortuitous event occurred. While reading the Milford School District *Bulletins* from the early 1950s we stumbled on to what seemed like a major conflict between the then Superintendent McBride and the President of the School Board. A casual conversation with the current Superintendent (as he was walking past where we were working in the Central Administration Building) raised the interpretation that 'Yes, there was a big fight in the early 1950s and McBride almost lost his job.' The observer made a brief note of the conversation and went back to reading the *Bulletins*. A few minutes later the Superintendent returned with a large bound book opened to the pages where the President of the School Board, Mr Lewis, had inserted several pages of 'charges,' essentially an attack on the ability and responsiveness of Superintendent McBride. This thick black book was one year of bound 'minutes' of the Board of Education, the legal record of the Milford School District. To the observer's question, 'Are there more of these?' the Superintendent said 'Yes, a whole closet full.' And to the immediate follow-up, 'Can I look at them?', he replied, 'Sure'. So began a long trek into the sixty-five year history of the Milford School District.

The guiding questions became, first, 'Why was the Kensington School built in the first place?' and second, 'What is the relationship between the Kensington innovation, as specific intentional planned change, and more general change in a school district?' These seemed to be worthwhile and powerful extensions of the original problem posed in our proposal, 'Kensington Revisited: A Fifteen Year Follow-up of an Innovative School and Its Faculty' (Smith, 1977).

To set the problems, the questions, and some of the themes which will follow, it seems appropriate to begin with one of the most potent stories from these records, what we came to call, 'The tangle of administrative succession.' This story seems prototypical of our thesis: history, politics, and agency in educational innovation and change, unusual only in that so many of the issues occur in such a short period of time and with considerable drama. The story was a startling revelation when we first encountered it. It provoked much of the analysis and interpretation of educational innovation and change that follows in this book.

The Tangle of Administrative Succession

Introduction

In a fundamental sense, the 1961–62 year was not only the end of the McBride Era, it was also the beginning of the era of his successor, Steven Spanman, Unbeknownst to anyone at the time, it was the beginning of a still later period, as well. For any theoretical model of innovation and change, the year is perhaps the most significant one in the history of the school district. Consequently, in our attempt at conceptualizing it is most critical. We go back to the Board minutes of July 1961 and tell the story in more detail. Into this we weave the CTA (Community Teachers Association) action and the two strands that take us out of the district to NEA (the National Education Association) and to the two highly visible consultants. Finally we return to a significant 3–3 tie vote in the Board on the attempted firing of a teacher.

The District Crucible: 1961–62

The Board's Action. On 11 July 1961, the Board met at 7 p.m. and went into executive session at 7:05. The first item (No. 3822) in the minutes:

> Mr. Osborn moved that the Board request Mr. McBride to submit his resignation as Superintendent of Schools. Mr. Henderson seconded the motion. *The motion carried unanimously.* (Our italics)

3

Mr. McBride was informed of the Board's action by Mr. Tompkins and the reasons the request was considered to be in the best interests of the School District. Mr. McBride asked for time to consider the motion and the request was granted with further action delayed until later this meeting. (7/11/61)

The Board then continued its activities, which had been started in April, of stripping the Superintendent of his formal duties. Then, the Assistant Superintendent had been put in charge of the instructional program and certificated personnel. He was instructed to report directly to the Board. Now, the Business Official was instructed to report directly to the Board on some eight functions, ranging from purchasing and distribution of all supplies to the execution of all phases of new construction. The motion also carried unanimously.

At 2:50 a.m., executive session was declared once again and the following minute was recorded:

> The Board asked Mr. McBride for his decision on the matter raised by the motion in No. 3822 above. Mr. McBride said that he had considered the request for resignation, but that he would not resign, basing his decision on the fact that approximately \$38,000[2] would be coming to him under his present contract. Whereupon, Mr. Henderson moved, in order to improve working relations among members of the administrative and instructional staffs, that Superintendent McBride be directed to act exclusively as advisor to the Board in such fields of educational policy and practice as might be assigned to him from time to time by the Board; that the Business Official and the Assistant Superintendent in charge of Instruction continue to discharge those responsibilities of direct operation of business and educational affairs that have been heretofore assigned them by the Board, that all of the above personnel report directly to the Board of Education and discharge any specific directives hereafter made to them and that office, stenographic and secretarial facilities be adjusted under the direction of the Board to reflect the changes in volume and nature of work that will occur under this reorganization of the detailed duties of the principal administrative officers of the district. The motion was seconded by Mr. Osborn and was carried unanimously. (7/61)

The meeting adjourned at 3 a.m.

The next meeting occurred six weeks later on 29 August 1961, the week before the autumn school term began. The minutes note that 'Also present was a citizen's group of approximately 115 people.' For Milford, this was a large turnout. After some preliminary general business the Board President introduced the Board Members, Administrators and school attorney to the audience. He then read a four page single space 'Statement on Changes in Administrative Setup' (No. 3868). Mostly he raised the issues we have already reported on, but he provided a context important for a number of issues in our analysis:

In reviewing the functions of the Board of Education, we find that under Midwest State Law, the Board is given the power to make all needful rules and regulations for the organization, grading and government of the school district. The law gives the Board a wide discretionary authority and actually the only basic requirement is the exercise of good judgment within the framework of the applicable statutes and court decisions. (8/29/61)

He then specified the financial aspects and professional aspects of Board activity and the need for confidence in the administrators to whom the responsibilities have been delegated. When the 'Board loses confidence in the administrator's ability and good judgment' it must take action in what is a 'difficult' and 'most unpleasant' duty. The Board President, Mr. Tompkins, made this specification of problems:

We recognize the long service Mr. McBride has given to Milford and this made the decision doubly hard. But this district has had an explosive student population growth in the last ten years, and we believe Mr. McBride cannot cope with the modern educational problems which confront us. No secrecy surrounds this action, but also there is no sensationalism in the fact that a man is no longer capable of dealing with the problems involved in a highly complex employment.

We believe that Mr. McBride is not now providing the necessary leadership as Superintendent which our teachers, our parents, and our students have a right to expect and in our collective opinions, he is incapable of providing such leadership in the future. He has failed to implement the desired policies and procedures of the Board. In fact, he has attempted to thwart these at every opportunity. His failure to cooperate with the desired changes has indeed been detrimental to the School District and has resulted in a lack of unity, harmony, and confidence on all subordinate levels.

The President indicated that this was neither a Summer phenomenon, nor a partisan political action since the April elections. Rather four of the current Board, who had voted for the three year contract eighteen months before '. . . have since realized that it should not have been given.'

After the presentation, the Board opened the meeting for discussion, questions and answers. These items were to be part of the official minutes. The meeting adjourned at 1:30 a.m. No record of this discussion appears. At the next regular meeting, they voted to delete the notes because of their incomplete nature. We have been unable to find any extant record of this discussion.

The CTA Action and Aftermath On 6 September 1961 the Milford Community Teachers Association, CTA, passed the following resolution:

Be it moved by the Milford Community Teachers Association that the Suburban County Teachers Association, the Midwest State Teachers Association, and the National Educational Association be asked to set up a fact-finding group which would study the current controversial situation

5

existing between the Board of Education and the Superintendent of Milford School District.

Such group to act as *impartial fact-finder and to submit a report of its findings and recommend actions* to the Board of Education, the Superintendent, the Staff, and the Community. (Our italics)

A copy of the motion and an accompanying letter dated 11 September 1962 was sent to the President of the Board. The letter indicated it had passed by an 'overwhelming majority.' It concluded with the sentence: 'We trust that you will hear from each of these organizations soon and will accept this resolution in the spirit in which it is offered.' The letter carried the signature of Ronald George, President of the CTA. The Board read the letter and acknowledged its receipt on this meeting of 12 September.

In the Board minutes, the next item in the controversy appeared in late October, the 24th, in the form of a motion by the Milford School Board to send a night letter to Mr. Leckey and Mr. Norman of the NEA Professional Rights Committee with copies to the CTA, Suburban and State Teachers organizations and all school administrators, principals, and local newspapers. The three page telegram began with a direct challenge:

> It has been brought to the attention of the Milford Board of Education that you will be in Central City on November 8th 'to make a preliminary study of the situation in Milford.' Unfortunately, all actions taken by your organization and the local association have come before the Board only through releases to the press or through verifaxed copies of correspondence between parties who have not seen fit to keep the Board apprised of actions being taken. These actions directly affect the educational system which is the primary responsibility of our local Board of Education.
>
> Let me state that we do not recognize the existence of any controversy between the Board and the Superintendent ...

Seven paragraphs then laid out the Board's perception of the situation, its responsibilities, and the courses of action open to the various parties. The concluding paragraph encapsuled their stance:

> To summarize our position, we do not recognize the existence of any controversy; we believe it is presumptuous for anyone or any group to attempt an independent investigation of the confidential relationship existing between the Superintendent and the Board of Education; we feel your committee is attempting to intervene in a situation which is not a part of the present relationship existing between the teachers, the administrators, and the Board of Education. While we have had no official request from you, but only the copy of a letter addressed to Mr. George and his unaddressed and unsigned request for a meeting place to be provided, we believe that no school property can be made available to you, that no subsidized time of district personnel can be provided and that there can be no official cooperation by the Board of Education with your committee.

Let me add however that, if you so request, we will convene a special meeting of the Board of Education to meet with you and further explain the foregoing position which we, of necessity, have taken. (10/24/61) (Our italics)

As a motion, the letter was seconded and carried unanimously. The Board adjourned at 2:05 a.m.

Internal Board Strife. On Tuesday 7 November 1961 the Board met in a special session at 3:00 p.m. with most of the Milford administrators, principals, and teachers. Mr. Thompkins opened with a five page statement. A fifty-five page transcript of the proceedings, prepared by stenotype reporters became a permanent part of the Board minutes. The meeting adjourned at 5:25 p.m.

The context of the proceedings sketch the complexity of the 'problem.' Immediately after Mr. Tompkins' initial remark as President of the Board, he commented:

There have been rumors, I know, that there has been a division among members of the Board partly upon the fact that a suit is presently pending between myself and Mr. Quigley[3] and at this time, in the context and for the reasons I have indicated, I wish to recognize Mr. Quigley to speak to the meeting of existing relationships among Board members.

Present day staff of the district who were present at the time recall the meeting as a public humiliation of Mr. Quigley, a forced apology to settle the law suit which Mr. Tomplins had brought. Mr. Quigley's words, at the time, were these:

Members of the Board have criticized my judgment on some issues and I, in turn have criticized them. I have disagreed with our Board President in his position on certain school matters and have expressed my criticism on public occasions, and I know he has likewise disagreed with me and criticized me. However, no Board member, to my knowledge, and certainly not I, have ever intended any difference of opinion or critical expression to be a reflection on any individual personally as distinguished from his official action nor to reflect upon his integrity or character. Specifically, the statements made by me at the Teachers Appreciation Dinner were not intended to in any way question the personal integrity of Mr. Tompkins and I regret that my remarks were phrased in such a manner as to possibly have created that impression.

Mr. Tompkins then commented:

... In line with the statement Mr. Quigley has made, particularly those that indicate no personal slights have been intended, wish to say now that the pending legal claim will be dismissed. (11/7/61)

We do not have any base rate data on the number of lawsuits filed between school board members now or twenty years ago. We assume that it is a reasonably rare event.

The Board's Stance with the Professional Staff. The meeting which contained the item of internal strife intended more generally to clarify the relationship between the Board and teachers in the context of the particular incident, the termination of McBride's tenure as Superintendent. Mr. Tompkins' formal statement as expressed in the following half dozen items:

1 Recognition of professional status of the teaching staff
2 Staff entitled to full support of the Board
3 Full support of professional activities and individual advancement
4 Free speech without fear
5 Full support for adequate salary levels and taxes under-girding them
6 Encourage individual professional advancement and proper intellectual climate
7 Teachers and administrators must participate in public relations and explain their work and program
8 The Board is the policy making group

These were amplified with brief paragraphs, long illustrations, and commentary.

In the later discussion, in response to a question by a staff member, no doubt appeared in the Board President's view of final authority and power:

> You are a teacher in one of the grade — elementary or high schools, between there you report directly to your principal who in turn is responsible to a supervisory principal, who in turn is responsible to the superintendent, who in turn is responsible to the Board of Education. (11/7/61)

As the meeting continued, positive comments were made by the staff about the Board's meeting with NEA officials. Also comments appeared about some internal Community Teachers Association concerns for the rapidity, if not hastiness, of the CTA action and the lack of advance notice to CTA members. The Board President adroitly stayed out of the possible entanglement in the internal affairs of the CTA. At several points he indicated that the CTA organization belonged to the teachers: '... the Board does not want to enter into the province of your association, this we feel is entirely up to you as professional people'. (11/7/61) For fear of suit and because no legal statutes demanded it, the Board refused to give reasons for its actions. The teachers were told only that the decision was unanimous. Actually, according to the Board President, the state statutes demand all personnel discussions to be in the privacy of executive session. The discussion ended with some residual unhappy remarks by teachers regarding the Board's action.

No record appears in the minutes of the Board's 'unofficial meeting' with the NEA representatives. The semester wore on and reports and policy statements on discipline and college study were reviewed. Community College developments and constitutional revisions for Midwest State School Boards Association appeared. The episode seemed almost to end by falling into a void.

In late November a letter and report arrived. In early December the Board met.

The NEA Action. The quarrel between Tompkins, the President of the Board, and Quigley, a long time Board member and former Board President, indicates the depth of feeling, the severity of the conflict, and the tremendous tangle of issues, events and personalities involved in any major political action. But it was Ron George and the CTA's earlier action which propelled, for the first time, outside forces into Milford and its day to day affairs. We return to our story with a set of questions.

When a decision to hire a new superintendent is made several questions come to mind. Why a new Superintendent? Why now? and Why this particular individual? Each instance has its own special circumstances, and, as our narrative shows, this seems true of McBride's 'departure' and Spanman's 'joining' the Milford District. The story continues to play in and out of the minutes of the Board of Education. The casual reader, as well as the serious inquirer might find a long ten page memo and an accompanying letter in late November, 1961, a vivid point to return to. The letter was directed to Mr. Everett Tompkins, President of the Milford Board of Education by Sterling Leckey, Chairman of the NEA Commission on Professional Rights and Responsibilities. The central substantive paragraph carried the tenor of the remarks:

> As emphasized in the statement, we hope you will recognize the need for deliberate action by both sides in the proposals made. The undignified treatment to which Mr. McBride has been submitted does not affect him as an individual alone, — it is considered an affront to all the professional personnel in the school system. Under the circumstances the Board of Education has nothing to lose and considerable to gain in finding a solution to the situation that will remove a good deal of bitterness from the present conditions and make possible an immediate step toward a more wholesome administrative situation. (PD[4] 11/19/61)

Copies of the report went also to 1) the Superintendent, 2) the Suburban Teachers Association, 3) the Milford CTA, and 4) the Midwest State Teachers Association. The Board unanimously voted that the CTA may distribute copies to all teachers and others, 'the same as the Official Minutes are now distributed'. The multiple constituencies in the community, already involved, continued to be informed.

The section of the report entitled 'Treatment of Superintendent' states the problem, as perceived by the Commission. We present this section in its entirety:

> On 7 April 1961, three days after the election of three men without previous board experience, the Milford School District Board of Education unanimously agreed that the Assistant Superintendent should report directly to the Board on items concerning curriculum and certified personnel. Until this time, it has always been the responsibility of the Superintendent of Schools to inform the Board concerning such matters. It is a surprising thing that an important decision of this nature, with such severe overtones, would be taken by the Board without more first hand knowledge acquired by official contact with the Superintendent over a reasonable period of time.

Three months later, on 11 July the Board, by unanimous vote, requested the resignation of the Superintendent. The Superintendent refused to comply. In a statement released at a subsequent meeting, the Board President stated that the resignation had been requested because the Superintendent 'had failed to carry out Board policies and procedures and had attempted to thwart them at every opportunity.' No specific examples of failures or resistance to Board wishes were stated.

At that time, twenty-four months remained on the contract which the previous Board had issued to the Superintendent. The Board, having been advised that it was questionable whether Midwest State law would permit the 'buying up' of the contract, made what it considered a reasonable monetary offer to induce the Superintendent to resign, but the offer was considerably less than the sum the Superintendent would realize from the full performance of the contract. When the Superintendent refused to accept the offer, the Board reassigned the duties of the Superintendent to other administrators. Both parties have remained adamant in their position on this matter since that time.

It was not the purpose of this inquiry to determine whether or not the Superintendent was capable of performing his total responsibilities. It appears to many members of the professional staff and to many citizens, however, that it is nothing short of tragic for a man who has devoted twenty-six years of service to the school system to end his career under extremely embarrassing and unhappy conditions. No information was presented from any source to indicate that there had been any dramatic change in the personality of the Superintendent or any abrupt loss of professional, mental, or physical ability that would warrant such contemptuous treatment of the chief administrative officer of the school system.

The persons conducting this inquiry do not question the sincerity of the Board of Education in their desire to strengthen the administration of the Milford School System. We do, however, question the choice of alternatives in dealing with the situation and deplore the indignity to which an important member of the school staff was submitted. It is to be expected that many members of the faculty of the schools would suffer a great loss of confidence in the judgment and good will of the Board, as well as the likelihood of proper professional treatment for themselves as a result of the Board's action in regard to the Superintendent.

The Superintendent's refusal to accept the Board's offer of partial settlement of the contract in view of the substantial amount due him under his contract is certainly reasonable. To the extent he has accepted conditions not to his liking in order to prevent excessive turmoil in the school system he is to be commended. It is to be hoped that the Board and the community will find a means to bring about a solution of the present situation that will restore confidence, that will be satisfactory to the members of the teaching profession, and which, should the resignation or termination be effective, would be reassuring to anyone who may succeed him in the position of Superintendent of Schools. (PD 11/61)

The Commission developed several lines of argument which sketched out the breadth and depth of the problem. We merely list them with brief comment:

1 'the controversy ... has reached a stage where no simple solution is possible.'
2 '... all parties to the dispute must be willing to make concessions, adjustments and sincere conciliatory efforts'
3 The teachers have developed 'doubt and uncertainty' concerning possible arbitrary board action to anyone who disagrees.
4 The long term difficulties in 'a system of multiple unit administrative control' and the tendency for board members 'to personally assume administrative responsibilities.'
5 The longer the conditions prevail the more difficult the resolutions.
6 The need to take a series of interlocking actions.

Several aspects of an overall solution were raised in the report. In the following we mix quotes and paraphrases:

1 Development of a Policy Manual applicable to all administrators, supervisors, and teachers.
2 One part would be 'a set of approved personnel policies, including particularly a Fair Dismissal Policy.' The latter would include written notice, an opportunity for improvement, and a hearing before final action.
3 Involvement of Board members, administrators, and teachers in the process.
4 Establish an office of Senior Consultant to the Board, equal in salary and coterminous with current contract.
5 '... secure the best qualified person available for the position of Superintendent of Schools. In view of the deep seated emotions that have developed over the present situation, it would be well to endeavor to find someone who has not been in any way involved in the present difficulties.'
6 The new Superintendent should be '... a man who will have the personality to win confidence, the background to develop a program of quality education, the integrity to stand for what he and his staff deem important as well as carry out the specific decisions of the Board, and the ability to win the cooperation and devoted efforts of all those responsible for the program of the public schools in Milford.'
7 To increase the likelihood of securing an able successor the report suggested setting up an ad hoc committee of several prominent educators to study the district, screen applicants and develop a short list of several candidates for the Board's final consideration.

Denouement. Real life events seldom follow totally the lines of classical drama. The denouement of the Board/Superintendent conflict and the district crisis appeared quickly and quietly, at least as reflected in the Board Minutes. On

12 December, agreements were reached between the Board and the Superintendent which reflected the substance of the Committee's recommendations: Senior Consultant — salary, office, travel, and duties as raised in the report; and beginnings of a committee to select a new superintendent. A detailed letter went to Mr. Leckey of NEA on the next day indicating the agreements. Responses were also made to the several aspects of the analysis and recommendations. In February the Board Committee reported the hiring of Dr. Theodore Jones and Dr. Russell Johnson as a two person screening committee to help in the selection of the new superintendent. The consultants were to solicit names from some twenty university officials and to interview at AASA (American Association of School Administrators) later in February. The Superintendents on the committee, Jones and Johnson, while from the midwestern part of the country, were nationally recognized members of the profession. They had access to networks of training institutions, leading figures in administration, and 'comers' in the field.

Latently though, the drama had a number of 'firsts.' In a sense they were innovations which became precedents and were to have long term important implications. They include:

1   major involvement of the CTA in district policy
2   appeals by teachers to their national organization
3   appearance of a national organization in local and district affairs
4   the national organization as a respected outside mediator whose proposals carried the weight of objectivity and fairness and whose substance formed the basis of the compromise and agreements

Several items seemed more of a continuation:

1   modernization
2   broadened scope of national consultants, advice, and reports
3   involvement in the 'national network'
4   continued community involvement, discussion, and debate.

Final Events of 1961–62.   The torrent of normal business poured down on the Board. Serious discipline problems, for example, discharging of firearms by several students at the high school, arose, were discussed, and settled. The Metropolitan Teachers Association became active regarding salaries here and in communities scattered throughout the county. Issues 'About Teaching Democracy and Communism in the Public Schools' appeared on the agenda. Teachers resigned and replacements were hired. The Senior Consultant developed a civil defense plan for the district. Work on buildings and building additions continued. The new junior high was opened in January, 1962. The problems of placing insurance at inexpensive rates and with some equity among agents in the community continued in the form of an 'insurance committee'; hours of discussion and a series of legal opinions were involved.

In April the two incumbents on the Board who were up for reelection were replaced by Mr. Wilkerson and Mr. Baskin. The two incumbents each received about 2500 votes, the two newcomers about 3600 votes. Mr. Wilkerson had been on the Board previously.[5] The first vote taken concerned Mr. Tompkins being returned to the Presidency. The vote was a 3–3 tie between him and Mr. Baskin. Mr. Wilkerson was elected Vice President unanimously. The Board adjourned at 4:00 a.m., 3 April. A week later Mr. Tompkins won on a 3 for, 2 against and 1 not voting. Unanimity was gone once again, but the change was not sufficient this time to save Mr. McBride, as it had a half dozen years before. In an unknowingly significant event for the Milford District, and in an illuminatingly significant item celebrating the interpretations that kingdoms hang by threads and that chance is a major antecedent of human events, Minute #4397 appears on 10 April 1962:

> Mr. Henderson moved that New Junior High School teacher, Ronald George, not be re-employed for the school year 1962–63, because of his *contemptuous attitude toward Board members, his irrational behavior in public, and his totally unprofessional behavior*. Mr. Osborn seconded the motion. Messers. Henderson, Osborn, and Tompkins voting 'yes' and Messers. Wilkerson, Baskin, and Quigley voting 'no.' The motion failed. (Our italics) (Tie vote on re-employment automatically fails) (4/10/62)

As one of Ron George's colleagues commented jokingly in an interview with us, 'If they had phrased it as 'rehiring' he would have been out.'

In late April, at a special session of the Board on a Saturday afternoon at 3:30 the Board, in executive session, voted 4–2 to offer Mr. Steven Spanman a three year contract as Superintendent. He accepted. Those voting for were Baskin, Henderson, Osborn, and Tompkins. Those voting against were Quigley and Wilkerson. No minutes were recorded of prior interviewing, the short list of candidates, nor the issues. The votes were along the lines of the the pro and anti McBride factions with Mr. Baskin as the swing member. Significantly, except for Mr. Baskin, the votes were the same on the attempt to fire Ron George. In May, Ron George, the not to be suppressed junior high school social studies teacher and president of the CTA, wrote a brief letter to the school Board. It is reproduced as Figure 1.

Figure 1: Letter to School Board

May 4, 1962

Gentlemen:

In keeping with the principle which I stated to you last September that this is the 'year of truth', the following is our exact copy of a letter which was sent to Mr. Sterling Leckey of the NEA today. It is submitted to you for your information. The letter was duplicated because it was not possible to get enough carbon copies.

Respectfully submitted,

Ronald George, President
Milford Community Teachers Association

On the same ditto sheet was the letter to Mr. Leckey in which Mr. George apologized for the long delay in writing, with the reason of awaiting the April School Board elections. He indicated that the new Superintendent, Steven Spanman, had been hired with the help of Drs. Jones and Johnson, the consultants to the Board. Further he indicated that:

> In the School Board election of April 3, 1962, the two incumbents, William Eads and Frank Oakes, were defeated by David Wilkerson and Stuart Baskin, who ran on the platform of dissatisfaction with the Board's handling of Mr. McBride and general interference in the administration. (5/4/62)

The final paragraph in the letter needs no explanation:

> Now to get to the real purpose of this letter. you will note in Items 4397 and 4398 that Mr. Iverson (a member of the CTA Executive Committee) and I are accused of 'contemptuous', 'irrational' and 'totally unprofessional' behavior. Mr. Iverson and I would like to have an opinion from you and Mr. Norman as to whether such accusations in these printed Board minutes which are distributed widely to the public, would be grounds for legal action against Mr. Henderson as the maker of the motion and against Mr. Osborn, who seconded the motion Number 4397.
>
> We will appreciate hearing from you on this matter. (5/4/62)

The Board acknowledged receipt of the letter and voted unanimously to attach it to the minutes. They added the comment: 'It was noted that Mr. George's letter was a personal one and was not participated in by the Community Teachers Association or the Executive Committee thereof.' (5/8/62) No other comments are recorded. Other business of the Board continued — discussions about the Civil Air Patrol, receipt of a survey on future plans of the Class of 1962, a fourth grade teacher's 'informative' presentation of a reading program, and bids on a senior high Language laboratory for $10,841. The Open House and dedication of the new junior high school were set for May 20th. The new Superintendent and his wife, Dr. and Mrs. Spanman, were to be invited. The gym of that junior high school, two years later, was to be a three month home for the fourth, fifth, and sixth grade students, the ISD (Independent Study Division) of the Kensington School. Among the half dozen new teachers hired for next year were Joe Harlan, an elementary guidance counselor, and Mary Radford, an elementary teacher who would be part of Kensington's staff two years later.

Ironies continued:

> Mr. Wilkerson called attention to Mr. McBride being honored by the Superintendents of the Metropolitan School Districts who presented him with a watch and fifty silver dollars, representing approximately a dollar for each year of service. Mr. McBride received an ovation from those present. (5/22/62)

In a special session on Saturday, 16 June the Board met with Dr. Spanman present. The item on the agenda was a discussion of the tender of offers for the land for the site of the Kensington Elementary School. Ten days later at the regular meeting, plans for an architect were tabled to await a later meeting. The Assistant Superintendent, Mr. Neal Unger, reported on a 'pleasant meeting' with Dr. Spanman on 16 June and that the new Superintendent approved the current plans and asked Mr. Unger to continue his efforts.

The Board's conflicts continued to shadow its activities. Mr. Tompkins submitted a three page letter indicating he would file for another three year term, the following year (April 1963), that he wanted 'to refute certain untruths and rumors' being circulated about himself, and that he 'unequivocally' was not running for higher political office.

Similarly, the press of regional and state politics continued. The Metropolitan Superintendents Organization had commissioned the School of Education of City University to prepare a study of School District Reorganization. A digest of its report was appended to the Board minutes. The report's objectives for reorganization focused on:

1 high quality programs
2 equalization of educational opportunity (economic) to an acceptable level
3 prudent expenditure of public funds.

The input-output analysis put together various combinations of district size, economic resources, and coordination of special services. 'Resolutions' of a 'final' sort were not achieved then. And, as we shall see later, district organization and reorganization is one of those political problems which are never solved finally, for changes have been in the air since the turn of the century and continue until today, where size and economic differences as issues have been replaced by issues of racial equity.

Ending Milford's Early History and Foreshadowing the Later History

The Spanman Era was to last but four years, 1962–66, including one year for a leave of absence. Dr. Spanman was Superintendent when the innovative Kensington School was built, staffed, and opened. The first year in the life of the school has been described and analyzed in detail in *Anatomy of Educational Innovation, An Organizational Analysis of an Elementary School* (Smith and Keith, 1971). The Spanman story intertwines with that story of Ronald George. Of all the twists and turns in human events in the Milford School District, the story of Ron George, the social studies teacher and president of the local CTA is perhaps the most dramatic of all. As we relate later, he became Spanman's successor as Superintendent of Schools, 1966 to the present. The details of those stories demand telling in their own right as well as telling as explanatory context for the changes in the Kensington School during its fifteen year existence. Essentially we have reported on the tangle of administrative succession. McBride, Spanman, and George were all involved, the latter in ways not clear at the time. But a tangle it was. Further, a complex context, partly moving under its own dynamics, occurred as well. Some of the elements of that context had been around for years. Some of it we tried to pattern and organize for the reader in the form of stories with multiple strands. Mostly these strands and stories stayed close to how they were perceived or might have been perceived by the participants engaged in the day to day action. Shortly we will distance ourselves a bit and look to some patterns and regularities which might be relevant to individuals and groups involved with communities and school districts in other times and places.

Implications for Educational Innovation

Without going into great detail, the foregoing 'vignette' raises a number of perplexities for the student of educational innovation. First it blurs the hard distinction between innovation and change. President Tompkins of the Milford School Board probably did not see what he was doing as 'specific planned change' when he was trying to oust Superintendent McBride from his position, after some twenty-six years as superintendent, even though it became the celebrated test case for such action in Midwest State. Nor would one think that Ron George, the social studies teacher and president of the local CTA (Community Teachers Organization) was innovating when he wrote to the National Educational Association (NEA) and brought a national professional affairs fact finding team into the locally governed district, for the first time. These were significant changes, ones that shade away from the usual connotations of educational innovation. The conceptual status of change, reform, and innovation seem to come on the agenda now.

Words like 'conflict,' 'state law,' and 'politics' leap out at the reader. One Board member, the current president, is threatening another member, a former president, with a suit, publically humiliating him, within the broader context of conflict with the Superintendent, and with the concurrent evolution of a fight with the teachers association. Technology, formal organization, and bureaucracy seem less central, although not irrelevant, to what is happening. Technocratic models of innovation, as described by House (1979) seem less important than the political models he raises.

Powerful individuals, Board President Tompkins, CTA president George, and Superintendent McBride seemed to be taking important action which changed the way things were in the Milford School District. Action and agency, in their farther reaches, are not in contradiction to the data in our story.

We were surprised too with the potency of an outside group of consultants and their recommendations, when their report is relatively calm, reasonable, and wise in a situation that is highly emotional, full of intense conflict, and when face saving alternatives are not immediately recognized or available. Consultants and innovation, as presented in the educational literature, have had a stormy relationship over the years.

The varying definitions of rights and responsibilites of the several subgroups or subsystems within the school district, Board, Superintendent, CTA, NEA, Midwest State Teachers Association and the Suburban County Teachers Association, are all evolving in only partially overlapping ways. At best there is a 'quasi-stationary equilibruim,' at worst there are misinterpretations and minimal dialogue.

A number of anomalous items which seem to fit nowhere in a theory of educational innovation, at least initially, run through the minutes — age of the Superintendent (late sixties), the long hours and amount of work for citizens elected to the Board, for example, the three in the morning adjournment times, and the need for a chronology of Superintendents who serve the District over the years.

For the student of educational theory, the problems raised by the relationship between 'facts,' 'fact finding,' and 'recommendations' for desirable courses of action seem well beyond the kind of 'objective,' 'value free' modes of thought and theory advocated by the logical positivists in social science, education, and educational administration.

The nature and quality of 'the tangle of administrative succession' episode suggests a 'drama' analogy or metaphor as a vehicle for exploiting the meaning of this event. What would philosopher Kenneth Burke, author of *The Grammar of Motives*, or drama scholar and critic Elder Olson, author of *Tragedy and the Theory of Drama*, or Erving Goffman, the sociologist who has given us a dramaturgical social science perspective in *The Presentation of Self* and other books, monographs, and essays, have to say about all this? Would it come out as a 'dramatist model of educational innovation?' And would it add another competing view to go with the technological, the political, and the cultural models of Ernest House, and the two additional ones, the biographical/personality and the historical ones we have suggested in our 'Reconstruing educational innovation' (Smith *et al.*, 1986)? Or, are we raising issues at the level of what Pepper (1942) calls 'root metaphors?' Sort of metaphors about metaphors?

Even as a partial agenda, all this seems to pose some striking and important problems for discussion of *Innovation and Change in Schooling: History, Politics, and Agency*.

The Problem and Its Context

Introduction

In a sense this book is really a book with several faces. In its first face, it is the third part of a trilogy of books, *Anatomy of Educational Innovation: a Mid to Long Term Restudy and Reconstrual*. The Trilogy is predicated on an initial intensive study of an innovative elementary school, the Kensington Elementary School in the Milford School district (Smith and Keith, 1971). The Trilogy as a series contains, as a first book, an account of the original members of the Kensington School in a fifteen year follow up of them and their careers. We have asked the question, What happened to the faculty of true believers after they left the Kensington School? The results we called *Educational Innovators: Then and Now*. The second book in the series is *The Fate of an Innovative School*. In that we did a fifteen year history of the Kensington School, anchored on each end with an intensive ethnography. The third book in the series, the present volume, fills in the historical and contemporaneous context of the school from the perspective of the Milford School District.

But beyond the fact that *Innovation and Change in Schooling* is a part of a trilogy, we feel that the issues of innovation and change, as we have tried to deal with them, make an important study in their own right. The book, we feel has a stand alone quality. Another face, as it were.[6]

The Relevance of History to Understanding Innovation

In an earlier circulation of the report on which this book is based we had reactions and comments regarding the need for such an intensive history of the Milford School District. In a sense we were asked, what is the question to which this long monograph is the answer? These remarks build a perspective which culminates in the phrasing of an answer to that question.

Several beliefs coalesced in our view. First, we felt that most educational innovators and researchers of educational innovation had not distinguished between educational innovation and educational change. Very simply we have come to see educational innovation as specific planned improvement. As such it is just one class of phenomena in the larger category of educational change. In this larger context of change, innovation takes on considerably different meaning. Our hunch is that most innovators have been so busy with their own problems and programs that they have not pursued the implications of events in the larger category.

As we thought about these issues, other related concepts entered our analysis. Educational reform became a major or large scale innovation. Utopian schools seemed like the broadest and most idealistic end of a continuum running from innovations through reforms to utopias. These clustered into change from an evaluative or ideological perspective. The genesis of a school district is a specific kind of innovation with a time referent. The evolution of a district implies gradual change over a period of time. Growth and decline suggest change in size and perhaps an evaluative disclaimer — growth as bigger and better and decline as smaller and lesser. These latter also implied a more organic or naturalistic metaphor as a general categorization.

Eventually, we settled on the conceptualization in Figure 2, an analytical context for the concept of educational innovation. Working through the data and analysis helped us 'see' the nature of Kensington School as an educational innovation. The magnitude of this insight is caught in the alteration in the overall title of our study. What began as 'Kensington revisited: A fifteen year follow-up of an innovative school and its faculty' has become *Anatomy of Educational Innovation: A Mid to Long Term Re-study and Reconstrual*.

The reconstrual continued. If educational innovation is only one kind of change and if it is your or my 'baby' as often is the case, and was in Milford, then a further idea follows. At a minimum, other individuals may have other interests and ideas which they see as desirable, special, and innovative. If their ideas and practices are not perfectly congruent with yours or mine then we begin to have a problem of

1   Educational change — the general category
2   Change from an 'evaluation' or 'ideological' perspective
      Innovation
      Reform
      Utopia
3   Change from a 'naturalistic' or 'organic' perspective
      Genesis
      Evolution
      Growth
      Decline
4   Change from a 'mechanistic' or 'technical' perspective
      Addition
      Subtraction
      Restructuring: Differentiation and Reorganization
5   Change from a 'contextualist' or 'political' perspective
      Interest
      Choice
      Conflict
      Negotiation
      Power
      Compromise

priorities, resources, power, and persuasion. In short, your or my innovation may well be just one small part of a political process. Goodness and truth may not lie in your or my project to the degree we had assumed. At this point, our specific planned change is more than a technical or scientific problem. Illuminating that cluster of events became very important to us. We began to talk of a 'political' or 'contextual' perspective.

It is our belief that many, if not most educational innovators, ourselves included, do not know much educational history. We believe that this is a tragedy for them and their ideas and a tragedy for many of the individuals in the schools within which they 'inflict' or 'save' with their innovations. This belief, as it relates to ourselves, is one of the major results of the study. As one of our colleagues commented upon listening to our enthusiasm and stories, 'You've discovered history.' And so we have. This concern for history in general and for the history of this district in particular is part of a major shift in our concept of paradigms or root metaphors underlying our approach to educational research, theory, and practice. We feel we are operating from a contextualist metaphor as Pepper (1942) and Sarbin (1977) use the term. With them, we believe the power of social science and educational inquiry will be enhanced as others move in this direction also.

Even so, there is still enough of the natural scientist in each of us to feel that an outsider's reasonably detached view of the 'natural history' of *a*, or better, *this* school district might be more important than just the pursuit of an idle curiosity. We believe that the genesis and evolution of the district from this more naturalistic perspective shades into our more contextualist, political perspective. As such, we can view 'the new elementary education of the Kensington School' as one superintendent's vision, in a history of five superintendents and sixty-five years of schooling in Milford. Where does Superintendent Spanman fit in the evolution of the Milford

School District? Where did he come from? Why did he build the innovative Kensington School here?

When we accidentally fell into the huge body of data, bound volumes of Milford Board Minutes reaching back to 1915, the practicality and possibility of this historical dimension became a reality. Beyond a Mount Everest being there to be climbed, we have found that vague, general and often ill-founded ideas take on another kind of vitality when they are moved into the concrete reality of data on human events. As we argue shortly, the Milford School Board minutes are public records of an unusual sort. Finding a closet full of them opened up unimagined vistas. The historical context was there.

One of the truisms in our field research is that 'the problem' evolves over the course of the project. This is the best of what is sometimes called responsive research design rather than pre-set research design. Rather than being a producer of anxiety, this becomes part of the excitment and joy of the unexpected in field research.

In short, this book, *Innovation and Change in Schooling: History, Politics and Agency*, is an historical context. It answers the question, 'Where does the Kensington School fit into the larger picture?' Because this picture is treated historically from the genesis and evolution of a school district to the political conflict of later years, it permits us to deal with the larger new phrasing of our problem 'Innovation and change in schooling?' By introducing 'schooling' in the statement we have gone from the instance of the Milford School District to a larger class or category of events, schooling in general. Further, we believe that one of the best ways, although not the only way, of understanding that larger set of events is to know intimately one highly detailed but integrated case. With such an image at hand, one can begin to come to terms with any other case and with the larger category. As we commented in jest with the current Superintendent of Milford, 'We know more about Milford than anyone ever has known and probably more than anyone will want to know.' That is, unless one wants to 'really' understand innovation and change in American education. Such is the question, and hope, of this book in the overall trilogy of books.

Historical Overview

Sometimes it's useful to sketch in broad strokes an overview, a broad but simple scaffolding or outline of the history one wants to tell in more detail. A number of choices exists in the nature of those broad lines of demarcation, for instance, general societal events such as wars and depressions and dramatic events, for example, Sputnik. Alternatively, the school district has had only five superintendents and one might speak of the Briggs era, the Grey era, the McBride era, the Spanman era and the George era. One is reminded of national history by dynasties, reigning kings, or presidents. Or one can capture periods around major local events, for example, district consolidation, which stamp the moments in the minds of participants. Finally the calendar permits a decade-by-decade striking of events. Perhaps to presage our larger analytical frame we have opted for a combination of these alternatives.

In Figure 3 we present a time line of six discernible periods: the pre-1925 common school district era, a long stable township period, the rapid expansion in district size precipitated by merger and the population explosion of the post-World War II suburban development, the brief four year period of Spanman's innovative lighthouse district gambit, a period of conservative consolidation and then the current era of community change characterized by three major themes — declining enrollments, social class shifts and racial shifts. Figure 4 presents the superintendent time line. Perhaps it is helpful, too, to recall our initial purposes. We are trying for a description and analysis of the changes in the innovative Kensington School between its opening in 1964 and its current status fifteen years later in 1979–80. As a piece of contemporary empirical research that represents a long time period. From an historical point of view it is not only recent history but also a relatively short time period. One aspect of our metatheoretical perspective assumes that a view of the history of the Milford School District will enhance our understanding of the changes in the Kensington School. More recently, as our data have accumulated, as new directions for inquiry have arisen out of available, people, documents, and themes and as analysis and interpretations have continued, we have found shifts in the very nature of our problem.

Contemporaneous Context

'Milford's Recent History: The School District as Contemporary Context of the Kensington School' aptly states the scope and intent of the latter part of our narrative and interpretation. A new superintendent, Dr. Steven Spanman, is just arriving on the scene in the Milford School District. The need for an additional elementary school in the District is apparent. That school will be the Kensington Elementary School. While the history of the Kensington School itself appears in another book, *The Fate of an Innovative School: The First Fifteen Years of the Kensington School* (1987), our approach here will explicate activities in the Central Office which bear on the origins and evolution of the school. In this way we pick up the threads of the history of the Milford District and we progressively move to a focus on the interdependency between the Kensington School and its contemporary context. But even as we do this we will continue our larger focus for our quarry is really broader than Kensington, that is, 'Innovation and Change in Schooling.'

The potentiality of the single case for an in depth rethinking of the problems of the evolution of schooling in American society provides another way of stating our agenda. In a sense, much of the professional talk of educational innovation and change over the last few decades strikes us as oddly off the mark, similar to what Gilbert Ryle (1949) once called a 'category mistake,' It's not a simple error of detail, nor a simple mistake in concept usage, but rather a fundamental misconstrual of the domain in question. It leaves one with a growing malaise and uneasiness, often an initial tacit feeling that 'something's all wrong.' Progressively we have tried to refine and make explicit our concerns.

As we became involved in the history of the school district, and especially as we

Figure 3: A Broad Overview of the History of the Milford School District

The Common School (3 Director Board)	The Long Stable Township School Period (6 Director Board)	Merger and Post-WWII Rapid Expansion	Spanman's Brief Innovative Lighthouse Era	Conservative Consolidation	Community Change: (Declining Enrollments, Dropping Socio-economic Status, and Racial Change)
	1925	1949	1962	1966	1972

Figure 4: Tenure of Superintendents

Mrs. Briggs	1928–1930
Mr. Grey	1930–1935
Mr. McBride	1935–1962
Dr Spanman	1962–1966
Dr. George	1966–present

tried to exploit the public record of the Milford School Board minutes, our uneasiness and reconstrual moved along in tandem. The explicit form of our research questions shifted from 'What has happened to the Kensington School?' and 'Why have the changes in the school occurred?' to the puzzlement, 'Why did they build such a school in the first place?' It seemed as though, an understanding of how and why the innovative school was built might help fathom some of the changes in the school itself. The biological and physical sciences look for 'mechanisms' to understand natural processes (Easley, 1974 and Easley and Taksuoka, 1968). Our bias toward social science is to look for actions, interactional structures and decisions of individuals living out their lives in multiple overlapping and sometimes conflicting groups. In our view these yield the 'mechanisms' of social change.

The central thread of our data continue to be School Board minutes. In Milford, the bound copies of the minutes also include the Superintendent's agendas, consequently one has a related, but still an additional record. This becomes exceedingly significant as one begins to contrast Superintendents — Mr. McBride, the long termed Superintendent from 1935–62; Dr. Steven Spanman, the Superintendent from 1962–66; and the current incumbent, Dr. Ronald George, 1966 to the present. Further, the Board on occasion included in the permanent record a variety of additional documents — long stenotyped records of significant meetings, reports of consultants, letters from patrons and so forth.

To these multiple records we have added several of our own. We have in the last few years attended a number of Board meetings and produced our own observational records, we have interviewed a number of patrons and staff and perhaps most significantly we have had brief focused conversations with Central Office personnel. In regard to the latter, as we worked in the Central Office reading and analyzing the Board minutes, staff would initiate a friendly 'How are things going?' We would comment with a general 'Slowly' or 'Painfully' and sometimes a specific 'In 1962 . . .' or 'In the Spring of 1968 . . .' On occasion this would stimulate an anecdote or story or two. Sometimes, when a puzzling set of events was occurring we would focus on a specific event or individual from the records, for example, 'Did you know a teacher named Nussbaum?' or 'What happened to you when the schools were closed down in 1970?' Some of our most vivid instances of the potency of triangulation (Denzin, 1970) or the multimethod matrix (Smith, 1979) appeared in these interchanges. They are raised and analyzed in detail in the discussion of methodology, to which we turn now.

Notes

1 All proper names have been coded for anonymity.
2 He had two years remaining on his contract, his salary was $17,000/year.
3 A Board member and at one time the President of the Board.
4 PD refers to project document, TI to taped interview, and SO to summary observations and interpretations. These uses are consistent with our earlier field research techniques and procedures.
5 The Board was composed now of Baskin, Henderson, Osborn, Quigley, Tompkins, and Wilkerson.
6 As we have commented on several occasions, the support by Dr. Ronald George, Superintendent of Milford, and by Mr. Frederick Mulhauser, our NIE Project Officer, has been overwhelmingly positive at every turn.

Chapter 2

Historical and Ethnographic Method: Blending Two Qualitative Strands of Inquiry

Introduction

An Overview

In trying to capture our method of inquiry regarding the historical and contemporaneous context of the Kensington school, we have elected to blend ideas from history and ethnography. Although the 'main' method is historical, we have moved from ethnography, our position of strength, to history, a method relatively new to us. Perhaps most significant is our view that the two strands are really quite compatible. Perhaps most surprising is the relative paucity of substantive research and methodological theory utilizing and linking the two. This chapter serves the dual purpose of first, acquainting the reader with some concrete aspects of how we did what we did, and secondly, indicating the beginnings of a rationale for that effort.

The key ideas to which we attend include a brief account of the social milieu in the Department of Education at Washington University, where Smith has taught for thirty years and where Prunty, Dwyer, and Kleine all received their PhDs. All of us have shared the joy of professional contact with Professors Callahan, Connor, and Wirth, our long time mentors and colleagues. We use the device of the 'interpretive aside, a comment in the field notes, to identify a number of anomalies, initial observations and reflections on doing ethnography and history. Basic to our efforts was the discovery of several sets of records, data, in the form of newsletters to patrons and especially school board minutes. We struggled with our 'contextual ignorance' and the problem of 'knowing how things turned out.' These are problems perceived as less acute or handled very differently in most of contemporaneous social science.

Finally we try to merge ethnography and history with a look at some of the diversity within each. This diversity is surprisingly similar in content and form. The power of triangulation and multi-methods, a cornerstone in our theory of ethnographic research methodology, reappears in our developing perspective in historical method. Our 'process' perspective in ethnography seems at the heart of the kind of chronicling done by historians. That provides a major instance of continuity across the methods. Finally, we move the level of abstraction of our concerns to the level of 'assumptions, metatheory, and paradigms' for a further attempt at integration. The root metaphor of contextualism seems to put to rest this part of our effort.

Origins of a Synthesis

Most essays have an interesting origin, a beginning, which helps give meaning to the substance they communicate. Among several, one brief story comes to mind in regard to these thoughts on the relationship between historical and ethnographic research in the study of schooling; it comments on the Department of Education at Washington University where we all have worked. Although most of us are quite individualistic, we do talk, banter and play a variety of friendly one-upmanship games. Several years ago Smith had been trying to understand the concept of explanation and began reading people like Scriven (1959), Dray (1957) and Gardiner (1959) on the nature of explanation in history. In the course of this he began to try to figure out how historians do their work. With his colleagues Arthur Wirth, Raymond Callahan and William Connor in mind, he came to the conclusion that historical method was just, nothing more than, 'participant observation with data fragments,' a kind of less adequate ethnography. We don't recall their specific reactions, beyond benevolent, tolerant smiles, and we are not sure that they believe Smith won that round. Cloaked in the jest, however, were two significant ideas. Essential similarities existed in the two approaches, that is, one is a form or instance of the other. Second, a major difference seemed to appear in the quality of the data that existed, that is, fragments. Malinowski's (1922) active ethnographic huntsman image seemed limited by the historical enterprise. This chapter is an attempt to explore the hunches caught in that bit of collegial humor.

Such humor and by-play suggest also that a more fundamental issue is lurking about. We knew one day we wanted to do a 'real' historical case study. At first, we didn't realize the extent of the opportunity which would develop around our Kensington Revisited project. In a sense, a fifteen-year follow-up is a kind of recent history. In 1964–65, we had studied the innovative Kensington Elementary School — open space, team teaching, individualized curriculum and instruction, democratic administration, pupil control of their own learning — and had written a participant observer monograph, *Anatomy of Educational Innovation* (Smith and Keith, 1971) on the first year in the life of the school. Now we proposed to return for an ethnography of the school today (1979–80) and a view of the further careers of the original faculty, a group of true believers, none of whom was still at the school.

In looking for some of the context of change it seemed reasonable to spend some time in the Central Office of the Milford School District, reading documents such as the Milford Public School *Bulletin*, and attending some of the School Board meetings. As we indicated, one day, while reading the file of *Bulletins* that the District sent to patrons, we happened upon some elements of conflict between the then Superintendent, Mr. McBride, and the Board. In talking with the current Superintendent, Dr. George, he indicated that the Board had tried to fire Superintendent McBride. He showed us the bound board minutes. Our enticement with these led to two years of intensive reading of minutes from 1915 to the present. It also led to contacts and interviews with older members of the community, a board member from the middle 1920s, members of the first high school graduating class of 1931, and a number of long term citizens of the community. Although we are still not 'historians' in a formal or professional sense, we have been busy developing a chronicle of the Milford District from 1915 to 1980, a sixty-five year period. The activity changed the definition of our problem, enlarged our final report to six book-length volumes, and demanded continued renegotiations with school district officials and with our project officer at the National Institute of Education (NIE) which has funded the effort. The concrete illustrations and substantive remarks in this book come from our experience in this part of our project.

Anomalies, Initial Observations and Reflections on Doing Ethnography and History

An 'interpretive aside' is a simple, practical ethnographic technique of writing in the fieldnote records a short comment to oneself about some hunch, bright idea or insight that occurs along the way in fieldwork (Smith and Geoffrey, 1968, p. 12). In the course of doing our history of Milford, a series of methodological observations, interpretive asides, and broader reflections arose and were noted in the fieldnotes and summary observations. We raise and elaborate a half dozen of them here. Mostly, the focus is on aspects of the data and the kind of thinking that seems to be occurring as one does a blend of history and ethnography.

The-World-Begins-in-1952 Phenomenon

One of the more interesting items we encountered is the 'the-world-begins-in 1952' phenomenon. Among the various sources of data on the history of the district the Milford Public Schools *Bulletin* became one of the most important. Volume 1, no. 1 appeared in August 1952. The *Bulletin* became the fulcrum around which the history of the district seemed to unfold. Each news item gave an indication of what had gone before and what was just beginning. It became a rock, a pivot point upon which inferences ran both backward and forward. For example, what was to become a deluge of pupils in the 1950s, changing the district from a semi-rural, semi-small town to a large suburban district, was just beginning. The Milford High School listed only thirteen faculty members with 'one or more years of service'; nine new faculty arrived in the Fall of 1952. The Milford Village Elementary School listed twelve faculty, plus six new members. The Marquette School of fourteen faculty was increased by four. The segregated Attucks School remained with a single teacher for all eight grades, In all, staff size increased by fifty per cent in that year. A two-classroom addition was being built at Marquette. Six classrooms were being rented from the Adams Street Community Church's Education Building, and the new Grant Elementary School was under construction. Overcrowding in the elementary schools was a real problem.

The substantive points are both interesting and important but our purpose here is to indicate that we found a rock on which to anchor our beginning story and analysis. The data produced an initial 'set of facts' and a beginning image of the nature and structure of the district. This record occasioned the raising of hypotheses about earlier years and the recency of the change from rural to suburban. It began to suggest linkages with the Kensington School and Milford District which we had encountered in our intensive observational study in 1964–65, *Anatomy of Educational Innovation*. To find a source which one could count on, at least initially, seemed very helpful. Because they started publishing the *Bulletin* in 1952, it seemed as though our world began in 1952.

The *Bulletins*, as data, had several other attributes which helped shape the label 'the-world-begins . . .', we gave to the phenomenon. First, the *Bulletins* were a large mass of data. Some years a half dozen were issued; they varied from four to eight pages in length. They have continued until the present. Second, by their very nature they were organized chronologically. They provided a kind of chronicle of the District for the latter-day reader. Third, they had a holistic quality — 'all' of the District news of interest to the patrons, at least as perceived by the administration. Fourth, the audience of patrons are the citizens who vote yearly for Board members, who legally direct the district, and the citizens whose support is needed for tax levies and bond issues — local democracy in action and, as we will see, with a vengeance. As we will discuss shortly, the *Bulletin* is the not the only perspective possible but is an interesting and important one for an ethnographer interested in historical documents as well as observations and interviews.

Discovering the Board Minutes

The initial interpretive aside leading to the previous section, 'the-world-begins-in 1952', was written before we got into the Board *Minutes*. These became an even more fundamental rock — earlier in time and with a peculiarly important decision-making format. It reminded us of the old story of the earth resting on a rock, the rock resting on an elephant, and the elephant on a turtle, and after that 'it's turtles all the way down.' The Board *Minutes* seemed to be 'turtles' all the way down. But even here, we had not studied the community newspapers and we thought we might find them to be 'the real bedrock of turtles' to continue to mix our metaphors. Actually we used those records more selectively.

Now the point we want to make is the nature of the cognitive processes involved in this phase of research as we are doing it. The finding of these sets of documents and the careful reading of them started several processes. First, as indicated earlier, it set a boundary, '1952 and onward.' Second, it indicated that those boundaries are always provisional and tentative as new sets of records appear. Third, by their volume, detail, and particular form — news items for the patrons in the one instances and legal records in the second — they gave an aura and confidence of 'reality.' Fourth, as we started to make notes we found ourselves chronicling specific events on a time line. Fifth, common sense strands — when buildings were built and the coming and going of superintendents — soon appeared. Sixth, some specific items related to contemporary events became themes, for example, a Black School, the Attucks, was built in the mid-1920s and reference was made to it in one of the first volumes of Board *Minutes*. This reference linked earlier resolutions of racial relations with the contemporary racial changes at Kensington and with what Myrdal (1944) long ago called *The American Dilemma*. Seventh, a developing gestalt or image of what the totality or whole is like began to form. Something called the Milford School District existed in the records, in the legal settings of county and state and in the minds of individuals. We found ourselves in the midst of the Griffiths (1979) and Greenfield (1978) debate on the social reality of educational organiza-tions. Eighth, a continuous inference process about 'unknown areas' based on implications from known items occurred. For instance, what was the relationship between faculty and staff turnover in Mrs. Briggs' early tenure as superintendent in 1928–30 and in her being fired after two years? What relation did the Board's stated reasons have to her personality and gender? What was the significance of pupils being called in by the Board to discuss the problems of the school? Finally, what alterations occurred in our intellectual processes as new information, and particularly new large bodies or sets of information arose, for example, finding the District *Bulletin*, then the sixty-five years of Board *Minutes* and then the extended oral histories of early Board members and students?

Each of those eight or ten cognitive processes has become an issue in our longer methodological analysis in our project. They seem very important for thinking about the relationships between historical and ethnographic methods at the level of a concrete practical activity of inquiry. Later, we found historians such as Gottschalk (1945) presenting examples of similar inferential thinking from documents.

In addition, finding and working for two years on the *Minutes*, of the Board of Education has been a most dramatic and emotional research experience for us, second only to Smith's original experience as participant observer in Geoffrey's class almost two decades ago (*The Complexities of an Urban Classroom*, 1968). The massive and relentless month in, month out, year in, year out quality of the data was overwhelming. The written at the moment and not to be changed record regardless of what happened later quality made for a powerful record. The moved, seconded, and passed quality of the data, focusing on decision-making, provided a 'reality' against which all other data could be compared, contrasted and triangulated.

Beyond those substantive intellectual processes, the personal consequences of this discovery of the *Minutes* seemed multiple. First, an energizing, exciting quality appeared. Motivation ran high. Day after day we returned to the new kind or genre of data for the surprises it contained both substantively and methodologically.

A related, but second aspect occurred. Creative thought was stimulated to a high degree. We were in a welter of new data, new formats, forms, and categories of data, new percepts and images, new items about which choices had to be made, and new construals or perspectives formulated. Continuously we asked, 'How do we cope with all this?' The materials were manifestly relevant, for little items kept appearing here and there and seemed to be connected. What were the patterns and structure of ideas which would encompass all this in some way relevant to our original problem and the way that too was evolving? The data transformed the problem from 'A fifteen year follow-up of an innovative school and its faculty' to what we later called 'Innovation and change in schooling,' a very different agenda. Finally overall the conception became *Anatomy of Educational Innovation: A Restudy and Reconstrual.* We were struck with the parallels to changes that occur in problem definitions as creative artists work (Beittel, 1973).

Along the way came the doubts about the degree of or levels of creativity — is it new to oneself versus is it new to the field? Were we just rediscovering old ideas? Intellectual journeys occurred into the nature of history, the philosophy of history, the methods of history, and into the substance of educational history — local, state, and national. Even book titles with a ring of the history of curriculum, teaching or schooling in England, Australia and elsewhere caught our eye and dollar — or pound — in the book stores. Conversations occurred with our historically trained colleagues. They were assaulted with concrete particular items and with abstract general items. What do you make of this? What do you think of that? What's the conventional historical wisdom on this, on that? And on and on.

When the energizing aspect collided with the creative aspect, the turmoil raced through all parts of our life. It got in the way of our teaching, although sometimes it blended in neatly, effortlessly and successfully. It made us impatient with committee meetings and organizational maintenance activities. It led to multiple new kinds of reading as we have indicated: further histories, biographies and autobiographies of historians, and books on historical method and philosophy of history. It awakened us in the middle of the night, impatient to get some new idea down, yet unhappy that if sleep didn't come, we would be too tired to push on for more than a couple of hours the next day. It meant drinking too much coffee and eating too much to dispel the sourness. It meant the need for heavy doses of exercise — handball, walking, gardening — to tone down the mania and to take the tension out of arms, legs and head. It was an incredibly important all-encompassing professional experience.

Eliminating One's Contextual Ignorance

Being new to historical research and coming at the task from our idiosyncratic brand of ethnography left us with a continuing problem of 'eliminating one's contextual ignorance,' and 'imagining one's self back into an historical period.' The phenomenon arose this way. In two separate interviews, one with a teacher who had been in the District a number of years and one with a former student of the Class of 1931, items were raised which we fumbled with because we did not know enough of the history of Milford and of Suburban County. For instance, with Mrs. Irma Hall, a Kensington teacher, we didn't realize that the Milford District and the Marquette District had merged as late as 1949 and that those two schools were the elementary school program when she joined the faculty. The interview put us on to some of the issues, which we've since explored, but we did not raise key items in that early history. Similarly, in talking with and later reading through the interviews with Mr. Elbrecht, from the early years of Milford High School, we did not have a view of the west end of Suburban County and Milford's relationship to the numerous other small three-director districts. Nor did we know much about education in general in Suburban County.

These 'fumbles' started us reading contemporary local histories and records from the turn of the century. Each source, as is true in all our academic work, tends to lead to several more, and in a few hours of searching one has three months of reading and a half dozen new problems. For example, we believe a need exists for a history of Black education in Suburban County. Similarly we believe a need exists for a biography of a Suburban County Superintendent who served for thirty-seven years in that office, an exceptionally long period in an era of incredible change. Each of these would clarify important aspects of schooling in Milford since the turn of the century.

As we have said, for individuals with minimal training in history, and with little training in historical research methods, one of the most difficult problems has been 'imagining oneself back into an historical period.' No images of Midwest State in 1870 or Suburban County in 1920 came to mind. The hurly burly of the rapid county growth in the post-war years clouds visions of an earlier more rural and small-town state of affairs in the state and county.

The two channels which seemed most helpful and fruitful in developing images were two of the main sources of data. As we indicated, open-ended, oral history type interviews with older residents of the community and professional staff filled in gaps regarding the coming of roads, electricity, volunteer fire departments and so forth. In addition, we started reading histories of all kinds. First were United States histories, particularly the splendid three-volume set by Boorstin (1978), *The Americans*. Second were books on the history of American education, such as Cremin (1980) and Butts (1978). Third, a variety of local histories appeared. A 'folksy' history of a Suburban County school district seemed very much like the Clear Valley School before Milford became Milford. Histories of 'Big City', its neighborhoods, its schools, its politics were sought. A centennial history of Midwest State University, and especially its college of Education, provided another look at the total state educational establishment, the training of teachers and the beginnings of educational research.

Lest our label, 'eliminating one's contextual ignorance', be taken too negatively, a few positive aspects seem latent in the approach and worth mentioning. The procedures follow the general inductive, interactive mode of our general research style. One learns a little here and a little there and those items play into each other and into later interviews, documents, reading, analysis and writing. This is tremendously motivating, in the sense that one is always discovering something new. Patterns emerge, flow and stabilize. It's very exciting intellectually, it keeps one at the task, hour after hour, day after day, month after month.

The particular configurations from established interpreters as they appear in

31

theoretical structures and in accepted descriptive formulations do not become overly potent filters as the new information is acquired or processed. At some point, what Hexter (1967) calls 'the second record', what the historian carries about in his/her head from general reading and knowledge must come into play. As we have argued elsewhere (Smith, 1979 and 1982; Smith and Dwyer, 1980) eventually that second record has to be well filled out and articulated with the specific problem under study and with the data being developed. We're arguing that 'too much too early' may be stifling to one's imaginative construing and reconstruing of the problem and the analysis. Unless it's eventually done, one may find one's only rediscovered the wheel, and probably a lopsided one at that. Even so, in the process, one keeps eliminating one's contextual ignorance.

Several substantive outcomes of this activity seem most critical. We were struck by the recency and the magnitude of educational changes. The basic change in Suburban County from ninety school districts to about two dozen happened since the Second World War. This was less than a dozen and a half years before Spanman was to build a space-age, open school. In the mid-1960s when we first came to the District and did *Anatomy*, that recency didn't even occur to us. Second, the 'catastrophic' current changes — race, SES, declining enrollments — seem less catastrophic when viewed from this longer perspective. Periods of high change, growth, complexity and specialization, as we report shortly, have been lived through, thought about and fought over. The current changes, modes of reaction and adaptation, will become later chapters in someone else's historical account. This is not to argue for change, reform or innovation coming too fast (for some individuals and groups) or too slow (for other individuals and groups). Rather it is to indicate that many of the hopes, aspirations, conflicts, disagreements and actions have had their counterpart in prior times and places.

Finally, and a point that first arose when Smith and Geoffrey were studying Geoffrey's classroom at the Washington School, is the realization that the world of urban education, at the classroom level and at the school level, has its own kind of pattern and order, and that this order and pattern could be observed, analyzed, reflected upon, lived with, and in some instances changed. This seemed a most important insight then. Now it seems that earlier historical themes, places, events and people could similarly be ordered and patterned. This seems an important part of 'imagining oneself back into an historical period.'

On Knowing How Things Turn Out

As we began some of our historical meanderings in the multiple kinds of records and data which exist in and around Milford, another issue or two left us a bit edgy. With our 1971 book, *Anatomy*, and with the ethnography of the 1979–80 year we knew beforehand how the historical story and some of the sub-stories came out. In a sense, we had some of the themes defined ahead of time and our search of the records was a clarification of the origins and development of those themes. Racial issues, the neighborhood school concept, demographic changes, the role of the Federal government, the nature of the curriculum, the importance of Superintendent Spanman, the issues around buildings and physical facilities suggest some of the themes from our contemporaneous studies. Somehow we seemed to be in a game different from the positivistic prediction and control social science we had grown up with. At the time, it left us with a question of the legitimacy of this new research effort.

Also, for a long time, we had been in debates with various colleagues over the importance of narratives, portrayals and stories (Stake, 1977) versus the importance of generating grounded theory (Glaser and Strauss, 1967). We tended to follow George Homans (1950) and argued strongly for both narrative and theory (Smith and Pohland, 1976; Smith, 1979; Smith and Dwyer, 1980; and Smith *et al.*, 1981). One of our recent joyful experiences has been to find that the historians split on the same kind issues. For us, Hexter's book, *The History Primer*, broke open the narrative/analysis dilemma by offering a third alternative. He took some of the edginess out of knowing the outcome. He presents an illustration of historical writing, an American baseball game, which has received considerable notoriety among sports buffs. American baseball is one of the most documented aspects of American life. Records exist on the details of every player, every game in the season and every aspect within the game — hits, runs, errors, and so forth. Newspapers chronicle each game daily. Daily, weekly and monthly papers and magazines offer commentary. For 'important' games, as in the final game of the 1951 National league season, the commentary is unending. This is the game Hexter, the historian, chose to write about as an illustration of history with a small 'h', the mundane and unimportant. In writing his history he ignored large masses of available factual data, omitted reference to star players who were unimportant that day and selected threads and incidents that culminated in the high drama of the game, Bobby Thompson's home run in the ninth inning. This example of what he calls 'processive explanation in history', a form of explanation, is an answer to the 'why' question which has plagued historians. He comments in summary:

> It is this outcome that warrants the substance, the structure, and the tone of the introductory section of 'The Last Game'. In other words, the outcome defines the appropriate historical macrorhetoric, and the macrorhetoric in turn dictates the selection of 'facts' or more accurately data to be drawn from the record. Or to put it more bluntly, amid a mass of true facts about the past, too ample to set down, historians choose not merely on logical grounds but on the basis of appropriate rhetorical strategies. (1971, p. 190)

In effect, he is making a case for the importance of rhetorical principles as part of the historian's craft. In the course of his analyses he raises concepts such as record, focal center, event clusters, fragments, promissory notes, judicious omission, universe of discourse, pivot points and unstable active explanandum. Although he would probably disown the label, he has a 'theory' of historical method. All this we found helpful in thinking about what we were doing in our Kensington Revisited project. Processive explanation gave us a rationale for what we had been doing in a social science which knew the outcomes. It bridged history and ethnography in a way which cuts to the heart of the logic of social science, the concept of explanation.

Merging of Methods in Ethnography and History

At this point, we want to back off a bit from the day-to-day data-based generalization of our activities that involved ethnography and history in our Kensington Revisited project. With this detachment came several broader ideas concerning the relationships among history, ethnography and the cumulating aspects of our work. These include: 1) diversity within ethnography and history, 2) some similarities and differences, 3) a concern for process as a mode of integration, and 4) a move to broader assumptions, metatheory or paradigms.

Diversity within Ethnography and History

As we began to ground our activities further in the methodological writings of historians and anthropologists, we found ourselves in a quagmire of diverse opinions. We had known the anthropologists did not agree with one another. In trying to write a general essay on ethnography several years ago, we were struck by the theoretical differences among such major figures as Bronislaw Malinowski, William Foote Whyte and Clifford Geertz. The differences among functional, social interactional and interpretive anthropology suggest that the 'real' problems in resolving their diversity lay in their assumptions, their metatheory, their underlying paradigm (Smith, 1982, Sanday, 1979).

Among historians similar differences exist. Morton White, an American social historian (1963) who is keen on narrative history, is a logical positivist seeking broad social laws. Jack Hexter, an American who specializes in British history, wrote, as indicated earlier, a book called *The History Primer* which is a long argument with Carl Hempel's (1942) classic paper, 'The function of general laws in history.' Lawrence Stone, an Englishman trained at Oxford and now at Princeton, has published a recent collection of methodological essays and reviews under the title, *The Past and the Present* (1981). Stone's first essay, 'History and the social sciences in the twentieth century', is a cautionary note to the historians. He feels the logic of the contemporaneous social sciences is in real trouble and they, the historians, should be wary of their borrowings from social science. The second essay is entitled 'Prosopography' and refers to collective biography or multiple career line analysis. He raises a set of issues undergirding our study of the original Kensington faculty. The third essay he calls, 'The revival of the narrative: Reflections on a new old history'. His new historians, after a flirtation with positivistic social science, quantification, and general laws are returning to narratives 'directed by some "pregnant principle"', which sounds a good bit like Hexter's processive history. Further, he argues they are more apt to look to the interpretive anthropologists (such as Geertz, 1973, and his thick description) as the more important kind of social science for stimulation.

Reading these materials by eminent anthropologists and historians suggests several tentative conclusions. 1) Intellectual ferment and turmoil are everywhere. 2) Guidance from other disciplines for educational theorists, researchers and practitioners is not going to be a simple '1 to 1' and '2 to 2' kind of borrowing. 3) Synthesis and integration, to whatever degree they occur, seem to involve a next level higher set of abstractions, a metatheory or paradigmatic level of discussion. 4) It probably should be left to philosophy, but we are reminded of Kaplan's (1964) argument of scientific autonomy. The working scientists, the crafts people of an area, must put their own intellectual house in order on their way to solving their own particular substantive problems. This would seem a worthy goal for any academic community.

Some Similarities and Differences

Rather than tackle directly this array of anthropological and historical methodologists, we have borrowed bits and pieces to illuminate some of the procedures we used and the ideas we developed as we tried to carry out and understand aspects of our Kensington Revisited project. Some of these have been noted along the way. The last volume of our NIE final report, the methodological appendix, is the fuller essay on methodology (Smith *et al.*, 1984). For the moment, we find the diversity and pluralism among historians and anthropolgists helpful in suggesting ways to do the inquiry and in giving ideas toward the rationalization of what one does. But the diversity is frustrating in not providing a logical structure of criteria for judging proposals and products.

As indicated in the introduction, one of our chief guiding hypotheses of the differences between ethnography and history was the dependence of the historian on data fragments. Now, especially after reading Gottschalk's (1945) essay on 'The historian and the historical document', we believe the hypothesis remains essentially true, but that it is a matter of degree. The ethnographer also deals in data fragments, but usually has a chance at larger and more relevant chunks.

A second difference seemed to exist in the 'active huntsman' role of the ethnographer, so eloquently captured by Malinowski; 'But the Ethnographer has not only to spread his nets in the right place, and wait for what will fall into them. He must be an active huntsman, and drive his quarry into them and follow it up to its most accessible lairs' (1922, p. 8) It seems that, too, is a matter of degree; there are historians and historians. The data oriented kind of historians chase the aforementioned 'fragments' in varied, creative and persevering ways.

A third difference, and one that now seems to be much more critical, is what lies behind the cliché of the ethnographer as the research instrument. In the historian's terms this has to do with the 'primary' and 'secondary' sources. For the historian a primary source is 'the testimony of an eyewitness.' A secondary source is the 'the testimony of anyone who is not an eyewitness' — that is, of one who was not present at the event of which he tells' (Gottschalk, 1945, p. 11). In this framework the ethnographer who observes is producing his own primary sources. He is the witness to the event. From the historian's point of view that has to be a powerful and important difference. Although the ethnographer still deals in fragments and although the ethnographer is a more active huntsman, it is the production of an eyewitness account by the researcher which is the devastating difference. Somehow we had never quite phrased it that way. But that in turn produces complications, for the eyewitness is also the 'detached' story-teller and analyst. Does one lose more than one gains?

Within his discussion of the historian, Gottschalk is very precise on the need to examine each document in terms of the 'particulars' of each item in any document. Some items may be based on eyewitness testimony, other items may be secondary, information that has come to the document writer from someone else. Again, to think of ethnographic interviewees and informants from this perspective casts new meanings on them and their reports. From a psychological perspective, we see parallels in the relationships between overall test validity and item analysis and item validity. A need exists for finer and finer documentation.

Note here also the contrast of the ethnographer who is an eyewitness observer and the ethnographer who uses an informant. The latter seems more like an historian. Similarly the ethnographer, or case study researcher, who relies on interviews is also more like the historian, and perhaps identical to the oral historian. Further, if one must use an interpreter or translator, one puts another screen between the event and the eyewitness. The commonalities keep suggesting ways to interpret the activities of each group of researchers.

But even here the issue turns complicated, as the ethnographer is apt to say to the historian. If 'the ideas, feelings, meaning of the participants' are the 'real data', as some more interpretive ethnographers and case study researchers argue, then the words of the interviewees might be 'more primary' than the observing ethnographer's eyewitness reports. This is complicated in at least two further ways. The observer, insofar as he or she is a participant observer, can observe and report on his or her own internal states thereby producing another kind of primary document. Secondly, at least since Freud, there is theory and data to suggest that an outside observation of slips of the tongue and unintentional mistakes may have a kind of validity that self-reports do not have.

Once the limits of the data are held constant, the ethnographer does his descriptive narrative and the historian does his historiography, which Gottschalk defines as 'the imaginative reconstruction of the past'.

In brief, and in spite of the pluralism and variety, reading historical methodologists has been a profitable exercise in rethinking the nature of what one does as an educational ethnographer.

Triangulation Between History and Ethnography

It is a minor matter at one level, but critical at another. Dr. George, the current Milford superintendent, gave us total access to the various sets of public records — the *Bulletin* to district patrons and the School Board *Minutes*. The latter exist in bound volumes and are stored in a locked closet just off the Superintendent's office. The minor point: we never took any of these out of the Central Office building. Concretely, we kept the two or three volumes with which we were working on top of filing cabinets in the secretary's alcove. We left the volumes there overnight which gave us simple access, early in the morning or late in the afternoon whenever we came up to work. When the Superintendent and secretary were on vacation, we had access through one of the Assistant Superintendents.

The major point, however, is that by working in the Central Office building, actually in a small conference room off the main hall, we gradually came to meet most of the secretaries, clerks and Central Office professional staff. They came to know the project in two forms, 'the return to the Kensington School' and a 'history of Milford.' The most general reaction was amazement at the long involvement in reading minutes — over the course of two years. With the legitimation of the superintendent and through our own efforts to spell out our activities, which included sharing the research proposal early and preliminary documents later, we gradually built a relationship that integrated a developing friendship and professional collegiality. These concrete activities and developing relationships set the occasion for some of the most striking instances we have encountered of triangulation or multi-method approaches to data and ideas (Smith, 1979). At this point, historical method and anthropological method merged into a general open-ended set of field methods.

Figure 5 illustrates the half dozen classes of data sources. First are the bound volumes of the Board *Minutes* themselves. We don't really know much about other districts and their *Minutes* and how they are similar and different, but Milford's volumes are fascinatingly diverse. In one form or another, these Milford District records go back to 1915, with scattered earlier records.

Beginning in the 1930s, each year of minutes is bound separately; before that the years are clustered. In terms of triangulation and multi-methods one of the most important aspects of the bound *Minutes* as records is that they contain other kinds of documents beyond the minutes themselves. This fact seems to make them a much more powerful set of records. For instance, at different times they included: 1) notes of other meetings; 2) original copies of letters to and from the board or superintendent to citizens, government agencies, etc.; 3) financial records: bills paid, budgets, bank loans; 4) superintendent's agendas; 5) reports on school issues by internal staff and outside consultants; 6) on several occasions stenotyped records (50–90 pages) of meetings involving severe conflict between and within staff and the Board. In short,

Figure 5: Classes of Triangulated Data and Data Gathering Activities

1 Multiple items bound into the Board *Minutes*
2 Other Central Office documents: historical and contemporary
3 Creation of data files to our questions and inquiries
4 MA and PhD papers — inside and outside Milford
5 Short-term conversations and long-term vivid memories
6 Other contacts and oral histories
7 Intensive interviews

the *Minutes* were much more than minutes, they were multiple kinds of primary documents with curious kinds of independencies and interdependencies, open to triangulation.

While working on the *Minutes*, a second kind of triangulation occurred. It blended document analysis with brief interviews. One of the most vivid of these is what we have called the 'Nussbaum story.' It goes like this. In reading the *Minutes* of the late 1950s a conflict arose in which the Board voted not to rehire a social studies teacher, Mr. Nussbaum. Allegedly he was having discipline problems and was too familiar with some of his students. He argued that they were firing him because he had distributed some literature on the teacher's union. The *Minutes* summarized the controversy, presented relevant information and contained some of the Board's allegations. Among the facts, Nussbaum was in his seventh year of teaching and he was chairman of the high school social studies department. In our experience, problems in teacher student relations — discipline and familiarity — are not problems typically of experienced teachers and department chairpersons. In the vernacular, things didn't smell right. It was at this point that the triangulation occurred. One of the Central Office staff wandered by the conference room in which we were working, as he was prone to do, and stuck his head in to say 'hello.' After the greeting, in our best non-directive style, we said, 'Say Bill, did you ever know a teacher named Nussbaum?' His response was immediate, direct and vivid. 'Oh, yes, the Board and the Superintendent were really on his case for union activities.' Then he proceeded to tell me an even more devastating story:

> At the time, I was teaching fifth grade at Milford Village School. The Community Teachers Association (CTA) President was teaching sixth grade in the room next to mine. One afternoon, the Superintendent, the high school principal and our principal all descended on him about the upcoming CTA meeting. He was told in no uncertain terms that he was to set the agenda beforehand, to have no additional items added, and under no circumstances was Nussbaum to get on the agenda. He couldn't sleep for three days. Later Nussbaum heard about it, called him, and said he wasn't going to raise a fuss at the meeting.

The triangulating point of the story is obvious: mixed data in the documents, incongruency with our knowledge of schooling, a Central Office staff member's immediate reaction, and then the very powerful story of teachers teaching together and the trauma faced by one's friend presented a powerful view of the events.

Instances of triangulation occurred with each of the other items in Figure 5. Other dusty documents appeared off of shelves. MA and PhD papers were loaned. In some instances the District began to accumulate data files in areas where we were searching for clear records, and the network of contacts grew and grew. As we have indicated, ethnography and history merged into a series of efforts to find credible data and to build a synthesis or view of the Kensington School and Milford School District.

Process As a Mode of Integration

One's origins seem both to help and hinder one's inquiry and thought. We came to ethnographic research from a measurement oriented kind of psychology. One of the texts we taught from was Remmers and Gage's *Educational Measurement and Evaluation* (1955). One of the parts of that book which we liked, as educational psychologists, was the unit on measuring the environment, including teaching and the classroom. About the same time we were enthralled with Cornell, Lindvahl and Saupe's *An Exploratory Measurement of Individualities of Schools and Classrooms* (1953), as well as H. H. Anderson's dominative and integrative teacher personalities (1945) and Withall's (1948) classroom climate index. All this was pre-Ned Flanders. A lot of this went into an *Educational Psychology* text (Smith and Hudgins, 1964).

One of the problems with this approach was that it was static, cross-sectional, structural. It was time-free. The larger problems in teaching, it seemed, were processual, sequential, longitudinal. Ethnography, or participant observation as we tended to call it, or the micro-ethnography of the classroom as Fred Strodbeck labeled it, seemed to put us next to the evolving and developing classroom over the semester. It permitted a view of the teacher and children as active, interacting human begins. This was one of the important lessons, for Smith, from his work with Geoffrey in the *The Complexities of an Urban Classroom*.

The most significant addition to our thinking occurred as we were trying to order our data from the Kensington Revisited project. There we began talking about 'a longitudinal nested systems model of educational innovation and change.' We had gone back to the Kensington School to see the longer-term fate of an education innovation, a specific planned change, in the Milford School District. We found the school different in a number of respects. One of the most obvious was a shift in the pupil population from 100 per cent white to 60 per cent black over the fifteen-year period. One of the obvious first answers to why this had happened was the United States Supreme Court decision in Brown versus Topeka in 1954. Before this time Midwest State law made it illegal for black and white children to be educated in the same schools. Without that decision, or an equivalent set of changes, the school would not have been different in this regard. The general model we present later in Chapter 9 is a simple grid. The nested systems are arranged hierarchically on the ordinate; the time line is constructed on the abscissa. The generic quality of the model is suggested by the possibility of inserting any set of nested systems on the vertical axis and any time line on the horizontal.

In effect, what started out as an ethnographic study of a school became something very different. In part, it became an historical study of a school district. As we struggled to order this world we ended up with a process type model which has close lineages in form and purpose with our earlier analyses of classroom interaction. At this point in our work, we believe that a diachronic or process mode is an appropriate and powerful way to integrate ethnographic and historical modes of inquiry. It handles well a cluster of important phenomena in the micro-world of Geoffrey's classroom and in the macro-world of the Milford School District.

Broader Assumptions, Metatheories or Paradigms

Another kind of serendipity also seemed to be in the offing. As our story telling and analysis was moving to a close, we found, lurking in the background, concerns that we have often labeled 'broader assumptions,' 'metatheoretical issues,' or 'the nature of one's basic paradigm.' Somehow we wanted a next level of consistency, which never seemed attainable. In fieldwork, at least as we practice it, the intensive literature search often comes relatively late in the inquiry process. On those occasions we use it to help see our data and ideas in a broader, intellectual setting. We try to generalize our findings. In part, this intellectual activity is the relation of the particular instance to a large, more general, more abstract class of events (Smith, 1979; Diesing, 1971). This becomes a practical task when one intersperses ideas and stories or when one views conclusion sections as offering the analyst and interpreter a variety of intellectual options.

As we were finishing a major piece of the Kensington Revisited project, what we called 'Milford's recent history: The school district as contemporary context of the Kensington School', and as we were doing our 'literature survey,' we were brought up short. We found ourselves stunned in reading Keith Goldhammer's provocative little book, *The School Board* (1964). We remarked to ourselves that our account of Milford's recent history, heavily an account of the board and su- perintendents, was quite different. In trying to isolate those differences we generated a list of a baker's dozen items. As we looked at that list, we felt that our tacit knowledge had been running well out ahead of our formalized knowledge — we knew better than we realized, a not unusual phenomenon in this kind of research. This led us into the broader, more abstract discussion in Chapter 10 which we label 'Intellectual turmoil in educational administration.'

We believe we have come out of our experience with a point of view that is quite different — not simply different in the sense of a substantive middle range theory of school boards, but that it has the potential for an integrated view of schooling across several levels of analysis. For instance, it encompasses the kinds of data one collects when one thinks about schools, the kind of methods and procedures linked to those data, the kinds of accounts one renders of those phenomena — both commonsense and technical — the kinds of concepts, propositions, principles and generalizations one uses in one's thinking, and finally a root metaphor, a world view, or metatheoretical perspective that is consonant with the other levels of analysis and synthesis. We believe this perspective to be the most fundamental intellectual achievement of this part of our research. Its test will be the degree to which it can subsume the substantive findings from the other parts of our study and several additional perspectives from the literature of social science and education.

Conclusion

This chapter has presented and argued two major ideas: a concrete view of our research procedures and the beginnings of a more abstract methodological integration of ethnography and history. Our major conclusion is that the two approaches have a considerable degree of overlap both practically and theoretically. Even the variability in perspectives within each of the approaches has a familiar ring and quality.

We found an easy flow back and forth between the kinds of data that we looked for an generated. Documents and interviews and observations seemed to demand many of the same skills and perceptiveness as their adequacy was challenged and as sense was to be made of them. Important modes of checking validity of information, such as triangulation, seemed equally appropriate within and across historical and ethnographic data. The historians' concept of primary sources enabled us to perceive the work of the participant observer in a fresh light.

We found the descriptive tasks of ethnography and the narrative tasks of history to be essentially comparable. Vignettes and stories of mundane and important human events had a similar kind of drama whether developed from the historical record or from contemporaneous sources. Regardless of source, the stories contained the potency that good stories have always conveyed. The historian's conception of processive explanation enabled us to reinterpret in a more powerful way the more usual issues in the nature of explanation in ethnography and social science. That is a powerful addition to our developing point of view.

The debate on the role of theory in social science runs through both history and ethnography. As we read the historians, we found no arguments which made us want to discontinue the enterprise. Our accent remains on sensitizing concepts and middle range models and theories which have a focus on specific difficult problems and which we feel give practitioners and other researchers working strategies for action. The generation of grounded theory remains a principal objective, although not to the extreme as that proposed by Glaser and Strauss (1967) who want to minimize, if not eliminate narrative accounts.

We remain intrigued with the turmoil at the level of metatheory, paradigms, or root metaphors. The historians, as well as the ethnographers, keep looking to the philosophers for help, which seems as slow in coming for the historians as it has been for the ethnographers. More and more we find ourselves leaning toward Kaplan's (1964) view that the research practitioners in each discipline and in each problematic area of inquiry must solve their own intellectual problems regarding assumptions, perspectives and metaphors. He calls it the principle of 'scientific autonomy.' Our writing of the methodology section in a kind of 'autobiographical mode' is our attempt to come to grips with that principle as we thought through the integration of ethnography and history. As our description and interpretation develops in the later sections of the book we will return from time to time to these problems. For the moment, we believe that we have achieved a workable integration between the evolving problems raised in the first chapter and a set of methods which will enable us to profitably explore those problems.

Genesis and Early Evolution of a School District

Chapter 3

The Origins of a School District

An Introductory Perspective

Beginning a school district is perhaps the most important educational innovation possible for a community. Our tour through the formal records, which began in 1913[1], was long after the beginning of the one room school in Clear Valley in the 1870s. When we entered the historical record, with the school board minutes, a several room school was already in operation. In addition, a one room 'colored' school was also a part of the school district. 'Separate but equal' was a part of Midwest State law and would remain so until 1954. It seems that no matter how far one reaches back into history, there is always a prior history and a contemporaneous context, at any point in that prior history. Later we will have more to say about all that. For simplicity's purpose we begin our chronicle in the 1920s when Milford was on the verge of three further major changes if not innovations — changing from a three director district to a six director district, beginning a high school program, and hiring its first superintendent of schools. For the contemporary student of educational innovation, one might ask, 'What do you make of all that?' What does a theory of educational innovation have to say about those changes? Is an educational theory of innovation different from a social science theory of innovation? Are there lessons that will be useful to the educational practitioner? Do these practical lessons vary according to the kind of position, role, or kind of activities to be undertaken? Is it the district, the school or the classroom that is the most important unit of analysis for this kind of discussion? Or, are all of these crucial?

In our view a first step toward answering those questions is the development of a chronicle of the events. Then we can begin to explore the chronicle and the substories from the point of view, the perspective, of the educational theorist and practitioner. It is to that chronicle we now turn.

The Early Chronicle of the Milford District

Among the very first recorded minutes of the School Board of the Milford School District is a three item account from February, 1924:

Board meeting called to order Feb. 6th, 1924, 8:10 pm by President Sand.

New school bldg. proposition discussed.

Moved and 2nd that 1000.00 fire ins. be secured on colored school bldg. Carried (2/6/24)

A week later, a four item set of minutes recorded the Board's activity:

Meeting called to order Feb. 14th, 1924, 8:30 pm at Mr. Gabriel's residence.

Moved and 2nd that committee of 2 be appointed to see Mr. Freedman with reference to making arrangements for purchasing land adjacent to present site. Carried. Mr. Connor and Mr. Gabriel appointed.

Moved and 2nd that committee be appointed to investigate site in Milford Village. Carried. Mr. Sand and F.K.T. appointed.

Moved and 2nd that we bring the proposition of a 6 Director district before the people and F.K.T. secure all necessary information concerning same. Carried. (2/14/24)

Several weeks later the third recorded meeting of the Board occurred. The minutes reveal several additional aspects of the School's functioning:

Clear Valley School
District #10
Board meeting called to order Wed. Eve. March 5, 1924.
Letter of resignation of F.D. Sand read and accepted.
Mr. Gabriel elected President of the Board.
Mr. Fred Emory appointed to fill unexpired term of F.D. Sand. F.K.T.
(3/5/24)

The minutes continue on in this fashion through the rest of the year. Eventually, year-in and year-out, they become more and more elaborate. The reader is left with an image of the school district developing before one's eyes. But even at this point several items are clear:

1   The district is a three-director rural or Common School District.
2   The Board meets in the home of one of the directors.
3   Concerns exist over school buildings, sites, and insurance.
4   A separate school for Blacks exists in the community.
5   Concern for a township school, that is, a 'six-director' school is on the agenda.
6   The Board elects its own president, and replaces its resigned members.

In subsequent minutes of irregular meetings of that Spring a number of items paint the story more fully. The Clear Valley School has a principal, Mr. Young, and two or three teachers including Mrs. Young. The principal is paid $160 per month and the teachers average $105 per month. The 'colored school' receives a name that spring and becomes the Attucks School.

In the Autumn of 1924, a new Board president appears, although Mr. Gabriel remains on the Board and F.K.T., Mr. F. K. Tholozan, remains as 'clerk.' The minutes continue to create a picture of schooling. Bills to a half-dozen book companies — American Book, Allyn and Bacon, Ginn, Little, Brown, etc. are recorded. Repairs to furnaces, hiring of janitors and general up-keep of the schools continue. 'The matter of electric wiring of the colored school was brought up. Motion carried that wiring be done.' In January of 1925,[2] four items appear:

> Moved and 2nd that bills be allowed. Carried.
>
> Moved and 2nd that bookcase be purchased by Mr. Young for colored school. Carried.
>
> Moved and 2nd that official strap, about $2\frac{1}{2}$ inches wide, for the infliction of corporal punishment be purchased. Carried.
>
> Moved and 2nd that 1 × 4 strips be purchased for tying desks together in west room. Carried. (1/13/25)

In the March, 1925 meeting three major items appeared:

> Moved and 2nd that the proposition of organizing this school district into a town school district with six directors be submitted to the voters at the annual election. Carried.
>
> Moved and 2nd that $.60 tax rate be submitted to the voters at the annual election. Carried.
>
> Moved and 2nd that plot of ground east of school yard be rented — rate of $50.00 per year. Carried. (3/12/25)

These went on the ballot in April with all due announcements, petitions, and indications that two villages — Milford and Pleasant Hill are within District #10, and also that '400 Scholastics'[3] reside in the District. On 2 April 1925, 130 citizens voted 'For organization,' fifty-one voted 'Against organization' and four were 'Questionable' (6/17/25). Clear Valley Common School District was now the Milford School District and would retain that name until the present. (6/17/25)

Milford: The Initial Six-Director Town School District

Very quickly the new Board moved to organize itself, voted a ten month school year, submitted a bond issue for $45,000 for a new four room school building, took options on four acres adjacent to the present school site, engaged a lawyer, and appointed a committee 'to make arrangements to provide an adequate building and equipment for the colored (Attucks) school.' (5/27/25) That committee reported out in the following summer: 'Moved and 2nd that committee proceed with alterations of colored school. Colored school to be increased to 32 ft. × 32 ft. with basement under west half. Motion carried.' (7/22/25) During this period, the Board minutes record pupil enumeration as:

420   White
 46   Colored
  4   Deaf, Dumb and Crippled
———
470   TOTAL   (5/27/25)

A year earlier, the enumeration was:

187   Male   )
                    White
196   Female)

 22   Male   )
                    Colored
 24   Female)
  5   f. m. & B[4]
———
434   TOTAL   (5/24)

The 1925–26 school year contained items which seem indigenous to schooling everywhere in America at different times. Property owners, who wanted more for their land than the School Board was willing to give, were subjected to the legal actions of condemnation proceedings. The first record of resolutions to problems of overcrowding also appeared that year. The Board minutes recorded it this way: 'On account of the crowded condition in some of the rooms it was moved and 2nd that parents who wished could keep their children home half day providing they gave them instruction at home. Motion carried.' (1/19/26)

On 13 April 1926, amidst actions on bills, levies and new Board members, several items related to staffing problems appear in brief enigmatic form:

Moved and 2nd that a man and his wife shall not be permitted to teach in our school district. Motion carried.

The question of renewal of contracts was brought up and was stated that there was considerable discord among the teachers. Mr. Craig and Miss Gurney advised Mr. Gabriel that they could not renew their contracts under present conditions, claiming Mr. and Mrs. Young did not cooperate with them. Several of the patrons, as well as the County Superintendent of Schools, called some of the Board members attention to existing conditions.

After much discussion it was moved and 2nd that Board shall not renew the contracts of Mr. and Mrs. Young. Motion carried unanimously. The President advised Mr. Young of the Board's action in its presence.

Moved and 2nd that Ronald Craig be appointed principal for the next term, 10 months, at a salary of $150/month. Motion carried unanimously. The President advised Mr. Craig of the Board's action in its presence. (4/13/26)

Two special meetings occurred in the last weeks of April. A group of six parents representing the Parents and Teachers Association requested the Board to 'reconsider the election of teachers.' While no formal general action was taken the Board requested and received a release from Mr. Craig of its offer as principal. At the second meeting, in two, 3–2 votes the board voted down the motion to consider 'none of the teachers,' and then voted not to reconsider its vote of the 13th. In brief, the decisions stood to terminate the Youngs and to promote Mr. Craig as Principal.

A variety of inferences might be drawn provisionally from these items. First, considerable problems must have been occurring for this is the first mention of the County Superintendent of Schools in over two years of minutes. Second, the nepotism rules seem to have arisen as simple solutions to ordinary day-to-day problems. Third, boards had total power over the teaching staff, that they moved initially in unanimity on such key issues, and that communications to key parties was carried out in the 'presence' of the entire Board. The clarity of direct observation and witness allowed no misconstrual of action. Fourth, appeals could be made and were made. Individual Board members were not locked permanently into voting patterns. The first split votes were recorded.

Amongst the 'heavier' items, appear motions which will become part and parcel of later approaches to small problems: 'Moved and 2nd that principal be authorized to purchase baseball equipment out of funds accumulated from sale of misc. stationery. Motion carried.' (5/5/26)

Whether many schools have engaged in money-making activities for years for 'fringe' items is not known. In Milford, the records indicate that this was the case from fifty-five years ago to the time of our study, 1979–1980.

While no clear mention is made in the Board minutes of the new school opening in the Autumn of 1926, bills for the builder, architect, 100 chairs, and $400.00 for a septic tank all were paid in the summer of 1926. The janitor was employed for ten months and 'permitted to use 2 rooms of the old building for living quarters.' It was moved and seconded that the builder 'give floors in the new bldg. 2 coats of heated linseed oil. Carried.' (8/11/26)

In the spring of 1927, the Board began it first action regarding high school education. Prior to this time youngsters had tuition paid to a neighboring district:[5]

> Moved and 2nd that the Board be appointed committee to see the parents of the high school prospects with the view of determining their attitude. Carried. (1/13/27) Moved and 2nd that special meeting be called for April 27th, 1927, for further discussion of high school work and employment of teachers. (1/13/27)

Two months later, action was taken: 'Moved and 2nd that the 9th grade of high school work be taken up for the coming year. Motion carried.' (6/8/27) The story continued immediately:

> Secy, instructed to write Supt. Jos. B. Michael whether or not a teacher can be employed to teach ninth grade high school work, and can alternate with lower grades, without affecting our standing as an accredited high school.

Secy, instructed to write Mrs. Claire Briggs requesting application. (6/14/27)

By 20 July 1927, Mrs. Briggs was hired, 'conditioned upon obtaining State of Midwest certificate to teach.' (7/20/27) Bids for renovating the old frame building were secured and the high school found a home and began. New programs bring unanticipated problems: 'Regularly moved and 2nd that some member of the School Board see Dr. Snyder[6] at his convenience to instruct whether or not we can admit a person to our school 21 yrs. of age, and married. Motion carried.' (9/14/27)

And the next item in the minutes speaks eloquently to another set of problems:

Regularly moved and 2nd that in the future if we should find it necessary to order any repair work done of any nature, that we secure at least three competitive bids, we to specify the work to be done and the materials used, and the lowest bid accepted. Motion carried. (9/14/27)

For the first time also, the bills were now listed by sequential number as well as by amount and biller in the School Board minutes.

At a September meeting the Board, which earlier had purchased a $2\frac{1}{2}$ inch strap for corporal punishment, now reversed itself: 'Regularly moved and 2nd that corporal punishment be abolished from the Clear Valley School. Motion carried.' (9/14/27)

The complications in this aspect of school policy and school functioning appeared within a month. A pupil was suspended. He and his parents appeared before the Board. He was warned and 'ordered' to return to school. The Board took a list of rules, infractions and penalties developed by the teachers and turned them into school policy. Although no copy of those rules exists, inferences can be drawn in part from the note of suspension. The note appears as Figure 6. Clearly the items of truancy, defying and disobeying the principal, lying, disturbing another room, and unruliness would be part of those rules.

Figure 6: Notice of Suspension

Billy Lamb, the eight-year old son of Greg Lamb, of R31 Box 29 was suspended from Clear Valley School on Wednesday September 21, 1927.

Charges:
1 He played truancy,
2 He defied and disobeyed the principal of the school,
3 He broke down the morale of the school by telling falsehoods,
4 He entered and created a disturbance in a room where he was forbidden to go.

Punishment:
Billy did not receive any punishment at school for his unruly conduct.

Signed by
Mr. Craig, Principal
Mr. Underwood, School Board Pres.
Mr. Matthews (Another board member)

The complications of 'policy in action' appeared in a lengthy item in the 12 October 1927 meeting:

> After a complete hearing of evidence and facts relative to corporal punishment inflicted on Kent Collinson, a pupil in Miss Gimble's classroom, by Mr. Craig, Principal, on Wednesday, Oct. 5th, the parents were advised that they would be advised at a later date of the School Board's findings. Mr. Craig was reprimanded by the Board and a general understanding effected that it is the desire of this School Board that corporal punishment be abolished from our school. While the Board is fully aware that the State Law gives the teacher the right to inflict reasonable corporal punishment, the Board wished the cooperation of the faculty in abolishing this form of punishment, using the suspension system as set forth in rules submitted by and signed by the faculty, dated Sept. 26th, 1927, referred to as exhibit A in minutes of meeting of Sept. 28th, 1927. (10/12/27)

Slowly, the high school program began to take on form and substance. Beyond the unlisted books which had been purchased and labeled only as 'High School books,' items such as these appeared:

Bills:

> 431 Central Scientific Co. — H. School Lab $149.91
> Regularly moved and 2nd that a cabinet for storing high school laboratory equipment be ordered by the Secy. as requested by Mrs. Briggs. Equipment necessary as set forth in the Bulletin on High School Organization, page #89. Motion carried. (10/12/27)
> Moved and 2nd that the necessary books to complete high school library requested by Mrs. Briggs in her letter of Oct. 12th be ordered by the Secy. Motion carried. (10/12/27)

Items relevant to basic dilemmas in public and private enterprise arose:

> Regularly moved and 2nd that Miss Wilma Mann discontinue giving music lessons in the school building pending a thorough interpretation by the Board of Directors as to the legality of her so teaching for profit. Motion carried. (11/9/27)

At the same meeting, the interplay among larger governmental structures, the local Board and the professionalization of teachers arose:

> Secy. instructed by the Board of Directors to advise Mr. Craig that schools in our district be closed Nov. 10 and 11th, to permit teachers to attend the State Teachers Convention, as per recommendation of Supt. Snyder in his note of 10/12/27. (11/9/27)

Similarly, the holiday structure was reaffirmed: 'Secy. instructed to advise Mr. Craig to declare Friday, Nov. 25th, a school holiday, being the Friday following

Thanksgiving. School closes this day as has been customary in previous years.' (11/9/27)

The final item on that busy November evening in 1927, helps keep the reader's image in perspective:

> Regularly moved and 2nd that a letter of complaint be written by the Secy. to Dr. Zeller, County Health Supt., concerning the odors, etc., arising from hog farm operated by Mr. Standish, which is endangering the health of our school children. Complaint filed by Mr. Craig with the Bd. of E. letter dated 11/9/27. Motion carried. (11/9/27)

The confusion over corporal punishment returned later that month: 'Regularly moved and 2nd that our rule abolishing corporal punishment again be instituted, teachers to use proper judgment and discretion in administering this form of punishment. Secy. instructed to advise Mr. Craig of this ruling.' (11/15/27)

The County provided some help regarding discipline and deportment. A Board action on 8 February 1928 commented this way:

> Regularly moved and 2nd that Secy. be instructed to write Mr. Snyder drawing his attention to the laxity of the Co. Truant Officer in re delinquency of children of this district — Jane Zellner — 2 other members — and Michael Gaines residing in Pleasant Hill (Chronic cases). Motion carried. (2/8/28)

For the first time, the Board raised an issue which remains a part of life in the Milford Schools: 'Regularly moved and 2nd that Secy. be instructed to request Mr. Craig to draft a plan whereby all teachers supervise playground during playtime.' (2/15/28)

And the Board also instituted the beginnings of school cafeterias and lunch programs:

> Motion made that Mr. Tomlinson and Mr. Nunn[7] be appointed to secure necessary equipment as suggested (they to use their judgment in the selections) for the preparation of food for the school children. Carried. (Mrs. Allen 7:30 to 3:00 p.m. @ $2.00 per day.)
> Motion made that Mr. Jennings and Newberry[7] be instructed to take care of the installation of necessary tables in the basement of the school. Carried. (2/15/28)

Housing, staffing, and keeping the lunch programs 'profitable' will be a regular item forevermore. Conventional wisdom in this domain, as we will see, is almost an internal contradiction.

At a special meeting of the Board, after the April 3rd elections, the new members were sworn in, and new officers were elected, 'by acclamation.' Other items were noteworthy for their first mention in the record: 'Committee of Mothers Club desires permission to plant shrubs and trees on school premises. Moved and 2nd that the committee be permitted to do their planting without Mr. Thompson's[8] deference. Motion carried. (4/14/28)

Two key items relevant to the educational programs arose:

> Regularly moved and 2nd that for the year 1928–29, that we organize a Junior High School consisting of 7th, 8th, and 9th grade school. Motion carried. (4/4/28)
>
> Regularly moved and 2nd that we offer Mrs. Briggs the position of Principal of this school at $175.00 per month, for 10 month term, 1928–1929. Motion carried. (4/4/28)

That salary was $35.00 per month higher than her teaching salary, $140.00, and $15.00 per month higher than the salary of Mr. Craig, the elementary principal who until then was the highest paid employee in the district at $160.00 per month. The median teacher salary at the time was $125.00. A week later, the minutes suggest that all was not well in staff relations: 'Regularly moved and 2nd that Mrs. Briggs be employed for the year of 1928–1929 as Principal of the High School and Elementary School, at $200.00 per month. 4 members Carr, Inman, Tholozan[9], and Ennis for. Opposed — Newport. Pres. not voting.' (4/11/28)

The next week six new teachers were offered contracts. Changes also occurred at the Attucks School. A new replacement teacher and an alternative were selected. The janitor was dismissed and a new janitor hired.

By Autumn 1928, the faculty of the Milford District consisted of nine professional staff, including Mrs. Briggs and a part time teacher. By November due to congestion and crowding the half time teacher became full time and an additional primary teacher was added. Only Mrs. Briggs remained from the previous year. High faculty turnover seems a part of the early years.

Milford Acquires a Superintendent: Mrs. Briggs

During the Summer of 1928, in this period of faculty change and turnover, the Board made an additional move: 'Regularly moved and 2nd that Mr. Carson write Mr. Tobias for permission to organize the Sch. Dist. under supervision of a Supt. Motion carried.' (7/11/28) The Board quickly heard from Mr. Tobias and a special session was called:

> Letter dated July 13th, 1928, from State Director of High Sch. Supervision, K. S. Tobias, read and unanimous approval of all Bd. members present expressed.
>
> Regularly moved and 2nd that on strength of this letter, Mrs. Briggs, our Principal, be appointed Supt, of our School Dist. to devote half of her time to the supervision of our schools and to organize the 7th, 8th, and 9th grades in a Junior High School, in accordance with the plans submitted to and approved by Director of H. S. Supervision, K. S. Tobias. Motion carried. (7/20/28)

In just one year (6/14/27 to 7/20/28), Mrs. Briggs had moved from being a teacher new to the district but organizing the high school, to principal, to becoming the first superintendent of the Milford Public Schools.

During the Fall months of 1928, members of the Board still carried out a number of miscellaneous activities: 'Regularly moved and 2nd that Mrs. Tholozan be authorized to purchase the necessary equipt. for hospital or first aid room. Motion carried.' (9/12/28) But the new superintendent began to take on broader responsibilities:

> Moved and 2nd that Mrs. Briggs write to Mr. Overmeier of the State University asking for one of the experts on building projects to call on us as soon as it can be arranged, our Board to pay his traveling expenses. Motion carried.
>
> Resolution introduced to give Mrs. Briggs general charge of the cafeteria. Seconded by Mrs. Tholozan and passed. Mr. Carr instructed to inform Mrs. Winter. (12/12/28)

In the Spring of 1929, an attempt was made to pass a bond issue for a school addition. It failed. Later, after a citizens committee was appointed, a plan for a new school was developed. It too failed. Finally in October 1929, a bond issue for a new school (four rooms), two new rooms at Clear Valley, and repairs and improvements at the Attucks School passed overwhelmingly — 438, 70, and 3. The new school would be closer to the population in the eastern part of the district. Passage of the bond issue meant then that architects, roofers, '. . . kindly consider the use of their asbestos shingles on the contemplated building' (12/11/29), and builders visited the Board. And the usual bills were paid, holidays for Christmas were set — Friday, 12/20/29 to Thursday, 1/2/30.

Staff problems seemed to remain. Mrs. Briggs raised complaints regarding the janitor and he was replaced in December 1929, with two weeks notice. On 8th January 1930 two teachers met with the Board:

> Miss Monet and Miss Greer representing our faculty — made a few remarks both for and against the present condition of the school system.
>
> Mrs. Briggs placed before the Board a few of the many difficulties that arise to hinder progress in the school work. Mr. Thomas had left us early in Nov. T. I. Wells took his place for a few weeks but failed to qualify and was discharged on that ground. Mr. T. M. Kane was hired and worked only a few days and he resigned. Mr. Fred Nolting was then taken in and appears to meet all requirements and we are hoping that he will stay with us the remainder of the year. (1/18/30)

In February: 'Miss Kelley and Mrs. Nolting, members of the faculty and *Hubert Click a member of the student body* were delegated to call upon the Board and make various recommendations.' (Our italics) (2/12/30)

In the week of 17 February the Milford Board held two special meetings in which the mid-winter drama reached a climax.

Mr. Nofsinger — Carr — Inman — Lawrence met informally with Mr. Peter Lake — superintendent of the Kennard School[10] for the purpose of obtaining information concerning a member of his faculty — who had been recommended to us as a likely candidate for our Superintendent.

Mr. Lake recommends highly Mr. F. W. Grey who has been in his system for 4 years in the capacity of Physical Education director and one whose ambitions and qualifications have outgrown this system and one that he (Mr. Lake) would be unable to retain.

Mr. Lake also explained quite satisfactorily the system of voting the tax levy in the two propositions. He also explained why our $.85 tax which was voted upon at the Annual School Election, April 1929 and was carried by a majority vote of the people — was ruled out of the County Court because a school of our classifi. on cannot vote more than $.65 for teachers and incidental fund.

Mr. Inman was instructed to extend an invitation to Mr. Grey to meet with us on Friday, Feb. 21/31 for an interview.

Our meeting was adjourned at 10:45 pm.

Within the week, the following Friday, the Board met with Mr. Grey. Only Mr. Edgar was absent. The verbatim minutes are presented in toto:

The purpose of the meeting was to interview Mr. Grey as a likely candidate to succeed Mrs. Briggs as Superintendent.

Our school district is growing so rapidly and we are in the midst of a building program this year and *we feel keenly the need of a man at the head of our school system.* (Our italics)

Mrs. Briggs has given good service and has done a splendid job of organizing a Junior and Senior High School, but the increasing demand is growing out of her power of control.

After a careful interview with Mr. Grey we naturally agreed that provided the additional tax of $.40 for building and repair fund (that we expect to vote upon at the next annual school elections) carries we would employ him — giving him a contract for 12 months, beginning July 1st, 1930, in order that he might be on the job during the building process this Summer.

In anticipation of the number of children that very likely will attend the school in Milford Village[11] Mr. Grey asks permission to make a survey of those living in the district and their preference. He was authorized to have blanks for this request printed and distributed throughout the district.

Mr. Mullanphy was authorized to inform Mrs. Briggs that we would not renew her contract.

Mrs. Tholozan was delegated to introduce Mr. Grey to Mrs. Briggs in order that he might become familiar with the school system — of what has been done and what needs to be done.

Meeting adjourned at 10:50 pm. (2/21/30)

The regular March 12th Board spent most of its time on the bond issue and bidders from eight financial institutions. Bills were read and approved. Names of Inman and Lawrence were submitted for re-election of members of the Board in April. At a special meeting, a week later, a number of items of business were handled — final architectural plans and bids for the contracts. Three items bear especially on several of our larger themes: 'The secretary read the application of Mrs. Briggs and after careful consideration we decided that it would not be wise to retain her in the system. Mrs. Tholozan was delegated to inform her of same. Her application is attached.' We have inserted her letter as Figure 7.

The next item in the minutes:

> G. W. Ford — colored contractor, was present and asked the consideration of the Board for the contract for the building of the Attuks School.[12]
>
> Mr. Grey submitted a report of the survey made just recently in regard to the number of pupils that will likely attend the Milford School and recommended the hiring of three additional teachers.
>
> Mr. Carr made a motion and seconded by Mrs. Tholozan to authorize Mr. Grey to proceed in getting teachers applications as per his schedule. (3/19/30)

Figure 7: Mrs. Briggs' Letter of Appeal

March 19, 1930

TO THE SCHOOL BOARD,

I am taking the privilege of submitting my application for a position as teacher in your high school next year. I think the previous experiences I have had here will render me more capable of efficient service than would be possible if I had not been at the head of the school for the past two years. I think you know me to be able to teach subject matter and at the same time maintain proper conditions in the room. I am familiar with the system and I know the student personnel, which is a decided advantage to any teacher. If I have the honor of remaining in the school, I pledge myself to cooperate to the fullest with Mr. Grey and the entire organization and to more fully convince you of this, I am willing to work without a formal contract, as this would enable you to remove me at any time I may not be entirely satisfactory.

I am turning over to your new superintendent a well organized school of which I am very proud. I think you may have acted very wisely in selecting a man instead of a woman as administrator, since the demands of the system will be very much heavier next year than they have been this year. At present I am succeeding in creating a very wholesome atmosphere for Mr. Grey in the high school. I have no ill feelings whatever toward anyone connected with the system, and I shall be more than pleased to remain with you as a part of your organization. I know I can render you a very valuable service. In addition to my teaching duties, I shall be glad to assist Mr. Grey in every way possible connected with the school.

Please consider this proposition fairly and discuss it with Mr. Grey. If I am retained in the system, I promise you will have no cause to regret it.

Very truly yours.

Mrs. Briggs

The Special Meeting in April reported the re-election of the two Board members and the overwhelming passage of the $.65 and the $.40 tax. The oath they and the earlier Board members took is reproduced as Figure 8. In simple language it places the local responsibilities in the state and national context.

Mr. Grey's Tenure as Superintendent

The hiring of a full time male Superintendent had a number of consequences. Two items from the minutes suggest the beginning of these implications:

> After careful consideration, Mr. Inman moved and Mr. Carr seconded that we give Mr. Grey a contract for 12 months beginning July 1, 1930 — at a salary of $2,500 per annum.
>
> Regularly moved and 2nd that Mr. Grey and Mrs. Tholozan proceed with the employment of teachers for the next year. (4/9/30)

Although the salary increase was a full twenty-five percent more than that paid his predecessor, the term was increased from ten to twelve months. The active involvement of the Superintendent in all kinds of activities originally a Board responsibility was to increase step by step over the years.

In the Summer of 1930, the Board, 'regularly moved and seconded,' that the new elementary school be named as Milford Village School and the high school be the Milford High School. Though the high school program was now in its third year, the financing remained precarious: 'Regularly moved and 2nd to raise the tuition of High School pupils from $40.00 to $60.00. Mr. Grey is authorized to notify patrons.' (9/10/30) Mr. Grey was given additional duties: 'Regularly moved and 2nd to appoint Mr. Grey as attendance officer for the district.' (11/12/30) The school's role in the larger community appears: 'A general discussion regarding tuition from other districts. Mr. Grey informs us that the payments are coming promptly and the enrollment is holding up well.' (1/14/31) The Board's involvement with the community also appears: 'Mutually agreed by the Board that we all attend the Annual County School Board Convention at Green City, Saturday Mar. 14–31.' (3/11/31)

In May of 1931, a series of items carried the flavor of Mr. Grey's growing responsibilities:

> Regularly moved and 2nd that the Board levy a tax of $.35 for Interest and sinking fund and to *accept the estimated budget for 1931–32 as submitted by Mr. Grey.* (Our italics)

Figure 8: Oath of Office of School Board Members

'I do solemnly swear (or affirm) that I will support the Constitution of the United States and the Constitution of the State of Midwest, and that I will faithfully and impartially discharge the duties of school director in and for the School District of Milford, to the best of my ability, according to the law, so help me God.'

Mr. Williams moved and 2nd by Mr. Easter that we approve the contracts for teachers as submitted by Mr. Grey and sign same.

Regularly moved and 2nd that Mr. Grey proceed with his plans for a school picnic.

Regularly moved by Mr. Williams and 2nd by Easter that we increase Mr. Grey's salary from $2,500 to $3,000 per year. (5/13/31)

The regular meeting of 11 June 1931, is noted for one major event: 'On account of having no quorum — no official business was transacted except the signing of Diplomas by the President and Secretary.' (6/11/31) In such auspicious circumstances the first high school graduating class was officially certified.

Items continue to appear in interesting juxtaposition: 'Mr. Grey explained in detail the New School Law relative to High School Tuition that was recently passed by the General Assembly, signed by the Governor and is to become effective Sept. 14, 1931.' (8/13/31) And:

> Mr. Inman moved, 2nd by Mrs. Tholozan that the Superintendent of Schools, Mr. Grey, be authorized to exercise general supervision over the janitors of the several schools and to prescribe their hours and the work to be performed by them. (8/13/31)

Mr. Grey, as Superintendent, is progressively more and more involved in both external relations and internal operation of the School District. At this point in time, if our inferences are correct, the Superintendent mediates between the State and the Board. He 'explained in detail' the evolving laws and regulations emanating from the State Capitol. In the past, one of the members of the Board wrote directly to the County Superintendent, to the State Department, and to the State University. As one reads the record of Board Minutes, one senses that the Board has hired a person it trusts and has confidence in, that it pays him increasingly well, and that it expects him to relieve the Board of a variety of chores and activities. While the Board retains 'ultimate' control, power, and authority, it now acts at a full step removed from day-to-day decision making in ever-widening areas of responsibility. The motion on janitors now reporting to the Superintendent follows by two and a half years (12/28), the responsibility given to Mrs. Briggs to supervise the cafeteria workers.

Although the Board minutes are not explicit in noting the Superintendent's regular attendance at Board meetings, it seems to have begun about 1931. Until then, each set of minutes indicates presence and absence of Board members but not of others. During this year, the language seems to shift from a particular Board member instructing or informing Mr. Grey to, 'Mr. Grey explained in detail the New School Law . . . .' and from not having been invited to be present to do so. Or:

> Mr. Grey explained that Mrs. Johnson's salary was below the legal standard required by the state in order that we get state credit for the extra High School work she is to carry out at Attucks School this year. In view of that, Mr. Inman made a motion — 2nd by Mr. Williams that we increase her salary $5.00 per month. Carried. (9/9/31)

In November, Mr. Grey joined the Board at a Saturday evening meeting of the
County School Board Convention:

> County School Board Convention held at Fairwoods High School. Our
> school was represented by Mr. Grey, Mr. Carr, Mr. Inman, Mr. Easter, Mr.
> Williams and Mrs. Tholozan. Mr. Snyder explained in detail the new
> school law in regard to consolidation and redistricting of rural districts
> recently passed. (11/7/31)

Between regular meetings of the Board, acts of nature occur, deliberately
organized community institutions respond, and the School Board takes notice and
responds with concern and good feeling, as well as its legal responsibilities:

> The secretary was instructed to write a letter of appreciation to each of the
> Fire Departments that responded to the call made on the night of Oct. 30
> when the frame school building caught fire due to overheating. Regularly
> moved and 2nd to give the Milford Village Fire Dept. a stove.[13] $10.00 to
> the Crescent Fire Dept. and 2 boxes of cigars to the Germania Fire Dept.
>   A report was made by Mr. Roundtree of the Fidelity Co. on the
> settlement for Insurance for the damage done to the school building in the
> recent fire. (11/15/31)

The role of specialist and generalist poses a problem at both the professional and
non-professional levels. The 'way things were' is captured in the minutes:

> Mr. Lawrence moved — 2nd by Mr. Williams that we purchase material
> for tables for the Milford Village Elementary School and have the janitors
> to make them at their spare time, also to place a storm door on the north
> side of the building. The motion carried. (12/14/31)

The same evening broader issues were brewing in the county and the Board, once
again, seemed to be tackling them in its usual direct common sense style:

> No further business to come before the Board at this time the meeting
> adjourned at 8 o'clock in order that we might attend a mass meeting of the
> Boards of Education of the adjoining district at Cummings Hall, Table
> Rock in regard to the consolidation and re-districting of school districts.
> (12/14/31)

These efforts at school consolidation have had a checkered history in Midwest State
and Suburban County. A local history of a part of Suburban County reports the
following:

> In 1933 a county districting board met 16 times and emerged with a plan to
> merge the 90 little three director districts in the county down to 16 . . .
> Wanting no part of this the board members campaigned against it and the
> measure failed all over the county. (PD 1977, p. 34)[14]

No records regarding these meetings appear in the Board minutes.
    In the first meeting of 1932, the format of the Board minutes took on a more

formal view. Instead of a flowing handwritten record, the minutes were typed in a professional looking style.[15] Items were paragraphed. Marginal identifications were introduced for the first time. Formal indication that the Superintendent 'was present' also appears. Bills were paid, old business was attended to, for example, the volunteer fire department was voted $15.00. And the Superintendent's role continued to be elaborated: 'Mr. Grey reported a temporary suspension of Michael Untermeyer and Joe Dolan on account of misconduct in classroom. A general discussion followed. The matter was left in the hands of Mr. Grey to dispose of as he sees fit.' (1/13/32) No longer did the parent and youngster appear before the Board. No longer did the Board directly decide on appropriate next steps.

The Board, in early March of 1932, accepted applications of two incumbents and later in March accepted two others. The next item was: 'Each member pledged to support the incumbent candidates and work hard for the tax.' (3/30/32) The iron law of oligarchy worked less than perfectly and one incumbent won and the other lost.[16] They were duly sworn in the following week at a special Board meeting.

Apparently the Board felt the reasoning and results surrounding Mr. Grey's appointment had been successful: '. . . we employ an additional man teacher to act as principal in the absence of Mr. Grey and teach Physical Education and Science at the salary of $1500.00.' (4/21/32) At the same meeting, one teacher was not rehired, and other teachers were offered contracts. One of the janitors, '. . . was dismissed on account of possession of liquor on school property. Motion carried unanimously.' (4/2/32) No mention of the economic depression occurs in the Board minutes. Although the Superintendent was rehired at $250.00 per month for twelve months, he was given a three year contract but with the provision that if the Board deemed it necessary to decrease (or increase) teachers' salaries the Superintendent's would be decreased or increased proportionately.

In August of 1932, at the regular Board meeting, one of our continuing themes, the education of Black children in the Milford School District, receives the following mention:

> The regular order of business was dispensed with to take care of a committee from the Waterford School District. The members of this committee present were Ben Olderman, President of the Waterford School Board; William Zener, Director of the Waterford School Board and Donald Day, Director of the Waterford School Board. Mr. Olderman was the spokesman and asked if they might be allowed to send the colored elementary pupils from the Waterford District to Attucks School in the Milford School District and what tuition would be asked. Mr. Grey explained that while the cost per pupil was much higher than $40.00 per year, that our present facilities would take care of these pupils without additional seating or teachers, and that, in view of this fact these pupils could be taken care of for $40.00 each for the school term 1932–33. This was satisfactory to the Waterford Committe and Mrs. Tholozan moved that we accept the colored elementary pupils from the Waterford District for the school year 1932–33 at $40.00 per pupil for a term of 10 months.

Mr. Roberts gave his 2nd to the motion and the motion carried unanimously. The committee then adjourned and the meeting proceeded with the regular order of business. (8/10/32)

Within a month, the County redistricting issue reappears and Mr. Grey and the Board members participated in the election of six members, one from each of the County's townships and one at large.

The interdependence of various public functions operating toward the common good appears in another minute: 'Mr. Williams moved that the Board of Education adopt a resolution that the Board go on record as not opposing the use of the school for a polling place. Mr. Roberts 2nd the motion and the motion carried.' (10/12/32)

In December, 1932, the Superintendent read the bills, #172–206, reported on fire insurance regarding the Clear Valley frame building, trucks on the school ground during school hours, and pamphlets available regarding the 'tentative redistricting program.' A transportation item appeared.

The Superintendent recommended a change on the manner of paying the transportation of the colored High School pupils to Big City High Schools by paying the parents directly instead of paying the drivers of the cars. After due discussion, Mr. Inman moved that the Board of Education pay the parents directly for the transportation of their children to Big City High Schools. The motion was 2nd by Mr. Williams and the motion was unanimous favoring the motion. (12/14/32)

At a later meeting checks from $3.00 to $4.17 sent to eight individuals for 'Col. H. S. Trans.' The 'busing' of students for racial reasons has a long history in the Milford School District.

The effects of the depression appeared in the Spring of 1933. In a series of split votes (3–3), a separating of issues and seeking advice of the County Superintendent, the Board finally voted to retain all of the teachers, to cut the salaries 10 per cent, and to retain a ten month school year. Each contract carries the provision, 'provided the school funds are available.' In addition the Board added a supplement to the teachers' contracts: '. . . it is the desire of the members of the Board that providing they can find suitable living quarters in the district, that they will be required to live within the district.' (5/29/33)

Conflict continued in the Board with some motions not carrying for lack of a second, others split 4–2. The issues involved insurance on the buildings, replacing a teacher getting married, and the equalizing of janitor salaries — one down from $135.00 and the others up from $75.00

In the Spring of 1934, discussion was held and a motion made and seconded that the Superintendent be given a new three year contract. The Board voted him a year's leave of absence because of illness. At that same meeting the first overall budget enclosed in the record of minutes appeared. It is reproduced in toto as Figure 9.

Figure 9: The First Extant Budget of the Milford School District

Estimated Budget for 1934–35		
Teachers Salaries	21,275.00	
Janitors Salaries	2,500.00	
School Supplies	600.00	
Janitors Supplies	225.00	
Playground Supplies	100.00	
Equipment	100.00	
Repairs and Replacements	150.00	
Libraries	100.00	
School Grounds	100.00	
Fuel	400.00	
Electric Services	325.00	
Telephone Service	200.00	
Water	175.00	
Insurance	500.00	
Colored Tuition	500.00	
Colored Transportation	300.00	
Board of Education	150.00	
Election Costs	50.00	
Enumeration Costs	50.00	
Miscellaneous Expenses	100.00	
Total Amount to be raised	27,900.00	27,900.00
1.20 levy will raise approximately	21,600.00	
State Revenue, railroad taxes, etc.	5,000.00	
Tuition, Int. on Bank Bal. and Miscellaneous	1,300.00	
	27,900.00	27,900.00

All fifteen teachers were retained in April, 1934, with small raises (most at $2.00 per month, for example, $105.50 to $107.50) although Mr. F. B. Newsome who assumed some of Mr. Grey's duties had a salary increase from $135.00 to $150.00 per month. Except for Mr. Grey whose salary was $2500.00 per year, Mr. Newsome was the highest paid employee of the district. In May the Board instituted the first fringe benefits to the teachers with the simple item: 'Mr. Lawrence moved and 2nd by Mr Easter that teachers be allowed 10 days per year with pay for sickness or death in the immediate family. Teachers to furnish a doctor's certificate of illness. The motion carried.' (5/9/34)

As the 1933–34 school year ended the Board took two actions which seemed to have long term significance. First the Board voted formally to admit visitors:

Mr. Easter moved and 2nd by Mr. Finley that we admit all visitors and let them voice their opinions or objections (sic) and then ask them to retire while the Board carries on its business. The vote was 3 for and 2 against. (6/13/34)

For the first time formal secretarial help is available to the Superintendent: 'Mr. Jennings moved — 2nd by Mr Finley that Mr. Grey employ someone as office assistant of $12.50 per week. The motion carried. Mr. Lawrence[17] voted against the proposition.'

The 1934–35 year started auspiciously in August. Discussions were underway regarding the acquisition of additional property adjacent to both the Attucks School, for playground space, and property adjacent to the Milford Village School. The third grade teacher petitioned to be released from her contract to teach in a prestigious community across the county: the Board so moved. A special meeting was called two weeks later:

> ... for the purpose of discussing the recent burglary committed in Clear Valley School.
>
> Mr. Easter requested Superintendent Grey to take charge of the meeting at this time Mr. Grey related to the Board and visitors[18] his stand, stating that his desire was not to prosecute to the extent of sending the culprits to reform school, but to sufficiently punish them, that there would be no accruence (sic) of their act.
>
> Members of the Board were asked to express their views. Mr. Finley was of the same opinion as Mr. Grey. Mr. Gottlieb, Mr. Easter and Mrs. Quales spoke briefly, their opinions being in harmony with Mr. Grey and Mr Finley. Mr. Ingersoll expressed his views, saying that if it could be so arranged, that the boys would be sentenced and then put on parole to some responsible person, he thought punishment would be sufficient. Mr Matthews[19] thanked the members for their attitude, promising that he and his son would make full restoration for what had been taken. Mr. Caroline made a brief talk equivalent to Mr. Matthews'. Mr. Carr[20] expressed his views and agreed with Mr. Grey and members of the Board on their stand.
>
> There being no further discussion on this subject, the visitors were excused at 8:45 pm and the Board went into session.
>
> Mr. Easter called the meeting to order, and asked for a motion to the effect that the Board support Mr. Grey in his stand on the subject. (8/14/34)

Three weeks later a brief item appeared in the minutes:

> At this time Mr. Grey briefly explained to the board the punishment meted out to the boys at the trial which took place August 17, explaining that the boys were put on a six month parole with the understanding that it would extend longer if full restoration was not made by this time. (9/5/34)

Continued progress was made on the property additions and a discussion occurred concerning enrollments:

> Under new business, Mr. Grey spoke on the enrollment of all three schools. Clear Valley was about normal, whereas Milford Village and Attucks had fallen off. Mr. Grey asked the Board's consideration of taking two elementary pupils from any one family in any district at the tuition of one and one-half. Mr. Easter moved and Mr. Gottlieb 2nd, that we accept pupils on the above mentioned rate. The motion carried. (9/5/34)

The array of miscellaneous items that make up Board activity continued as usual: the school kitchen showed a profit of $3.91 for September, the monthly bills were read and approved, $3,000 was borrowed form a local bank to pay October and November bills, a motion was made and passed that a secret ballot be taken on coal bids, the vote was 4 to 2, a discussion was held on, '. . . the necessity of laying sidewalks along the front of our school properties for children's safety,' and finally: 'Mr. Lawrence moved, 2nd by Mr. Finley, that we have school room sprayed each evening after school has been dismissed to rid rooms of flies. The motion carried.' (10/3/34) Later in the Autumn it was moved, seconded and carried: '. . . that we leave the use of the school building by all organization in the hands of Mr. Grey.' (11/7/34)

In January, the regular meeting on the 2nd failed for lack of quorum. A special meeting was called for January 9th, and it was noted: 'Mr. Grey being absent due to illness, Mr. Inman read the current bills.' (1/9/35) Three weeks later, a second special meeting was called:

> The Board of Education of the School District of Milford met at Clear Valley School January 29, at 8:00 pm, for the purpose of determining the Board's desire to fill the vacancy caused by the death of our Superintendent, Mr. Grey. (1/29/35)

By Friday (2/1/35), after interviewing seven candidates, eliminating four, and taking two votes, Mr. McBride was elected on a 4–2 split vote. On the following Wednesday (2/6/35), it was noted at the regular meeting of the Board of Education that, '. . . with our Superintendent, Mr. McBride, also in attendance.' An era had ended, a new one had begun.

Summary

Our chronicle started as a brief account of the transformation of a three director school into a six director school, the organization of a high school, and the hiring of the first superintendent, three major innovations. Before we were done we found ourselves involved in stories of the principalship, the huge array of administrative tasks in the day to day maintaining an entity called a school, administrative succession, teacher turnover, race, gender, and classroom discipline. These items passed through our purview in the form of items in the Board of Education minutes: actions, decisions, and votes.

Notes

1 Later we found a volume of mixed records labeled 1914–1919 which has school board minutes dating from 10 September 1913 — 28 September 1922 and minutes of the Annual School Meetings from 7 April 1914 to 7 April 1925.
2 Minutes are available only for single meetings in September, November, and January, February and March.

3   Scholastic refers to pupils, but it's not clear the age limits in the enumeration. Midwest State law indicates 0–21 years at present. It seems that approximately 120–150 pupils are actually enrolled.

4   No indication occurs regarding the meaning of these symbols. Our guess is 'feeble minded' and 'blind.'

5   The minutes are not exact on this point. Records indicate that Black high school tuition was paid.

6   Suburban County Superintendent of Schools. Other records indicate he was a formidable school man and held office for thirty-six years from 1916 to 1952.

7   Board members.

8   The school janitor.

9   The wife of an earlier Board member, F. K. Tholozan.

10   Kennard School is an adjacent district where some Milford high school students had gone to school over to years and where Milford had rented in the last year a basketball court for use by its pupils.

11   Milford Village, by name, was an unincorporated village. When the town school district was organized the School District took its name.

12   Six weeks later (4/30/30), the contract was accepted; no record exists of the amount nor of taking of bids. A later bill of $255.00 to the G. W. Ford Hardware Co. is listed.

13   In January the Board voted the Milford Village Volunteer Fire Department — $15.00.

14   Other data suggest the year was 1931 and the ninety three director districts were really seventy-five plus fifteen consolidated or six director districts. PD refers to 'Project Document.'

15   Some of the very early minutes had been roughly typed.

16   The law was not totally less than perfect for the outside winner had been on the Board earlier but had lost the previous year.

17   Lawrence was frequently in the minority on the Board, for example, his candidates to fill positions regularly lost. No inference could be made from the minutes as to the reasons.

18   Parents of the youngsters involved.

19   While no first names are recorded, the names are the same of earlier Board Members. Both Mr. and Mrs. Matthews attended.

20   A prominent local citizen.

Chapter 4

The Early Evolution of a School District as a Series of Innovations

A Thesis

In considerable detail we have followed the particulars in the early history, if not the genesis and evolution, of the Milford School District. To ourselves we talked about 'chronicling' the district. These concerns follow upon our earlier suggestions that 'innovation' is a concept embedded in multiple language systems, theories, metatheoretical perspectives, and metaphors. In our view, 'change' is the broadest and most general of these terms. 'Genesis,' 'origins,' and 'evolution' assume a more naturalistic process, if not a biological or growth metaphor. Intentionality, particularly in the sense of reflected–upon action, seems foreign to the metaphor. In our utilization of the Board of Education Minutes we have tried to report as relatively detached, naturalistic observers of the scene, with only an occasional commonsense interpretation. We might have called ourselves, after an earlier label, 'natural historians.'

The thesis we want to begin to examine is that each step in the origins and early evolution of the district might be seen as an innovation, 'a specific, new, planned, improved change' in the district. The three changes we were particularly interested in were the changes in the school district from a three director rural elementary district into a six director township district, the beginning of the Milford High School, and the hiring of the first Superintendent of Schools. These were changes in one sense but not changes on another.

Milford was a district before 1925 and a district afterwards, that did not change. It is a six member district now; before it was a three member district. Among other things, Midwest State now put it into a different category and permitted and required different things of the District. The citizens felt different before and after.

Milford had been offering an educational program to its citizens since the 1870s. The one room school had increased in size and had become a several teacher school with a principal. All innovations? Or only changes? Now the instructional program was changing once again and a high school was started. Youngsters stayed longer, new subjects, as we will see shortly, were 'added' and the district had 'innovated' once again. These were local innovations, for in other places in the metropolitan area, the state and the country, these were old hat institutions, not new to the larger community and culture. But are they still innovations — at least to Milford? The use of the concept seems bounded by a reference to a particular community of understanding. Is the Milford community different from the Midwest State community, and is the latter different from the readers of this report who want to think about innovation in their schools?

Finally, Milford now had a superintendent, but it had always had someone looking after the particular tasks, more recently principals and board members who seemed to take on differentiated roles as they made the educational system happen. Is it merely a new position and role in an old structure? And is 'merely' a way of damning or trivializing something important?

Our point is simple. The definition of what is change and what is not, what is a specific planned change and what is not is always open to some question. Now, as we ask questions reflecting reasons and causes for the innovations, we must be a bit cautious about the power of the interpretations and the generalizations for they rest on key conceptions more like sand or quicksand than concrete.

Even as we present that conclusion, and use the metaphorical language of sand and concrete, we accent an additional point that the language we use, genesis and evolution versus innovation and change, brings a considerable number of latent images and metaphors that give meaning to what we say. That meaning may run unintentionally beyond or short of where we want to go. And this, too, can be a problem for anyone concerned with schools and their improvement.

We have depicted, heavily with quotes from the minutes of the Board of Education, the early years in the genesis of the Milford School District. The chronicle continues much the same year after year in the Board's record. At this point, as we are moved to state some preliminary generalizations arising as we read the accounts, a further reservation occurs. We hold these interpretations tentatively because they overlap heavily some of the thoughts that began in our study of the Alte School District (Smith, 1978 and 1986) and our study of *Federal Policy in Action* (Smith and Dwyer, 1979). To us we seem to be moving to a codified coherent point of view. Others may see us 'finding what we were looking for.'

As we moved inductively from items arising in our reading of the Board minutes, and later from *Bulletins* to the community, other documents, and a few interviews, several large categories arose. The first cluster involved the community or series of communities of which the school district is a part. One item is, for example, the changing population of the district. Second, a number of items were a part of the evolving processes and structures of the organization qua organization. For example new positions — principal, superintendent, and secondary teacher appeared. Rules and regulations and standard operating procedures were codified. In turn these items flow into, but can be discriminated from a third, an educational category — classrooms, curriculum, and teaching.

Community Items

In an important, perhaps major sense, the school board lies between the school and community. In modern jargon it is the interface. For some analytical purposes the board can be clustered with the community, for other purposes it is part of the school system. But in its mediating, interfacing position and role it provides a view of both. Its minutes are full of items permitting generalization and speculation of key items in developing a perspective on the community.

County and State Government and Agencies

In the very early years of the district, the state influenced the Milford District mostly as a set of laws which indicated procedural rules, both opportunities and constraints. From 1910 through the 1920s, when the School Board Records began, the Clear Valley School operated as a 'Common School District.' When the Board sought to become a town school district it proceeded under Section 5618 of the Revised Statutes of Midwest State, of 1919. The County Clerk regularly audited the District treasurer's accounts. On occasion appeals for help were made to the State Department, for example, procedures in becoming a district with a superintendent or to the State University for expert help on school buildings.

The potency of the state rules appears in another document, a brief history of the Milford High School, written by a Board member, Mr. Carr, for the first high school annual published in 1931, as the first group of youngsters received their diplomas:

> Milford High School has a prehistoric period; an effort which, apparently failed, yet helped to make a path for the later success. In the Summer of 1924 a young man, Principal of the Clear Valley School, made a proposal that three of the four teachers would teach four ninth grade subjects during the following year for a stipulated increase in salary. The Board was inadequately informed as to the credit requirements of a High School but trusted the knowledge and ability of its principal and thought any venture forward was worth trying.
>
> Only 5 pupils started and when about mid season it was learned that the school had failed to receive credit from the State Department some of these dropped out. The venture was abandoned next year, but one of these pupils stepped into the second year of High School at Kennard and ultimately was graduated there. The effort was not wholly a failure. (*H. S. Annual*, 1931, p. 5)

Very little of this information appears in the sketchy Board minutes from the early years. What does appear is the constant checking of requirements with the State Department by the Board and by Mrs. Briggs at the Board's request. Having been burned earlier, as the above quote indicates, would not have been a bad inference from the minutes themselves. Mr. Carr returned a few paragraphs later to the theme of state control. 'After the regular inspection of the State Department had put its stamp of approval upon our first year of High the Board began to plan for the next year.' (*H. S. Annual*, 1931, p. 5) The state government continues to exercise its responsibilities.

Suburban County contained some seventy-five small school districts, all governed by three member boards and most operating one room schools. The education of adolescents was problematic in those districts. The beginnings of Milford High School had a flavor of 'rural cosmopolitanism.' As one member of the first graduating class Mr. Elbrecht commented:

> The interesting thing, I think when this high school was started, it, as you know, it drew from that end of the county and it drew one or two students from almost each one, like maybe one from Rhodes School and another from Morrison School and then there two of us from Union School. (TI 2/80)

In an important sense, Milford High School, was to serve these functions for its end of the county until a wave of post–World War II consolidation swept the county — and the state between 1949 and 1952.

Educationists, growing up, being educated and later teaching in large urban or metropolitan areas, seldom appreciate the role played historically by the county superintendent of schools. In the 1920s and 1930s, in Suburban County, which was then heavily rural, his communiques appear from time to time in the school Board minutes — giving advice, informing the Board of meetings and generally playing the role of expert and communication link with the outside world of organizations, laws and rules affecting local public education. On one occasion, actually the first mention of the County Superintendent, he was brought in to help and give testimony regarding the dismissal of the principal and his wife who both taught in the school. Later he was instrumental in the initiation of the high school:

> On the recommendation of our County Superintendent, a teacher was secured with the necessary educational credits to teach four ninth grade subjects: English, Science, History and Mathematics. Mrs. Briggs, the new High School teacher, coming from Western Tennessee, took hold of her job with energy and decision, made herself familiar with the requirement of the State Law and gave the Board much needed assistance in the purchase of the required library and scientific apparatuses. (*H. S. Annual*, 1931, p. 9)

In short, those governmental units provided not only legal constraints but methods to help carry out the desires of the Board and indirectly the community.

The Annual Election

While a Newtonian metaphor is out of favor among some post positivist epistemologists, a clockwork regularity appears in the annual school board elections in the Milford School District. Each spring the minutes report on who has filed for the election, the selection of judges, the votes garnered by each individual, the swearing in of new members and the election of officers within the Board. As we have indicated, state laws governed the very format of size of Board, for example, three director common school or six director township school, the procedures for changing from one to another, the requirements for an annual election, and the procedures to govern those elections. The annual election is an important element in democracy in the schools.

Community Participation in the Annual School Meeting

Grass roots democracy and local control of schools appears in its most vivid form in the set of records entitled 'Record of annual school meetings,' the first category in the E. F. Hobart new edition of 'Records of school district.' The items that appear in the earliest extant record, 7 April 1914, and reappear year in and year out are:

1   Election of a director — usually one of three person board
2   Voting the length of school year — usually ten months
3   Authorizing building use for community groups 'as specified by Law'
4   Voting for County Superintendent of Schools
        Coleman — 5 votes
        Snyder — 3 votes
        Taylor — 0 votes
        Quinn — 0 votes

                                                  (4/6/15)

5   The small number of voters present
        1914 (director elected by 17 vote majority)
        1915 (8 votes for County Superintendent)
        1916 (29 voters present)
        1917 (63 voters voted for Directors)
        1920 (142 votes cast for Directors)
                (153 votes cast: 94 for, 34 against building a new school house)
        1922 (53 votes in director election)

The small size of the community, the direct involvement of a small coterie of citizens, and the resolution of community differences by 'voting' appear and reappear. A School Board member, E. K. Tholozan, from the 1920s commented this way as he recalled his early experiences:

EKT: We started you might say from the ground up — all we had was a
    two inch water main in the streets and cinder roads.
Obs: So nothing was paved at that time.
EKT: Nothing was paved at that time. We didn't have any electric, we
    had to come out to outside toilets and we had to come out to coal oil
    lamps and gasoline stoves in the summer time. So we organized the
    Milford Village Improvement Association. And after that was organized

then the next thing the school problem came along 'cause people started moving out and they had children. Well, we found out where the school was and Herbert Jackson, he was the school director at that time and he come over to our meeting one night and explained the school and told us that it was Clear Valley District. So after that we decided that since we were starting to grow in the community we needed a — we wanted a member on the school board.

Obs: Oh, in Milford Village apart from the Clear Valley area?

EKT: Well, Clear Valley District covered everything. It covered everything from the city limits up to the highway and out to about Richmond Road and down to the city line and so the Spring election in 1920 the Improvement Association nominated me to be candidate and filed its candidate for school board and I was elected in April 1920.

Another citizen, Mrs. Tholozan, who attended Clear Valley School reflected back on this aspect of the community:

Mrs. T: What they had — this was all farms over here — that was sort of — in the people's minds it was two sections — Milford on that side of the railroad tracks was the poor people and on this side of the railroad tracks was the people with just a little bit more money.

Early on, with the assertiveness of the Milford Village Improvement Association the belief seemed to be accepted that one member of the Board should come from each of the three main geographical and population areas of the district.

Obs: Now, when you said you were part of that Milford Village Improvement Association — where did the other school board members come from at that time?

EKT: The other two come from this side — from Rowlings Hill and from the — the west side of the Carleton Boulevard.

Obs: Okay — and you were on the east side?

FKT: Yeah — I was a mile east of the school.

Obs: Okay.

A Rolling Structure of Power and Authority

Reading Board minutes may be a very limited way of viewing the nature, genesis, and consequences of power and authority in school affairs. In the early years and the long period of the township school several reasonably concrete generalizations seem evident:

1 Incumbents mostly won elections.
2 The Board mostly supported incumbents.
3 New members often had run unsuccessfully earlier or were appointed to fill out terms for resigned members.

4   The Board picked and released superintendents.
5   A changing Board brought changes or threats of change in superintendents.
6   Superintendents recommended, hired and fired faculty but teachers also were consulted from time to time regarding superintendents.

The view that comes forward is a gradual or rolling structure of power and authority. Mostly there is stability and gradual change within the structure. Occasionally a cataclysm occurs. Partly, that stability seems to be built into the very structure of the Board in that two of the six members are up for election every year. Consequently, except for resignations, it takes three years to replace totally the incumbents on the Board. Majorities can change more readily, for two new members coming on to a split Board can shift a minority to a majority opinion. Later instances of this occurred and not only make for drama, but clearly present an image of our label, 'a rolling structure of power and authority.' Obvious historical models for this kind of structure appear in the federal Constitution and in state governments. People in power in an earlier era wanted change to be possible but wanted it to come gradually.

Conflict and Politics

Historically, according to some analysts (Iannaccone, 1967, Tyack and Hansot, 1982), public schools have often been stereotyped as a non-political institution. Our recent experience (Smith, 1978, Smith and Dwyer, 1979) suggests that the stereotype is not true. Our reading of the Milford documents suggests that this was not so fifty years ago, at least in the Milford School District. Earlier we had commented upon the crowded conditions in the schools in the late 1920s, and difficulty in getting a bond issue passed for the second school, the Milford Village School:

> But opinions differed as to the proper place for the new building and the proposition was defeated. Later in the Summer (1929), another differently worded proposition met with like fate and it became evident that the school year would be a hard one. (*H. S. Annual*, 1931, p. 6)

Conflict existed. The political processes of majority votes were at work, to the dismay of the Board and faculty. The alternative solutions were also in debate, as were the implicit perspectives related to the solutions. The account continued:

> An obvious and *rather frequently heard* solution for the crowded conditions in the school was to discontinue the High School, or at least, to halt its advance at the tenth grade. But the board, in conference with the Superintendent, agreed that such a step would have a very discouraging effect upon *the forward looking elements* of the district, and it could not bring itself to *desert, midway,* that *expectant, persistent class* of boys and girls now ready to enter the eleventh grade. (*H. S. Annual*, 1931, p. 6) (Our italics)

The pervasiveness of the conflict received mention a bit further on in the account: 'As the year (1929–30) rolled on the discord which had arisen in the district found a

71

counterpart in the faculty and to some extent in the Board and among the pupils.' (*H. S. Annual*, 1931, p. 6) A perspective on the nature of conflict resolution also appeared: 'Fortunately there were *enough cool heads* scattered around to prevent any open breaks, though the tension was keen enough to impair the efficiency of the system. (*H. S. Annual*, 1931, pp. 6–7) (Our italics)

The interplay of events essential to our analytical position continued to receive mention: 'However, the annual State inspection again gave its approval of the School as of accredited rank, though accompanied by criticisms of the inadequate physical facilities'. (*H. S. Annual*, 1931, p. 7) The continuous impact of resources — their absence, limits, or presence, aroused emotions one might expect:

> Even then, relief was in sight, for, during the Fall a compromise bond issue had been passed which would provide eight new classrooms. And when, at the Spring election of 1930, a tax was voted sufficient to carry the burden of a four year High School, a sigh of thanksgiving escaped some of us that our worst year was behind and that better times were at last in sight.

Mrs. Briggs, described by a former student[1] as 'abrasive,' 'aggressive' and 'difficult to get along with,' was replaced that year. (TI 2/13/80). Another graduate of the first class, in reflection back over fifty years commented with good humor, 'When she said frog, you jumped.' (TI 2/26/80). A number of new teachers were hired. The new building and additions to the old were available. And, 'A new superintendent was in charge of the entire system.' (*H. S. Annual*, 1931, p. 7). A clear perception of his role appears in the wake of the trying and conflictual time just prior to his appointment:

> The new head, Mr. Grey, *assumed no teaching duties*, his *whole attention* being directed to the organization of the faculty, the curriculum, and the student body into an *efficiently working* educational institution. He permitted himself only one activity other than administration and that was the High School athletics. (Our italics) (*H. S. Annual* 1931, p. 8)

The second superintendent was to resolve the conflicts within the school; the Board continued to be both a forum for that debate in the community and a resolution, through elections, of those differences.

Demographics: The Press of Population Growth

While just a trickle compared to the flood which will come in later years (the 1950s and 1960s), the population growth in the early part of the century forced the school from its initial one room frame building to a three room frame building to the first brick and stone building built in 1926. Later, with increasing population, secondary classes were added year by year. People who argue the potency of demographic variables in understanding schooling — its nature and changes — will find us among them. Early on, demographics fueled in part, the gradual development of Milford School District.

Much later, actually in the present years of the District (1979–80), the community is faced with declining enrollments. Two elementary schools have been closed; a 'housing committee' has under discussion possible additional closings. As one central office staff member commented, 'If people thought building schools was difficult, they ought to see what closing one is like.' In our view, as we will elaborate later, declining school enrollments, is the front edge of much larger societal problems — zero population growth, stable GNP, zero sum games in reallocating the material goods and benefits in our society, and general decline of natural resources on 'space ship earth.' Solutions to societal problems under these new conditions will amount to 'a new ball game' with a new set of rules. Educators are among the first community professionals to try to solve these problems, and in so doing to actually try to define and re-define the problems, the rules, the criteria, much less the solutions. Small wonder, that frequently there is a beleaguered quality among school people these days. But, as we said, those were to be problems for a later generation of Milford citizens and educators.

Changing Technological Quality of Life

Item by item, the schools changed with the increasing technological development of the community. Notes about wiring for electricity, septic tanks, attaching water lines appear throughout the record of the mid and late 1920s. The schools keep playing leap frog with the material standard present in the community at large. Frame buildings gave way to brick and stone buildings. Wood burning stoves became coal furnaces and later were to become gas and oil central heating plants. The public utilities, for example, water and telephones, reach the schools and assume a regular or 'natural' place in the order of things. A comment by an early resident, Mr. Tholozan, who had moved to the community about 1920 gives a picture of this part of the world:

> *Obs* Yeah — so and at that time, the community was pretty much a rural area except there was a little community in Milford Village itself?
> *EKT*: Yeah — yeah.
> *Obs*: A few hundred people or how many would have been there?
> *EKT*: When I moved out here we didn't have I don't think a hundred people.
> *Obs*: So just twenty-thirty families maybe?
> *EKT*: Say fifty — about fifty families at that time but then it started to continually growing — in other words, it came fast after that — by 1923 we made an arrangement with the Metropolitan Electric that if most of us bought an electric range we could get our service installation free. In 1923 they erected the electric lines and we got the telephones and the electric service from 1923 on and then from on — later on the roads came and so forth.

In this context, the later conflicts at the Kensington School over carpets and air conditioning take on a much different quality (Smith and Keith, 1971). They seem to us now as one more item in making the schools more and more like life in the rest of the community. Sometimes the community is more or less supportive or antagonistic to these changes. Irrevocably, if not 'naturally,' we would argue, the schools change toward congruency with the general technological changes.

The Vividness of the 'American Dilemma'[2]

From the first recorded minutes of the Board of Education which mentioned fire insurance for the 'colored school bldg.,' we were surprised by the quantity of continuing references to the 'colored school.' Education in Midwestern State was racially separate by state law. Whether it was 'separate but equal' is only slightly less clear. Item by item both schools improved; item by item the Attucks School seemed to change only after the Clear Valley School changed. Within what would now be called institutionalized racism, for example, there was frequent reference to the 'colored school' even after the school had received a formal name, the Attucks School. It is also true that the board did concern itself regularly with the education of Black children.

With a vivid *déja vu* quality, the hiring of Black teachers, the sending of Black high school students out of the district, the receiving of out of district Black elementary pupils as a help to the other districts and as a means to fill rooms with low enrollments, and all the problems of transportation and its financing, appear in the minutes of early Board meetings.[3] The curriculum of the Attucks School received no more notice in these minutes than did the curriculum of the Clear Valley and Milford Village Schools. Mrs. Shields, a teacher[4] at the Attucks School in the late 1930s, commented favorably upon the teaching arrangements. It was her first teaching job. She was picked from a class of a dozen and a half, eight of whom had been interviewed:

> The Attucks School was a one through eight school for Blacks, There were two teachers there, one teacher taught grades one through three, then after that the grades skipped and then was a four, six and eight one year, then a five, I guess a three, five and seven the next. . . . I had only fifteen students and from there on we had a graduation class every year. . . . Now I taught there for five years, and there were only thirty-five students in the school. There was no contact at all that I recall with the White schools or any of the White teachers or any of the White administration. It was a totally segregated situation and the only person that I ever saw was Mr. McBride who was the Superintendent. (TI 8/15/80)

Many of Mrs. Shields' comments involved a comparison with the Metropolitan City School District where most of her college classmates taught. Those comparisons give a further flavor to the Attucks School within Milford:

> When I graduated they (Metropolitan School District) had a surplus of teachers so you were on a waiting list and the rating list was on the basis of

your rank in class and as vacancies occurred then you were called. Well, at that time in the Black grade school there were 45 and 50 students per grade in the room perhaps. Well, I had friends who had 45 children and 15 books. Supplies were bad in the Black schools.... I never did teach in Metropolitan City.... I stayed in Milford because even though I had multiple grades, I had a small number. I had all the supplies I wanted. I had a community, the school was a community and I liked that. I had all kinds of parent cooperation, no discipline problems hardly, really ever. So those were all pluses to me so I just — when I was called I just never went to Metropolitan City. I didn't want to go and then I got married after about a year anyway. And I couldn't teach — at that time — because you still couldn't teach married. (TI 8/80)

In short, a small isolated community of families, mostly working in a local factory, and living in company houses, seemed to go about its business in a fashion isolated from the larger community. The American dilemma played itself out in a variety of ways. This was Milford's way.[5]

Summary

Neither did we not start out to be historians, nor did we begin as community sociologists. Nonetheless, the data and our curiosity dragged us in those directions. The lessons we were learning seem important for other educators, and especially for other educational innovators. The schools are enmeshed in multiple communities — local, state, and national. These communities have organized themselves, over the years, and that seems very important as well, to accent both stability and change and to accent both local and distal (central) power and responsibility. As values, as issues, and as procedural structures, these are very old problems, topics, and themes in political science and community sociology. While our analysis may not be especially novel or illuminating to scholars in these disciplines, we have been surprised by our own lack of awareness and even more, the naivete of some of our colleagues advocating change.

Organizational Structure and Process

Our initial study of the Kensington Elementary School, *Anatomy of Educational Innovation* (Smith and Keith, 1971), carried the subtitle, 'An organizational analysis of an elementary school.' Any school as an organization fits into a larger organization, the school district. As we read Milford School District records and constructed a chronicle or narrative, we began to form slightly more complex abstractions regarding 'organizational structure and process.' These abstractions seemed applicable to the genesis and evolution of any school district, as a series of innovations. This provides a context for understanding not only the Kensington School as an innovation but innovation in schools in general.

The School Board: Pervasive, Potent and Responsible Agent

The narrative of the School District, based heavily on the early minutes of the Board meetings, leaves little room for doubt concerning the Board's pervasiveness, potency and responsibility for conducting schooling in the Milford School District. Occasionally the minutes record a meeting that captured, in microcosm, that interpretation. The evening of 28 September 1927, was one such occasion. Further, the minutes seemed to capture some of the style of the Board at that time. After approving the payment of some fifteen bills the minutes moved this way:

> Regularly moved and 2nd that laws marked exhibit A[6], as submitted by the teachers of the Clear Valley School dated Sept. 26th, be multigraphed and the penalties of disobedience or any infraction on said rules be thoroughly explained and a copy thereof be sent to the parents and guardians of each and every child attending the Clear Valley School. Motion carried.
>
> Regularly moved and 2nd that rules marked Ex. A be approved and adopted by the Board and a copy be furnished each teacher.
>
> Billy Lamb, a pupil in 2nd grade under teacher Miss Grace, appeared before the Bd. of Ed. with parents to answer charges preferred by Mr. Craig as to why suspension of Sept. 21st should not be affirmed. After a complete hearing and a warning, the suspension was lifted and parents ordered to return child to school 9/29. Charges as submitted by Mr. Craig dated 9/28 marked Exhibit B attached herewith.
>
> Regularly moved and 2nd that the Secy. be instructed to inquire of the School Faculty why the necessity of homework or home studies. Motion carried.
>
> Regularly moved and 2nd that the Secy. be instructed to order 12 copies of 'Windmills of Holland' from Myers and Carrington as requested by Mr. B. N. Earlhem. (9/28/27)

Two additional items from these minutes related to hiring a teacher and seeking competitive bids on repair work.

Several interpretive comments seem in order. As noted earlier, the Board approves and pays each item of expense of the district. It 'elects,' literally a vote, early on, each teacher hired in the district. Now, almost for the first time, the Board establishes the rules of behavior in the school and holds a hearing and dispenses final judgment on deviance. In addition it inquires into issues of 'homework' and approves the purchase of multiple copies of a particular book, *Windmills of Holland*. The Board seemed in close communication with the teachers, accepting rules and penalties as policy and inquiring into their views of home study. A closeness and directness with purpils and parents existed as well.

At several points we have interpreted Board action as having a style, using words like, 'direct' or 'common sense.' The image which kept appearing over and over again is that the Board was able to cope with the problems as they perceived and defined them.

But it is the image of 'pervasive, potent, and responsibile' agent that is our main point here. While we don't have interviews from the individuals at the time and only a few documents such as the nine page history from the first High School annual, the inference we came to was one captured in the general label. If that is correct, it seems important to compare and contrast with Boards in succeeding years and in other communities.

Incrementalism and Muddling Through

School policy seemed to evolve, item by item as the Board faced particular concrete problems. Beyond those enumerated above, the records are a litany of: 'Moved and 2nd that Safety signs for road be investigated. Carried.' (9/18/26) And, 'Moved and 2nd that sign be made reading "Vehicles not permitted on school grounds during play period". Carried.' (9/18/26) And, 'Moved and 2nd school be dismissed Fri. 24th acct. exposition Day.' (9/22/26) And, 'Moved and 2nd that in case of any contagious disease in a family the other members of family be excluded from school until disease is over. Carried.' (1/19/27) The most general statement capturing this kind of organizational development and processes is what Lindblom (1969) has called 'muddling through' or 'incrementalism.' He contrasts this to the 'rational' actor model of organizations.

While this incrementalism and muddling through concept 'jumps out at us now,' our data gathering and interpretation came in time, after our *Federal Policy in Action* research (Smith and Dwyer, 1980). Perhaps, too, the ideas are most relevant to new, small, growing, developing, creative organization. When one has a history, a social structure, a standard way of doing things, a policy handbook, or an entrenched establishment, perhaps the point is less well taken. But, the environment always keeps changing, the district always keeps responding — sometimes proactively and sometimes reactively — and, perhaps, keeps muddling through. Lindblom generalizes his gradualist position as the heart of democratic policy making.

Specialization of Positions and Roles

When the school was a Common District School, and even before, if our set of records is correct, a one room school began in the 1870s, a single teacher taught in the school. By the mid 1920s, a teaching principal is at the school and teachers are elected, 'hired,' for particular grades, one and two, five and six, and so forth. Later, in 1929, as a high school is begun the district hired secondary teachers and the principal became a half time superintendent.

Gradually, specialization of positions and roles occurred. Today the district central offices buzz with assistant superintendents, public relations officers, night school administrators, federal contracts specialists and a dozen assistants, secretaries and support personnel. Part of our later analytical task will be to sort out the antecedents for these changes. Is it primarily simple growth and expansion? Or are the objectives and domains of schooling broadening as well? Is there a simple paralleling of the complexity of American society? What happens to these processes and their specific positional outcomes if our current image of declining enrollments, dropping socioeconomic status and racial change is true, not to mention, our speculations regarding zero population growth, constant GNP and scarcity of natural resources? These questions run far beyond our current data and conjectures regarding innovations in Milford and other communities.

We might ask also, what are the limits of specialization. In the current era, the Kensington School has a materials center coordinator, remedial reading teacher, speech therapist, counselors, special education teacher and teacher aide. On several occasions current principals and teachers have speculated in a way which suggests that specialization may have outrun its benefits in the School and the district.[7]

Resources for Schooling: Finances

If, as we argue shortly, that a dearth of discussion in school Board minutes occurs surrounding curriculum, the opposite can said for discussions of money and finances. Those appear at every meeting, usually in multiple guises, strands, and events. Whether this is a broader economic phenomenon, an outgrowth of the mixed monopolistic capitalist system which characterizes the country as a whole or whether it is a religious phenomenon, a Protestant view on original sin and the depravity of mankind, or a simpler moral/political view that financial bases of power are the most corruptible forms and hence need to be guarded against the most, or perhaps it's just that early great American trait of being close with the dollar, we do not know. Regularly the Board raised resources through tax and bond levies voted by the citizens of the community. On occasion they borrowed money from banks in nearby Metropolitan City to meet expenses when unevenness in tax collections occurred. The dispensing of funds occurred through serially numbered checks following a reading of bills by Board members and later the superintendent. The Board treasurer carried a $20,000 bond in the early years. Once a year and with every change in treasurer of the Board, the county treasurer audited the district's books.

In such context, it is not difficult to see the easy possibility of the school superintendent being very busy with and concerned about finances. Nor is it difficult to see him being recruited for and developing a businessman's orientation and perspective. Financing schooling returns in our story in multiple forms.

The Evolving Role of the Superintendent

The story of Mrs. Briggs, the half time first superintendent, has been told earlier and only a few mysteries remain. Why did the Board solicit her to join the faculty and begin the high school? Why were her promotions so rapid? Why did the Board refuse to retain her as a teacher when the new superintendent was hired? Her story, and those questions, soon become context for the image of Mr. Grey, the first full time superintendent and his gradually enlarging the position and role of superintendent. Item by item he took on, at the Board's direction activities, duties, and responsibilities which earlier had been done by individual members of the Board or by the Board as a collectivity.

The role of these two early superintendents of the Milford School District seems closest to what Callahan and Button (Button, 1961, Callahan, 1964, and Callahan and Button, 1964) call 'the superintendent as business manager (1910–1929),' or 'school executive' although none of the labels seems to quite fully capture Briggs, Grey or McBride. Perhaps 'jack-of-all-trades' or 'Topsy' would be closer. The superintendents seemed to gradually be given the multiple responsibilities for administering the school system. This 'generalist' role seems to be its own kind of specialization, that is different from teaching self-contained fifth and sixth grade, different from teaching high school Latin and English, and different from cooking in the cafeteria or being a maintenance worker.

Callahan has commented:

> Beginning about 1900 the conception of the role of the chief administrator of the schools began to change. This change occurred not because of any change in the nature of the work or the quality of preparation of the teacher nor because of any basic change in the purpose of the school. Rather, the change was a direct result of the impact of powerful social forces on the one side and the institutional weakness of education, and especially the superintendent, in the public schools on the other. (1964, p. 7)

While this may be true of the large city superintendency in the early twentieth century, it docs not seem to capture the empirical reality in the origination and evolution of the role in the Milford School District, and possibly other rural districts. Several aspects seem to be important. The school system *was* changing. Milford was growing larger, more buildings and more teachers. Its 'purposes' were expanding — a high school had been created. It's noneducational activities had increased — a cafeteria and lunch program was instituted. Finally, its relationship to outside groups — especially the county and the state — was becoming more complex.

The vulnerability thesis — powerful social forces and institutional weakness of educators — seems a shade off the realities of Milford. In the 1920s and 1930s, before the rise of labor unions, social security, and due process, every working person seemed vulnerable. In Milford, janitors, teachers, principals and superintendents arrived and departed at the pleasure of administrative superiors and ultimately the potent school Board. And school Board members 'came and went' at the annual pleasure of the citizenry. The vividness of teacher turnover and janitorial firings under Mrs. Briggs, and her replacement by the Board (after hearings from pupils and teachers), we found to be high drama.

As our later superintendents are introduced and their stories told, we will try to move toward more abstract interpretations. At that point we will review more intensively the Callahan and Button perspective. For the moment, we are struck with the political nature of the position, responsive to the Board and community, and with the broad array of managerial tasks which the Board gradually was delegating to the incumbents of the position.

Fate of Old School Buildings

Unlike old soldiers, school buildings neither die nor fade away, they are sometimes reconditioned and used forever. The original frame building of the Clear Valley School, according to the Board meeting in the Summer of 1926, became the residence of the custodian. A year later, pressure for a high school program arose and the Board looked for a place to house the new program: 'Committee of all Board members to meet at the Clear Valley School Sunday afternoon July 17th, 1927 at 2 pm to consider the necessities of reconditioning the old school for occupancy of 1 room to be used for high school work.' (1/13/27) Immediately thereafter bids for roofing, carpentry, and painting were accepted for the remodeling.

The following autumn (10/12/27) partitions were ordered constructed 'in rooms occupied by Mr. and Mrs. K. Talcott as living quarters' and to '. . . change room arrangements for smaller children to the new school building and 7th and 8th grade pupils to the old school.' (10/12/27)

These processes of changing utilization continued and are captured in a delightful quote from the account of 'Boys' Basketball' in the first High School Annual in 1931:

> The first thing confronting the boys when their thoughts first turned to basketball was a place to play. This did not stump them very long. There was the old building with a partition separating two large rooms. Bringing up tools with which to work the boys tore out this partition, put up goals at either end and — lo and behold — a basketball court 50 feet long, 30 feet wide, and 13 feet high. (*H. S. Annual*, 1931, p. 41)

Summary

When the school district is conceived as a system or an organization several key items or elements capture most of the phenomena and events in our story. The boundary of the district as an organization can be drawn as including or excluding the school board. As we indicated, sometimes it is best conceived as part of the community system and sometimes as part of the district as a system. In Iannaccone and Lutz' (1970) analysis it would be a point of tangency, a part of both and mediating between the two. To anticipate our later discussion of the 'longitudinal nested systems model,' the Board mediates control of one system upon another. In the District, in those early years, no questions existed regarding authority and social power. The Board 'moved, seconded, and voted' on resources, personnel, organizational structure and procedures. The district seemed to change by a process of incrementalism or muddling through. Problems arose, both in the environment and within the organization. Discussions were held, common sense inquiries occurred, decisions were made. Sometimes the organization increased in size — new buildings — in complexity — new positions, rules and procedures — and in specialization.

Classrooms, Curriculum and Teaching

The Dearth of Educational Talk: An Introduction

Whether it's the nature of the Board's discussions, the nature of minutes which record decisions and actions, or the particular secretaries, the School Board record is remarkable for the dearth of items regarding curriculum, teaching, or educational philosophy. Perhaps, too, and in spite of the Deweyian revolution going on in the intellectual centers, the common school is a common school in the rural and small town communities of America in the 1920s and 1930s. From time to time references to science equipment and bills to book companies and map companies occur. Later accounts of the consideration of sewing machines and a movie projector which would show both silent and talking pictures appeared. And, early on, money for balls, bats and gloves and a reference or two to renting a neighboring basketball court appeared. (The varsity football team didn't arrive until 1954). Occasional references were made to teachers teaching particular grade levels in the elementary school and to subjects — science, math, English and social studies at the High School.

But no reference occurred to controversies such as evolution in science nor were there any discussions recorded concerning the limits of literary realism nor of the economics and politics taught within social studies. As we've indicated, the basics seem to have been taught and no debate was recorded over phonics, project methods, or the whole child.

One final speculation, and it is a speculation, it's almost as though the Board provided the resources: taxes, buildings, material supplies, teachers and administrators and they, the teachers and administrators, were to bring the ideas, the structure, shape and scope of the curriculum, and the methods of teaching from their normal school training and their own experiences. In general, except for discipline perhaps, the local society was reasonably homogeneous on the one hand. On the other hand, the social structure of the small town was accepted rather than problematic. As a result education went along easily and 'naturally.' Perhaps, too, that's the serene part of what people often mean by the 'good old days.'

Currently, in 1979–80, the board spends one of its two monthly meetings on curriculum. Presentations are made by specialists, by teachers, and by principals. Sometimes, problems, 'squeaky wheels,' receive attention. Other times 'slide-tape' shows of special events are celebrated. These changes came slowly as we will note in later chapters.

The Gradual Expansion of Programs

When our story began in the 1910s, the Milford District was a small two teacher elementary school. The record is one of gradual expansion of programs. The initial major focus was continuing the programs for adolescents by establishing a high school, year by year. The curriculum grew subject by subject. Extra curricular or play activities originally were a bat and ball, later basketball came in and still later (1954) varsity football was to appear. Similarly, a night school program for adults began at the Attucks School in the 1930s, later a kindergarten program was initiated. Accounts of sewing machines and cooking stoves indicate the rise of a home economics program.

Teacher Role and the Organization of Instruction

The earliest Board records we've been able to find indicates that Clear Valley School was a two teacher school in 1913[8]. Miss Witteman was paid $75/month, Miss Butcher was paid $60 per month.

During the earliest years for which we have records, the organization, the school, the multiple jobs of the teacher, and aspects of the governance of the school are caught in brief notes from the board minutes. For instance the comment: '... procure ... more desks in the primary room' (12/18/13) clearly implies that the eight grades were broken into a primary and upper grade room. Later comments in the 1920s about the 'colored school' used a similar analytical scheme. A further comment from an early Board meeting stated:

> Resolution drawn and ordered given to the teachers — requiring teachers to be at school 20 minutes before nine each day and give careful attention to heating and ventilating *and also to give them the Christmas Holidays on condition that they comply with this request.* (12/18/13) (Our italics)

Not only were custodial duties part of the role but vacations were *quid pro quo* for the time in those morning, before school duties. In these minutes, and in later months as well, note was made of the contingency between teacher reports and their monthly salary payments: 'Teachers warrants for next ensuing mo. ordered drawn when report is properly made.' (12/18/13)[9] Some kind of record keeping, 'paperwork,' has been a part of teaching for a long time — at least in Milford, As we read accounts of the history of schools in Suburban County, these records are required by the County Superintendent, who in turn is acting on the basis of laws enacted by the Midwest State Legislature.

While the label 'inservice training' either was not invented, was unknown to the Board, or perhaps just not used, the phenomenon was present. The minutes phrased it simply: 'Day or two to be allowed teacher to visit schools.' (9/27/16) No reciprocal demands on teachers were noted, in contrast to some of the other aspects of the expansion of the teacher role.

The Student Body

The Board minutes speak only of enumeration of pupils and the desire for educating the children of the community, at least at the common school level — reading, 'riting and 'rithmetic plus a little more. The genesis of the high school drew selectively an unusual group of youngsters. We have already commented that they came from nearby districts as well as Milford. When looking at a photograph of their classmates during an interview with two individuals the following exchange occurred:

> *Mr. Simmons*: . . . he's president of an insurance company, and he founded a publishing company, and like I said, this gentleman here up on top of the flag pole there, he was president of the Metropolitan Public Commission. . . .
> *Obs*: A pretty interesting bunch of people.
> *Mr. Elbrecht*: I was going to say that it was sort of an elite group of students because, not to throw bouquets or anything but there were only, like I mentioned before, one or two of us from each of these outlying schools plus a few from the Milford area. And we really wanted an education because it wasn't easy in those days. We didn't have bus service and all the facilities that we have now. I mean, it was very primitive you might say. (TI 2/1980)

Initiatives in change came from multiple quarters.

Class Size

The Board records contain few particulars related to class size. In 1922, the following appeared: 'Moved and 2nd that new room or north room be equipped with 40 chair desks, 1 teacher's desk, and 1 bookcase to be purchased from American Seating Co. see contract on file. Motion carried.' (9/28/22) Our general impressions from the records of numbers of teachers and the discussion from time to time of adding a half time teacher or converting a half time teacher to full time is that the Board implicitly viewed small classes as important educationally. The high school graduating class of eleven youngsters in 1931 supports this interpretation. In the late 1930s, Mrs. Shields, a teacher at the Attucks School, contrasted her dozen to twenty youngsters (at four grade levels, fifth-eighth) with her teachers college peers who taught classes of forty-fifty in Metropolitan City. The class size difference was one major factor in her staying at Milford when an opportunity came to teach in the City.

Free Text Books

Milford took a giant stride in increasing the availability of public education in the Spring of 1914: 'Ordered printing up of Annual Meeting notices with a clause to have meeting vote on the proposition to have free text books for all pupils.' (3/16/14)

Some sixty years later, Superintendent Spanman would be in trouble for assessing special fees for materials and the Kensington School would be envied for 'free-free' books, for example, thirty sets of encyclopedias, that is, books given to the district by book companies. But in 1914, progress continued: 'Ordered spending of $10.00 for library books. Mr. Brock a committee of one to attend to purchasing or contracting for textbooks for school — free textbooks.' (4/30/14)[10]

These issues received further clarification and presumably elaboration in 1922: 'The principal was authorized to order textbooks and misc. school supplies and present bills to Clerk. Maximum for the textbooks 200.00. Misc. school supplies 60.00.' (9/28/22) In short, the partially graded school (two teachers) possessed textbooks as one of its major instructional tools. The graded elementary concept appears early also: 'Fourth and sixth grade books for next year's use to be ordered before close of this school term.' (4/4/18) An image of an 'assign–study–recite' text book based curriculum and instruction emphasis seems a congruent inference from the Board minutes.

Instructional Time: Days and Hours

Reading early school Board minutes takes on special meaning when one has a vision of items from Kensington's beginning and the superintendent's mandate regarding the length of the school year and the length of the school day (Smith and Keith, 1971, pp. 23–25). His vision of the twelve month year and the individually tailored length of the school day ran up against long term precedents. For instance: 'Next term of school to be 10 months by a unanimous vote.' (4/7/14) Year in and year out the community argued for what might be described as a 'full year' of schooling for the youngsters. Occasionally minority votes would be cast for an eight or nine month year. Even in the worst of the depression, ten months was voted, but with a disclaimer 'provided sufficient funds are available.' Never was a longer year voted.

Records on the length of the day are more difficult to come by. In 1913 the teachers were to be present twenty minutes early to 'heat and ventilate' the building. In 1916, standardization arrived: 'Ordered that school is not to be opened for children before 8:30 when teachers are to arrive. Teachers agreeing to arrange this with pupils.' (1/24/16) No mention was made regarding the closing hours. Presumably three or three-thirty was the hour.

The High School Curriculum

The two best sources of data on curriculum and teaching are the first High School Annual and several oral history interviews with former pupils, a teacher, and a board member from the 1920s. A summary from reading and analyzing the High School Annual is presented in Figures 10 and 11.

Figure 10: High School Curriculum Defined by Teacher Responsibilities

1	Helen Hamilton —	English
		Latin
2	Betty Harrison —	History
		English
		Commercial law
3	Ann Peters —	Science — Text
		Laboratory
		Biology
		Music
4	Susan Kelley —	Math
		P.E.
5	Fred Grey —	Athletics
		Typing

Figure 11: Extracurricular Activities as Informal Curriculum

1 Class officers structure
2 Dramatics — 'Gypsy Rover'
              'Prairie Rose'
3 Glee Club
4 Athletics — Basketball — boys and girls
              Baseball   — boys and girls
              Tennis   — boys and girls
5 Participation in school elections
6 High School Annual
  High school Monthly News
7 Parties   — Valentines
              Junior-Senior
              Cafeteria Supper
              Christmas Festival
              School Picnic
8 County Playday (Girls)

The formal curriculum seems, by present standards and diversity, to be both limited and traditional. It did represent the basic disciplines of history, science (mostly biology), math (algebra and geometry), and English. Latin was the only foreign language — taught initially by Mrs. Briggs and later by Miss Hamilton. Mr. Grey developed a set of lessons and exercises in typing and loaned the pupils his own typewriter. One former pupil, Mr. Elbrecht, who later became a journalist, remembers this with considerable positive feeling — both in its curricular importance and in his feeling for the Superintendent:

> Yeah, when he found out that I was planning to go to college, why, he told me, he said 'You should learn to type.' And he said 'We're not giving a course in typing but I used to teach typing years ago, and if you'll get an old typewriter at home I'll type out....' But once a week or so I would go in his office and he would type out a sheet of finger exercises. Just like they do in typing class. Then I would go home and practice that. Then when I got a perfect sheet I'd bring it in to him and then he'd type out another sheet for

me. And that's how I learned to type. And I'm eternally grateful to him. (TI 1980)

Presumably because of the source of data — the High School Annual and the monthly newspaper — the array of informal or extra curricular activities seems quite broad.

Physical Education. Small amounts of money for bats and balls seem to be a regular part of rural schooling everywhere in America. Milford had some interesting differences and specialities as well: 'Necessary material for tennis court allowed.' (4/30/17) Aspects of that were elaborated on by an early High School student:

Mr. Carr was a tennis player and he had a tennis court at his place . . . he made a tennis court there . . . I learned to play tennis there. He was quite a player and he taught the boys around, those that were interested in tennis. And we'd gather there every weekend on Sunday and we'd play all day long there. And we would take care of the court then. We'd roll it and then we'd mark it and so on, and patch the fence if it needed patching and so on. (TI 1980)

Mr. Carr became Clerk of the Board, without salary in 15 April 1918. In 1922 he was a member of the School Board.

Basketball seemed popular early in the life of the school:

Mr. Elbrecht: Yeah, we made our own basketball court. We leveled off a spot, you know, and then they put up some backboards and we played outside because — until such time as they were able to tear the partitions out of the old building. And then we used that as a basketball court.

Mr. Simmons: It was all mud, you know, and whenever it rained and anybody would run through it or something they would leave tracks and of course it wasn't good for dribbling a basketball in it. But we didn't know the difference. (TI 1980)

Music. Today, the Milford School District has a strong program in music. The Kensington School continues in that tradition. Although particular events often can't be interpreted causally, the specifics do conjure up images. In 1916:

Acceptance of piano offered by the Baldwin Piano Co. Miss Bird to be allowed use of same and after school hours to give lessons in music.

Stone (a Board member) to haul same from piano store to the school house. (9/27/16)

Later, in the High School, a 'one person music department' appeared in the form of one of the students, who later played professionally:

Mr. Elbrecht: We put on a play every year I believe.

Mr. Simmons: That's right, yeah, we had one every year . . .

Mr. Elbrecht: Then we had Gypsy Rose or Sweetheart, or — no we didn't have the personnel for that.

Nothing in the arts. Now we didn't even have a music teacher but Cliff had taken music lessons and he was an excellent piano player. We had one fellow who was good on the sax and that was our band essentially.

Obs: Nobody played a bass or anything, just the sax and the piano?

Mr Elbrecht: No, I remember we needed a drummer. And one of the teachers came in and she said 'Do we have a drummer?' Johnny nudged me and said 'Tell her you're a drumer.' And I said 'I'm a drummer.' I couldn't, I never even handled a drum stick, so a couple of times at noon, Johnny took me up in the room and showed me how to keep the beat. And well that — sometimes I didn't do too well and she (Mrs. Briggs) tapped me on the head, 'You're a drummer?'.... (TI 1980)

The interview continued with some mention of the several teachers who supervised at different times with different productions:

Mr. Elbrecht: We all sort of pitched in.

Mr. Simmons: Yeah, it was, like I say, the whole thing was always a family affair. We had some of the lower grades that — there weren't enough in our class to fill out roles and so we had to use part of the other classes....

Mr. Elbrecht: Well, I mean, we were so short of help that, I guess you'd call it help, that I could never sing you know, and the farthest from my mind was singing and I had to sing a solo in the *Gypsy Rose*, I think, you know, it was kind of embarrassing for me, I'd say, but....

Mr. Simmons: Well, an interesting thing was in that one operetta, they do it in, I guess, in movies and what not there, the one girl was supposed to sing a solo and she couldn't sing and ... so my niece she sang ... so she stood right behind her in the wings there and she sang, you know, and the other one just moved her mouth and no one knew the difference.

Mr. Elbrecht: I wish I'd had someone to do that for me, it would have been much more successful. (TI 1980)

Library Books. The concept of the 'Perception Core' in the ultra modern Kensington School (Smith and Keith, 1971) seems rooted in the concept of 'Library Books.' As early as 1915 the Board was spending small amounts, $10 to $15, for library books. A typical item in 1917 indicated the importance of the teacher's judgment as well: 'Library books to be ordered as per list furnished by Miss Olin amounting to $10.20.' (4/30/17) Scattered references appeared regarding small amounts of money for library purchases. In 1922, it was noted: 'Moved and 2nd that we purchase 1 set of the World Book. Motion carried.' (4/28/22) A bookish pupil in High School, a decade later, reported a multiple set of experiences:

Mr. Elbrecht: I remember we had a small library. Just a little bookcase. And in view of the high school starting they — I guess the Board, probably Mr. Carr was as responsible as anybody because he was quite a reader and a well-educated man — they brought in a selection of books, some of the classics like some of Dickens and *Kenilworth* and *Silas Marner* and so on and then I believe we had a . . .

Mr. Simmons: We had good library dictionaries. . . .

Mr. Elbrecht: And we had a set of encyclopedias. . . .

Obs: In the high school room?

Mr. Elbrecht: Yeah, and then each year then of course, they added more new books to that. But I remember that I always liked to read. I read almost everything they had in that limited library. But it was good material, what they had. (TI 1980)

Community Models and Resources

In one of our interviews we were struck with the community resources open to a personable, bright, bookish, and multi-talented youngster. Mr. Elbrecht's account from the interviews reads this way:

Obs: I guess I was struck by your comments both about Craig and about Carr, in the fact that their influences came initially throught the Boy Scouts and that kind of thing and I guess I'm curious, were there other figures like that in your life and then your neighbor with this fine library and so, that seemed to make a difference in your education?

Mr. Elbrecht: Yeah, I would say that Mr. Carr made a tremendous difference in the education of not only some of us that went to the high school but to the young men in general in the community. It seems to me that anyone that he came in contact with he left his mark and not one — we were talking about it some time ago, a few of us got together, not one of the young men that he had been in contact with ever got into any trouble and they all seemed to prosper. He was quite an individual, now, he also was interested in sports and he sort of sponsored the baseball teams out here and of course he got a bunch of us interested in tennis, he was an avid ice skater and in the winter time he'd teach us how to skate and he was a good figure skater and he taught us figure skating and things like that and reading — he was a Sunday school teacher also and he wouldn't just — I don't think we ever cracked the Bible in his class but we talked about literature and philosophy and things of that nature and he really broadened us, I mean, you know, in fact knowing him and being with him was a bit of liberal education in itself and something that I value very highly, I mean, I feel that I almost got as much education in contact with him as I did going to high school.

Later in the interview, he related the story of a neighbor:

Mr. Elbrecht: I thought we were — I thought I was extremely fortunate to know somebody like that and then I was again fortunate to have this access to this tremendously wonderful library across the street from my place.

Obs: Talk a little — let me make sure we're going here — tell me a little bit about your neighbor with the library and stuff. . . .

Mr. Elbrecht: They moved out and built shortly after we did. I was — we moved out in 1921 and I guess they moved out about 1923 or 24, in those years, anyway, I know that when I was in grade school, probably the eighth grade or so, then I knew them and I started getting books from their library. . . . This was a tremendous library, they had practically all of the classics, the French and Russian writers and the English like Thomas Hardy and Dickens and Thackeray and boy, I just waded through a lot of that. I had a tremendous knowledge of literature by the time I got to college, I mean, which helped me considerably but I always did like to read and I'm going back and still reading — yeah, I'm going back and reading some more Dickens and Hardy and Thackeay and the whole thing.

Obs: Did you learn to read before you went to school or did you learn at school?

Mr. Elbrecht: No, no, I — in fact, it was a funny thing — when I was a youngster I talked German until I went to school so that actually threw me back about a grade until I learned English — I don't know, my folks talked German and I mean, that's the way things went in those days, you understand.

Obs: Yeah, I understand that. . . .

Mr. Elbrecht: And then when I got to college then I took a year of German up there because I had no trouble with the pronunciation at all but . . .

Family factors mixed in for him, in a way different from some of the youngsters with whom he grew up:

Obs: Were you parents supportive of your literary kind of interests along the way?

Mr. Elbrecht: Oh yes, I was going to say, most of the parents I suppose in those days were not too supportive of any education beyond the eighth grade and especially in a community like we were in. There wasn't any high school nearby for the children to go to, but when I indicated to my parents that I would like to go on, why, they were very supportive and they liked the idea very much. In fact, they supported me all the way through. Now I had an aunt, my father's mother's sister, and I know we visited them one day when I was in high school and she said, 'What does he need with more education?' You know, that was the attitude in those days. I mean, you had an eighth grade, you could read, write, compute and that was it.

Obs: Your Father was a farmer also?

Mr. Elbrecht: Yeah, he was farming. He did some farming and building. He built a number of houses, he was a builder in addition to farming.

> And, as I say, both parents were very supportive of me getting more of
> an education if I wanted it. (TI 1980)

The importance of that community member continues through multiple activities:

> *Obs*: But in that sense and with parents who had minimal education — did
> your Father go beyond the eighth grade for instance?
> *Mr. Elbrecht*: No, Mother didn't either.... That (Mr. Carr) was a
> stimulating experience. I mean, he broadened our minds that there were
> a lot of other things in the world, you know, than just this little
> community and he recommended books that we read, you know, and
> things like that. Just to give you a for instance, I remember when the
> Scout troup met up in the old church yard one Halloween night, with
> tombstones all around, and he had a flashlight and he read the book of
> *The Hound of the Baskervilles* which was quite an experience, you know,
> and he read that to us out there in the church yard. I mean, that was the
> type of thing that he would do and then in Sunday School class, maybe
> we would discuss a book like *Beau Geste* or something like that or we'd
> discuss philosophy of government. I mean, there were a whole gamut of
> civilizations, I mean, was sort of — he would draw us out — what did
> we think or so on and so forth. It was so much more than just a cut and
> dry Sunday School class, you know. I think he figured if we wanted
> religion we could get that in the church and he was intent on our minds.
> That's what he was intent on and I know I have some very good friends
> from the little select group that I was with and we are all most
> appreciative — what he did for us.
> *Obs*: Well, the lessons were falling obviously on fertile soil....
> *Mr. Elbrecht*: Right — So yes, I see what you're driving at — you're
> attempting to see what other forces were active in forming us even
> though we had this limited educational facilities so to speak. Of course,
> for those days, it was adequate really.
> *Obs*: And as you say, most of the people, if you could read and write and
> compute and do the farm work or the shop work or whatever ...
> *Mr. Elbrecht*: Right, that was all that was necessary. (TI 1980)

Summary

In conclusion, at the time of the first commencement in June 1931, the pride of the
district in its high school is well indicated in a story told by Mr. Carr, the Board
member in the brief history of the school:

> When the annual inspection of the school was made by the State
> Department of Education it was given full credit as a first class four-year
> High School. Talking with the Superintendent and several members of the
> Board, one of the Board members remarked, 'You think then, Mr.

Inspector, that we have a pretty good school.' 'No,'replied the Inspector, 'I wouldn't say just that. I would leave that 'pretty' out, you have a good school, no qualifications at all.' (*H. S. Annual*, 1931 p. 9)

From an able student's point of view the criterion was a simple one, access to the next step in the educational leader and later into a career:

Actually, we had the basics that we could get into college if we wanted to go. As I recall at that — at that time, most colleges required two years of a foreign language and two years of math and two years of science. Well, we had all of that plus we had four years of English, we had two or three years of history and I believe we had a course in civics, that's probably in our junior year . . . and then in our senior year then we had our biology and English and commercial law and commercial arithmetic I believe, and one other course, probably in social studies of some kind. We had a fairly good curriculum I would say for that type of school, you know, from coming from scratch. (TI 1980)

One further concluding thought comes to mind. The several lines of data which draw the picture of the early high school might be an accent of small size rather than rural America fifty years ago. The Barker and Gump *Big School, Small School* (1964) volume suggests that small schools retain many of the social, nonacademic, and academic positions and roles of the large high school, but have many fewer individuals competing for those positions. Consequently, the kind of experience — musician, athlete, scholar — tends to be much richer for the average student. At issue, fundamentally, is the kind of citizen adult the community desires to see facilitated, a theme running through much of our analysis.

In brief the high school was designed to fit state regulations, it was approved — lauded by a state inspector, and it permitted at least one student to meet the entrance requirements to the State University. Beyond that considerable latitude seemed possible. Further, for some, family or community gave schooling a potent if not unique kind of support.

Summary and Conclusions

We seem to be following a progression of a chronicle, mostly in the words of one group of the participants, the school board members, and even here in their formal documents. But even here not totally so, for we have letters and we have conversations and interviews with some of the members of the community, from fifty years ago. Then we begin to organize these comments into larger categories, items related to community, items related to school organization, and items related to curriculum and teaching. Now, in this concluding section we need to make comments more specifically bearing on the issues of innovation and change.

We are struck with how easy it is to speak of 'genesis and evolution' of the school district, but we are puzzled as to why that is so. It may be that the ideas we carry in our heads, 'the second record' as the historian Hexter calls them, are so pervasive and so a part of common sense or the conventional wisdom that they have a non problematic quality about them. Perhaps, too, the records which make up most of our data have a 'naturalistic' quality, that is they seem to have a natural regularity, much like the seasons of the year. There is a rhythm of the school year, at the board level in the April elections, and at the school level with openings after Labor Day in the Fall, the Thanksgiving and Christmas holidays and the closing in the early summer after Memorial Day. Perhaps, also, similar events are happening all over the country so that what might be called 'innovations' at the local level are occurring throughout the country as well. We are reminded of the distinction regarding 'creativity,' that which is new to the individual as opposed to that which is new to the larger community. At Milford, the innovations, 'the specific planned changes,' have previously occurred elsewhere in Midwest State and in Surburban County. Consequently, the basic process seems to be finding out how it is done, what the laws and the regulations are, and borrowing the procedures and formats.

Among the many innovations, the three most profound are the move from a three director district to a six director district, the creating a position of school superintendent with the hiring of an individual to fill the position, and the beginning of a high school which extended the instructional program to adolescents and which altered the organizational structure of schooling. The three are interlocked legally through state law. They are expressions of community growth and changes in size and social backgrounds. And they represent political interests in the actualization of visions of the good life in the minds of the local citizens.

The dynamics or driving forces underlying the creation of the high school as an innovation were a combination of an increasing number of adolescents and the image of a better community. The initial difficulty which arose regarding the creation of Milford High School seemed more a lack of knowledge of state law than anything else.

Similarly, the increasing size of the district and the attendant growth in the number and complexities of the administrative tasks seemed to foreshadow the need for a superintendent. These same forces, and some stereotypes regarding gender, 'the need for a man,' seemed to be at the root of initial administrative succession of superintendents. Again, there seemed to be networks of local knowledge of people in neighboring places, the Kennard School District, which brought Mr. Grey to Milford. Illness and death, a kind of 'natural' event 'drove' his succession.

Overall, we were struck with the events in the chronicle being part of a legal and political process. The local school district seemed nested in Surburban County and received guidance from a county superintendent with a long tenure, thirty-two years as we would eventually discover. The Milford District and Suburban County were nested in Midwest State. The latter had laws which governed the shift from a three director to a six director district and laws that said that one third of the board stood for election every April. Somewhere in the more distant past, these, too, were innovations. Now they were merely conditions which set the ground rules for the changes, the innovations, in the local districts, such as Milford. If we were to amend. House's (1979) analysis of innovation into the technological, political, and cultural, we would want to accent the subdivision of the political into 'legal' and into various levels of the 'micro-political,' the local, the county, and the state. These distinctions seem very important for understanding innovation and change in schooling.

It is difficult to articulate an 'image.' But that seems what we are about. The innovations and their causes, in Milford's early years, seemed part and parcel of a political process, within rural and small town democracy, which have been part of the American scene since the inception of the Republic. We are reminded of Tocqueville's classic statement of early nineteenth century American society, *Democracy in America*, a volume that we had been introduced to as undergraduates and hadn't read in years. As we looked back at it we discovered that he had 'found Milford.'

> In America the force behind the state is much less well regulated, less enlightened, and less wise, but it is a hundred times more powerful than in Europe. Without doubt there is no other country on earth where people make such great efforts to achieve social prosperity. I know of no other people who have founded so many schools or such efficient ones, or churches more in touch with the religious needs of the inhabitants, or municipal roads better maintained. So it is no good looking in the United States for uniformity and permanence of outlook, minute care of details, or perfection of administrative procedures; what one does find is a picture of power, somewhat wild perhaps, but robust, and a life liable to mishaps but full of striving and animation. (pp. 92–93)

It sounds as though E. K. Tholozon and his wife were two of his interviewees and Milford was one of the locales he traveled through. We find ourselves beginning to generalize the interpretations that we are making. Most significantly for the discussion of educational innovation, our historical, natural history, perspective takes away some of the 'glamour' and the 'unusualness,' which are among today's connotations of the concept of innovation, and links the concepts back to the more ordinary political, organizational, and administrative processes. Of these intertwined strands, we are impressed with the political as the most important driver of innovation. And lurking behind that we see community change, especially the demographics of population and some need for or rationale of congruence among the parts of a community and society driving the political process. For those of us, for example Smith and Keith (1971), who have focussed on the 'principal' as a change agent, we now have a context and disclaimer to his power. Increasingly we will see that as the professionalization of teachers and administrators occurs, legitimate conflict over 'innovation' will arise with these very fundamental democratic processes and the political interests of the Board and the community.

Our excerpts from the School Board minutes, documents such as the High School Annual, and a few retrospective interviews synthesize into an image of the instructional program in the early Milford Schools, and into an image of innovations in that program, and further into an image of the dynamics of how the instructional innovations occur. The picture is a common school curriculum of 'readin', 'riting and 'rithmetic,' the basic skills taught in an 'assign, study and recite' pedagogical mode, in a self contained classroom. Innovations seem more of the order of slightly increased specialization as the school increases in size. Extensions in the form of high school instruction for a small and select, highly able and motivated, group of students from local and neighboring elementary school districts. Carl Elbrecht's stories of a neigboring family and their 'lending library,' and even more significantly, Mr. Carr, one of the community's most well to do, educated, and philanthropic citizens provided the young Carl Elbrecht with a stimulating, bookish, liberal high school education. We are not sure of what conceptual sense to make of his comments, but we are struck with what Merton (1957) might have called 'functional equivalents.' This language of the functionalist and positivist social science seems an initial point of departure for further interpretation.

The dynamics of innovation, observed by us mostly by inference from the documents and conversations are two fold, individual initiative and dialogue, talk among the various individuals and groups of individuals in the setting. That seems so commonplace and so natural to the situation that it might escape notice. From our perspective it is so fundamental, so powerful, and so in tune with our interpretation of democratic values that it needs isolation and emphasis. Part of the power of these early images is that they are the 'bare bones' of education, education without all the idiosyncracies and complexities of the later years. Thus they enable us to see the emperor's 'innovative' new clothes without all of the blinders. We feel that that is a very powerful reason for looking at the historical context of innovation.

Notes

1 Mr. Elbrecht commented that as a student he was one of several students who appeared before the Board to discuss school problems. In his view Mrs. Briggs had problems with the students, the faculty, and the Board.

2 Our reference here is to Gunnar Myrdal's classic on race relations, *An American Dilemma* (1944). His work hovered over us constantly as we read, observed and tried to make sense of the Kensington /Milford experience.

3 We have not been able to find a comprehensive history of Black Education in Suburban County. For some interesting similarities see our study of the Alte School District (Smith, 1978).

4 Mrs. Shields later helped integrate another community school system after 1954, has been a successful and respected elementary and high school teacher, and won a 'teacher of the year award.' She left the Milford District because of declining enrollments and a desire to start a family.

5 For some similar comments on other schools in other communities see Peshkin (1978, pp. 203–206).

6 No extant record exists of these rules.

7 We raise this issue in some detail in Book II of our trilogy, *The Fate of an Innovative School* (Smith, Prunty, Dwyer, and Kleine, 1987).

8 A secondary source indicated a one room school existed in the district from the middle or latter part of the nineteenth century.

9   Washington University night school and summer school, interestingly enough, still adheres to this procedure. It does get the grades reported.

10 The record of the annual meeting indicated that the vote was 'unanimous' of all citizens attending.

Section Three
The Longer Rhythms of Stability and Change

Chapter 5

Chronicling McBride's Tenure as Superintendent: 1935–62

Introduction

In the description and analysis of educational innovation from an historical perspective, it is important to see the phenomenon in various contexts. McBride was superintendent of Schools for twenty seven years, a long period by any standard. His tenure enables us to look at the evolving and changing Milford School District from a point of view different from that of the innovative Spanman who later was to build the Kensington School and from the earlier administrations of Briggs and Grey, who defined the superintendent's role as the first incumbents and who participated in the organization of the Milford High School. The latter effort might be seen as the last 'big' innovation in the early years, for it came after the District became a six director town district and it came concurrently with the designation and filling of the new position of Superintendent.

As we tell McBride's story and then try to interpret it we are doing so in the context of a national economic depression in the 1930s, a World War in the 1940s, and postwar population growth and suburban development in the 1950s. Also there was a quiet state department of education which had spent itself in the early 1930s on a failed attempt to consolidate local school districts, but later was to regroup more successfully. Locally, a relatively stable small town, not quite suburban community, was to last until the early 1950s when the suburban population explosion occurred in Metropolitan County generally and particularly in Milford's stable local small town community. One might argue that 'survival' rather than innovation was the issue at hand. Phrases, if not clichés, abound for talking about the context, 'the temper of the times' and 'the way things were' and 'swimming upstream' or 'rolling back the tide' are a few of these. We find the ideas significant. The proactive innovator be he or she in the community, on the board, in an administrative position, or in the classroom, must be able to see, read, decide, and act in such contexts. There may be 'strategic moments' for significant planned changes, innovations. And there may be 'normal processes,' politically, organizationally, and educationally, connected with schooling that have to be respected. It is to all this we now turn as we tell and interpret Superintendent McBride's story.

In relation to our overview of the broad historical sweep in the chronicle of the Milford School District, the McBride era splits into three major periods: 1) a long period of stability and gradual growth that is a continuation of Milford as a six director township school system; 2) a period of transition and 3) a long period of rapid post World War II population growth, really a population explosion when the district was building 'a school every year,' until there were a dozen. We speak of long periods, for the McBride era lasted almost twenty-seven years. The stable period began in January 1935 and lasted until 1949. In 1949, the Marquette School District merged with Milford and in 1952, the first post World War II school, the Grant Elementary School was built. From 1952 until 1962, building a school a year, the District grew rapidly, McBride aged, and the Board wanted him to step down. Amidst considerable controversy Steven Spanman came in 1962. But that part of the story comes twenty-seven years later, even though we know something of it as 'the tangle of administrative succession.'

The Long Stable Era (1935–49)

The continuity in district affairs appears in the rapid socialization of the new superintendent. Within two months of his appointment he 'reads the current bills for the month of February'. His work was commented upon: 'Mr. McBride then gave a very satisfactory report on conditions, in relation to improvements and progress for the past month.' (3/6/35) And it was moved, seconded and carried: '... that the Board accept estimated budget plans for 1935–36 as submitted by Mr. McBride.' (3/6/35) The educational program of the District continued to grow gradually, like Topsy, this time in adult education:

> At this time a Mr. Smith, representing the advanced adult education program of Suburban County, was invited to consult with the Board on situation prevalent at the Attucks night school. Mr. Everhart moved. seconded by Mrs. Quayles, that Mr. McBride make inquiries with the proper authorities at Capitol City as to what can be done about compensation for teachers teaching at the Attucks night school. The motion carried. (2/6/35)

The interplay of state and local activities continues: 'Mr. McBride explained the merits of House Bill 21 now before the General Assembly at Capitol City.' (3/6/35) The Board went on record in support of the bill.

Adult education appeared to be more general for the Board moved, seconded and passed the recommendation in April of 1935: 'Under recommendations by Mr. McBride ... that we leave the question of letting the Adult Education group have a room at either Milford Village or Clear Valley School in the hands of Mr. McBride to act on as he saw fit.' (4/3/35) Amidst some controversy three of the high school teachers submitted their resignations for the following year. With a split vote the Board accepted them. Later a group of patrons sought a reconsideration. The Board saw it as 'closed business.'

With the consultation of an official from the State Department of Education the Board made plans to solicit Federal funds for a two to four room addition to the Milford Village School and a gymnasium building at Clear Valley.[1] (6/17/35) Letters went to President Roosevelt and three congressional representatives. On 2 October 1935, the Board met at its regular time:

> The first order of business for the evening was the letter from Mr. T. N. Poser, acting State Director for the Federal Emergency Administration of Public Works, notifying the Board of Education of Milford that the application for a government loan of $28,000 and a grant of $24,763 had been approved by the government, and that immediate advice of the approval and acceptance be forwarded to Mr. Poser. On the advice of Mr. Thompson, Mr. Everhart moved, seconded by Mr. Eason that the following resolution be forwarded;
>
> > Be it resolved that the Secretary of the Board of Education immediately notify the Federal Emergency Administration of Public Works that the *Board of Education of Milford, Suburban County, Midwest State hereby accept the loan and grant referred to, based upon the PWA rules and regulations imposed by the President of the United States,* and be it further resolved that a work schedule be also immediately forwarded as required. (Our italics)
>
> The motion carried. (10/2/35)

Interestingly the federal-local relationship also included transportation: 'A committee of patrons of our non resident pupils met with the Board to discuss plans and means whereby these children may secure transportation with some government aid.' (9/4/35) Most of the Board's time in 1935–36 involved the multitude of details in financing, contracting and building the addition.

The interrelation among present buildings, their size and structure, additional new building space, the housing of children, the structure of the educational program, and the concerns of parents appear dramatically in that 1935–36 year. The election of new Board members in April was strongly contested although we have no data on the issues. The votes by order of filing were 332, 342, 291, 216. One incumbent won with 342 votes and one lost, with 216 votes. Within a week, at a special meeting, Mr. McBride, the Superintendent, received a new three year contract. In the third special meeting in April, the report of the Superintendent as summarized in the Board minutes included: 'The discussion and explanation to parents about the moving of elementary school children to the school building on Pearl Drive. It was agreed that Mr. McBride take care of the date for meeting.' (4/28/35)

In June: 'Mr. McBride spoke on the probability of moving all elementary grades to Milford Village School. A group of patrons from Meramec Road[2] met with the board at this time, expressing their views.' (6/3/36)

In July, formal actions occurred: 'Under unfinished business, Mr. Everhart moved, seconded by Mr. Yates, that all elementary grades from first to sixth be moved to the Milford Village School. The motion carried.' (7/1/36) This consolidation of all elementary pupils into one building was a several month process. While discussions went on within the Board and in public meetings between the parents and the Board, apparently no organized opposition arose. The arguments pro and con did not appear in any of the Board records.

That summer the Board and the Superintendent for the first time seemed to run headlong into the mix of federal money for equipment (PWA), the complications of varied equipment characteristics and varied prices on the bids, and the need for care regarding rules and regulations, what today might be called red tape:

> The Board of Education of the School District of Milford met for a special meeting July 17, 1936, at Clear Valley School, for the purpose of reconsideration of some of the awards made on equipment for the PWA Project No. 1956-R at their July 1st meeting, 1936....
>
> The following resolution was adopted by the Board....
>
> WHEREAS, there appears to be some unsatisfactory conditions in regard to the recent award at the July 1st meeting, and WHEREAS there has been objection on the part of some bidders in that some awards were made to high bidders instead of the low. Be it therefore resolved that due to these existing conditions that the Board of Education reconsidered or rejected bids that were not satisfactory and reconsidered Items 2 and 3, under Section I, Item 1 under Section II, and Item 7 under Section II. (7/17/36)

In a series of ten more specific motions that Board reaffirmed its earlier action with explicit reasons that low bids did not 'meet specifications.' For example:

> The Board specified the Medallion wire basket No. 397 as equal.... The Board is ready to show why the Metal Equipment Company basket is not equal to the Medallion basket.
>
> First: The basket is not as heavy and durable
> Second: The basket contains four wires around which makes it weaker
> Third: Sharp points on corners of Metal basket make it dangerous to hands
>
> These will be brought along for your examination. (7/17/36)

The purchase of Medallion steel lockers involved *ten* reasons, mostly related to durability and safety. The Board' minutes, before adjournment, closed with:

> I certify that the above is true, conscientious consideration and action of the Board of Education of Milford School District, July 17th, 1936, on school equipment awards, P.W.A. Project Number 1056-R, and action was taken subject to approval of PWA.
>
>   F. N. McBride
>   Supt. of Schools
>   (7/17/36)

It looked as though the Superintendent had been busy, done his homework, was assuming a larger and larger role as business manager and executive officer of the

District, and was learning to cope with 'the FEDS.' As with water dripping on stone, the role of superintendent is being defined. In the middle of this process, and without our understanding the causes or reasons, an item appeared in the minutes: 'It was agreed by the Board that Mr. McBride take a leave of absence for a few days rest when his judgement saw fit to do so.' (7/1/36) He seemed to be working hard, doing what the Board wanted, earned some days off, and was trusted to use his own discretion in taking that time.

When a nation is in a depression, when school needs seem never ending, when District resources are scarce, as always seemed the case in Milford, and when a President of the Nation is calling for 'A New Deal', and when one had successfully won support for a building and equipment, it probably shouldn't be a surprise to find an item in the minutes such as the following:

> Mr. McBride then gave the Superintendent's Report. A resolution was proposed, asking the government for an additional grant on the extra money spent on our building project. Mr. Yates moved, seconded by Mr. Ellis, that this resolution be adopted. The motion carried. Some discussion on heating problem. It might be possible to get a WPA project on this with Mr. Galvern supervising. If done by WPA work, we could get work done for about 10% or 20% of what it would cost otherwise. Mr. McBride is to go ahead and look into this WPA project.[3] (11/4/36)

One doesn't have to be a reinforcement theorist to see and understand the rapid learning of grant application skills nor a cognitive theorist to see and understand the changes in perspectives occurring in the minds and behavior of the Board members. Whether these shifts are a long jump or a short step to the habits, perspectives and organization structures of 1979–80 can be debated.

In a series of three items, presumably related, the Board acted on 1) the resignation from the Board of Mrs. Quayles who had been secretary; 2) the hiring of a Mr. W. Quayles as janitor; and 3) the hiring of Miss Needles as secretary to the Board.

> The question of Secretary of the Board was discussed, and the discussion resulted in the following action of the Board. It was moved by Mr. Yates and seconded by Mr. Ellis that Miss Needles be Secretary of the Board until further arrangements are made by the Board of Education, at a $5.00 additional salary per month. The motion carried. (9/22/36)

Now, for the first time, the Superintendent's secretary was also the paid secretary of the Board, 'Further arrangements' weren't made until March, 1944, almost a decade later.

In October, the Board voted '. . . to stand the expenses of Mr. McBride . . .' to both the state and national teachers meetings. In December the school picnic increased in scope and status, as the Board signed a contract with Mark Twain Amusements, a Metropolitan City amusement park to hold the School Picnic May 6th.

In June, 1937 the Board minutes indicated for the first time that Milford considered the audio visual approaches to teaching: '. . . to have Mr. McBride investigate the purchase of a Visual Education machine, and that we join the Visual Education Program.' (6/2/37) These discussions continued on into the Autumn. A new machine which played both sound and silent films was soon to be on the market. The Board decided to wait for that.[4] Anticipating a later discussion we would mention that twenty-five years later, Superintendent Spanman would arrive with a persuasive style, masterfully utilizing an overhead projector with charts, graphs, and alliterative topic words, and make Kensington, in plan at least, '. . . an elementary school which would give them the most modern audio-visual program in the nation.' (Gillespie, 1967, p. 15) One might ask, when is an innovation really an innovation?

During these years, business and organizational items flood the minutes: insurance, boilers and stokers, and radiators, bids on major and minor maintenance, hiring and firing of custodians, cafeteria profits, wages for cooks ($1.25/day), bids for coal, salaries for new staff and amounts of increase for old. Even the children and parents became a part of this:

> There are still some children who have entered Milford Village School, in the 1st grade, and who have not presented birth certificates. Mr. McBride is to write another letter to these parents, stating that these birth certificates must be turned in to Mr. Ulrich by Monday, October 18, or the child will be sent home, until a birth certificate is received. (11/6/37)

During these years the purchase of bits and pieces of equipment suggest that curricular and extra curricular activities were part of the discussion in Board meetings. Concerns were expressed about sewing machines, Sousaphones in music, storage lockers for Boy Scout equipment and so forth. And then, dropped into the minutes in the section entitled 'Monthly Report' or 'Report of the Superintendent,' is an occasional major curriculum item:

> There was some discussion on having a kindergarten at Milford Village Elementary School for the last three months of this school year. Mr. McBride is to investigate the number of children who would attend the kindergarten, and if there are sufficient number, he is to go ahead with plans. Motion made . . . seconded . . . and carried. (2/2/38)

A month later, a $4.00/month tuition rate for non-resident kindergarten pupils was established.

The Board minutes suggest the continuing influence of the county superintendent and the possible collegial aspects among superintendents:

> Mr. McBride then gave his monthly report. There was some discussion of the question of a survey being made, which was brought up at the County Superintendent's meeting. As we do not know enough about this, the Board decided not to pass on same. (3/2/38)

The hypothesis we are reaching toward is the gradual development of relationships between the relatively isolated superintendents of small county districts which culminated many years later in the formation of the League of Superintendents of Suburban County. Intertwined in this is the gradual decline in importance of the County Board of Education and the County Superintendent of Schools.

On Wednesday, 9 March 1938, a special meeting of the Board was called. Amidst minutes of lumber buying, insurance company contracts, restarting heating and electrical systems, and discussions of classes which are usable, the reader makes the inference that the West end of the old High School building has burned down. The rebuilding was complicated by differences with the insurance company $17,000 vs $9,000, the possibilities of WPA money and the role of union labor. A week later the insurance differences were adjusted and compromised to $13,000. Outside resource possibilities were reported as:

> A visit was made to the State WPA office in Capitol City by Mr. McBride and some of the Board members yesterday, and were informed that there is not much chance of a WPA project with skilled labor. It was decided by the Board to forget the WPA. (3/16/38)

One of the Board members who is in the construction business offered to manage the rebuilding for 10 per cent of the contract. This necessitated his resignation from the Board, after which he received the contract.

Besides rebuilding parts of the High School, additions to the elementary school, for a kindergarten, and remodeling of Attucks were on the agenda. Mr. McBride made another visit to Capitol City and was told that bills for school aid were in Congress in Washington, DC and that district voting dates should not be set until the bill passed in Congress. The Board then resolved:

> That the School District undertake a building project looking to an addition to the building, and that we seek whatever Federal aid is available, and authorize the President of the Board and the Superintendent of Schools to fill in the preliminary questionnaire in order to get the project underway, and to execute the necessary applications. The motion carried. (5/16/38)

The Board also moved for a special election for the bonds for the school. The vote was 8 to 1 in favor (329 to 40). The Board President, Mr. Brock, resigned in order to accept the contract as one of the architects for the new building.

We have not made an exhaustive study of the economic importance of school business for a local community, nor the evolution of sealed competitive bids as a technique for controlling favoritism in awarding contracts. In Milford, the main bids were so let. This kind of local 'economic politiking,' if we can use such a label, is openly reported in the minutes. Presumably it's 'just good business.' A strong case can be made for a local citizen representing and advocating for the district as architect. A touch of irony appears in another item labeled 'political meetings' which follows right after the contracting discussion of the school building items which were awarded to the two former Board members:

> In regard to political meeting, it is the unanimous opinion of the Board that the auditorium at Clear Valley School, the Milford assembly hall, and the

Attucks School be made available for a reasonable number of times to the political parties for political meetings during the Fall, provided they make arrangements with the Superintendent a reasonable length of time before the holding of the meetings. (8/3/38)

School systems in rural areas and small towns in pre World War II America were fascinating community institutions.

The application for Federal aid was written and rewritten several times as ideas changed, possible amounts of the contract changed, and as union minimum wage rates for the metropolitan area were incorporated. Additional land was bought, competitive bids received for the construction and contracts let during Summer and Autumn of 1938. Two of the final touches were the Board's resolutions that: '. . . the architect be authorized to design and secure an appropriate bronze tablet to commemorate the assistance furnished by the United States Government.' (3/8/39) And the Board's resolution: 'A motion was made . . . to sell the shed that has been used by the WPA to the WPA, for $30.00. The motion carried.' (5/22/39)

In its beginning at least, 1939–40, seemed noteworthy only in someone's afterthought. The Board minutes for that year were bound with those running from July 1939–July 1948. The gathering war storm in Europe obviously didn't enter into the one page per meeting sets of minutes. Nor was the ebbing of the 1930s recession much in evidence. Rather, on 5 July 1939 the agenda consisted of the roll call (one absence), the secretary and treasurer's reports (approved with a balance of $9,368.66), the cafeteria report was read and current bills paid, the Superintendent's monthly report (a thank you to Dr. Evans[5]) and the hiring of Miss Engle as home economics teacher (at a salary of $1,274.70 for ten months and an extra $127.30 for the eleventh month), the coal bid was accepted, eight book shelves for the library were purchased from a local school and business supply company, and repairs were authorized for the Milford Elementary School. '. . . two doors replaced, cement step in front of the building repaired, new downspout on the North side of the building, and tuckpointing.' The meeting was over in an hour and ten minutes, at 9:10 p.m. On 6 September 1939 the enrollment was:

45 Attucks
255 Milford Village School
247 High School

which represented an increase of forty-five or fifty pupils. The Board also did not support Patricia Talbot's petition for another half year of high school tuition and transportation which she needed because she had failed to graduate in the usual four years' time.

The legal context of public education appeared and reappeared in Milford in quite explicit ways. Patricia Talbot's case was reconsidered two weeks later:

The Board reconsidered its action of a previous meeting in the matter of paying the tuition and transportation for one-half year for Patricia Talbot, a colored girl. After listening to a report of investigation as conducted by the Superintendent, and after consideration of the law, the Board came to the conclusion that it was unauthorized to pay any further tuition or transportation for Patricia Talbot. (9/18/39)

The day to day business of running a small school district continued with items related to a neighboring one room school district and the local codes of morality:

A motion was made by Mr. Coser, seconded by Mr. Yankel, that we permit the Whitcomb's PTA to hold a program this year only; in our gymnasium, and that they be advised that the Board has established a policy against the use of the school building by school districts and other organizations outside the territorial limits of this school district, and that holding public dances in public school building is absolutely forbidden and against the policy of the Board. The motion carried. (10/4/39)

Once again, the gradual extension in scope of school services appears in the minutes when the changes demand financial resource: 'A motion was made by Mr. Coser, seconded by Mr. Yankel, to pay Mr. Smith $100.00 for trips made to different colleges with students last Spring. The motion carried.' (12/6/39)

A month later, three items of note appeared. The Superintendent reported on personal and real estate taxes 'stricken off' school districts 1935–39. Second, a committee was appointed 'to survey the district for future school building sites.' The third suggests the vagaries of policy with neighboring districts: 'It was decided to entertain the members of the rural school boards sending students to our high school, and their wives, at a dinner on Saturday night, February 24, at 6:00 p.m.' (1/3/40) A month before, and a month later, the Board reiterated its policy of non-use of buildings by outside schools and organizations. The final item dealt with 'Sex Education': 'Miss Gaynor, Mrs. Kelly, and Mr. Smith gave quite a discussion on sex education as it is carried on in our school, and on the health program in general.' (1/3/40) This seems noteworthy in several regards. The controversy over sex education continues through the county now some forty years later. Second, the Board has initiated formal curriculum reports by staff to the Board. Eventually this becomes institutionalized as on a rotating once a month emphasis. The following month, the minutes included a similar item: 'Mr. Smith, Miss Palm and Louis Yankel gave quite a discussion of the guidance programs as carried on in our schools.' (3/6/40)

A month later bills for 'band uniforms' were paid. Earlier a bassoon had been purchased. Music education continued in full splendor.

The Board extended its program to include a 'playground this Summer at both schools' and appointed Mr. Reynolds at a salary of $100/month 'to take care of the playground.' At the next meeting the school nurse, Mrs. Kelly, was rehired.

Home economics was handled by a contract with the State Department of Education (8/7/40). Major outlays for shop equipment — 'double shop benches,' tools, metal stools, were made. And the Superintendent was requested to investigate the number of students who would want to take chemistry, the cost of equipment, etc., and report at the next meeting (8/27/40). And at that next meeting the Board voted 'that we put in a chemistry course in the high school this year' (9/4/40).

World and national events did come directly to Milford in September of 1940. Perhaps, the form should have been anticipated by any observer and theorist:

> It was the sense of the meeting that it will be necessary to adopt proper regulations concerning leaves of absence for teachers now in the military service or those hereafter called, and provide for their re-employment upon termination to their military service. (9/4/40)

Later a leave of absence policy was adopted. During the 1941–42 year references to 'defense children' and possible Federal aid,[6] the selling of 'defense stamps' and the departure of the secondary principal and a few teachers appeared.

For over a decade, since Mrs. Tholozan's leaving the Board, the membership had been all male. On 4 November 1942, Mrs. Bester was voted in by the Board to fill a vacancy caused by resignation. That Spring she was re-elected in an uncontested race. A month later she resigned because she moved out of the district. She was replaced by Susan Jones.

As we have indicated at several points in our discussion the source of several of our 'themes' in this history of the district are the concerns, problems, and issues in contention and manifest in the Kensington School and Milford District today. The involvement with the Federal government is one of those major themes. Today it's a concern for PL 94–142 and the Office of Civil Rights. In anticipation are concerns about court ordered desegregation, busing, and hiring policies. In 1941, the flavor was very different:

> Mr. McBride gave an explanation in regard to the defense aid that is being given by the Federal Government. Quite a bit of discussion on this. A motion was made ... that we authorize Mr. Bestor to prepare application to the Public Works Agency covering certain improvements in the existing school facilities, with the understanding that if we go ahead with the work, we employ Mr. Bestor as architect. The motion carried. (7/21/41)

The activity went forward in the next few months, and at what now seems like an incredibly quick turn around time at a special meeting on Friday, 3 October 1941, the minutes record the 'success' of Mr. McBride and Mr. Bestor:

> Mr. Bestor and Mr. McBride attended a meeting in the PWA office, and they are ready to offer us a $70,000 grant for the building of a new elementary school. After quite a bit of discussion on this, a motion was made..., that we write a letter to the Midwest City office that we are ready to accept their offer in the amount of $70,000, but that it will be necessary that we revise our building set up. The motion carried. If advisable Mr. McBride and Mr. Bestor are to make the trip to the Midwest City office for a conference there. (10/3/41)

Three years later (6/26/44), Mr. McBride read a telegram to the Board indicating they had received $12,500.00 from the Federal Works Agency for construction costs of a two room addition to the Milford Elementary School. Twenty thousand dollars of bonded indebtedness was approved 48 to 2 in the special election of 13 July 1944.

In August of 1943, a note was made on a phenomenon that presumably was occurring all over the country: 'Mr. McBride gave a report on the Suburban County Planning Commission's post war program. Quite a bit of discussion on post war planning for our school district.' (8/4/43) No record appeared at this time. One of the generalizations we would make is simple but potent. Common sense units of time often are broken into chunks around memorable events, such as a war and 'post war planning.' Implicit also is a dimension of special times, that is, the war years and more normal times. Further, implications seem to exist for these as occasions in which initiatives might be taken.

The Board continued to receive requests for releases from contracts. Most seemed to be handled quickly and easily as teachers had husbands who were moved by their companies or were moving for better employment, were marrying, or were having children. Seldom were other reasons stated. The Board eventually requested each teacher to make a personal appearance as part of the procedures. One instance was noted of a teacher moving to a university position: 'A motion was made . . . that we accept the resignation of Katherine Masters, to accept a position at the University of Minnesota.' (1/5/44) After nine years Mrs. Tackie left her post as School Board secretary. She was replaced by Julia Openstein.

Transition and Change: The Modernization of Milford

Transition Years

The arbitrariness in selecting any year, for instance, 1949, 1950, or 1951 as the cut off period in the two phases of the long tenure of Mr. McBride is clearly seen in the events of the Spring of 1949. Mr. Lewis, a man who was to become a major figure on the Board for a number of years, was elected. A series of items with far reaching significance arose early:

1   The Superintendent was authorized 'to sign teachers up as he finds them without the Board's approval when necessary, in order to be sure of getting them.'
2   'A discussion was held on the Education of Handicapped Children in the community.' Within a decade, a county wide program would be 'the' resolution until PL 94–142 appeared in 1975.
3   Inquiries regarding a neighboring Vocational School were instituted. This problem, too, would be solved with a Suburban County wide program in another decade and a half.
4   The remodeling of the new Attucks School has been noted. That lasted only until 1955, the year after the Brown and Topeka decision.
5   A Drivers Education Program was considered.
6   The continuing general question of church–state relations arose: '. . . the Gideon Society had requested the privileged of giving out Bibles to all the

school children from the 5th grade up that wanted them. It was agreed to let them do so.'

7   The first recorded item and formal 'instructing' of the Board arose: 'Mr McBride mentioned that he would have "What the High School Ought to Teach," a pamphlet by Mr. Charles W. Boardman for the Board members at the next meeting.' (5/10/49)

8   Arrangements were made to have buses driven by full time District employees. The problem of transportation was to remain with the District, seemingly forever.

9   Questionnaires were sent to teachers soliciting their opinions on a number of matters. Teacher influence on District policy will have a fascinating but stormy history in the District.

10   Responsibility for granting use of buildings by outside groups was delegated to the Superintendent. The role of Superintendent and the varied incumbents over the next thirty years have been equally fascinating and stormy.

11   From the first time also, the Superintendent's Report to the Board was now prepared in mimeographed form and bound in to the Board minutes. The data, for later generations of practitioners and researchers, has been elaborated, and hence, transformed.

The annexation of a school district is a major innovation in any school district. It became an important defining element in the transition and modernization of the Milford School District. A number of proposals circulated throughout Suburban County for the reorganization and consolidation of the some ninety school districts, many of which were still three board elementary districts with just one school. A few of the districts had actually closed their schools as enrollments had made them totally unfeasible. Considerable county 'politiking' occurred in some areas. Milford's Board eschewed all this except for the adjacent Marquette District which had several hundred pupils in its elementary school and which had sent most of its youngsters to Milford High School for a number of years. In the several years between 1949 and 1952, the consolidation did occur and the massive suburbanization of the metropolitan community had a 'modernized' district system to cope with the huge new housing tracts, the young families, and the thousands of children to be educated. But it is to the detail of our one district, Milford, which we return.

Throughout our account of the evolution of the Milford Schools we have noted a gradual extension of goals and functions, for example, establishment of the High School, the Kindergarten and so forth. As these have occurred new structures and processes have appeared in buildings, positions, rules and regulations. Another aspect of 1949–52 as a transition period is the formalization of organizational structures and processes. We noted already the formal mimeographed report of the Superintendent. In May of 1949 the word came from the State Department of Education that in the 1950–51 year all schools would be classified as A, AA, AAA. The word to the wise included:

1 formation of written policies
2 development of philosophy and objectives
3 certification of all teachers
4 school librarian in place
5 purchase of supplies and equipment.

In the same meeting, Mr. McBride presented a 'how-to-do-it' outline which Engelhart and Engelhart had published in the *American School Board Journal*:

1 Organization, procedure and duties of the Board
2 Office and duties of the superintendent
3 Personnel
4 General policies

In addition seven rules of thumb were presented by Engelhart and Engelhart regarding the preparation of the rules and regulations. In paraphrased form they are:

1 be consistent with the law
2 be guiding principles rather than collections of detailed instructions
3 reflect board policies not administrative procedures
4 be framed by executive and professional staff and approved by board
5 not restrict initiative but define range of duties of individuals and groups
6 recognize 'professional character of the workers'
7 be part of minutes record of board and not modified without board's consent.

One doesn't have to be a student of classic social scientists such as Max Weber, nor of his more recent interpreters such as Peter Blau (1956) to perceive the rise of bureaucracy as part and parcel of Milford's move into another aspect of mainstream modern American society. The spring of 1949 reeks with formalization of systems of rules and policies, with definitions and specializations of roles, with hierarchies of power and authority, and, a bit more implicitly, with impersonalization of actions and relations among individual staff members. The State Department of Education has a hand in this, the professional and academic educational community, for Engelhart and Engelhart have been a part of Columbia University's Teachers College community and its expanding network of educational administrators, also is a part of the shift. The *American School Board Journal* is publishing their work. And, as we will see in considerable detail shortly, Mr Lewis, a newcomer to the Milford School Board, has strong interests in modernizing Milford's schools. Superintendent McBride is in the middle of these major events in the transition of the Milford School District.

In June, the array of 'summer items' continued to appear in the minutes. On 14 June, a half dozen teacher contracts were issued. The discussions continued with Quaker Company over the dynamite blasting at Pleasant Hill and relocating of the Attucks School. The Board went to a lawyer for a legal opinion. Continued blending of finances between the Marquette School and Milford Schools occurred. The janitors' salaries were increased. The five per cent boosted them ($2,520, $2,184,

$2,310) above the salaries of some of the new teachers. The elementary teachers were paid less than the secondary teachers.

Regarding curriculum, instruction, and school affairs, it was noted that Mr. McBride distributed the pamphlet 'What the high school ought to teach,' He noted also that the High School had thirty-three and a quarter units of credit approved by the State Department of Education. And a final item appeared regarding student activities in the high school:

> A discussion was held on the recent 'M' Club invitation. It was decided that rather than stop it entirely and drive it underground, that something of a milder nature be substituted to satisfy the majority of club members. (6/14/49)

The results of the survey of teachers were also reported. This seemed important in several regards:

1   The Board continued the tradition of soliciting teacher opinions
2   For the first time, a formal questionnaire was used
3   Elementary Teacher results were separated from that of the High School Teachers
4   The nine questions covered issues of governance, curriculum, and teacher evaluation.

Question #1 asked 'Do you feel that the formulation of an educational program in Milford has been a democratic process involving you of the professional staff?' (16 yes, 1 no). Question #9, 'Have you ever been asked to do anything that you could not consider being completely ethical?' (1 yes, 16 no). The only item with split views concerned teacher evaluation: 'Would you welcome the opportunity of aiding in the establishment of a system of teacher evaluation?' The split was 3 to 5, yea and nay in the high school and 5 to 3, yea and nay in the elementary school.

The Continuing Themes

During the 1949–52 period, most of the stories we have been telling and the themes we have been exploring continued. Rather than detailing these at length, we will allude to them only briefly and illustratively. For instance, on 7 April 1949, with the new Board members, Mr. Lewis and Mr. Norton, agreements were reached on several aspects of the Superintendent's report: 'It was decided to determine if more than 1 candidate is available for our vacancies in teachers. If more than 1 is available the Board will consider the qualifications of the candidates.' (4/7/49) This sounds as though efforts were starting to increase the size of the pool of teacher candidates and thereby the quality of the staff.

The problems continued with the Black school and the Quaker Manufacturing Company over land usage and rebuilding the school: 'It was determined to do some additional studying before deciding just what has to be done about the Negro building situation including that of future usage and possibility of paying tuition in Metropolitan City.' (4/7/49)

The negotiations with Quaker Company continued. On 22 October 1949, the Board voted to ask for $18,000 for a new two room frame building for the Attucks School. A month later, it was reported that the Company made the payment. In the next few months plans were drawn, bids were let, and the low bid was accepted (2/7/50). Construction began immediately. Ironically, Metropolitan City rejected Milford's overtures. The Superintendent's Report contained the brief item 'Negro children — the City will not accept them.' (5/10/49) Today, after a new school building had been built, a 1954 Supreme Court Decision handed down, and changing population migrations in the metropolitan area, discussions are underway about a metropolitan, City-County, desegregation plan.

The cafeteria continued along:

> The suggestion from the County Board of Health that silverware be divided, that we improve fly control in the cafeteria, that granitework be replaced, that only one individual handle straws and that garbage cans be washed weekly will be followed.' (4/7/49)

And finally another of the neverending events: 'The school bus and drivers were discussed and it was decided to check further into the matter.' (4/7/49)

Concerns for handicapped youngsters continued to be raised, not only in Milford but all over the Suburban County: 'Mr. McBride reported on a committee that was being formed in order to find out whether or not a central school could be started to care for all handicapped children in the county.' (11/11/49) Similar concerns arose over vocational education:

> A discussion was held on the Vandeventer Vocational School. It was decided that Mr. McBride again talk to Mr. DeLuca regarding whether or not there would be any students here that would benefit more by going to the vocational school half time than by staying here all day. (11/11/49)

Discussions on school reorganization, circulation of literature, and Board resolution in favor of reorganization (9/13/49) all occurred. The community opposed the idea:

For	690	
Against	1700	
Total	2350	(11/11/49)

The Milford District as a geographical educational unit remains this day as it was decided on that day thirty years ago.

In December of 1949, another 'first' occurred in the District. Plans were underway to establish a citizen's committee regarding school finances:

> School Finance Committee. An extensive discussion was held on the way to select the original committee to study the school finances. Mr. Lewis moved to send a post card to the community with a return card attached to

return if interested in serving on the committee, to try to get a representative group. Mr. Jennings seconded the motion, which carried. (12/13/49)

On February (the 14th), the Board decided to meet jointly with the new citizen's committee to discuss ways to present the new school levy to the people of the district. The levy passed in April and a new 'Lay Committee' was formed.

More Evidence of Transition

In the Summer of 1949, the first Board minute appeared regarding what was to be the population explosion:

The building of a new subdivision on the southwest section of our school district and suitable site for another elementary school were discussed. It was decided that we would try to get more data on other subdivisions as to how the number of children run in proportion to the number of homes. (7/12/49)

The enrollments that Autumn were 1151 students. Subtotals appear in Figure 12. A few high school students were enrolled in neighboring districts where they had started before the merger between Milford and Marquette Districts. The minutes mention a handful of special education students in private schools.

Report after report on new subdivisions appeared. For instance, Wooded Valley — 'A total of 733 homes in the next two and a half to three years' — appears

Figure 12: Enrollment in Milford in Autumn 1949

	Milford	Marquette	Attucks
Elementary	305	439	17
Kindergarten	49	58	
1	48	54	
2	58	63	
3	44	53	
4	39	43	
5	32	38	
6	35	56	
7	—	39	
8	—	35	
High School	390		
7	37		
8	34		
Freshman	109		
Sophomore	73		
Junior	77		
Senior	60		

in the Superintendent's Report of 11 October 1949. The magnitude of suburbanization kept appearing in vivid numbers:

> Mr. McBride reported on the new Edinburg Estates subdivision, stating
> that 2400 homes were to be built within the next three years, beginning this
> July, and that a tentative site for a school of about 4 to 5 acres had been
> discussed. (6/13/50)

A variety of temporizing actions were taken and they illustrated the inter-
connected complications which must be considered by the Board and administration
as the District changed:

> An extensive discussion was held concerning the grade organization of the
> three schools. It was decided that an extra room be built at Marquette
> School and also to bring Marquette's eighth grade to the high school. It was
> further decided to prepare an extra room at Milford Elementary School,
> leaving the seventh grade at Milford Elementary. The problem of
> transporting the eighth graders from Marquette was brought up for
> discussion; it was decided to talk with the Suburban Bus Company to see if
> something could be worked out with them. (5/16/50)

One of the appeals of radio and television 'soap operas' is that they do capture
some of the realities of stability and change in the everyday lives of people. New
variations on old themes appear, and old variations on old themes remain. On
occasion the Board minutes in several successive items suggests the Board also
captures the realities of stability and change in the everyday lives of school people.
After the litany of approval of minutes, presentation of the treasurer's report,
reading of the bills, the next four items from 14 August were these:

> Mr. McBride mentioned that the first general faculty meeting would be
> held at 9:30 a.m. Monday, September 4th, suggesting that the Board be
> present if possible and also that invitations be sent to presidents of the
> various organizations affiliated with our schools.
>
> Mr. McBride mentioned some disciplinary problems to be taken up at
> the beginning of school, such as excessive smoking on school ground,
> loitering in automobiles in front of the school, etc.
>
> After an extensive discussion Mr. Gordon moved to pass the following
> resolution:
>> 'Actions and practices of very small minority in the past have
>> made it necessary for the Board of Education to pass a resolution
>> directing the administrators and faculty to take whatever steps
>> necessary to provide a wholesome, orderly process of education.
>> The Board fully recognizes the need for full co-operation of the
>> student body in providing this process.'
> The motion was seconded by Mr. Lewis and carried.
>
> A discussion was held concerning entrance of non-resident students
> living in another high school district. It seemed to be the consensus of

opinion that the Board follow the Midwest State School Laws, Section 10340, concerning admittance.

It was decided that the transportation contract between the Board of Education and the Suburban Bus Company be signed after the addition of the word 'average' in the phrase 'with a guarantee of a minimum of,' paying the bus company on a monthly basis. (8/14/50)

Two weeks later the board held its now 'regular monthly meeting of the Milford School Board for the discussion of Educational Program and Procedure.' Since a quorum was not present, the three members and Mr. McBride attended the meeting of the 'Lay Committee.' That Committee was active with other citizen's groups and was looking into policies, rules and regulations for Board and students. The Board also looked to them for suggestions about school site recommendations. The composition of the Lay Advisory Committee occurred by each director nominating five citizens. *Noblesse oblige* occurred and the thirty individuals were unanimously appointed. (6/13/51)

The education of Black students took a novel twist which raised problems that had been settled for several decades. In the Superintendent's Report the agenda item stated: 'Negro High School students. City has announced that they will not receive any students from County. Have had meeting and Mr. Cunningham is to confer with Mr. Ives.' (8/15/51) The Board minutes stated it this way:

A lengthy discussion was held concerning the admittance of Negro students to Metropolitan City Schools and further action was withheld pending an attempt to get Metropolitan City Board to accept students from the county. Other possible places for sending these students were to be investigated by Mr. McBride. (8/15/51)

Almost a year later (5/14/52) this problem was 'solved' according to a note in the Superintendent's Report: 'Aubuchan Woods will accept Negro pupils for high school next year; trying to work out transportation with two other neighboring schools. (Item #9)' (5/14/52) The Board minutes phrases it this way: 'The situation on colored students was discussed with the understanding that they would be accepted at Aubuchan Woods Schools and that transportation would have to be looked into.' (5/14/52)

The special problems of being a minority child with a handicap appear vividly:

Mr. McBride reported on a five year old deaf Negro child whose parents want to send him to Metropolitan City Turner school unit for the deaf. It was agreed to try to help them as much as possible through a welfare agency but that from an educational standpoint the Board could do nothing. (9/12/51)

On 12 March 1952: 'Upon a motion by Mr. Quigley and seconded by Mr. Lewis, it was unanimously agreed to allow Mrs. Porter $300.00 toward the tuition on her youngster at the Institute for the Deaf.'

Mr. McBride made continuing reports on building and public relations from several meetings he had been attending. Federal Aid continued to be sought: 'On a motion by Mr. Lewis and seconded by Mr. Gordon and a unanimous vote the Board formally ordered another application to be filed for Construction Aid under Public Law 815' (10/3/51)

The formal resolution was adopted on (10/22/51)

The 1951 calendar year ended with continuing discussions of several more school sites and visions of soaring expansion. One subdivision development described:

250 homes now	1951
250–300 more by end of year	1952
total of 800–900 by	1953

And for the first time a note was made to: '. . . pay our pro-rata share to the Co-operating Schools,' a county wide organization in audio-visual and other activities, and a group that was to expand considerably in later years. Bonds and tax issues moved along accordingly.

The expanding population continued to have a variety of effects beyond the immediate crowding of buildings and classrooms. It meant long discussions:

> After considerable discussions it was decided to investigate three possibilities for expanding our room for next Fall, namely: rentals, temporary arrangements in present cafeterias, or permanent structures that could have future use as multi-purpose rooms at both Milford Elementary and Marquette Schools. (3/12/52)

In the Spring of 1952, while the community voted for increases in levies for the incidental fund and the teachers' fund, the citizens voted *against* (470 to 556) transportation for pupils.

Pupil attendance and promotion policies of several sorts were formalized in the Spring of 1952: 'Further action on non-resident elementary students was tabled until the June meeting.' (5/14/52) This was after a vote in April that denied admission to a pupil from Morrison School District because of overcrowding:

> The situation on colored students was discussed with the understanding that they would be accepted at Aubuchan Woods Schools and that transportation would have to be looked into. (5/14/52)
>
> It was moved by Mr. Lewis and seconded by Mr. Quigley that the Board adopt the policy that children must be five years old by the first of January in order to enter Kindergarten and six years old by the first of January in order to enter the first grade, which carried with the Board's unanimous approval. (5/14/52)
>
> A letter from Dr. Davidson regarding equivalency certificates was brought to the Board's attention. After considerable discussion it was decided to grant diplomas on the basis of passing the USAFI test to those (who) have had one year's satisfactory record at Milford High School and on the basis of passing the GED tests to those who have had two and a half years satisfactory record at Milford High School. (5/28/52)

The promotion policy was discussed at length. It was moved by Mr. Lewis, seconded by Mr. Quigley and unanimously agreed that Mr. McBride ask the classroom teachers organization whether it is their opinion that a percentage of students feel that work is unnecessary for promotion. (5/28/52)

The 1951–52 year closed in June with several items which suggest that transition periods are in the eyes of the beholder more than the reality of the world of schools and school boards:

1   A survey of special education needs within and between neighboring districts received attention.
2   The High School principal Mr. Green resigned and was replaced in two weeks by Mr. Clark.
3   New regulations on Federal Aid were read by Mr. McBride. (6/25/52)

The major point, though, is that Milford is in transition. Marquette has been annexed. New central office positions have been created. A strong Board member, Mr. Lewis, has appeared; he is traveling to professional meetings, reading educational documents, and crowding the Board and the Superintendent. Finally, population increases in the form of post war suburban subdivisions are looming as a tidal wave on the horizon.

Demography Fueling Innovations

In our attempt to achieve some coherence in our chronicle, concepts and hypotheses tend to creep into our account of the development of the Milford School District. Our section title, 'Demography fuels innovations,' is one of these. The rapidly increasing population of the Milford community pushed the district, through Board actions initially and primarily, to undertake all kinds of 'new' activities. As we have indicated, the 1949 to 1952 period seemed to be one of those times when enough other elements were also involved to speak of 'transition' in this period and to speak ultimately of the 'transformation' or the 'modernization' of the Milford School District. But it is the change in the demographic variables which we see as so important to the 'driving' of innovation and to the rippling of its effects to which we turn in this short section.

It seems appropriate to picture the decade of rapid growth with a minute from the Board's record indicating the kinds of problems and their attendant resolutions which occur in times of rapid population expansion:

After two informal get-togethers involving the two whole evenings of June 16th and June 30th with members of the Milford Baptist Church committee, it was decided to enter into lease agreement with said Baptist Church and the following resolution was passed:

Resolved: That the Milford Board of Education in the name of the School District of Milford enter into lease agreement with the

> The Milford Baptist Church, A Corporation, for the purpose of
> using a portion of a brick building, known as the Milford Baptist
> Church Educational Buildings, for school rooms. (7/16/52)

Concomitant with the 'innovative' special arrangements for temporary housing
were plans for the new schools which were being built. These plans ran into delays
because of general regulations. A special meeting of the Board was called for 23 July
and a resolution was passed:

> The need for meeting special federal requirements before proceeding with
> our opening of bids was brought to the Board's attention by Mr. McBride.
> It was agreed to recall bids and postpone the bid opening date upon advice
> of a letter of July 16, 1952 from the Federal Security Agency on Project No.
> 1085, concerning Federal Fund Reserve for final approval of said project
> and from telephone conversation with Mr. Frank Olden, District Engineer
> of Community Facilities Service and Housing Home Finance Agency. It
> was moved by Mr. Metcalfe that all previous plans and commitments be
> held in abeyance so that we may fully comply with federal regulations.
> Motion was seconded by Mr. Lewis and unanimously adopted. (7/23/52)

A notice went to the architect, to the newspapers and to the bidders. Further contact
with the federal authorities for specifications also occurred and word was sent also to
the State Department of Education.

Old issues do not disappear just because new ones are arising to crowd already
busy agendas. Discussions were held on transporting Black High School students to a
neighboring county district and discussions continued on 'a visiting teacher for shut-
in children.' Tuition help, $300.00, was paid for a disabled child to attend a special
school in Metropolitan City. The usual kinds of items arose for cafeteria, building
maintenance (termite control!), building insurance, replacing teachers who resigned,
resolving janitorial problems. Technological changes interacted with county population increases and with other sources of educational innovation. Consideration was
given to county wide instructional TV which was coming on the scene. Additional
rooms for kindergarten children were rented from another church, near the Milford
Elementary School. Last month's innovation is now this month's accepted practice.
Arrangements continued on additional property for schools in areas where builders
were developing large tracts for new houses.

If a further generalization is needed at this point we are once again reminded of
the huge number of 'logistical decisions,' many of which are part and parcel of
innovation, which pass in review by the school board. These are preceded and
followed by countless telephone calls, discussions, and meetings. The volume of this
kind of interaction seems both to require certain kinds of personality structure in
central office staff, and in Board members and, in turn, takes its toll on those same
individuals.

In addition, an important mode of thinking, about which we commented
earlier, reappeared in two instances. The Superintendent reported on teacher pupil
ratios of districts comparable in size and economic level to the Milford community.

Similarly: 'A salary schedule for Suburban County was brought to our attention and same indicated that we are in a fairly good position.' (10/29/52) The first item seemed to precipitate the hiring of a variety of additional teachers, both full and part time as the Milford average of 25 pupils to one teacher was higher than most of the districts surveyed. A similar survey on birthday cut-off dates for kindergarten children was conducted in January. This comparative mode of thinking, 'How are we doing vis-a-vis our neighbors?', seems important politically and normatively (ethically). It contrasts with more idealized conceptions of what 'ought-to-be' and more scientific or technical conceptions of 'research data show . . .' As a conceptual problem we will take that up at several points in our theoretical analyses for it underlies a major issue in innovation. The Milford records indicate an awareness of the issues, although no great significance is attached to it in the minutes.

Finally, we might end this introduction to the new decade with a note on some of the descriptive factual data included later in our analysis of 'the strong board member.' Mr. Lewis' attack on Mr. McBride came in February of the 1952–53 school year. One period flows easily, and sometimes not so easily, into another. Time segments are artifactual and often more in the eyes of the observer than in the eyes of the day to day participants. At the next meeting, 17 March 1953, the Board voted to attach Mr. Lewis' comments to the minutes. Other large and small items continued to appear: a change order for 'sand painting the walls of the new Grant School' was issued. And: 'It was agreed that we lay plans to build a new high school unit rather than to add to the present unit.' (3/17/53) One sentence for a large major decision.

We do not know if there is any broad national consensus on the strategy and tactics of the Board and Superintendent regarding the buying and selling of property for schools sites, nor if such actions qualify as an innovation or a consequence of innovation. But if the Milford experience is at all typical it seems to come down to that great American custom once known as horse trading. Foresight and insight, bargaining and negotiating skills, and more than a bit of entrepreneurial zest for the game seem to be the ingredients. Earlier, we recounted bits and pieces of the drawn out discussions in which the Board finally got the Quaker Company to trade property but also contribute eighteen thousand dollars toward the building of a new two room frame building with basement for the Attucks School. The company needed the land for expansion; presumably it had considerable value to them. Even earlier we have seen the give and take regarding lots next to the present schools and acreage for the Milford elementary School in 1930. The arrival of the post World War II big subdivision developers shifted both the stakes and the nature of the game. The Board's gambit is reflected in the minutes:

> In a letter from the Suburban County Planning Commission it was brought to the attention of the Board that a meeting was to be held on Tuesday, April 21 at 8:00 p.m., on a petition by Waller-Evans, to change the zoning from 7500 square feet to 6000 square feet, on a 165 acre tract on Richmond Road near Downing Drive.

If our arithmetic is even approximately correct that's a twenty per cent decrease in size of the lots and opens the potential for a twenty per cent increase in the number of homes at a cost of less than three per cent of the total parcel of land. The Board seems to have appreciated the significance of this for the next entry in the minutes stated: 'It was agreed by the Board to have Mr. Udall contact Waller-Evans and tell them that the Board will not oppose this change in zoning, if they make provision for a suitable five acre site for a school building at no cost.' (4/9/53) The Company seemed to enter the spirit of the discussions for a week later at the regular monthly business meeting of the Board it was noted among discussions of several pieces of property for separate new schools:

> Upon a motion by Mr. Metcalfe and seconded by Mr. Youngman, offer number one from the Waller-Evans Realty Company as to site in the Richmond Road and Downing Drive vicinity should be accepted, which would be a 500 foot frontage site to be graded level, built up so that there would be no overflow at cost not to exceed $12,000.00 to the school district. (4/15/53)

This seemed in keeping with amounts being quoted for other sites. A month later the developer countered with an offer to sell the Board five acres of 'developed land' for $27,000. The Board called this 'unreasonable.' The developers returned for a brief private conference and offered $15,000 as a figure. The Board accepted.

But modernization doesn't happen all of a piece. Changes are occurring elsewhere, as we raise in detail in the next chapter. Strong Board members don't disappear early, nor is conflict ever settled once and for all. At the 9 April meeting two new Board members were elected and sworn in. It was a close election with both incumbents losing:

Trotter	1123
Gordon	1047
Youngman	1248
Dawson	1236

The minutes contain these items as well: 'Mr. McBride, as Superintendent, made the statement that if there was anything that the Board particularly wished him to do, he would be glad to cooperate.' For a reader of years and years of minutes, that is an unusual item to be recorded. Something beyond demographic changes seems to be underway. The next two items seemed to bear on several key issues which continued to provide an undercurrent to the deliberations:

> Mr. Lewis recommended a special meeting to be held on the functions of the school board and the Superintendent to have a more democratic procedure in the relationship of the two, as brought out in 'School Boards in Action.'
> It was agreed that three copies of the following school publications should be purchased to exchange among the Board members: *The School Board Journal, The School Executive* (4/9/53)

Superintendent McBride has held the office for almost two decades. It seems a strange time to be talking of 'democratic procedure in the relationship?' A touch of 'country' still seemed to remain: 'Upon a motion by Mr. Randle and seconded by Mrs. Carrington, it was unanimously agreed to pay the bill for material for pants for band uniforms made by the Home Economics Department.' (4/15/53) Curriculum and instruction initiatives for innovation appeared from within the system: 'Mr. McBride said that Mr. Unger was anxious that one of our elementary schools should become a pilot school for a new course of study coming out for elementary schools. This was mutually agreed upon.' (4/15/53) Technology also continued to win out: 'It was agreed that bids should be obtained for a power lawn mower.' (4/15/53) Accord between the Board and the student body seemed to continue:

> ... it was unanimously agreed to accept the rules set up for the Junior-Senior Prom ... and to compliment the students on their rules and hope that they would make this a congenial affair and encourage all guests to remain until the end of the evening. (4/15/53)

School boundaries are always items for debate and contention. New schools re-open these discussions. Milford's new elementary school, the Grant, is located in the middle of the district, between Marquette and Milford Elementary. The Board handled it this way:

> The next order of business was to determine the boundaries of the Grant School.
> Mr. Unger, Mr. Ulrich, Miss Idler were all present and presented 15 possibilities for the consideration of the Board.
> After much consideration, Plan #2E was adopted upon a motion of Mr. Randle and seconded by Mr. Dawson.
> Boundaries in Plan #2E consist of Richmond Road on West, Doleman on South, Carleton Boulevard to cemetery East, cemetery North along railroad. (5/13/53)

The Board moved forward with the bond issue for building new schools:

> Proposition
> To authorize the Board of Education of the School District of Milford, Suburban County, Midwest State to incur an indebtedness of said District in the amount of Eight Hundred Thousand Dollars ($800,000) for the purpose of purchasing school house sites, erecting school houses and furnishing the same, and building additions to or repairing old buildings, in said District, and to evidence such indebtedness by the issuance of bonds of said District in said amount for said purpose. (6/24/53)

Transition and change, the modernization of Milford, fueled heavily by population increases, is well under way.

The Remaining Years of McBride's Tenure

In an attempt to maintain the development of the narrative of Milford and to keep some of our interpretive and analytical themes close to the time, place, and circumstances of their occurrence we have looked for common sense, if not logical, breaking points to divide our discussion. Nineteen fifty-five seems one of those points. Mr. McBride has survived the threat to his superintendency, the 'potent outside report' has become an historical document, the strong Board president lost his bid for re-election, the boundary problems between and among the new elementary schools have revealed the localist roots of neighborhood schools, the Attucks Elementary School is being closed, and the new high school has been conceptualized, designed, and readied for construction. These issues, only mentioned in passing here, are the core of the next chapter, 'modernization as innovation'.

In the early Autumn of 1955, reports from NEA platform and resolutions were included in the bound Board minutes. Political educational action at the national level was under way as well. The Board, with reports from the Superintendent, was cognizant of those positions. The Board approved the structuring of the seventh and eighth grades as a junior high school and the housing of the youngsters in the new high school, to be opened the following year. Temporary buildings were readied at several of the new elementary schools: 'Mr. McBride reported that the temporary buildings at Edinburg Elementary School are ready for occupancy as soon as the gas is turned on and that six of the eight rooms would be used right away.' (10/11/55) Bus transportation was being discussed with the State Department of Education. And other discussions were under way 'with regard to unionized custodial employees' (10/11/55). Teacher recruitment trips were made to the State Colleges in the rural parts of Midwest State. In the already existing older schools, the Board continued to make and actualize plans to build 'multi-purpose rooms' for the use of teachers and pupils. These discussions were unanimous. They equalized the facilities across the elementary schools. They also suggest a part of the district history that later administrators, Spanman, Cohen, and Shelby were to be in conflict with in their analysis and label of 'multi useless' rooms as they planned and later defended the design of the Kensington School. Copies of a 'revised official salary schedule for teachers' (11/29/55) was developed but no action was taken. Again we seem to be foreshadowing issues of Superintendent Spanman's tenure for in less than a decade he was to break the salary schedule to bring in staff he wanted for Kensington and for district curriculum development efforts. Motions also were passed to continue to solicit Federal Building Funds, this time approximately $350,000. A bond issue of $1,830,000 was passed.

When the district pupil population is growing and buildings are being built at the rate of one per year, and the same events are happening in most other districts, it doesn't take much figuring to see a teacher shortage in the making. In December 1955, the County Superintendent of Schools wrote a mimeographed letter to the President of Milford's Board of Education and presumably to all the Districts in Suburban County indicating the magnitude of the problem. The supply of new teachers from the colleges and universities was not going to be sufficient in Midwest State, nor in neighboring states. Recruitment tactics and pressures, both from out of the state and within the state, were described. Alternative sources of teachers and financial inducements were part of his concern.

Innovative programs continued to be created and implemented in several ways.

The County Health Department began a 'parent education program in mental health' which was available for two schools in the district. A proposal for a 'supervised summer activity program' for the district was submitted, and passed, after discussion later in February.

Accidents and acts of God still happened. A fire destroyed most of the Marquette School in February. That same afternoon at 3:00 p.m. the Board met in special session, made plans, and voted to implement several decisions. Round the clock security was provided by the custodial staff and county police. Several churches offered the use of their facilities. One of these was accepted. Some classes went on double shift for which approval was sought from the State Department of Education. Insurance, inspections, and reconstruction moved forward. The cause of the fire was to be investigated by 'whatever County Department that handles such investigations.'

Inserted in the February minutes was a detailed set of materials (ten plus pages) describing a neighboring district's competition for an architect to design a new junior high school. One's neighbors seem always present for a variety of comparative purposes.

In March 1956, discussions began with a builder over a school site in the Wooded Valley area, for he was planning on building some 350 homes in the area. Kensington School, for the first time, was in the offing, although a half dozen years away.

In April, the last two of the 'anti-McBride' faction did not stand for re-election. Mr. Rainey and Mr. Eads joined the Board with large majorities. Immediately following their installation and the voting for officers, Mr. Quigley remained President of the Board, Mr. McBride presented a new 'Administrative Organization.' Dr. Stechman remained but as 'School Business Official.' A 'Director of Services and Information' was created. Two 'Administrative Assistants,' one for elementary and one for secondary were listed, as was a principal and assistant principal of the high school and a junior high school principal. Each elementary school continued to have a principal. Most were offered two year contracts. A formal organization chart spelling out these arrangements also appeared. Mrs. Iller, a former principal remained on the staff in an unspecified position. Later she returned to an elementary classroom. It would be twenty-five years before another woman would be appointed principal in Milford.

Curriculum issues floated by the Board in May. The Board voted not to be involved in the Metropolitan Educational Television Programs. A welfare program was raised and Mr. McBride was to represent the district in the discussions. In response to a P.T.A. request: 'A discussion as to special education for above average students was held at some great length.' (5/15/56) Plans for a summer school program at a fee of $24.00 were proceeding. Special education students were identified. A class for mentally retarded and employment of a speech correctionist were recommended and passed, as were supervisors for art and physical education.

The Summer of 1956 was spent on the usual kinds of problems: buying buses, black topping playgrounds, hiring last minute teachers, working with realtors and property owners on possible schools sites, reviewing bids on equipment and materials, attending to insurance, and seeking legal opinions on a variety of items. When school opened, 1000 youngsters were being bussed. By the end of September parents were to be told: 'Since there is no State Aid furnished for the transportation of kindergarten students all those students wishing to ride the bus must pay the required set fee.' (9/25/56) And the renaming of schools also occurred that Autumn. The two oldest educational figures, Mr. McBride and Mr. Unger, the superintendents of Milford and Marquette prior to the merger, were honored by having schools named for them. Prairie School, named for the beauty of its geography, later was altered to Williams, upon the request of the School P.T.A. and Mother's Club. Later the Mothers' Club requested: '... consideration of a name sign for the Williams School.' (3/12/57) This led to the general issue of signs for all elementary schools, appointment of a committee, and later approval. Local democracy (of the people, by the people, for the people) had its way again in Milford.

Formalization of programs continued. Under the title of 'Those extra educational services other than regular curriculum' appeared accounts of the testing program — achievement (California), general and special abilities (DAT), interests (Kuder and Strong) and the array of clubs (twenty-five) athletics (six boys, four girls), music, dance, publications, etc. Modernization was continuing. One could almost see the shadow of Mr. Lewis, the former President of the Board. Administrative salary schedules were developed as ratios of teachers salaries: 1.4 for elementary, 1.45 for junior high and 1.5 for senior high. Teacher retirement programs defined at the state level moved from four per cent contributions by teachers and by the district to six per cent by each. A new position, for example, Director of Music, was created; another, Director of Guidance, was lengthened from ten to eleven months, and also: '... an additional secretary be employed for the central office to work on federal records.' (2/11/57)

Architects' conferences, changes in plans and special conditions (sewers, structural steel, roads, etc.) appeared with great frequency as new buildings were planned and built and as old buildings were renovated. For the first time, the minutes included comparative cost figures — by rooms and by square footage:

School	Per Room	Per Sq. Ft.
Unger	$28,700	$15.80
McBride	28,500	12.05
Field	22,400	11.00–$12.00
Williams	21,500	' — '
Edinburg	20,500	' — '
Grant	17,600	9.04

Cost cutting items were raised. All bids on the new Unger School were rejected by unanimous vote: '... due to the high cost and sufficient funds not being available.' (11/27/56) 'Specs' were to be reviewed, government regulations considered, and new advertising for bids. A form of data and argument was crystallizing and would appear with great force in later years as debates arose on the Kensington School. A January bond issue for $890,000 passed 1345 to 157.

Tucked away in the minutes in January was an enigmatic item: 'A discussion was held on the consolidating all the County School Districts.' (1/16/57) In February, another minute referred to the letter from the County government regarding consolidation: 'The matter was tabled by the Board until more information is available.' (2/11/57) Much later, December 1957: 'Mr. McBride read a letter to Mr. Quigley from the Secretary of the County Board of Education stating that they had agreed not to submit a plan for further school district reorganization at this time.' (12/10/57)

Annual school Board Electisons found the incumbents unchallenged and Mr. Tebeau was re-elected. An anomaly occurred. Mr. Quigley and Mr. Edmond each received three votes for President. Mr. Edmond withdrew and Mr. Quigley was elected unanimously by acclamation.

Early in our account of the district's history we commented upon the gradual accretion of equipment and supplies — baseballs and bats, a piano, and movie projector. Obviously through the years new items were added. Occasionally items in the minutes provided striking comparisons and contrasts. In the summer of 1957 in anticipation of the opening of the new high school this item appeared: '. . . the Administration be authorized to purchase Wood Shop, Metal Shop, Mechanical Drawing and Mechanical Crafts Equipment for the total amount of $33,368.49.' (7/9/57) The motion carried unanimously.

Also, like an old friend, the 'National School Lunch Program' reappeared, the papers were signed, upon a unanimous vote of the Board. Also like an old friend, special education issues returned in the form of a multi district regional unit for handicapped children. Petitions were required. While these discussions and activities were underway, the local resolutions continued on their idiosyncratic way:

> Mr. McBride asked the Board's opinion on keeping a handicapped child in the Marquette School.
> The Board agreed with the Superintendent's decision to let the child stay in school as long as he could get around in a normal classroom and handle himself without too much inconvenience to the teacher. (11/26/57)

The Exceptional Children District program in Suburban County was established in the Spring of 1958. The Board signed the appropriate contracts. A new era began.

Occasionally, an item of curriculum and instruction appeared, as with a demonstration of a second grade reading in the Autumn of 1957. It was noteworthy because of the contrast in the overwhelming presence of items for buildings, additions to old and new buildings, and equipment. Architects, contractors, and insurance agents seemed to have established permanent residence in the Board's meeting room. But still the Board attempted to keep one eye, or better, a glance from one eye, on issues of curriculum and instruction.

The recurring issues surrounding custodians, the nature of their work and working conditions, reached a new plateau when the Board went on record for a forty hour week: '. . . but not between Monday and Friday . . .' (7/14/58) with insurance, salary schedule and increases also formalized. The School Board attained a degree of formalization and cosmopolitanism as well. The National School Board Convention was to be held in San Francisco in January, 'three tentative reservations' were made. The National School Administrators Meeting would be in February; 'three tentative reservations' were made for this meeting.

Dropped into the October 1958 minutes was a long detailed document of twenty-three, single spaced, typed pages entitled 'Board of Education policies, School District of Milford.' The struggles, over clarification of policies, begun a decade before by Mr. Lewis, the former President of the Board, had now borne fruit. Among the numerous items, several seem worthy of mention or quotation. The initial paragraphs contain these elements of a preamble:

> The Milford School District is governed by state law. In the absence of such laws of control the Board has power to make needed policies for control and operation of the school. . . .
>
> The Board shall have the power to make all necessary rules and regulations for the organization grading and government in their school district. . . .

An outline of the major headings appears in Figure 13 and indicated the scope of the document. No discussion of the document, beyond the expenses in having it printed were contained in the minutes.

Another of our reappearing themes, school district merger and consolidation appeared in a brief minute in January 1959: 'A motion was made by Mr. Tebeau and seconded by Mr. Eads that we go on record as opposing any plan of merging the city and the county school districts so there would be one school district. The motion carried unanimously.' (1/13/59) The long history of localism continued.

In February the Board raised Mr. McBride's salary (to $18,961), gave him a new three year contract, and passed unanimously 'a resolution commending Mr. McBride for a job well done' (2/25/59). Later in the Spring the CTA's slightly revised salary schedule for teachers was passed by the Board. All teachers would go on the schedule. The statement was mimeographed in form available for distribution.

Increased enrollments hit the junior high school level and the first of the split shifts were planned for 1959–60. Beyond the horrendous scheduling problems with eighth grade classes running from 7 a.m. until 11:45 and seventh grade classes from 11:55 to 4:40 p.m., special problems were anticipated around: 1) Public relations; 2) Transportation; 3) Field trips; 4) Intramural programs; 5) Building cleaning and maintenance; 6) Cafeteria. Plans for resumbitting the failed bond issue were readied.

Figure 13: Formalization of District Policy

I	Operating Procedures and Policy Relating to the Board of Education	$6\frac{1}{2}$ pp.
II	Policies Relating to the Administrative Staff	$7\frac{1}{2}$ pp.
III	Policies Relating to the Instructional Staff	3 pp.
IV	Policies Relating to Non-Instructional Staff	3 pp.
V	Policies Relating to Use of Buildings and Properties	$\frac{1}{2}$ p.
VI	Policies Relating to Students	1 p.
VII	Miscellaneous Provisions	3 pp.

Among the comments raised were that the split shift junior high youngsters were also among those who had been in 'Churches and Basements' in their primary grades. A long report on projected enrollments suggested that during the 1960–64 years a need for forty-one elementary classes (1–6), forty-three in junior high (7–9), and seven in senior high (10–12). Total district enrollment figures (K-12) were estimated to increase between 1960 and 1969 from 7558 to 10,289.

An anomaly in the general negativism toward consolidation occurred in October 1959. The Board indicated a favorable reaction of Milford with Kennard District and Appleby Estates. No details were presented. The Kennard District was one of long association — for example the high school youngsters rented the basketball court there in the 1920s and the second superintendent of Milford, Mr. Grey, had taught there. Nothing was to come of the initiative.

Much earlier we had commented that old school buildings neither die nor fade away. During the 1959–60 year, the Attucks School building was under discussion as a facility for handicapped youngsters. The Marquette School was considered as a renovation candidate for a second junior high school. The anticipated split shifts of double sessions had been held off until Autumn of 1960.

During the late 1950s, the minutes read along easily and rapidly. Two impressions appear. First, the building-of-buildings activity, item by item, keeps moving along. It represents huge expenditures of energy. Second, no conflict appears. Everyone, including the patrons in their votes for bond issues and tax levies, seems to agree that housing the youngsters and supplying them with desks, books, playgrounds is essential and of the highest priority. In the midst of this Mr. McBride is clearly initiating activities, responding to Board inquiries and making acceptable recommendations. His immediate staff, Macon in secondary, Unger in elementary and Fairfax in business seems competent and in full cooperation. The principalship incumbents are stable and mostly have been in the district for a number of years. No minutes occur indicating community displeasure with any of these men.

Beginning the Denouement of McBride

In February 1960 three visitors to the Board meeting were identified by name, Mrs. Wilkerson, Mrs. Stork, and Mr. Tompkins. Mr. Tompkins and a Mr. Hackworth filed for the Board elections later in the Spring. The Bond issue passed four to one. In March principal contracts with two year extensions and salary increases were recommended and passed unanimously. Mr. McBride's contract was redrawn with a three year extension and salary increase. Mr. Tebeau, a board member of six years who was not running for re-election, was commended for his services. Mr. Quigley and Mr. Tompkins were elected. Mr. Quigley became president by unanimous vote. Then, in what looked like adroit moves regarding the Vice Presidency of the Board, two nominations (Crocker and Eads) was made, a unanimous vote to close the nominations occurred, and then one candidate withdrew and a split three to three vote for and against the candidate (Crocker) resulted:

Crocker	Yes	Edmond	No
Eads	Yes	Trotter	No
Tompkins	Yes	Quigley	No

A similar split occurred over the Secretary position. Finally a compromise of sorts was worked out. Eads became Vice President and Tompkins became secretary. From even a casual reading of minutes, a not too distal inference might be that 'something's afoot.'

In executive session during the same evening a motion was made that the column on principal's salary for 1960–61 should read as stated in the 1961–1962 column. This involved a 'double bump,' for example the 9600, 9900, 10,100 would read 9600 to 10,100 to 10,400 in the case of the high school principal. The motion passed but two members, Eads and Tompkins abstained. Later in the meeting, Mr. Crocker submitted his resignation from the Board. The next minute was enigmatic: 'Mr. Crocker made a statement that, while he was resigning, there would be no interference in regard to it and that he would be glad to help in any future Board issues or like matters.' (4/8/60) The final item of the evening: 'A special meeting is to be held April 19, 1960 to explain to Mr. Tompkins, the new Board member, the need for split sessions at the junior high.' (4/8/60) A charitable gesture to a new Board member? Or political manoeuvring?

The special meeting on 19 April drew 'a number of visitors,' involved presentations by the local chief of police, a parent (Tillman), and the Assistant Superintendent, Dr. Macon on 'the double sessions.' After the presentations and discussions the Board worked its will in this fashion:

A motion was made by Mr. Tompkins to direct the administrators to again study the idea of double sessions, with the purpose of eliminating them and pursue the use of our present facilities. The motion failed, due to a lack of a second.

Mr. Trotter offered a substitute motion to proceed with our basic plan and take into consideration the following objections:

1 Social impact (disruption of home life, working mothers)
2 Leisure time of child (delinquency problem)
3 Additional crossing watchmen
4 Additional police
5 Traffic hazards.

The motion was seconded by Mr. Edmond and carried unanimously. (4/19/60)

At the regular 17 May meeting, the Board controversy erupted again, and strangely:

Messrs. Quigley, Trotter, Edmond and Superintendent McBride. Mr. Eads and Tompkins were present in the lobby but declined to take their seats in the meeting. The business of the meeting was delayed while Mr. Tompkins called Mr. Trotter, the secretary to the Board, into the lobby. Upon his return to the room Mr. Trotter reported Mr. Tompkins had attempted to bargain with him on what matters should be taken up in the Board meeting before Mr. Tompkins would participate in the meeting. Mr. Trotter stated he did not agree to the suggested bargaining, because he felt it was improper procedure. Mr. Edmond said that Mr. Eads had made a similar proposal to him and that he likewise refused to agree. At approximately 8:45 p.m., Mr. Tompkins and Mr. Eads left the building without being in the Board room. (5/17/60)

The meeting continued until 12:15 a.m. The minutes were not signed by Tompkins and Eads.

In late May Mr. Wilkerson, Mr. Edmond's nominee in a group of three nominees, was elected to the Board. Mr. Tompkins' and Mr. Eads' nominees were defeated three to one.

Meanwhile, in an aura of strangeness to the reader, the Board was submitting and passing bond issues, planning the new junior high school, building the next section of the high school, and carrying on the multitude of small item decision making. Multiple strands of district activity, building activity, and perhaps most of all classroom teaching and learning, seem to go on in spite of the heavy strand of politics over governance. The implication of this for the theoretical analysis of schools as organizations seems very important. Even amidst large scale conflict and political manoeuvring, the work of the Board and the administration continues.

The 1960–61 year began in the summer and once again involved the usual broad array of issues: bids for work on the new junior high school, discussions and correspondence with the County Water Department on connections for water at the junior high school, notification that the district had received a triple A rating for its K-6-2-4 program and approval of sixty-two and a quarter units of credits, and information from another district on their 'financial studies' to help the board decide 'what can the district afford to pay for schools' and on and on and on. The Board minutes continue to reflect the wide array of items which entered its purview.

Another of our continuing generalizations had been the breadth of the range of items reflecting the human condition that passes through the filter of a school board and its decision making processes:

> A discussion was held concerning Board policies for married students, etc. . . . it was the opinion of the attorney that a Board of Eduction has the right to establish its own policies.
>
> Mr. Eads made a motion that the Board not admit married or divorced students, etc., and the administrators write policies implementing this decision . . . carried unanimously. (8/30/60)

The point we are reaching for here is that the Board has a much larger social role than that of educational guardian or policy maker for the three Rs. The administrators, almost irrevocably, share in this larger role. Implications, often latent and unnoticed, seem to ripple in multiple directions — for professional training, for schooling in a democratic society, for the reproduction of society.

On occasion, simple arrays of figures suggest the magnitude of problems on their way. The report enrollment in September 1960 raises the continuing crisis in population growth. Figure 14 presents the data. The kindergarten contains a number of children who will enter parochial schools as well as public schools. But the first few grades are averaging over 600 pupils while the last two years of high school about 350. The tidal wave will continue to inundate the district.

In February 1961, the membership of the School Board shifted again. Mr. Wilkerson and Mr. Edmond, both incumbents, indicated they would be candidates for re-election. Mr. Trotter resigned. From six names to fill the unexpired term, two were nominated. On a four to one vote Mr. Oakes won over Mr. Osborn. The vacancy would be filled for a two year term in April.

In April, the two regular incumbents of the Board lost in a strongly contested election:

Edmond	2197	
Wilkerson	2022	
Osborn	2827	
Henderson	2642	
Oakes	4344	(4/7/61)

Mr. Tompkins on a four to one vote, with only the past president, Mr. Quigley, voting no, became president of the Board. The Board had been transformed.

Also, significantly, one of the long term administrators, Dr. Macon, formerly the high school principal and more recently the Assistant Superintendent for secondary, resigned for reasons of health.[8] Interestingly, the Board split its votes, four to two, to accept the resignation. The 'new majority' were among the 'four.' Mr. Neal Unger was 'elevated' to Assistant Superintendent.

Figure 14: School Enrollment, 1960

Grades	Number of Pupils
K	1055
1	713
2	632
3	524
4	581
5	500
6	494
7	502
8	507
Total K-8	5508
9	505
10	404
11	357
12	340
Total 9–12	1606
Grand Total K-12	7114
	(9/12/60)

Four days later, the real meaning of 'elevation' appeared. In executive session, at 10:20 p.m.:

> Mr. Tompkins asked Mr. Irby, school attorney, to read opinions as to assignment of administrative duties, etc.
>
> Mr. Osborn moved that Mr. Neal Unger, in his duties as Assistant Superintendent, is to have the primary responsibilities of the direct supervision of instruction and curriculum in the primary and secondary levels and of all certificated personnel and will report directly to the Board of Education as they require. Mr. Unger is to assume his respective duties immediately rather than July 1, 1961, the date shown on his contract. Mr. F. M. McBride is to be Superintendent in charge of administration and all non certificated personnel. The business official will continue to report to Mr. McBride. It is the desire of the Board that there be mutual respect and harmony in the administration of the school system. Mr. Eads seconded the motion. The motion carried unanimously ... (4/11/61)

Mr. McBride had run up against another 'strong school board president' and was in another fight for his professional life.

In a series of motions, immediately afterward, the Board moved for a study of the organizational structure of the district, for reports by all the central administrators on policy, procedures, and positions, and for one year contracts for all principals and supervisors. The winds of change were blowing hard.

Summary and Conclusions

We have phrased Superintendent McBride's career in the Milford District into three periods: early, transition, and late. The early period was relatively stable and allowed us to focus on what we initially thought might be 'normal' processes of district functioning. Now we are much less sure of words like 'normal' or 'usual.' Shortly we will make terms such as these problematic and look into their meaning.

The transition period made us more conscious and articulate about several ideas. First, it broke the implicit generalization we had worked under since first becoming acquainted with the Milford School District and its then Superintendent, Steven Spanman, that the individual most responsible for innovation was the Superintendent. In very dramatic form we saw that that role or function can be played by other individuals in other positions. Mr. Lewis was such an individual on the school board.

Second, the potency of population changes for innovation now is very much in our minds.

The very nature of those generalizations set up an 'obvious' third generalization: educators interested in school improvement must look to mulitple sources of innovations. We began to think in terms of open systems with multiple sources of action and 'origins of interaction.' Long shadows appear from early anthropologists, Elliott Chapple and Conrad Arensberg (1940).

The fact that there was so much conflict between Mr. Lewis and Mr. McBride and later Mr. Tompkins and Mr. McBride suggested a fourth generalization, that different individuals have different ideas about what is good and desirable for the district. That is, one individual's conception of an innovation, a specific planned change for the better, may not be universally seen as good. Individuals who 'resist change,' to use a recent if not current concept in the innovation and change literature, are not necessarily 'bad' or 'negative' as the resistant to change label implies or connotes. In our view questioning this concept changes the very construal of innovation theory. Innovation moves from being 'natural' or a 'technical' concept to an 'evaluative' and 'political' concept. That, we feel, is a major difference in the construal of innovation.

The biggest innovation in the Milford Schools in these years was the consolidation of the District with the Marquette District. Why this succeeded in 1949 in Milford, not to mention consolidation's even greater impact in other parts of Suburban County, when attempts had failed at the turn of the century and in the early 1930s has important implications for a perspective on educational innovation. Political movements in the larger community have major consequences on local districts.

Finally, the post World War II suburban population growth, which was occurring all over the country, if not the world, set the stage for a decade of building new school buildings. The mix of Mr McBride's advancing age and the increasing size and complexity of the Milford District, and the rise of a community reform movement ushered in Dr. Steven Spanman, the 'tangle of administrative succession,' and the building of the innovative Kensington Elementary School, the original focus of our interest and inquiry into educational innovation. As we indicated in the first chapter, this succession brought a number of additional innovative 'firsts' to the District.

It takes only a sentence to refer the reader back to the first chapter and the initial story of our saga, the tangle of administrative succession. The winds of change did blow hard upon McBride. He was ousted in his late sixties in a series of bruising political battles within the community, the board, and the professional staff. While that larger and perhaps more dramatic political theme wanders all through our account, and is one of our major findings regarding innovation, a number of the 'smaller' aspects must be looked at more finely now. We do this as we talk about 'modernization as innovation' and look again, more analytically, at the long tenure of Superintendent McBride, and what his story tells us about innovation and change in schooling.

Notes

1   The grant proposal went to the Federal Emergency Administration of Public Works.
2   The Clear Valley School was on Donaldson's Road near Meramec Road.
3   On 3 November 1937, discussion occurred regarding renting a concrete mixer 'for the WPA project on the grounds.' Some success apparently occurred.

4   On 3 November 1937, a Bell and Howell 'picture projector' was purchased.
5   On 4 March 1940 he became medical director of the district at a salary of $300/year.
6   In 1941, the Congress passed the Lanham Act which gave aid to communities facing hardships due to expanding war factories and military bases.
7   Other items from these early years will appear in the next chapter in more thematic discussion.
8   In an interview, a former teacher indicated there were additional personal reasons for his departure.

Chapter 6

Modernization as Innovation

Introduction

We have told Mr. McBride's story in brief form. The theme of that story might well have been labeled 'modernization.' Milford went several long steps from its small town, almost rural status, to a large suburban district. Exemplifying this best, in the last ten years, the district built nearly a school a year. Mostly we tried to convey these changes with a minimum amount of emotion, considerable detail, and with occasional humour and irony as the stories contained those elements. Along the way we alluded to several 'key' items which, in terms of our macro rhetoric of innovation, require additional discussion. Our thesis, modernization as innovation, requires that we retrace some of our steps.

As we explore these issues in what was a quite long era in the district, we believe that the 'anatomy of educational innovation' will take on a quite different image than many of the more specific time bound analyses of innovation or innovative programs provide. Historical analysis offers subtle contextual concatenations of ideas that are precluded in other accounts. Part of the benefit in this analysis is that McBride's tenure encompassed what we have called 'a long stable period' as well as a long 'expansionist period' in the life of the district. As our story indicated, and as the interpretation will enhance, the periods present both comparisons and contrasts, and even more importantly, the two periods are related in a number of ways.

The basic strategy we utilize is to present different parts of the 'social system' as agent, that is, as innovator. We let the events progressively build a perspective about innovation.

The Principal as Innovator: Personality Conflict

Personality conflict is one of those widely used common sense labels which everyone understands but which social scientists have great difficulty rendering clearly, Mr. McBride seemed to have growing and continuing problems with several of the men who filled the high school principal position in the 1940s. In 1945 when Mr. Smith was principal a minute was recorded: 'It was agreed by the board that Mr. McBride use his judgment in regard to the problem of the high school principal.' (1/4/45) In April, 1945 one of the new teachers, Mr. Hightower, was hired at a salary of $3000, an amount greater than any other teacher and principal in the district. Among the five '... teachers to be notified that they were not reemployed' (4/5/45), was Mr. Smith, the high school principal.

The following 15 November 1945, a minute appears:

> Mr. Hightower, Principal of the High School, presented his reactions in his new position to the Board, Superintendent, students, parents and teachers. Several special committees of teachers have been functioning, one of which, the Curriculum Committee, is seemingly displaying commendable professional interest and zeal. The subject of Curriculum Planning will be considered at a dinner to be given at City University and it was moved ... to pays for the plates of any teachers interested in this phase of work and who would care to attend. (11/15/45)

In short, a new principal has appeared. Major curriculum activity is underway. Within two years he would be in difficulty with the Superintendent and within three years he would be subject to a major inquiry and would be relieved.

But in the Spring of 1946, things were presumably going well, for the Superintendent recommended Mr. Hightower for a $300 raise to a salary of $3300, more than ten per cent higher then the elementary principal who was the next highest paid staff member at $2970.00. Mr. McBride's salary was increased to $4800/year. In March of 1947, Mr. Hightower's salary was increased to $3600/year by the Board. No mention was made of the Superintendent recommending the increase, as he had in the previous year.

Teacher turnover, partly voluntary due to pregnancy, illness, or moving but mostly due to Board decision not to 're-elect' continued. In 1945 seven teachers were not reappointed, from a group of twenty-five. (Eighteen were given contracts.) In effect, between a fourth and a third were not rehired. On 2 April 1947, the Board terminated the appointments of five teachers. The phrasing of the letter included the following notice:

> *According to state law* the Board of Education must notify teachers of their failure of re-election to the Milford School Faculty before April 15, and this is your official notice that you are not being retained. (Our italics) (4/2/47)

Once again the importance of the legal context for school action appears. Most applied social science theory seems to have omitted this as a major set of variables. Without question, in our view, an educational innovation theory cannot afford to continue such neglect.

A month later the high school principal was having his problems: 'After discussing the situation of the High School Principal it was decided that if he does not secure a new position and thereby resign he will personally appear before the Board at the June meeting.' (5/13/47) The next step involved a citizens group:

A committee representing the Mothers Club — Mrs. Jay, Mrs. Cento, Mrs. Houston — appeared before the Board to voice their opinions on the work and duties of the High School Principal. Messers. Jay, Gones and Cento were also present. (6/1/47)

These items, brief as they are, actually were among the most extensive in the very sketchy minutes kept by Miss Susan Jones who had become secretary in September of 1945. Some kind of resolution to the 'trouble,' undefined at this point, apparently had occurred.

Some six months later, in February 1948, personnel discussions were underway: 'The estimated budget and the election of teachers and administrators were considered. Action is to be taken at a future meeting.' (2/48) Things hadn't improved in the administration of the high school and it was noted in April: 'After considerable discussion a motion was made by Mr. Smith and seconded by Mr. Hamilton to accept the recommendation of the Superintendent not to renew the contract of Mr. S. K. Hightower.' (4/2/48) In less than two weeks, with a new school board installed on 6 April, a special meeting was held on 12–13 April. Only one item appeared in the minutes:

Upon the recommendation of the Superintendent a motion was made by Mr. Norris and seconded by Mr. Hamilton to rescind the notice of April 2, 1948 and that a new contract for $3900 per year be offered to Mr. S. K. Hightower. Said contract to be returned within fifteen days or per Article 2, Section 10342A of the Midwest State School Laws. (4/12–13/48)

The unusual double date reflected a long evening meeting and a resolution from the wee hours of the morning. On that evening of 12 April, 1947 a 'Meeting of Board of Education and Citizens Committee, Milford, Midwest State' was held. This meeting produced a *ninety-eight page stenotyped report* on the conflict between McBride and Hightower and culminated in the aforementioned rescinding of the 2 April action and the offering of Mr. Hightower a contract. It's not clear whether Mr. Hightower returned his contract or whether he decided to quietly fade away. In a special meeting in July:

Superintendent McBride recommended the appointment of Mr. Donald T. Green as Principal of the High School at $4100.00 per year for the school year 1948–49, contingent upon his acceptance by July 14, 1948, and also his release from his present position at Ashland[1] in Midwest State. (7/9/48)

In February of 1949 Mr. Green's contract was renewed for two years at a salary of $4300. But it's the issues in the McBride-Hightower conflict which need to be raised, and it's to these we now turn.

It seems important to take up this case of 'personality conflict,' report it briefly and make the beginnings of an analysis. 'Personality conflict' has appeared and reappeared in Milford. Presumably other districts have similar problems. The data are mostly from the long stenotyped report of the evening of 12 April which has been bound with the Board minutes.

The issue is initially phrased by the Board Chairman: 'We will now open the special meeting. Last Friday night we had a special meeting to talk to this committee from the mass meeting and we had Mr. McBride state his different points of non co-operation of Mr. Hightower.' (p. 1) A second citizen's committee, favoring the Principal, wanted to be heard. As tax payers they 'demanded' a hearing:

> We ask of you to allow us and give us a hearing. We ask it, and as tax payers we demand it. We are not interested in personalities. We want to know the facts of the case and what is going on. We think we have that right as tax payers. (p. 2)

As the preliminary fencing occurred about 'open meetings before the entire community,' mass meetings, two committees, fairness to all and so forth, Mr. McBride commented: 'Mr. Chairman, if an open meeting would result in the kind we had at the last two mass meetings, I am not in favor of going before any open meetings.' (p. 5) One of the citizens referred to: 'The children went on strike for one day.' (p. 5) The context continued to unfold in another citizen comment:

> But this was your suggestion. I say these men are certainly entitled to hear this, and so are the people downstairs and so are the teachers downstairs and everyone else that pays taxes in this district.
>
> Let's open the whole thing to the public down in the gymnasium. You have got police protection. These people aren't fighting. (p. 6)

The Board decided to go ahead with representatives of the two committees. Mr. Hightower was upset because he had to answer charges 'on the spot' without knowing the specifics before hand. The first charge against Mr. Hightower was stated by Mr. McBride:

> Last Fall in connection with the operation of organizations such as PTA and Mothers' Circle, it seemed that he took over the contacts in dealing with them in the arrangements of meetings and so forth. These contacts and arrangements should be handled through my office because of the fact that the organizations represent both elementary and high school.
>
> I called him in and told him about that.
>
> He had been advised at the beginning of the year to come in and talk with me on problems of these schools and he did not come into my office until a month and a half after school started.

Mr. Hightower gave a long reply which seemed to capture from his perspective a number of elements in the personality clash. Again we quote the entire response verbatim:

> The executive committee of the PTA had a meeting at which Mr. McBride was not present. He was ill at that time, and at that meeting I was asked by both the president of the Mothers' Circle and one of the officials of the PTA — I don't know whether it was the president or not — if it would be

possible for me to prepare cards for mailing announcements announcing the meeting, and I said I would be glad to do that.

I went ahead and prepared the cards. That is the only way I had anything to do with arranging meetings of the PTA or the Mothers' Circle.

When Mr. McBride called me in, as I recall the interview, the first thing he said to me was how I thought things were going. I said I thought very well. He asked me how I thought we were getting along, and I told him very well. And he assured me that he felt the same way.

Then he went on to say that he was greatly disturbed by the fact and he wondered why it was that he had not been and was not being consulted by the officials of the PTA. That they were the people — I am quoting this as I recall it — who had supported me in our disagreement last year and now they were asking me the questions instead of him, and at that time I gave him every assurance I could, that I thought those people were not intentionally slighting him, and I told him further that in the future when anyone asked me to do anything for the Mothers' Circle or PTA, I would refer them to him since that was his request.

The interchange went on:

Mr. McBride: He is referring to one specific instance. As far as I recall I said nothing about the people that were supporting you last year or anything about that and I know there were a good many telephone calls and things of that sort which seemed to me could have been referred to my office.

Mr. Hightower: May I say this. It is rather difficult to be in a position with a man who is so jealous of his authority that when you try to work with a duly organized group in your community and support their activity, that he writes down what you do word for word and puts you on the carpet. (p. 15)

The charges, over forty, the replies and counter replies went on page after page. They included items such as:

1 The Principal didn't bring any problems to the Superintendent.
2 The Principal talked publicly 'that there was something radically wrong with the Milford Village School,' the elementary school which his son attended.
3 He was part of a meeting in which the high school teachers criticized the guidance program.
4 He invited the Milford Village School and some rural school in for a matinee.
5 In the High School '—— foul writing on the desks, in the room, on top of desks and school furniture, and they are badly marred.'
6 On Saturday morning, after a play, three girls worked on the stage and no teachers or principal was present.

Each of the items received a reply, an explanation couched in terms of the nature of the school, the Principal's responsibility, and his efforts to administer the school.

Then an item arose which had major consequences for the remainder of the meeting. The Superintendent charged that the Principal had made a statement about a pupil: 'We can't have him around here. Short on teachers anyway. Can't be bothered.' And, in addition, the Principal hadn't talked to the Superintendent about the case. The Principal countered with: 'I deny it.' The Superintendent rejoined: 'You are wrong, for I heard it over the telephone.' At the time in the district's history, the Superintendent was housed in the high school building. Also at that time the telephone technology or the type of service purchased was a system with several telephone receivers all connected to the same line. McBride, Hightower, and later we were to discover, several secretaries all used the same hookup. McBride's listening in on the 'private' and/or 'professional' calls of his employees both professional and non-professional became an important issue in its own right.

The tangle of incidents went on and on. Issues such as transporting youngsters for hearing tests were perceived by the Superintendent as 'not informing me' and by the Principal as 'accepting responsibility' in some cases or as 'delegating responsibilities' when he had teachers take charge. Some involved the Principal's priorities in going to his Church Board meetings instead of PTA executive committee meetings. And some charges involved issues that had strong community aspects such as raising the price of admission to the high school basketball games without talking it over with the Superintendent.[2] Other items included complex issues of multiple authorities and chance events. For example, on one occasion, youngsters were being transported to an athletic event, a mix-up occurred on who was to ride on which bus, one bus broke down, the students had dinner in a restaurant connected to a tavern, and everyone got home late.

Through the long litany of charge, explanation and counter interpretation, Mr. Hightower spoke of his 'good faith and interest in your school' and 'I would say they are foolish criticisms' (p. 38). At other points, Mr. McBride is saying:

I have another note, hard to work with in promoting things for the school. In connection with the music department, too independent about high school, can't get him to talk over work. I have another note, when I asked him to come into the office he may never come in until I call him again or send for him. (pp. 39–40)

The list of items continued on through page 62 of the stenotyped notes. Images of Captain Queeg and the Caine Mutiny court-martial arose in us. Mr. McBride concluded:

And those are notes mainly on which the basis of non co-operation is made. And I have had to illustrate through those to show a point of why we think that there is non co-operation, and, of course, those notes are dealing with this year. (p. 62)

An extended discussion occurred among the representatives of the two citizen's groups, student representatives, and members of the Board. Most seemed to argue that 1) the problems should be settled that evening; 2) co-operation required efforts and good faith by both parties; 3) that last year's conflict had erupted again this year; 4) that both men were assets to the district; 5) that specification and separation of duties needed to be made; 6) that neither was totally in the right or wrong; 7) that the Board because it contained no professional educator could not lay out the specific 'duties' of each office; 8) that a third party might be brought in as a consultant; 9) that if the two couldn't come up with a workable specification of duties and areas of authority then one or both should be removed; 10) conciliatory language appealed again and again to 'the betterment of the school,' 'all of us want a good school'; 11) that the two parties themselves need to work out problems.

The culmination was:

> Upon the recommendation of the Superintendent a motion was made by Mr. Norris and seconded by Mr. Hamilton to rescind the notice of April 2, 1948 and that a new contract for $3900/year be offered to Mr. Hightower. Said contact to be returned with fifteen days as per Article 2, Section 10342-A of the Midwest State Law. The motion carried. (4/12–13/48)

In short it seemed a 'fair' hearing. Charges were made and answered. Considerable information about the high school and the district appeared. Images of Principal and Superintendent were created. The Superintendent's 'listening in on the phone' seemed to be a breach of professional standards which undercut the instances of 'non co-operation.' The Principal seemed to respond as an articulate, hardworking school man. The various parties listening to the give and take were not convinced by the Superintendent. In turn, at one point the Principal seemed to attempt to force the Board to make a choice between the two:

> I am trying to make a point here that the basic philosophies are different.
> It would seem to me that when that comes up the Board, as I understand it, is the rightful one and must decide what the policy will be. They are the policy making body. Now, if you agree with what Mr. McBride's policies are, the ones you want, it is my duty to see that I do it. If you agree that my policy is the one you want, then it is my duty to see that he lets me do it. (p. 81)

Discussion continued back and forth regarding the responsibilities of Superintendent and Board and options such as third parties to help settle the issues.

We have spoken of the events as a 'personality conflict.' Members of the meeting used such adjectives and norms as:

friction	p. 6
one man's word against the others	p. 64
a misunderstanding or overlap of authority	p. 64
where one's authority starts and where the other's begins	p. 65
last year there was trouble and this year again we have troubles	p. 65
some misunderstanding there that can be corrected	p. 66
differences of opinion	p. 67
this isn't a fight over personalities, we are not after Mr. McBride's hide	p. 69
these two men were not getting along	p. 71

We presume that when phrases such as these appear in the conversations and discussions of citizens, communities, and school board members then much larger issues exist regarding authority, status, and self-esteem.

School drama tends to be less like classical drama, where conflict arises, a crisis appears and the denouement arrives, and more like theater of the absurd, where one walks in and out of a drama which seemingly has no beginning and end. In July a Mr. Donald T. Green was recommended and hired as Principal. Mr. Hightower disappeared from the scene.

Turning a 'personality conflict' into an instance of innovation may be stretching the latter concept a bit. The points we want to make are severalfold and seem to gradually clarify aspects of 'planned change.' Mr. Hightower in trying to take the high school in directions not shared by Superintendent McBride was acting like 'an agent.' In so doing he challenged the power and the authority of the Superintendent. Over a three year period, high praise for his curriculum development turned into a litany of charges that seemed to amount to a threat to the incumbent Superintendent. The ultimate challenge was a 'him or me' statement by the Principal. The Board chose the Superintendent and the Principal left. Risk taking can have its costs.

Perhaps more than any other lesson from this episode we are struck with the legal constraints on educational action, with the skein of power and authority relationships among the law, the Board, the Superintendent, the Principal, and the citizenry, with the human drama involved, and with the length of time for episodes to run their course. The image of 'politics' in both its pejorative sense and in the sense of people resolving conflicts in a reasonably orderly, fair, and democratic way also comes to mind.

The Community as Innovator: District Consolidation

On Thursday, 19 May 1949, the Milford School District increased in size by fifty per cent. A neighboring school district, Marquette voted to 'become attached or annexed' to Milford. Milford had twenty-eight teachers and 667 pupils. Marquette had eleven teachers and 317 pupils. In a sense, this, too, argues for the 1949 year as a key demarcation point. The geographical boundaries of the District have now been set for the next thirty years, that is, to the present. Further attempts at consolidation will be resisted — successfully. The formal steps seem quite simple. First, a petition was presented to the Marquette Board of Education on 2 May 1949. A copy appears as Figure 15. Second, the Board held a public meeting: 'The Board then went on record to have a mass meeting of the district so they could explain and answer any questions which could be in the minds of the people of the district.' (5/2/49) Third, the election was held, as indicated by the announcement presented as Figure 16.

The vote was reported in the minutes of the regular Board meeting on the evening of 19 May:

> The secretary at this time read the results of the election which was held at the school on the attachment or annexation to the Milford School district (as per attached Ballot).
> The result was as follows:
> For Annexation   240 votes
> Against Annexation   7 votes
> Void Ballots   4 votes
> The President then instructed the secretary to notify the Milford School Board of the results of today's election and to await their reply. (5/19/49)

At that time there were 380 pupils in Grades 1–8, and an additional fifty-one in kindergarten. The number of graduates that Spring was twenty-four. There had been thirty-two the previous year.

The Milford Board met in Special Session, 31 May 1949. It voted unanimously to 'annex and attach' the boundaries, property and monies of the Marquette District.

Figure 15: Petition for Annexation

PETITION FOR ANNEXATION
To THE BOARD OF EDUCATION
SCHOOL DISTRICT OF MARQUETTE

We, the undersigned, qualified voters of the School District of Marquette, County of Suburbia, State of Midwest, desire that the School District of Marquette be attached to the adjoining School District of Milford, for school purposes, in accordance with and under the authority of Section 10484, Revised Statutes of Midwest State, 1939, as amended, and do hereby petition you to call a special meeting or election according to law, to test the sentiment of the qualified voters, voting at such election, upon such desired attachment.

(28 signatures)

Figure 16: Notice of Election

NOTICE OF SPECIAL SCHOOL ELECTION

NOTICE IS HEREBY GIVEN to the qualified voters of the School District of Marquette, County of Suburbia, State of Midwest, that a special school election of said district will be held at the School Building on Downing Drive in said District, on Thursday, May 19th, 1949 commencing at 7 o'clock AM, and ending at 6 o'clock PM on that day, at which meeting or election the following will be proposed and voted upon:

PROPOSITION: That the School District of Marquette become attached or annexed to the adjoining School District of Milford, for school purposes, as authorized by Section 10484, Revised Statutes of Midwest State, 1939, as amended.

By order of the Board of Education of the School District of Marquette, Suburbia County, Midwest State, this 2nd Day of May, 1949.

William D. Metcalfe
Secretary, Board of Education
School District of Marquette

The County Board of Education had recommended, at least as one alternative, the consolidating of five additional elementary districts into the Milford District. The Milford Superintendent's Report to the Board on 10 May 1949 under item 11 referred to: 'Report of County Board of Education to State Board of Education on proposed reorganized district: Milford, Marquette, Union, Caldwell, Morrison, Rhodes, Dudley.' Three of those small districts had two teachers, one had one teacher and one had no teacher, not even a school. Several were schools which had sent pupils to Milford High School for a number of years, several of whom were in the first high school graduating class of 1931. The Board chose the simpler alternative.

With the consolidation of Milford and Marquette in 1949, the District, in one stroke, increased in size by fifty per cent. The geographical area increased, which meant some of the youngsters had long distances to travel to the high school. In addition, the Superintendent/Principal of Marquette joined the consolidated Milford staff and became Principal of the school. By virtue of his prior position one might argue he was over qualified for that job alone. The post war suburban growth was beginning, each year fifty to 100 additional youngsters were coming into the schools. Rooms were added. New curricula and teachers were added. Finally, the projections on increases in student enrollment were of the order of 500 youngsters per year. Literallty a school a year was to be built. That process, as we have indicated elsewhere, demanded hours of time in an array of activities by the Board and the administrative staff. One way to handle these needs is the creation of a new central office position. After some discussion on the nature and scope of the work, Mr Unger was given the post of Director of Elementary Education and was made responsible for the several elementary schools. The minutes read this way: 'A discussion was held regarding having Mr. Unger as half time principal at both elementary schools. It was decided to delay action on his contract until this could be discussed with him and with the State Department of Education.' (2/27/51) In a related move the contract of the Principal of Milford Elementary School, Mr. Langwell, was also held up. Two months later:

> . . . that Mr. Langwell be notified that he is not being re-employed for next year due to the following reason: that the Board has discussed as early as three months ago the plan of setting up a Director of Elementary Education and that an assistant be employed in the person of a young man to be trained and work with the Director of Education. This notification is to be tendered before the 15th of April according to Section 10342A of Midwest State School Laws, 1947. Motion carried. (4/10/51)

Immediately afterward Mr. Unger was tendered a new contract as Director of Elementary Eduction.

If one looks a bit more abstractly at these events they can be conceptualized. We have developed a model, Figure 17, to represent the sequence of events. District consolidation and district population increase caused an increase in district size and led to projections of further increases. This precipitated at least four kinds of tasks and activities: plans and arrangements for new buildings, temporary facilities,

Figure 17: Antecedents of Organizational Change: The Creation of a New Position

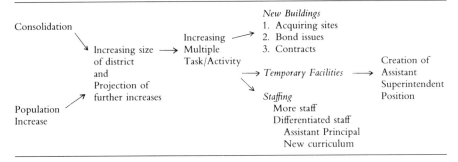

staffing needs and changes, and the ambiguous transportation problems. Someone has to do the enlarging quantity of work, and a new position is created. The presence of Mr. Unger, formerly a 'superintendent,' argues for his becoming the incumbent.

These events and processes seem so much a part of common sense, they seem 'natural.' Further, a look back at Mrs. Briggs' arrival as teacher and principal for the new High School and her later becoming Superintendent had much the same quality.

School District consolidation, the formal changing of school boundaries looks easy when everyone wants it. It was resisted at the turn of the century, in the early 1930s, in larger form in 1949, and later for reasons of tax equalization and still later for racial equity. Community votes are the central procedure. State law provides a format and set of rules for carrying out the process. The 'innovation' lasts a long time. In this instance, the Milford District continues in its 1949 form down to the present.

Consolidation and population growth also changed the internal administrative structure of the Milford School District. The new position of Director of Elementary Education was created. It, too, would last for a long time, eventually being converted into an Assistant Superintendency, and still later being eliminated when district enrollment fell, when several elementary schools closed, and when a long term incumbent retired. These innovations all seemed to have a 'natural' quality, ones that were not problematic but followed on large demographic population shifts.

The School Board as Innovator

Prologue

It should come as no surprise at this point in our monograph to have a section on 'the school board as innovator.' By state law the Board is duly elected to be responsible for the education of children in the geographical catchment area. The early history showed the Board acting as agent and creating the district. In the late 1940s and the early 1950s the Milford Board of Education's actions produced some 'wrinkles' in our analysis of the context and process of innovation. One of these was the arrival of 'the strong board member.' Another was the use of social science, an outside social science survey, in the pursuit of innovation.

The nature and magnitude of the Board's agenda led us to see these innovations under the larger rubric of 'modernization.' By this we mean two kinds of changes, a recognition of changes in the outside world, the different ballgame, in today's cliches, and a recognition that other places had ways of dealing with those changes. The implication was that 'we, too, should be doing those new things'. When the Board takes a hand in such events, it is a very powerful one. But, as we shall see, it is not all powerful. In American education, there is no such 'all powerful' agent. And that is a very important finding, so we believe.

The Strong Board Member: A Major Event

As we indicated, at a special meeting of the Board on 9 July 1948, a new High School Principal was hired, Donald T. Green. Teachers continued to come and go as two new staff were hired. Building maintenance remained a continuing problem and a plumbing contract was let. Technology continued to invade the schools — a liquid duplicator was bought for the elementary school and an electric stove was purchased for the Attucks School (8/3/48). In the March discussions of the coming elections, the Board voted for a kind of 'insurance': 'A motion was made by Mr. Jay and Mr. Norris to first place the names of the incumbents, in order of length of service followed by other candidates in order of date of filing on the official ballot. The motion carried.' (3/8/49) But 'insurance' sometimes doesn't work. A month later the minutes record the votes:

Incumbent	341
Incumbent	416
Incumbent	92
F. J. Lewis	529
M. T. Norton	509

Mr. Lewis and Mr. Norton were sworn in.

At times it is difficult to judge whether the Board took on new vigor with the election of new directors of whether a shift in secretaries engendered a new style in reporting. Probably some of both. When Mr. F. J. Lewis joined the Board and became secretary, the minutes doubled or tripled in length, the Board seemed more active, and Mr. Lewis seemed in the middle of that action.

A further image arose gradually in reading the minutes after the election of Mr. Lewis. Notes occurred of his involvement in AASA, traveling to Atlantic City, bringing back ideas, inserting them into Board discussion and action. Attempts were made to define the responsibilities of the Board, the Superintendent, the Principals, as major positions in themselves. Further, attempts were made in definitions of the other positions, and even more critically in Milford, of the relations among the incumbents of each of the positions. Gradually, an evaluative aspect of this arose and reached several climaxes. Mr. Lewis voted against a salary increase for the Superintendent and presented a long bill of particulars. Later, a call for termination of Mr. McBride's contract arose, and became a community issue of considerable magnitude.

The data fill in the overview this way. In March of 1950 a special meeting of the Board was held:

> Board action on the petition from some of the children was discussed. The Board then passed the following resolution:
> > The Board of Education goes on record as reaffirming all policies of the Board and the School and that all problems must be taken up with the proper Teachers, Supervisors, and Administrators. (3/21/50)

At the next meeting, the two new Board members were sworn in, and then nominated and voted in as President and Vice President. The agenda was full:

> The Board recommended that Mr. McBride send letters to the parents of the pupils through the mail and by the pupils and also put an open letter to the people in the Village News and the Township News, with Mr. Lewis and Mr. Norton working with him on it. (4/6/50)

Two items later in the same evening: 'Mr. Lewis moved that on April 25th a general meeting about our education program be held, which was seconded by Mr. Norton and carried.' (4/6/50) In the executive session that same evening: 'It was decided that a general report be kept on teachers throughout the year, both good and bad reports, by the Principals for the Board's attention.' (4/6/50) That meeting was held after the regular Board meeting: 'After adjournment an hour of open discussion was spent with the people who were present as visitors.' (4/25/50)

In May, 'Mr. Lewis moved that the Board spend up to $1500.00 for library books for the high school, which was seconded by Mr. Norton and carried.' (5/16/50) The meeting was introduced and thereby labeled in the minutes as follows: 'The first meeting of the Milford School Board for the discussion of Educational Programs and Procedures was called to order....' (4/35/50) A month later: 'The Regular Monthly for Educational Programs and Procedures was called to order.' (5/31/50) The main items of business:

> The President read the various lists of recommendations for the Lay Committee.
> > It was agreed to have the Lay committee ready to go at the next meeting for Educational Programs and Procedures.
> > After adjournment over an hour of open discussion was spent with the people who were present as visitors. (5/31/50)

Several items had a jarring ring to them as one read along.

> Mr. Trotter suggested that a survey be made of other schools concerning the custodial standards as to age, health, etc. Mr. Lewis suggested that a

survey also be made concerning how much work a custodian can do. It was suggested that Mr. McBride get a book on custodial help. (6/13/50)

The nature and quality of information related to school functioning shifted during this period. Three kinds of data seemed involved: comparative data from neighboring districts, an increase in meeting attendance and reporting back by administrators and Board members, and an appeal to published statements.

More specifically, a letter from a prominent local Superintendent regarding fund raising organizations was read and the policy statements accepted. The Superintendents of Suburban County were developing their own internal leadership, to a degree independent of the County Superintendent's office. Names of books and pamphlets, *The Custodian* by Viles and *Developing School Plant and Programs* were being purchased, read and discussed. The Superintendent's Report of 1 September 1951 mentions 'Midwest State Schools' (the state NEA journal), *Nations Schools* and *School and Community* and articles such as 'A message to boards of education' and 'The nation reaches a verdict.' And thirdly:

> Mr. Norton moved to send Mr. Lewis as a member of the school Board with Mr. McBride to the National Administrators Convention in Atlantic City in order to get both a professional and a layman's viewpoint of the convention, which was seconded and carried. (1/9/51)

The Board seemed to be arming itself in several ways.

The Board's thrust for upgrading school programs continued. Not only were there now regular Board meetings on Educational Programs and Procedures but the Board divided itself into three sub-committees: House, Insurance, and Education. Mr. Lewis and Mr. Gordon were members of the Educational Committee (4/10/51) Two weeks later (4/24/51), on a motion by Mr. Lewis and an unanimous Board vote a Diversified Occupations Course was approved for the Fall term. On 16 May, on a motion by Mr. Lewis the Board unanimously: '. . . agreed to have a three day work shop before school starts and to pay teachers for these three days.' (5/16/51) Two weeks later, the thrust continued:

> The following three goals from Mr. Lewis' recommendations to the Board as the result of his attending AASA convention in February were discussed and it was decided to implement them as quickly as possible. They are:
> 1 An adequate building program.
> 2 A public relations program that will not only keep the public continuously informed but will engender a democratic attitude in the community that will carry over into the schools.
> 3 Complete information on:
>   a Teacher conferences with administration
>   b Guidance results
>   c Testing program. (5/29/51)

The intensity of concern seemed exhibited in another two lines: 'Several hours were devoted to the discussion of part of Mr. McBride's report of the Denver conference.'

(8/29/51) The Denver Conference was on Public Relations and Mr. McBride had been expensed there as well as to a State Meeting at State University (5/29/51).

Correlated with those moves by Mr. Lewis and the Board were the increasing formalization of state regulations. Inserted in the Board minutes is the State Department's moves regarding 'Classification and Accreditation.' Milford High School offered thirty-seven and a half units of approved credit and was due to receive a Triple A classification in the next year.

As one reads along, page after page in Board minutes, images of other, more contemporary school boards come to mind, as do images of other small groups and their dynamics. The 'strong personality' or the 'strong board member' conveys in the schoolman's common jargon the first level of meaning. The constellation of elements includes: 1 outspokenness, 2 often in opposition to the superintendent, 3 strong community base or voter support, 4 a willingness to entertain confrontation and conflict, 5 intelligent and articulate, 6 needs for power or dominance, 7 major commitment of time and effort. These events came to a head on 25 February 1953:

> After considerable discussion, a motion was made by Mr. Metcalfe and seconded by Mr. Quigley that Mr. McBride be offered a contract at $9000.00 per year for three years. Messrs Trotter, Gordon, Quigley, Metcalfe, and Mrs. Cooper voting for and Mr. Lewis voting against this motion.
>
> Upon a motion by Mr. Gordon and seconded by Mr. Lewis it was unanimously agreed that the Superintendent give study and make recommendations for administrative assistance, so that the Superintendent may be freed for closer relation with the Board on education program. (2/25/53)

The minutes were followed by a one page formal conract, the first ever enacted in the minutes. It was prefaced by reference to the appropriate sections of Midwest State School Laws. But even more signficant for our analysis of the 'strong school board member' is a two page bill of particulars in which Mr. Lewis presented his rationale for dissenting on the new contract. It was a broad scale attack. We reproduce it in its entirety. The first part seems almost a preamble or set of assumptions:

> The American Association of School Administrators in booklet 'What to pay your Superintendent' say: 'The Board of Education is responsible for ascertaining as accurately as possible the degree of success attained by the executive over a period of time.'
>
> Evaluative Criteria says: 'The Superintendent of Schools keeps the Board of Control informed through periodic reports, regarding the schools objectives, achievements, needs and plans for the future.'
>
> The School Board Member in Action booklet of the AASA says: 'The Board should discuss the educational problems. It should not limit itself a business and financial affairs. Often Board members do not feel themselves

qualified to talk about educational policy. So far as technical detail is concerned this is generally true. On the other hand, the aims and purposes of what schools are doing and the human results they are accomplishing are things which any intelligent American is competent to judge. One of the Superintendent's important tasks is to keep Board members informed about such things. In times when school business problems are so pressing, care must be taken that the Board's trusteeship for educational progress does not go by default.'

Davies and Hosler in 'The Challenge of School Board Membership' state (in the chapter — Follow the School Program): 'Rely on your Superintendent as your professional advisor and co-ordinator for the enterprise. His regular reports to the Board are indispensable.'

They further state: 'There is something wrong when Boards meet two or three times a month and meetings last from 8 to 8:30 to midnight or after. There is no need for making such demands upon the valuable time of Board in a well organized and well run school system.'

The AASA School Boards in Action sums up the responsibility of the local Board in relation to the educational program in three sentences:

1. The Board should know the characteristics of a good educational program.
2. The board should know what is going on in the local schools and in the best school systems in other parts of the country.
3. The board should constantly be evaluating and improving the work of the schools.

They further state: 'The function of control of the educational program should never be delegated by the Board of Education.'

The next entry moves the broad preamble into the middle of Mr. Lewis' personal perspective on the local situation:

In striving to introduce education matters into Board actions, I two years ago, after considerable study in addition to attending the National Convention of the American Association of School Administrators, as Board representative, presented a program of goals for our school system. Several of these goals were adopted in May 1951, but no report on progress on same has been made and no further discussion or additional recommendations have been made. Last year I agreed to the increase to $7500.00 for the Superintendent, only on the understanding that administrative reports outlining progress during the 1951–52 school year and plans for additional progress during the 1952–1953 school year be presented.

Those goals included three items: building programs, public relations program and information regarding testing, guidance, and teacher/administrative conferences (5/29/51). The comments by Mr. Lewis continue:

It was agreed by the Board that these reports be made at the May, 1952 meeting, but so far no reports have been presented.

An analysis of the preceding comments leads me to conclude:

1   That the Superintendent has not kept the Board regularly informed regarding the educational program and because of this our
Board has not fulfilled its responsibility in relation to the educational program.

2   That my wishes for education information are not new, as they
were expressed in my report of 2 years ago and repeated in my
request for administrative reports last year.

3   That a system of regular reports to the Board, permitting constant
evaluation of our educational achievements be made a part of
Board procedure, so that decisions regarding administrative results
of our school may be made on facts and not on opinions or
feelings.

4   That it is necessary for the Board to make certain that the
formulation of the educational program is a democratic process
involving the Board of educated interested laymen, the Superintendent of schools, the professional staff and student council (as
recommended by the AASA).

In view of the above conclusion, I cannot agree to increase expenditures for our chief administrative office until such time as I am assured that
this increase in expenditure will bring increased benefits to the boys and
girls of our district.

Some of the questions which I feel should be continuously answerable
to insure a proper evaluation of our educational program include:

What are the statistics on Drop-outs? (from challenge of school-
board membership)

Are there clearly established and recognized channels of communication between individuals and groups? Between Board,
administration, teachers, custodians, pupils, parents! (the challenge of
School Board membership)

How adequate are provisions for pupil participation in school
government? (evaluative criteria)

Is the Superintendent accepting the personal responsibility for
planning, co-ordinating the school's public relations program? (as
suggested in the AASA's year book on 'Public relations for America's
schools')

How adequate is the general organization of the pupil activity
program? (evaluative criteria)

Is the formulation of the educational program a democratic
process involving the Board of education, interested laymen, the
Superintendent of schools, the professional staff and student council?

Do our courses of study draw attention to moral and spiritual
values? (as suggested in 'Moral and spiritual values in the public
schools')

What efforts are being made to provide wider counselling? (evaluative criteria)

Is our library being used effectively? (evaluative criteria)

How adequate are provisions for follow-up service or guidance? (evaluative criteria)

How extensive is the information concerning scholastic progress? (evaluative criteria)

This then extends the meaning of our conception of 'the strong School Board member,' an item of considerable importance in the analysis of the history of the Milford School District, and, presumably of any school district.

The analysis has been developed around two central concepts. The first of these is the potent or strong school board member, another kind of agency in innovation. The second is the cluster of innovations which we have called modernization. Getting in touch with the times and with practices developed elsewhere, in the county, across the country, in professional meetings and in the professional journals.

Drama exists in the analysis for the denouement is yet to come. Mr. Lewis and Superintendent McBride are in a kind of conflict that might be described as a death struggle. They seem beyond the usual mechanisms of discussion and compromise. This seems beyond the farther reaches of innovation as technical processes of planned change.

The Potency of the Outside Survey — Or the Strong Board Member Revisited

Setting the Stage. The educational scene in the 1970s and 1980s seems strewn with reports, and evaluations. Considerable disagreement exists on their impact, usefulness, and purposes — latent or manifest. Amidst the growth and expansion of the district, the pressures to modernize, the arrival of two new Board members, Dawson and Willman, and the presence of 'the strong Board member,' the idea of a school survey arose. Three interrelated items appeared in the minutes:

Mr. Lewis suggested that a possible survey of the school district should be made.

Upon a motion by Mr. Dawson and seconded by Mr. Youngman it was decided to write to several universities who might make a complete comprehensive survey of the District, so the School Board may decide which one will be best for their purpose.

Several universities and colleges mentioned were Columbia, George Peabody, Chicago, and Central State University. (5/6/53)

Amongst items regarding custodians, publicity for bond issues, and motions to pay bills, an item of concern regarding the administrative and organizational plans occurred:

Also in the meeting of May 27, we should talk over and discuss a working relationship for the general improvement of the school system as follows: 1) the definition and explanation of areas of responsibilities of the principals of the high school and elementary schools, of the superintendent of school and his relationship with the Board of Education, the teachers with each other, the principal and superintendent with the Board, and, 2) what should the administration do? (5/13/53)

Reports were presented by the Superintendent, Director of elementary education and the high school Principal. All these were to be attached to the minutes. None was. A special meeting was called for 8 June to continue the discussion.

In the 8 June meeting, examples of surveys, correspondence with several institutions, and a decision to write to Dr. Thoelke from Central State University occurred. Several specific ideas regarding shortening Board meetings, indexing the minutes, developing a 'follow up date file,' and semi-annual reports to the Board were raised and discussed: 'It was decided to delay any further action on the subject until a well-laid plan is worked out, possibly by September.' (6/10/53) Amidst a huge agenda of building plans, contracts, building of temporary facilities, and conflict in firing cafeteria staff in the Summer of 1953, the Board interviewed professors from three universities regarding the survey. They settled on Dr. Thoelke of Central State University. His staff had completed 'sixty surveys in the last five years.' The minutes accented several items.

> Three general phases of the survey were emphasized:
> 1   Every survey is based on a careful analytical study of the community.
> 2   ... a representative lay group to be used in an advisory capacity.
> 3   ... emphasize the future ...
>   This type of survey is a basic instrument in policy, a foundation for procedure, and there is no standard to check against without a survey....
>   Dr. Thoelke further stated that the survey does not evaluate personnel, but they advise the Superintendent on personnel records; the length of time covered by the survey is usually a complete school year in order to see the whole span; and within the survey they do follow-up work on graduates. (7/6/53)

The cost is $2.00 per pupil. Fifty copies of a report are submitted. The staff is available for further consultation.

The Survey Proceeds.   After the decision on 3 August several ongoing activities, for example, evaluation of results of education, and groups, for example, the Lay Advisory Group, were integrated into the survey plans and procedures. One of Dr. Thoelke's pamphlets and several references in his bibliography were ordered by the District. Some jockeying over citizen membership on the survey team occurred; each Board member was to contribute names. Visits by the survey team began in the Fall with some conflict, 'Some of these people (the survey team) were not very courteous to our personnel' (12/16/53).

In early January (1/4/54) the survey team made a progress report to the Board. Several items were stressed:

1 Involvement of citizens and citizen groups,
2 Teacher survey, its importance for further inquiry, further teacher involvement,
3 Completed report on buildings; including a suggestion for early purchase of a high school building site: twenty to thirty acres and close to center of district,
4 Solicitation of Board questions: seven were listed, for example, Board-administration relations, broad aims, School Board activity, student progress, and advances in moral and spiritual education,
5 Development of teacher committees — supplies and budget priorities, text book selection and salary schedules, and teacher reports to Board on outstanding work and new ideas.
6 Leaving administrative budget detail to administration so that 'the Board could have more time for the more essential items.'

A seven page, single spaced report on the high school placed Milford High School near the median of some sixty high schools surveyed by the team. Instructional space for science, home economics, and industrial arts was limited. Overall acreage also was limited, as were a variety of overall service provisions. The expanding district very much needed a new high school.

Shortly after the meeting the Board held its regular meeting and a special meeting (13 January and 16 January). Among the agenda items were concerns over the selection of the teacher salary committee. The Superintendent was rebuked by the Board for 'selecting' rather than 'electing' teachers to the committee. 'The salary schedule of the teachers was discussed at great length. Two main factors were involved — the democratic selection of the teachers' committee on salaries, and the suggested program of teacher evaluation.' (1/16/54) Upon a unanimous vote the following went to the teachers:

> The Board wishes to go on record in favor of increased salary schedules. The Board feels that the committee drawing up a salary schedule should be elected rather than selected. The Board would like to suggest that a schedule be worked up on an evaluation system to insure greater opportunities and benefits for individual teachers and the school district. This would also assist the Board in obtaining the necessary two-thirds support for increased teacher fund levies. (1/16/54)

In short, and in retrospect, it seems a complex political statement recognizing four groups: Board, teachers, administration, and citizens whose interests overlap only partially. It suggests also a tying together of issues — salary and evaluation which many teachers' groups might oppose. It seems to have a carrot type appeal to the teachers — teacher election to the committee and two-thirds majorities — and a stick to the administration. It unites an earlier theme, the strong board member, with the current theme, the outside survey, toward a larger synthesis, a political model for understanding innovation and change in schooling. Mr. Lewis, with Mrs. Cooper's help, led the attack at the prior meeting. Mrs. Cooper made the motion here. New business, that evening, concerned a budget committee and teacher involvement.

In the 27 January meeting, the plot took an interesting turn. The teachers from all the elementary schools sent letters to the Board:

> All of these letters stated that the teachers were satisfied with the person who was representing them on the salary committee, and they were opposed to teacher evaluation for salary purposes. They were in favor of the salary schedule as presented. (1/27/54)

After an initial split vote, a detailed discussion occurred and the Board unanimously passed a motion accepting the scale as presented.

The Board continued to work through the recommendations of the outside survey committee.

The Board kept after the knotty problems of governance and administration in the school with a special meeting of the Board and a long discussion on 'the suggested division of Powers and Duties of the School Board, the Superintendent, the Principal, and the Teachers' (2/5/54). The basis was a University Bulletin article 'Suggestions for procedures for Midwest State Boards of Education.' Some fifteen points, from publicity to special education, were raised.

At a busy regular meeting, after a series of passed motions on salaries and contracts for principals and central office personnel, the Board, on a split two to four vote, did not recommend a new three year contract for the Superintendent, whose current contract had two years to run. The gauntlet was thrown down.

Another ten items were discussed on 24 February as part of the continuing concerns over 'Powers and Duties.' The intertwining of our themes continued: 'Mr. Lewis thinks we should go ahead with the school policy until we get the recommendations of the University survey; working on the ones that are necessary, then taking up the ones that the survey brings up.' (2/24/54) For the first time, a formal written report by the Superintendent on the AASA meetings was submitted and incorporated into the minutes. In addition, mimeographed copies of key speeches were included also.

In March, the Superintendent submitted a detailed four page public relations program. The Board continued to make suggestions on the format and quality of production of the *Our Schools* newsletter. Reports were filed by the high school principal on the secondary principals' meeting, by the elementary director on the remedial reading programs, and by Midwest University on the guidance program (2/24/54).

The Citizens' survey took on an explicit political quality because the Chairman of the committee had his name and position printed on campaign literature. Henceforth all campaign literature should be submitted to Dr. Thoelke at Central State University.

When Consultants Conflict. But Professor Thoelke was not the only consultant brought into the district. In May, Mr. Murphy of Lloyd, Lloyd, and Murphy, a prestigious firm of educators and consulting engineers from the east appeared before the Board, presented his credentials, and made the following comments:

> He suggested a high school of at least three units to be used, for instance music, gym, library, and lunch room. In this way the noise will not disturb the other classes which are in session. He thinks that our present high school site is too small, and that it should never be used for a senior high school. A tract of land of at last forty acres would be the smallest a community of our size should consider.
>
> The customary fee for consulting work is one half to one per cent of the cost of the construction of the building. . . . A minimum charge of $1000 would be made to draw up the program of requirements. This would take several months. (5/19/54)

The Board thanked Mr. Murphy and indicated no action would be taken at the moment, 'but will think it over.' At the regular meeting five days later, the Board, at the recommendation of the Superintendent voted to hire Lloyd, Lloyd, and Murphy as consulting engineers for the proposed new high school.

At the regular June meeting, a letter from Dr. Thoelke 'that the report on the survey would be available the week of July 12' (6/9/54). Also, at that meeting a ten page, single spaced revision of 'Policies, rules and regulations' written by the Superintendent, and distributed earlier in April: '. . . were read and discussed in detail. They were not adopted, but will be presented again as corrected.' (6/23/54) Lengthy mimeographed reports of substantive school issues as raised in National meetings and prepared by one or another of the administrators continued to be presented to the Board, discussed and bound with the minutes. These professional activities, which started in the transition period, seemed to be impelling the district toward modernity.

Mr. Murphy of Lloyd, Lloyd, and Murphy returned for a special session of the Board. He and his colleagues were urging the immediate hiring of an architect, additional sites for a high school and three elementary schools be sought immediately, and the proposed high school site be used for a junior high school. Mr. Murphy urged a common questionnaire to go to all architect applicants. A six page 'tentative outline of spaces' was provided. He also recommended that the architect, when selected, and several members of the staff might visit two communities in the south eastern part of the country: '. . . as these areas have a number of most interesting high school buildings.' (6/23/54) In the accompanying letter Mr. Murphy indicated he had read the Thoelke Report, supported the need for the three elementary schools and argued for the conversion of the present high school into a junior high and the development of the recently acquired property into a new junior high. Further he argued for a third junior high in the western part of the district.[3] He argued also for anticipating housing developments and buying ahead of them because it was considerably cheaper.

Appearing, almost as counterpoint to the modernization and growth frenzy was a minute regarding a twenty acre tract of recently purchased land which someone had sown in wheat: 'The wheat on this same property is to be harvested and the school district will be paid $10 per acre as agreed with the previous owner.' (6/30/54) In addition, an old barn on the property was to be torn down.

Reports from each high school department were filed regarding space and equipment needs in a high school of 1500 students.

The Potent Report Arrives. On 14 July 1954, the Board Room was jammed with fifty patrons concerned about a newspaper article which stated: 'Lack of effective leadership by the Milford Superintendent, survey charged.' A variety of aspects appeared. The Board was split four to two on much of the voting. At least one member of the Board and the Superintendent had not received a copy of the report, even though City Press, the local newspaper, had a copy and was allegedly quoting from it. The Board President, Mr. Lewis, had released it to a reporter. He neither authorized the story nor did he 'think it was a completely false one,' nor had he done anything to retract it. Mr. McBride was represented by a lawyer. At least two members of the Board had been asked about giving it to the papers. A motion was made and seconded by Mr. Lewis, the School Board President, that the Superintendent be asked to resign. It failed two to three, with the President not voting. A Board member, Mr. Quigley, wrote Professor Thoelke criticizing the report. In scathing tones, three typed pages, a former principal of Milford High School did also. As Dr. Thoelke was on sabbatical and out of town, the acting head of the University Bureau of Research and Service responded. On 28 July the Board argued about the Report's distribution, voted four to two to circulate it, and sent copies to several University Education Department Chairmen as well as State Education Officials. In addition the Board voted to have Dr. Thoelke appear before the Board, to invite Mr. Murphy of Lloyd, Lloyd, and Murphy to attend, and to keep a record of the distribution of all copies of the report.

A lost letter (dated 28 June) from Thoelke to Lewis finally found its way into the minutes of 11 August. The key paragraph underlying at least some of the misunderstanding was this:

> It is customary for the Board to accept the report by official action at the first regular meeting subsequent to the receipt of the report. This acceptance does not imply endorsement or adoption of the recommendations contained therein. I see no harm in presenting the report to the papers previous to the July 14 meeting with the request that they withhold publicity until such time as the Board has officially accepted the report. This will give them time to study the report and will also insure that release is simultaneous. (6/28 from 8/11 minutes)

The debate that evening involved also a letter from Dr. Thoelke declining to attend because of his sabbatical. He suggested the collation of reactions and a response from a staff member of the Bureau of Educational Research and Service. Mr. Murphy, the architect, indicated he would be happy to attend.

The Vice President of the Boosters Club presented a petition signed by 1066 residents of the district stating: '. . . our unqualified endorsement and appreciation for the leadership of Superintendent F. N. McBride in the educational and administrative operation of our school system . . .' The last paragraph of the petition urged 'constructive publicity,' 'close cooperation,' and 'harmonious operation' in the interests of the 'welfare of our school children.' The Board voted unanimously to make that district policy. The Superintendent indicated areas of advancement and improvement neglected in the survey: educational planning committee, guidance study, study in elementary curriculum, evaluation programs, and publicity programs, Further discussion by administrators, teachers, and the Board was also approved unanimously. A motion was also made to tape record discussion at the next meeting 'so that misunderstandings do not arise over comments made.'

Reports as Political Ammunition. Warfare metaphors and images, in discussions of schooling, are viewed as inappropriate by some individuals when one's first concern is the 'boys and girls of Milford' or 'America's children.' But reading minutes of Board meetings conjures up varied reactions. Item Number 632 from 29 September 1954 is offered to the reader:

> Mr. Lewis read a statement to the Board about the manner in which the Superintendent was discussing the Central State University Survey at various public and teacher meetings. President Lewis read the following recommendations to the Board:
>
> I, therefore recommend that this Board of Education direct the Superintendent to prepare for Board approval at the next regular meeting of this Board, information for distribution to the Teachers and to the public in which he recognizes that:
>
> 1 The Board of Education is responsible for evaluating administrative results.
> 2 That a comprehensive survey is a recognized means of assisting a Board in its evaluation of administrative results.
> 3 That the Central State University Survey was an unbiased survey of a comprehensive nature.
> 4 That the purpose of the Midwest University Survey was not that of a comprehensive one and cannot therefore be compared with the Central State University Survey.
> 5 That we have had excessive teacher turnover as indicated by the Central State University Survey.
> 6 That there has been an unusually brief tenure of high school principals over a nine year period.
> 7 That the problem of drop-outs is a serious one in the secondary school and that some steps must be taken to improve the situation.
> 8 That there must be more faculty involvement in guidance and that there be a follow-up of drop-outs and graduates as recommended by the teacher committee.
> 9 That the administration must become much more effective in educational leadership as recommended by the Central State University Survey.

10 That the Superintendent will accept and administer all policies adopted by the Board of Education including all that may be developed as the result of the recommendations made in the Central State University Survey.

The gauntlet was thrown down again. It was moved and seconded to adopt the recommendations. A countermove to adjourn, because the meeting was running past agreed upon times, was made. It was defeated. The debate went on for over an hour. The discussion terminated with a unanimous vote: 'That the Board of Education and the Superintendent recognize the Central State University Survey as an evaluation of the Milford School District and will study it with an open mind.' (9/29/54) The meeting adjourned at 12:30 a.m.

At the next meeting, a counterattack appeared in the form of letters from the teaching faculty of each of the elementary schools. They expressed approval and support of Mr. McBride and his administration. One was: '. . . expressing concern over a rumor that the Board of Education contemplated removing Mr. McBride'. Confidence and support of the Superintendent was expressed. (10/13/54) No word came from Milford High School.

The debate continued and finally ended with a motion that no action would be taken until after the April election. In the interim everyone would work together to prepare a blueprint for the future of the Milford School District. Two weeks later the majority changed its mind and on a four to two vote they rescinded the vote on the clause: '. . . that no action will be taken on Mr. McBride's status until after the April election.' (10/27/54) The reason was that the motion was a possible violation of their oath of office. The Board stayed in executive session and the next motion was made by Mr. Krist, seconded by Mr. Youngman:

Whereas Mr. F. N. McBride has failed to fulfill his obligations as Superintendent and Administrator of the Milford School District, Sub-urban County, and

Whereas F. N. McBride has grossly exceeded his legal authority as Superintendent and Administrator of said School District

Now it shall be resolved, that this Board of Directors shall consider the contract between F. N. McBride and the Milford School District, as terminated forthwith and that no further warrants payable to F. N. McBride be issued against the Treasurer of Milford School District. (10/21/54)

The motion passed with a four to two majority. Concerns about the legality of the vote were raised. The next motion recommended the high school Principal be made acting Superintendent. The Superintendent was brought in and notified. He indicated he had a legal contract which ran until 1 July 1956. He wanted a list of charges and a public hearing. The Board voted no, four to two. If one has any doubts as to the severity of emotion and feeling the next minutes give an exclamation point to the affair:

Mr. Lewis asked Mr. McBride to leave the Board room and he refused to leave.

Mr. Krist stated that if Mr. McBride would not leave of his own accord, he would call the police and have him moved forcibly.

Mr. Krist then called the police and Mr. McBride decided to leave of his own free will before the police arrived.

Mr. Lewis then asked Mr. McBride for the keys to the building and he turned the keys over to Mr. Lewis. (10/27/54)

The high school Principal, Dr. Macon, was brought in and offered the Acting Superintendent position. He wanted a day to think about it. A press release was prepared. The votes continued four to two. The press release itemized fifteen specifics ranging across failure to comply with Board Rules and Regulations, permitting out of district pupils to attend, failure to submit annual reports, lack of response and action over principal turnover, teacher turnover, and pupil drop-outs, and items regarding leadership raised in the Central State University Survey.

At the Board meeting the next evening, Mr. McBride, through Dr. Macon, presented a statement, upon the advice of his legal counsel that the Board couldn't terminate the contract. Dr. Macon couldn't take a position that might not exist. The Board then voted to test its case in court. Two days later, at 9 a.m. the Board passed a series of motions changing who could sign checks and documents for the district. On 10 November the Board moved forward legally and found that Mr. McBride had already initiated legal action. The attorneys and the judge reached an agreement to let Mr. McBride continue in office until the case was settled. At this meeting also an eighth grade teacher submitted his resignation: '... because of the existing situation between the Board of Education and the Superintendent, which he feels is impairing his services as a teacher.' (11/10/54)

In December, letters from the Board's lawyer indicated that the legal status of the Board's 'discharging' of the Superintendent would have pro and con briefs filed and he prepared for oral arguments before the judge.

While the county judge deliberated on the Board-Superintendent conflict, or at least the Board's power to fire him, the minutes remained silent on the affair. In late March 1955 the activities surfaced in several items:

Since Dr. Macon had been appointed Acting Superintendent 28 October 1954 in the instance the position of Superintendent was vacated by court action, President Lewis asked Mr. Macon if he had anything to bring before the Board:

He did. It was this resolution:

We, Mr. Neal Unger, Director of Elementary Education, for the School District of Milford, Dr. Phillip Macon, Principal of the High School, and Dr. Earl B. Steckman, Assistant, for the School District of Milford, do hereby propose the following recommendation;

We, the above, are of the opinion that someone or some group of persons must assume the responsibility for the educational leadership of the educational program within our School District. We believe that this can best be accomplished during this interim period by we as a group; and that each member should function within his own designated area of authority as now delegated to us as administrators by the Board of Education of the Milford School District.

Problems affecting the entire school system would be resolved by the above mentioned group through conferences and any problems requiring Board approval would be submitted to the Board of Education through the office of the Assistant to the Superintendent. (3/29/55)

It was signed by all three individuals. The Board then voted four to two on two items 1) rescinding the appointment of Macon as Acting Superintendent and 2) accepting the resolution presented by Dr. Macon.

The Democratic Resolution. One week later, all these actions were for nought. The control of local schools in America lies in the participatory democratic procedure known as voting. On 6 April in the presence of some seventy-five visitors, the Board reported the election results:[4]

Lewis	1111
Krist	1053
Edmond	2475
Irwin	537
Trotter	2506

The voters rejected 'the potent Board president,' as we have labeled him, and one of his more recent supporters. The four to two majority was now a two to four minority. Mr. Quigley became the new president. The long conflict was now over.

But, as with many real life stories, a postscript existed. A resolution was passed to continue to seek the court judgment on the case for it was of interest to varied groups of teachers and educators, both local and state. Since it was also possible for Mr. McBride to act as Superintendent during this period he was reinstated by a four to one vote (one absence). A further postscript appeared a week later in a motion: 'Be it resolved that the interim committee, consisting of Dr. Macon, Dr. Steckman, and Mr. Neal Unger, to supervise the schools, be dissolved and a vote of thanks given herewith for a job well done.' (4/14/55)

The issue did not die with that resolution for a major judicial decision was being sought by a number of local and state parties to the question 'Can a Board fire a Superintendent who has a legal contract with time still to run?' on 19 April 1955, the Board attorney indicated the legal route from county court to appeals court to State Supreme Court. Further questions arose of personal liability of Board members for any salary paid 'illegally.'

On 16 August 1955, the Court ruled that the Board could not fire the

Superintendent; Section 168.090, 1949 was the only ground for dismissal. Two weeks later Mr. McBride, on a four to two vote, received a new three year contract at $10,000/year.

Conclusion

Concluding an episode as long and as dramatic as this one seems an affront to the images we have tried to create. In keeping with the general tenor of this chapter, we have chosen to look here at the School Board as an agency of innovation. The rise and fall of the 'strong board member,' during nearly a decade of service, suggests again the need for conceptualizating the long and the short time lines involved in educational innovation. Even here the lines will run out much farther in time, for as we shall see, Mr. Lewis' attempt to get Mr. McBride to formalize policy in the form of a codified statement will finally find a resolution in the 1960s when Superintendent Spanman will introduce a commercially published system, a policy handbook, which he had used in his prior position as Assistant Superintendent of Southeastern City. That would be Spanman's most successful innovation, both in terms of acceptance and longevity. It would last until the present day. That part of 'modernization as innovation' was one of the critical problems of the late 1940s and early 1950s, identified by Mr. Lewis and reintroduced a decade and a half later. As observers and analysts we are left humbled by this image of innovation.

But the humbling process is even more pronounced when we look to the 'unbiased,' 'scientific' survey carried out by well regarded school administration researchers, trainers, and practitioners at a nearby University. The move from social science data to policy statements seemed so simple in the eyes of Thoelke and associates. Their action precipitated in us considerable thought on the nature of the interplay among educational research, theory and practice. Ultimately it was part of the stimulus for the reconstrual of the nature of thought in educational innovation, in educational administration, and in education in general. That will appear in our more general concluding interpretive chapters. The twist given the report by Lewis is as good an illustration of the use of social science knowledge in the service of political interest as one might find. The 'on sabbatical' stance of the principal investigator has its own kind of ironies.

The resolution of the conflict over modernization in the annual April voting of the community and the loss of the election by School Board incumbents, Lewis and Krist, is another of the most powerful images in our data of the context of educational innovation. The playing of local politics had an exemplar of no mean status in Mr. McBride. It forces one to rethink the various conceptions of the Superintendent as educational philosopher, as businessman, or as administrator. Rather, it is politician par excellence, if not political leader, that comes to mind in the instance of Superintendent McBride. Even though he 'lost,' Board member Lewis is not a simple tragic hero. The Board itself, and its community origins, remains a major agent in innovation. Our historical data and analysis keep pushing us toward a political and community model of educational innovation.

The Supreme Court as Innovator: The American Dilemma in the Milford Schools

Origins

More than any other innovation, the desegregation, and in Milford's case, the integration of Milford's Black and White students, has a history that runs back in time and that runs outward into the community. Following Gunnar Myrdal's (1944) classic phrasing we speak of it as 'The American Dilemma in the Milford Schools.' We make the Supreme Court decision in 1954 as the fulcrum for the consideration of these changes as an innovation, an innovation of major magnitude. The story goes this way.

From the first recorded minutes of the Board of Education which mentioned fire insurance for the 'colored school bldg.,' we were surprised by the quantity of continuing references to the 'colored school.' Education in Midwestern State was racially separate by state law. Whether it was 'separate but equal' is only slightly less clear. Item by item both schools improved; item by item the Attucks School seemed to change only after the Clear Valley School changed. Within what would now be called institutionalized racism, for example, there was frequent reference to the 'colored school' even after the school had received a formal name, the Attucks School. It is also true that the board did concern itself regularly with the education of Black children.

With a vivid *déja vu* quality, the hiring of Black teachers, the sending of Black high school students out of the district, the receiving of out of district Black pupils as a help to the other districts and as a means to fill rooms with low enrollments, and all the problems of transportation and its financing, appear in the minutes of early Board meetings.[5] The curriculum of the Attucks School received no more notice in these minutes than did the curriculum of the Clear Valley and Milford Village Schools. A teacher[6] at the Attucks School in the late 1930s commented favorably upon the teaching arrangements. It was her first teaching job. She was picked from a class of a dozen and a half, eight of whom had been interviewed. As we noted earlier she found the working conditions better in Milford than her classmates found in the segregated schools of Metropolitan City. Many of Mrs. Shields' comments involved a comparison with the Big City School District where most of her college classmates taught. Those comparisons give a further flavor to the Attucks School within Milford. In spite of multiple grade levels in her class, the class size was smaller and supplies were plentiful. The school was intimately and cooperatively related to the immediate Black neighborhood. In short, a small isolated community of families, working in a local factory, living in company houses, seemed to go about its business in a fashion isolated from the larger community. The American dilemma played itself out in a variety of ways. This was Milford's way.[7]

The American Dilemma Continues

By the mid 1940s, the Black enrollment had dropped steadily. One teacher, Clara Reynolds, remained for many years. She was the lowest paid member of the teaching staff through these years. Further, one of the largest industrial plants in the district sought to move the Attucks School for the company's expansion. The Board, the Superintendent and the Company planned and negotiated for several years. Plans were in motion for Federal aid in the construction of a new school (as well as for the Milford High School). In the meantime maintenance problems were acute enough to bring a citizens committee to the Board:

> A committee representing the Patrons Association of the Attucks School ... brought before the Board requests for needed repairs and equipment — insufficient heat in the south room, broken windows, water in the basement, and broken furnace pipe; a clock and additional playground equipment. The committee was assured that these requests would be taken care of as expediently as possible. (10/16/45)

The next mention of the Attucks School appeared in the March 1946 minutes and dealt with discussions between the Board members and the Company that wanted to move the school. The negotiations foundered on who would pay for the new school, and in June the Board noted: 'After due consideration it was decided to have the Attucks School building repaired sufficiently to put it in usable condition before the September school term.' And, 'The Quaker Manufacturing Company is to be notified that at present the Board is financially unable to bear the expense of erecting a new building.' (7/17/46)

Some problems don't fade away. In the Spring of 1949, with two new Board members, Lewis and Norton, a variety of items were raised including one relevant to the Attucks School. 'It was determined to do some additional studying before deciding just what has to be done about the Negro building situation including that of future usage and possiblity of paying tuition in Big City.' (4/7/49) The situation complicated itself further in that the Quaker Manufacturing Company activities involved dynamiting in one section of its building program.

> A discussion was held about the Attucks School and about the Quaker Manufacturing Company blasting during school hours. It was suggested that we check to find out about the blasting and register a complaint, getting legal advice on it first and then approaching them through an attorney. Mr. McBride was instructed to inquire from the Negro Improvement Association about blasting, etc. (5/10/49)

In the Superintendent's report of 10 May 1949, now mimeographed and bound with the Board minutes, Item #21 contained a one line statment: 'Negro children — the city will not accept them'. (5/10/49)

The Supreme Court Decides

In the Spring of 1954, the Supreme Court handed down the decision, in Brown vs. Topeka, that 'separate but equal' was unconstitutional. Shortly thereafter in the Board meeting it was noted regarding desegregation:

> Mr. McBride explained that many of the county schools are planning to continue as they are now until a final decision is forthcoming from the Attorney General. No action can be taken at this time concerning the Negro students of our District. (5/26/54)

Amidst all the controversy described in the potent report concerning the Superintendent, other major items of business occurred:

> The decision of segregation is up to the Board of Education according to the letter from the Commissioner of Education pertaining to the Attorney General's opinion in regard to the US Supreme Court decision on segregation in the public schools.
>
> Dr. Steckman recommended that the Board make a decision soon, but not to permit the colored children to come into the schools until September 1955.
>
> A motion was made by Mr. Quigley and seconded by Mr. Tebeau that plans to end segregation in Milford School District be made so they may take effect 1 September 1955. The motion carried unanimously. (7/14/54)

A month later the Board received a petition from 'thirty-five Negro families.' No copy of the petition appears in the records: 'It was decided to wait until September 1955 to admit colored pupils in the elementary schools because of our crowded conditions and it would be to their advantage to continue at their present school until that time.' (8/25/54) The Board also voted unanimously to meet within a week (8/30) with the parents.

Rental of more rooms at the two local churches was decided on. A deadline was set for signing the agreement on property for the new high school. If the owner is unwilling to sign, then the issue will be turned over to the school attorney for condemnation procedures.

The special meeting of the Board on 30 August 1954 dealt mainly with the petition by Black residents of Milford. The minutes are reported in their entirety:

> The meeting was called as a result of petition represented by certain citizens in regard to the decision of the Board to postpone integration of colored students until September 1955. The Board had agreed, previous to the meeting, that if the group of citizens represented by the National Association for the Advancement of Colored People wished integration of the High School students in September of 1954, then the Board would be willing to begin this part of the program but postpone elementary until September 1955 because of crowded school conditions. If any colored high

school student wished to continue his education at Green City High School, the Board would continue to pay tuition and transportation.

Mr. Lewis opened the meeting by presenting a statement in accordance with the agreement stated above.

Many of the signers of the petition were present. Mr. Yancey acted as spokesman for the group, explaining that *it was felt unfair for high school students to spend 30 hours a week in the classroom and 25 hours transportation time.* The elementary situation was felt to be satisfactory for this year. Mr. Ragan, State President of the NAACP, also spoke and expressed approval of the Board's revised plan of action for high school integration.

Mr. McBride stated that in the future all citizens must work together for the school system and there would be no distinctions made between any of the students in the total school program.

The group of citizens who were present approved the decision reached by the Board and left the meeting well satisfied (Our italics) (8/30/54)

The ironies of rational arguments, 'thirty hours in the classroom and twenty-five hours on a bus,' in the service of short term political interests and long term equity and justice at different points in time seem part of the human condition in Milford and elsewhere.

A Tentative Conclusion

The American Dilemma is Gunnar Myrdal's classic phrasing of America's continued perplexity over the relationships between and among its Black and White citizens. From the mid 1920s until 1955, Milford maintained a small elementary school for the children of Black families who resided in the district, and, on occasion, for children from adjacent districts whose numbers were insufficient to support a school. Midwest law prohibited the children from the two races to be educated together. Black adolescents attended high school in Metropolitan City or in Green City, the one suburban community that maintained a separate Black high school.

The story, as a Board of Education issue, ended for the moment in the 1954–55 and 1955–56 years with the series of decisions by the US Supreme Court, rulings by the Midwest State Attorney General and decisions by the Milford Board of Education. The issue remained dormant for over a decade, then with all the twists, turns, and convolutions typical of social change, conflicting values, and the continuing tensions between majority will and minority right, it arose once again in the mid 1960s. This time it would have the form of a series of skirmishes. The time after it would be with all the force of one of the major issues in the district in the mid and late 1970s. It is an imperative issue for us in our understanding of 'innovation and change at the Kensington Elementary School,' for Kensington which was 100 per cent White in 1964–65 when we first studied it, became 60 per cent Black and 40 per cent White by 1979–80, the year we returned to the school. For the 1980s even larger issues seem on the horizon as mandatory desegregation of the metropolitan area moves through the courts, judges' orders, legislative action, and a groundswell of conflicting public opinion organizing into political action are all in contention.

When emotion, prejudice, and multiple moralistic stances are so much a part of an issue, as they seem to be with this one, and so cloud the 'realities' of an issue, it seems important to present, as well as we can, the particulars of one school and one school district. We are neither so naive to believe we can be 'objective' in some ultimate sense nor to believe that intense, strongly held and conflicting political issues can be solved by such 'objective' data and analyses. But situations change, old participants leave the scene and new ones arrive. Human action often shows flashes of creativity, insight, and compassion. Integrative and compromise solutions appear, and democracy staggers along. Vivid, clear, and somewhat detached images, stories, and interpretations, so we believe, can be a helpful part of these processes.

The Teacher as Innovator

Into the flow of the narrative comes an item which captures another major change in the district — a teacher of some half dozen years was fired. The 'to-do' surrounding the event reflects important differences from the early on 'good old days' of the 1920s and 1930s. On 10 April of 1959 the Board noted that the tax levy passed (1936 to 553), swore in the two unopposed incumbent Board members who were re-elected, and attended to the series of decisions involved in placing all teachers on a salary schedule and the recommendations from CTA, a Community Teacher Association Committee which had been meeting in regard to the January 1958 schedule. Most of these were moves in accord with the position established by the National Education Association. The Superintendent listed those teachers recommended for rehiring, those teachers 'not wishing re-employment,' and three teachers not recommended for re-employment. The latter were to be officially notified immediately. One of the three was Mr. Nussbaum from the high school.

At the 28 April Board meeting, his letter was read asking for a hearing 'regarding the non renewal of his teacher's contract.' 'After considerable discussion' the Board voted to grant him an audience. The next evening, 29 April in special session the Board heard two teachers, including Mr. Nussbaum. In his opening remarks he indicated he had been in the district for seven years and that there was no change over those years. He also indicated he had consulted with a lawyer and had brought him along for consultation even though this wasn't strictly a legal hearing. Mr. Nussbaum thus read a February letter from the Principal. Mr. Nussbaum's reply to the Principal was then read. We have included these as Figures 18 and 19.

The minutes gradually unfold the complexities of the issues and the several perspectives on those issues. We include, *verbatim*, the several pages:

Mr. Nussbaum stated that neither one of the principals gave him the guidance he asked for.

Mr. Ramsey (the lawyer) said that Mr. Nussbaum never received a

Figure 18: Letter Regarding Points of Concern

February 25, 1959

Dear Mr. Nussbaum:

I wish to confirm our conference which was held on February 19, 1959 regarding your major weaknesses as a teacher at Milford Senior High School. At this conference we pointed out various aspects of your professional career.

Mr. Ritter has had conferences with you at various times concerning your status. They have not produced the desired results, therefore, I feel it necessary to inform you about these points that are of a serious nature. It is evident that the following areas are of major concern:

1   Your absence from assigned duties
2   Negligence in showing proper leadership in a classroom
3   Poor class control
4   Familiarity with students.

It is our desire to be of assistance, and we trust that you will avail yourself of our help. Please feel free to contact me at any time if you have questions regarding the above points.

Sincerely,

Allen R. Eastman
Principal

cc: Macon
      Ritter

Figure 19: Letter Requesting Clarification

Dear Mr. Eastman:

After our conference on February 19th, and upon receipt of your letter of February 26th, I gave much thought and consideration to the four points raised in your letter.

It has been, and still is, my sincere belief that I have always willingly and satisfactorily fulfilled my obligations as a teacher to both the administration and the students. However I would appreciate your writing in detail a clarification of the four points set forth in your letter, and would be grateful also for any suggestions you might care to offer for my future guidance.

Sincerely,

N. E, Nussbaum

cc: Macon
      Ritter

communication after 4 March 1959, in regard to his replying to the letter.

Mr. Quigley asked if he had any conferences. He replied yes, one in January of 1959. This was in regard to switching of hall duty with Miss Dalton without the Principal's approval.

Mr. Trotter asked if he had any previous conferences of last year, and he replied yes; in regard to punctuality. He had one conference.

Mr. Nussbaum said as to Point 2 in the letter which is 'Negligence' in showing proper leadership in a classroom, that he felt he had very good leadership. He stated that he was a departmental head of a group of teachers and is looked upon as an experienced teacher.

He felt that during one of his social drama presentations, if one were to go by the room, one would think that it was not good leadership in the classroom. However, he felt that what he was trying to do was good for the students.

Mr. Nussbaum stated that on Point Three, which is 'Poor Class Control,' that he felt he had no discipline problems in the classroom at all.

Mr. Nussbaum stated on Point Four, which is 'Familiarity with Students,' that at one time Mr. Ritter said a youngster did come up from behind and flip a bow tie combination that he had on. He did not really notice this and this is when Mr. Ritter claimed he had familiarity with students.

Another time when the bell was about to ring he asked some youngster to erase the blackboard. He was little and could not reach the top. Mr Nussbaum said he gave him a boost and Mr. Ritter saw this and felt he was too familar with the youngster.

Mr. Nussbaum felt he is an experienced teacher, that he handled his duties fine and that his punctuality was fine.

Mr. Nussbaum stated that seven (7) years ago he was to have talked up the Union with the teachers. He says he did not do this.

He did join the Union three years ago and has not talked up the Union at school. He did invite some teachers to a post-Christmas Meeting. He thought they would be favorable members. The men did attend this meeting and asked him for membership application cards and he gave them to one of the men. But, never did he hand out a card on school time. Mr. Eastman heard of this and found out that Mr. Nussbaum was a member and was *white with rage*. This was in mid 29 January 1959. He stated that Mr. Eastman told him that he was plenty shrewd because he did not do the dirty work; that he was clever and underhanded in giving out these cards. (Our italics)

Mr. Nussbaum feels that because of the Union incident, his position changed with Mr. Eastman.

Mr. McBride asked Mr. Nussbaum if at any time he was told that he was being dismissed because of the Union.

Mr. Nussbaum answered 'no.'

Mr. Trotter said there was no dismissal involved. Just no renewal of contract.

Mr. Nussbaum stated that he has not been doing all these things and he is capable of continuing to teach as he has done in the past six and a half years.

Mr. Nussbaum said he hoped the Board of Education can reconsider and re-employ him for the coming year and give him an opportunity in giving the service that he feels he capable of giving.

He stated that both parties are bound by this agreement.

Mr. Quigley explained that no teacher is bound to a contract. He can resign in the middle of a term and the Board does honor such resignation.

Mr. Quigley stated that since the state law was quoted several times, he would like to read it for the benefit of any concerned.

Mr. Quigley stated that the Board would take both Mr. Nussbaum and Mrs. Andrews' statements and that they would be given consideration by the Board of Education and notified of their decision. (4/29/59)

On 12 May the Board asked the Superintendent and Assistant Superintendent if they had changed their minds: 'Mr. McBride stated that after careful consideration they still have decided that in the interest of our orderly process of education, Mrs. Andrews and Mr. Nussbaum are not to be re-employed.' (5/12/59) The Board discussed the earlier statements and reaffirmed their decision.

At the 16 June meeting: 'Mr. Eads said he had received a telephone call from Mr. Nussbaum, stating that the Board of Education is to be sued and that they would be served with notices at the next Board meeting.' (6/16/59) In July Mr. McBride indicated that Mr. Irby would represent the Board members in the suit. In August Mr. Irby filed a memorandum of a 'Motion to Dismiss.' The case carried throughout the 1959–60 year and the dismissal date was set for 9 May 1960. Because of a change in Board members, the defendants were changed. Through all this (and other business) the school lawyer was on a $200 per month retainer. On 18 May 1960, Mr. McBride reported the case dismissed but that Mr. Ramsey, Mr. Nussbaum's lawyer would appeal.

The Board lawyer, Mr. Irby was on a regular $200 per month retainer. For legal services on the bond issue Mr. Irby's firm was paid $6000, of which $3000 was to Mr. Irby. In December of 1960 Mr. Irby's summary bill for the Nussbaum case was $1529.25. The Board tabled it. In January it was paid on a five to one vote. Mr. Tompkins opposed it. The negative vote questioned the legality of the payment in the absence of a written contract.

Mr. Nussbaum was gone.

The significance of the events falls mainly in the area of personnel policy and relative power of the several groups making up the school system. First, state law, as interpreted by the courts, sets boundaries and parameters to the discussion. At this time, a tenure law did not exist, the Board had the power to not re-employ teachers as the Board saw fit.

Second, for the first time in Milford, the non re-employment of a teacher involved a lawyer and extended legal proceedings.

Third, the beginnings of more formalized due process procedures were in place. The Board's recently adopted and amended policy statement on 'salary schedules' was broader than salaries and began to address a variety of conditions of employment. Conferences had been held with Mr. Nussbaum. Formal letters were exchanged and entered into the record. A hearing, which had long been a Milford procedure, was granted.

Fourth, the Board, while retaining formal power had, from the earliest years of the district records asked for teacher recommendations for all kinds of items, for example, school rules and discipline in the mid 1920s, had entertained teacher ideas and suggestions, and often, in the best collaborative manner sought to jointly work things out. At one point, during President Lewis' conflict with Mr. McBride, the Board had moved to have the teachers elect members of their own group to be representatives on a teacher committee. For whatever reasons, the teachers and especially the elementary teachers backed off and presented written letters indicating their support of Mr. McBride's selections. Most teachers seemed to want to teach and to leave administrative and policy issues in the hands of the administration and the Board.

Finally, the 'union issue' crossed uncomfortably in the episode. Reading the minutes — seven years service, department chairman, and only a few instances of lack of punctuality, teacher/pupil relationship concerns — leaves one with the feeling that more is going on than instructional problems. The 'white with rage' remark about the Principal's reaction and the Superintendent's concluding judgment 'in the interest of our orderly process of education' are also less than reassuring. Interview data from a retired elementary teacher evoked a comment about the Nussbaum affair: 'Mr. McBride was scared to death of the union' and 'he wouldn't have them in Milford.' No record appears of the Community Teachers Association's action in the matter, although later interview data indicated that in the eyes of one teacher, the head of the CTA was pressured to stay out of the conflict and not to provide a forum for Nussbaum. Nussbaum apparently knew of this and elected the legal route rather than professional peer action.

For anyone familiar with the labor movement and the long efforts to organize for collective bargaining, the establishment of salary schedules, and the establishment of tenure for teachers, our Nussbaum story will be an old tale. We include it for several overlapping reasons. First it represents the real and clear difficulties of attempts on the part of teachers to innovate in the area of democratizing schooling, in the sense of formally shifting power relationships in the schools.

Second the story also indicates the difficulties in getting clear knowledge of what is happening. Nussbaum's firing, in our latter day view, was for trumped up charges of classroom control and familiarity with students. Charges that sounded 'funny' regarding a teacher with seven years of service and who was a departmental chair, when we first read them in the minutes. The triangulation of data from two retired teachers regarding the administration and the Board's feelings on the status of unions in the Milford Schools is one of our most potent illustrations.

Our third point, mostly by inference, concerns the phrasing of the teachers' role. The comments allude to a number of small items which suggests a constrained quality regarding the nature of teaching in Milford: switching of hall duty, the defensiveness regarding a social drama presentation, the limits in informal relationships with students, and the controls over what one does out of school in one's private life.

In short, the teacher as an innovator, at this point in time, in Milford, seems like a contradiction in terms. Contrasts with the later Spanman era and similarities with the later Georgian period emphasize our systemic view of innovation and the fact that every part of the system is context for every other part. One simple moral for teachers is that there are times and occasions for cautiousness and care.

A Conclusion: The Politics of Innovation as the Most Basic Process?

As we have observed and thought about Mr McBride, Milford's long serving Superintendent, and the issues of innovation we are left with several conflicting images, almost negative cases in the area of 'planned change.' Innovation is not the label that comes the mind. Yet he was engaged in multiple 'specific planned changes' as we have defined the term. Rather it is the word 'politics' that comes to mind. Webster is enlightening here: 'the theory or practice of managing affairs of public policy or of political parties; hence, political affairs or the like; in a bad sense, dishonest management to secure the successes of political candidates or parties.' As the two meanings shade into evaluation an image of McBride as innovator appears.

One way to innovate is to bring new people to a position or a task. Our first illustration concerned the high school principalship and several of the incumbents. McBride sought changes to improve the school according to his vision of a good school. He ultimately was trapped by some of his administrative tactics.

Another way to innovate is through the action of a stong or 'potent' School Board member. Mr Lewis did that in several ways, by trying to urge Mr McBride into action and through the use of an outside social scientific survey. He was not successful, at least at the moment. A decade later, another Board member, voicing many similar concerns would be successful.

A third way to innovate is for a teacher to organize like minded colleagues into a union. Whether there was a push for staff power, colleagial authority, or democracy in the workplace in Milford at this time is not clear. This kind of political innovation, which we return to later as well, is one of the most far reaching for it seeks to change the form of governance as well as possible substantive changes in schooling *per se*. Mr McBride, with the support of the school board, did not want such innovations, and acted to prevent them.

In short we have several pictures of the politics of innovation, mostly *vis a vis* the position of the Superintendent, who valued alternatives other than those being proposed. We have not used the term 'resistance to change' because it assumes that everyone, except some ill-informed or ill-willed individuals, agrees on what is good and desirable. In presenting Mr McBride we wanted to see the world more from his perspective. His 'innovativeness' and 'resistance to change' was more complicated than is usually implied by those terms.

But, in a sense, all this is preamble to a more positive way of phrasing the issues of innovation. In keeping with the overall subtitle of the monograph, *History, Politics, and Agency*, we have looked at the multiple parts of the Milford School District and posed a critical illustration or two when each acts as innovative agent, the origin of specific planned change. The political interests of each is often brought into conflict with the others, and sometimes it is high conflict worthy of tragic drama.

We stayed, roughly, with a chronological time line even through this long analytical chapter, for part of history is the development of social structure. Each later innovative attempt occurs with an enlarged and enhanced backdrop of people, relationships, understandings, and rules. We have always liked the label, 'quasi-stationary equilibrium,' a set of identifiable relationships among the elements of any open social system, which provide a context for any purposive individual or collective act, innovative or recurring.

Overall, the improvements in Milford seemed part of modernization. Item by item the school system changed in ways that eventually made it less rural and less isolated and more and more like the contemporary scene in American social life. The 'progress' of the twentieth century was rapidly being brought into the Milford Schools.

Notes

1   An outstate small town.
2   Reading Peshkin's (1978) account of rural Mansfield, its High School and the centrality of athletics to the community clarifies how important such an issue might be perceived to be by the Superintendent.
3   To anticipate our story, these changes did occur. The third junior high was never constructed.
4   In addition the tax levy for the teachers fund and for the incidental fund were both deafeated. A third issue, transfer of a small piece of Milford property to another district was also defeated.
5   We have not been able to find a comprehensive history of Black Education in Suburban County. For some interesting similarities see our study of the Alte School District (Smith, 1978).
6   Mrs. Shields later helped integrate another community school system after 1954, has been a successful and respected elementary and high school teacher, and won a 'teacher of the year award.' She left the Milford District because of declining enrollments and a desire to start a family.
7   For some similar comments on other schools in other communities see Peshkin (1978, pp. 203–206).

Radicalism and Conservatism: The High Drama of Innovation

Chapter 7

Milford's Shooting Star: Steven Spanman

Prologue

Where to begin? This seems both our problem as social scientists now as it had been Milford's problem as locale for Steven Spanman, the individual most responsible for its most noteworthy innovation, the Kensington Elementary School. The slightly pejorative term, 'shooting star,' belongs to a latter day Kensington staff member, who felt that the Spanman era had been given too much prominence in our early reports on the school, and that Spanman's quick coming and going, and as brilliant as the fire, if not light, had been, was less than the contributions of others to the history and present status of the school district.

Further, we have already introduced him as McBride's successor in 'the tangle of administrative succession' in the introductory story of this monograph. In addition he appeared at many points in *Anatomy of Educational Innovation*, Smith and Keith's (1971) earlier account of the first year in the life of the Kensington Elementary School. Even more significantly he is a central individual in the analysis of the original faculty and staff of the Kensington School and the Milford District in *Educational Innovators: Then and Now*, and of the history of the school, *The Fate of an Innovative School: The First Fifteen Years of the Kensington School*. These are Books I and II in the Kensington Revisited trilogy.

As we recounted earlier, a new era began in the Milford School District in the Summer of 1962. Dr. Steven Spanman was now Superintendent. He had not arrived for the July School Board meeting. Business was attended to as usual with Mr. Fairfax representing the administration. Messrs. Baskin, Osborn, Quigley, Tompkins, and Wilkerson were present. Mr. Henderson was on vacation. The only directives to Dr. Spanman noted in the Board minutes concerned enrollment. Dr. Spanman was to contact the Superintendent of the Catholic Diocesan Schools to: '. . . ascertain the enrollment plans in the elementary schools for the next three years, as it would affect the Milford School District.' (7/24/62) and to: '. . . submit a complete report and recommendations on the projected enrollment patterns and the area need for school building programs.' (7/24/62) This, too, passed unanimously.

174

A minute existed on the purchasing of lots for a building site. A letter from a local architectural firm, Marland and Enright, which had built the Hillside School, indicated their desire to design any new schools, possibly adapting an existing plan. What was to become the Kensington School was in the offing.

The First Board Meeting

The new Superintendent was present at the 28 August meeting. The agenda was long and the minutes were full of items carrying the phrase 'as recommended by the Superintendent.' Each item passed unanimously. Perhaps, our knowledge of Spanman clouded our views, but we believe anyone reading the minutes would come away with a feeling that an active, take-charge individual was the new incumbent in the Superintendent position. The Superintendent's mimeographed agenda was now enclosed with the minutes 'for purposes of reference.' Sixteen items were elaborated in the twenty-three page, typed single space, statement. Our intent is to explore this first meeting in some detail for it seems to capture much of Spanman's personality, perspective, and administrative style. These make up our growing conception of agency, the individual as agent.

The Content of the Agenda

Item by item, the content varied in importance and breadth of impact. Item one dealt with a longstanding inequity in Suburban County's tax rate. The Board was urged to go on record in support of the attempt for equalization. Milford, as one of the larger and less wealthy districts, would profit thereby. With his recommendation, Spanman moved directly into a major issue in Suburban County, equalization of resources for the schools. Beyond the content itself, we are left with an image of Spanman's ability as a 'quick study.' During our investigation, casual conversations and interviews with Central Office personnel, both professional and nonprofessional, reveal perceptions such as 'brilliant' and 'imaginative.'

Item two dealt with the 'Organization of the Administrative and Supervisory Staff.' The Assistant Superintendent and business officials who were reporting directly to the Board since the McBride conflict, were now to report to the Superintendent. Illustratively:

2.2 All recommendations and formal communications to the Board of Education will be made through the Superintendent.
2.3 State reports and other official communications from the school district, including press releases, will go out over the Superintendent's signature.

The concerns for rethinking the district's organizational structure led to a concluding recommendation:

   ... authorize the central staff to examine critically the present organizational structure to determine whether it fulfills the needs of the school system and to make suggestions for the improvement and development of its structure.

For all the noises about 'democracy' in the Kensington School, and that was a real and important issue (See *Anatomy*, Chapter 8, pp. 235–278), Spanman's action at the district level left it very clear that he was to be the center of power and communication. Further, organizational structure of the district had been a problem plaguing Mr. McBride, the prior Superintendent, in his major quarrels with the two Board Presidents, Mr. Lewis in the early 1950s and Mr. Tompkins in the early 1960s. The main lines were now clear in reporting to Spanman. Other pieces of possible change would be studied and reported on by the Central Office staff, always through him.

Item three requested authorization for the hiring of a 'communications secretary.' This was part of a larger effort to have a professional educator responsible as Director of Communications:

> In the opinion of the staff, communication is one of the most important aspects of administration. The quality of the program depends greatly upon a school district's ability to communicate with its own members as well as with its patrons and interested citizens.

An incumbent for the secretarial position, Mrs. Virginia Fillmore was named and approved. Her story will flow into broader district events for later she became secretary to the Superintendent and to the Board, probably the most important nonprofessional staff position in the district, and remains in that position to the present.

Item four, Invitation Extended to Metropolitan Superintendent's Association for the Fall meeting to be held at the new Milford Junior High School. 'This item is for information,' so read the minutes. Spanman seems to be testing the local superintendency waters. They are invited to his turf and to see Milford's new Junior High School. At a minimum the inference is that he moves quickly in contacts with his peers.

Item five, Amendments to Transportation Policy Recommendation, eliminated a controversial $1.00 surcharge over the $36.00 bus fee for students who lived less than a mile from school. Little items become big issues on occasion. Transportation has been one of those never ending sore spots in the district for three decades. Eliminating the dollar fee seemed an attempt to ease one of those 'little' problems. As we discovered earlier, a school district engages in many tasks beyond or subsidiary to its central educational functions. Transportation is like insurance, cafeterias, maintenance, and leaking roofs, problems which never really get solved but require continuing, steady attention. More than some of the others, it contained an important aspect of impinging directly and daily upon the patrons.

Item six responded to the request of a parent to have his son admitted to first grade. The problem involved an 12 October birthdate; school policy required the child to be six on or before 15 September. The extenuating circumstances were a move from another community where the child had had six months of nursery school, a full year of kindergarten, and a recommendation for promotion to first grade. The Superintendent recommended that the parents' request be denied. These realities contrast sharply with the idealism later articulated at Kensington in its ultimate goals of individualization as to entrance, graduation, hours of daily attendance, and days of yearly attendance.

Item seven reported on the Summer Instrumental Music program which served 200 youngsters and for the second year showed a slight financial profit for the district. As we have indicated, music has been a major part of Milford's curriculum from the beginnings of the District.

Item eight reported on a meeting between Spanman and the Superintendent of the Archdiocesan Schools, 'the meeting was very profitable and beneficial.' The Milford community has always had a large parochial population. At a prior meeting of the Board, they had directed the Superintendent to inquire regarding enrollment projections. He responded immediately.

Item nine was a request by the Superintendent to permit his acceptance of an invitation to make an audio visual presentation, at no expense to the district, to a seminar of '. . . a most interesting and especialy well-informed cross section of military, academic, governmental, and industrial personnel.' Dr. Spanman is both an engaging lecturer and a proponent of technology in the schools. National exposure was a part of his continuing agenda. Cosmopolitanism was part of his style. Technological innovations were part of the promise of education's future.

Item ten, Consultant Services of the Architectual Design Institute (ADI) plays directly into what will become the Kensington School and extends our understanding of the organizational and administrative roots of educational innovation; consequently, we reproduce verbatim the several paragraphs in the agenda:

Dr. James Holland, Director of the Architectual Design Institute, has indicated that he and his staff are interested in giving assistance in school planning for the Milford School District. The cost to the district for such services would be $2000 which would include consultant fees, travel, lodging, etc. The amount paid by the school district would be supplemented in the sum of $7000 which would result from a grant from the Olds Foundation. The $2000 contributed by the Milford School District would allow for the necessary consultants as well as pay a portion of the cost of the whole project. This amount is consistent with that charged to other school systems by the Architectual Design Institute. No direct payment to any individual working on a project would be made by the Milford School District as the ADI would make payments out of its funds for all travel and lodging as well as for publication of educational specifications or other reports.

The Architectual Design Institute is interested in school systems searching for new knowledge and wishes to leave to others who have more money (like the federal government) to help people who have no ideas. Many new ideas are currently under investigation by the District's Curriculum Study. (Our italics)

In terms of actual building cost, the ADI consultants would be a saving. As a more important consideration, such consultant assistance would enable the administration and staff to design the facilities that would reflect the educational needs of the school district. At present, the school system has indicated that assistance by the Architectual Design Institute would enable the staff to define more precisely and efficiently those programs already under consideration by the Milford School District. Of tremendous importance, such consultant service would equip our staff with valid criteria upon which to make sound evaluation of our existing and proposed programs.

The Architectual Design Institute would provide the much desired consultant services for assisting the staff in determining the educational specifications from which the most efficient architectual plans could be developed for the proposed Kensington Elementary School.

Recommendation: It is recommended to the Board of Education by the Central Staff that the consultant services of the Architectual Design Institute be secured at a cost to the district of $2000.

As with all the recommendations in the meeting, this, too, passed unanimously. The new Superintendent was moving the district into contact with national organizations, resources, and ideas. Our italicized paragraph presents an item suggesting hypotheses of both an elitism and an anti-federal government perspective.

Item eleven, Progress on the Language Laboratory, seems to carry multiple messages as well. It, too, is reproduced verbatim:

Upon their return from vacation during the first week of August, members of the administrative staff were greatly disappointed that very little work had been done on the Language Laboratory during the month of July. Vacation, an accident to one of the workers, and the lack of an essential part were the reasons given by the company. The Superintendent of Schools, the Supervising Principal of Secondary Education, and the Coordinator of Curriculum Research were in repeated telephone conversations with the company. Each time, the company gave assurance that the installation would be completed during the following week. However, each time a new deadline approached, very little progress was apparent.

In a letter dated August 20, the Superintendent of Schools informed National Technology Corporation that, if they could not give written confirmation of the installation date, the School District would be reluctant to implement the program after August 27. In response, a representative of National Technology Corporation met with members of the administrative staff and informed them that the earliest possible completion date would be September 4. The company was again informed of the school district's position. After a phone conversation with his general manager, the company representative assured the school district that the laboratory would be completed no later than August 27. The administrators felt that this was a satisfactory completion date as it would still allow four days for the teachers to conduct their scheduled workshop.

Friday, August 24, four workers renewed the progress on the Laboratory. They were scheduled to continue all day Saturday and Sunday to complete the installation by the August 27 date.

'A shaker and a mover' is another label which has remained as part of Spanman's reputation with Milford school personnel. Lurking behind that was a sense of efficacy, a view that the education world was malleable through his efforts.[1]

Item twelve dealt with Inservice Programs and indicated that scheduling was underway for the programs outlined in the June Board meeting. Shortly, the pattern of these will appear as the specific items are listed and then actualized.

Items thirteen and fourteen were one line acknowledgements of the Treasurer's Report and the Payment of Bills. Item fifteen requested five administrators be expensed to the State Meeting of Secondary School Principals. At their best, professional meetings are a means of peer education — usually in pleasant circumstances and surroundings. Spanman was involved personally and expected his Board, his administrative staff and his teachers to be involved. Such education was expensive. In this instance, the principals were to travel with District Funds. The Board, on this occasion, approved.

Item sixteen, Population Building Study Recommended, raised the issues of long term planning, an analysis of current facilities and their adequacy, population projections and additional space, and curriculum evaluation and development regarding the instructional program. This large scale effort also provided for the involvement of the former Superintendent who was now a senior consultant: 'It is further recommended that Mr. McBride be appointed to serve as coordinator of the study, reporting directly to and responsible to the Superintendent of Schools.' The activities and treatment of a prior Superintendent who had been relieved of his responsibilities is no mean problem. In the eyes of most observers, Spanman had restored some of the dignity and respect due to McBride.

Item seventeen involved a continuation of a Depository Agreement with a local Bank and Trust Company.

Item eighteen, Employment of Architect and items nineteen and twenty on the school site for Kensington fall together. The parcels of land were being accumulated lot by lot. The move toward the selection of the architect was a part of a larger strategy:

> Considerable amount of educational planning must be done by the administrative and supervisory staff before an architect is engaged to design the building for the Kensington Elementary School. It is the opinion of the staff that obtaining the services of an architect as a first step toward the acquisition of a new building is a mistake. An architect should be engaged only after the staff and the Board know exactly what educational program it wishes to offer the children and what spaces are needed to house the program. It is at this point that the talents of an architect can be utilized

most advantageously. The more information the architect is given in the form of educational specifications, the better job he can do toward satisfying the educational needs of the pupils served by the school. The Architectual Design Institute (assuming approval of the recommendation submitted in Item ten) will assist the staff in determining the educational specifications.

The Superintendent presented an explicit procedure for selecting an architect — publicizing the District's intent, initial screening by administrative staff, final evaluation and selection by the Board. Almost for the first time, education, the curriculum,the goals, and the content were to be taken as problematic. Prior to this an unquestioned consensus seemed to exist as conventional wisdom in the Milford community. Buildings followed 'naturally' upon that wisdom. In our effort to understand innovation and change, more and more we have been struck with the importance 'of what one makes problematic.'

Item twenty-one involved the distribution of an Audit Report which would be discussed at the next meeting. Item twenty-two involved personnel: three resignations, eight elections, six contract changes (for example, finished MAs), and announcement of six remaining vacancies. Item twenty-three reported on a Superintendent's meeting with the State Commissioner of Education.

Item twenty-four dealt with 'Real Estate Development: Implications for Future School Planning.' Discussion was specifically on the Islington Apartments. Already thirty-two elementary age pupils are in eighty rented apartments, 190 units are completed, another thirty will be ready by Christmas, and 440 will be the final total. A survey of ten developers indicate that 702 additional school age youngsters will appear.

Item twenty-five presented a safety engineer's report and Item twenty-six described the Williams School's Landscaping Plans using $500 raised at last year's 'Fun Fare.' The Williams School Committee had altered its original plans somewhat, because of expenses. The Superintendent's recommendation was simple: 'It is recommended that the Williams School PTA and Mothers' Club alternate plans for landscaping be approved.'

The Structure of the Agenda

One doesn't have to be a McLuhan fan to appreciate that much of the message is in the medium. A half dozen items accent the perspective. First, the materials were organized and well written. Each point was made in a topic sentence or short paragraph. The next paragraph or two spelled out the sub issues involved. In an important sense, one might infer that the Superintendent was educating his Board with clear, concise, well reasoned items.

Second, each item culminated in recommendations. The Board was to go on record to take quite specific action. Discussions were background reasons and arguments. They were not idle chatter. They led to actions which were to improve the education of the youngsters of Milford. Concepts such as practical reasoning and theory of action spring out at the reader.

Third, the comprehensiveness of the agenda, the quantity of issues, and the detail were overwhelming. To disagree would take considerable study, strength of character, and intellect. The Superintendent was creating an image of strength and power, a man who knew what he wanted and how to get it.

Fourth, the Superintendent was opening up relationships with the many people, facets, positions, and organizations of his world. These include the other superintendents, the archdiocesan schools, and national corporations supplying new educational technology. He was going to be centrally involved. And that's the position from which things get done.

Fifth, those social scientists who focus on interaction would discern that the 'origin' or 'initiation' of interaction had an exemplar in Spanman. Clearly he was in charge of administration within the District.

Antecedents of the Meeting

But full agendas such as the one of August 1962 do not arise from the ether. Rather, as in the performance of a symphony, they are orchestrated and involve considerable effort. Two letters from the President and Director of Programs of ADI indicate a bit about antecedents of the meeting. For practioners, the antecedents build images of practical action that might be taken. The President's letter is dated 19 June before Spanman arrived in Milford.

Prior to coming to Milford, Spanman was part of a network out of Eastern University. People who knew people had put his name on the short list for the Milford superintendency. In addition, we now see that he knows people who know people, people who are doing things, and people who want to do things. The leaders of the Olds Foundation and the Architectual Design Institute (ADI) are of that order. They seem entrepreneurial, flexible in agendas toward their goals, and a bit on the elitist side. A tenor of excitement in the air pervades the letter and the assumptions behind the stated items. Spanman's quoting in his agenda the pungent line on 'significant ideas' versus 'government money' suggests that he has a talent for playing the game.

Figure 20: Letter from ADI President

Dear Steven:

Bill Hastings called me a few days ago to tell me the good news of your move to Milford. He described it as a first rate system.

I indicated as far as ADI is concerned, we leave the choice of communities in which he works entirely up to him. He was worried about the distance but I told him to disregard distance if the idea being pursued is sufficiently significant. As an Institute we are *interested in new knowledge, and leave to others who have more money (like the Federal Government) to help people who have no ideas.* (Our italics)

From meeting you in Atlantic City, I would guess that Milford, with you as Superintendent, would not be classified in the latter category.

With every good wish for your new administration.

Cordially,

An 11 July letter from the ADI Director of Programs began this way:

> It was nice to hear from you and to learn of your continued interest in the possibility of us giving some assistance in school planning. We have talked with Jack Hullings and found that he was very anxious to get someone started in Midwest since no one had asked for any help from there.

He went on to spell out the agreements of $2000 and $7000 and his arrangements which Spanman had quoted verbatim into his Board agenda item. The concluding paragraph suggested the longer reach of the waltz: 'I would like to add too, that we would like very much to continue to work with you on a continuing basis in the event we reach an agreement for the first year's services.' The commitments while small in dollar amounts were large in two ways. Spanman, the Milford District, and ultimately, the Kensington School was to be ADI's exemplar in Midwest State and the Central Region of the country. Second, the initial contract was not only just that but it was also a gambit for a continuing relationship beyond the first year. Each side was investing tentatively with longer term options.

Conclusion

A detailed presentation of the agenda of a single Board meeting invites a consideration of pros and cons. The totality of a single meeting conveys just that, a totality. Second, the reader, and the Board as well, is capturing a first look at the Superintendent in action. Primacy effects in perception and attitude formation have earned a place in many summaries of research. Third, and as later data will document, the first meeting is not an atypical sample of Spanman in action. As a side show barker or TV commentator might say, 'What you see is what you got, and what you got is what you bought.' Spanman has a large agenda, he knows what he wants, he tried with considerable care with his Board to persuade-through-education.

The Year Continues

Planning and Doing

Visionaries are sometimes accused of missing the steps between the bottom and top of ladders or between their present location and the vistas on the horizon. Spanman didn't have that problem — at least initially. A tentative program for curriculum presentations to the Board was submitted and approved at the September meeting. Figure 21 suggests the scope and sequence of that agenda. A similar agenda for Inservice Teacher Education Programs appeared also. Not only were children to be educated but so, too, were Board members and teachers.

The Board presentations were all by Milford teachers. The workshop courses and

Figure 21: Tentative Program for Board Curriculum Meetings 1962–63

September	Mathematical Experience
October	The Principals' Role as Instructional Leaders
November	Social Experience: the Study of Man
December	Guiding Life in the School
January	Educational Specifications: Kensington School
February	Evaluation of District Programs
March	Creative Experiences
April	Scientific Experiences: Developing Scientific Concepts
May	Vocational Experiences
June	Evaluating Change in Children and Youth

Figure 22: Format for Curriculum Presentations to the Board

   I   General Overview of Present Curriculum
  II   Problems Inherent in Present Curriculum
 III   Promising Practices and Proposals
      A   Incidental Teaching (Elementary)
      B   Modified Platoon School (Elementary)
      C   Correlated Studies (Junior High School)
      D   Cooperative Teaching (High School)
      E   Instruction on Totalitarian Ideology
 IV   Question Period—Members of Board of Education and Audience

consultancies were all by individuals outside the district. Some were for graduate credit, others for local inservice credit.

In September the Board approved: 'Notice was given that the Superintendent has been extended an invitation to membership on a national educational organization Conference Planning Committee.' (9/62) A motion supporting this activity was made, recorded, and approved unanimously by the Board. In addition, 'central staff responsible for curriculum improvement and development' were expensed to the state ASCD meeting. Similarly, released time was provided teachers and guidance counselors for attendance at state meetings. The latter was not unusual. The image is that everything and everyone is on the move.

The upper echelons of the Central Office staff were in place immediately as indicated on the letterhead of district stationery. In effect, the staff reorganization was accomplished immediately.

The curriculum presentations, entitled Curriculum Orientation Series, seemed, at least in their outline and titles of presentations, something a little different. For instance the social studies program in October was listed this way, as presented in Figure 22.

This outline, we would contend, is an exemplar of practical reasoning. Further it is a reform oriented way of reporting. Innovations are its outcome. The 'general overview of the present curriculum' gives the status quo proponents a chance to state their case. The 'problems inherent in the present curriculum' gives the critics their day. The 'promising practices and proposals' has a double edged cut — ideas and practices, abstract and concrete manifestations. 'Promising' suggests the lure of the tentative and the hopeful. And, finally, the Board and interested community patrons have their day, to raise questions and to comment from whatever perspectives they care to raise and share.

It seems important to note also that while we have focused our account of 1961–62 on the Superintendent's initiatives and shortly on issues related to building the Kensington School, life went on in the schools. The busy agenda continued — as always.

Personnel Policies and Practies

Among the various policies discussed in the Autumn of 1962, one of the most far reaching involved 'selection of personnel.' In the Superintendent's agenda it was stated this way:

> Employees of the school district shall be appointed only upon the recommendation of the Superintendent. Should a person nominated by the Superintendent be rejected by the Board, it shall be the duty of the Superintendent to make another nomination.
>
> It shall be the duty of the Superintendent of Schools to see that persons nominated for employment shall meet all qualifications established by law and by the Board for the type of position for which nomination is made. (12/11/61)

Historians of Milford, and presumably other districts as well, will see this as a long jump from the early days when the Board recruited, interviewed, and elected teachers at their own initiative. Now the Superintendent possessed this initiative. The bureaucratic details, for example, delegation and specific procedures, were spelled out in a twelve page document. Shortly thereafter a nine state teacher recruiting program was implemented.

Throughout the first year the Board received announcements of the Superintendent's national activities as speaker, consultant, and active role-player in professional organizations. Consistently they supported these activities with released time away from the district sometimes they contributed expenses as well. At AASA, he chaired one program and was panelist on a second. The Board expensed him and two members to the annual meeting. The Superintendent modeled the active national stance. On occasion he educated his Board by taking them along. The record contains also numerous items: announcements, letters, requests, and thank you notes from personnel at all levels of the professional staff regarding similar opportunities at local, state, and national levels. The spillover of stimulation and reinforcement flowed in multiple directions.

Internally a major shift occurred in the Central Office staff. Mr. Fairfax, the Business Official, upon the recommendation of the Superintendent, was 'reassigned from his present duties to the substitute teacher pool, effective immediately.' Mr. Ranson replaced him as 'Administrative Assistant for Business Services.' The Board gave its approval unanimously.

The Superintendent seemed to be using the array of options available to his position in moving the district internally. First, he adjusted the bureaucratic conditions, to use a phrase of Blau's (1956) as in reorganizing the interactional arrangements of who reports to whom and in clarifying policy. Second, he educated everyone in the system — himself, the Board, the Central Office staff, the principals, and teachers, Third, he selected, both hiring and firing, key personnel. Playing those strands in harmony seems a very sophisticated set of administrative skills.

Ending the First Year

The Spring of 1963 juxtaposed ironically several events which emphasize the human dimensions of the educational enterprise. Mr. McBride, the long term Superintendent who was ousted in a bitter fight and who served out the remaining two years of his contract as a Senior Consultant to the district, received a testamonial dinner in March. Shortly thereafter, on Superintendent Spanman's recommendation, Mr. McBride was granted a leave of absence with pay for the last three months of his contract. Second, in March the Board moved and passed unanimously a Certification of Appreciation to Mr. Quigley, a Board member for twelve years, for his service to the District. The President of the Board was Mr. Tompkins, a long term opponent of his. Superintendent Spanman received a new three year contract on a unanimous vote. A week later, Mr. Tompkins, the only incumbent running for re-election was defeated at the polls. Politically, one of Spanman's opponents retired, one of his supporters lost at the polls. Consensus and unanimity in the community and within the Board seemed not a part of the scene.

The new Superintendent continued to lecture at national educational meetings and he continued to publish articles in educational journals on such topics as: 'The Superintendent's concern for curriculum and instruction' and 'New directions for elementary education.' Meetings held in the local metropolitan area provided opportunities to bring visitors to the district, this time for a view of the recently completed but award winning high school building.

The continuing energy being poured into the District by the Superintendent and staff can be seen in these other activities recorded in considerable detail in the minutes and agendas on auditing, insurance and a policy handbook. The latter, the policy handbook, was built around six 'policy study committees':

1 Community-School Relations
2 Organizations and Administrators
3 School Finance and Business Management
4 Staff Personnel
5 Pupil Personnel
6 Instruction and Curriculum

These committees met for several years. They labored valiantly. The product was a large blue covered, looseleaf policy handbook. It remains in the district to this day, with some regular updating. In some ways, it might be argued that this was one of Spanman's most important and lasting innovations.

Proposals for the first summer elementary school also appeared. Its functions were simple but classic:

1   Opportunities for participation in areas of interest (enrichment).
2   Opportunities for strengthening basic skills such as reading, listening, writing, and speaking (5/14/63)

Insofar as individual differences among youngsters is a major reality, extending the more able and raising the minimum competencies of the less able seems an important set of educational alternatives.

The Remaining Years of Spanman's Tenure

The detailed account of the first Board meeting set the tenor of Spanman's Superintendency. The flow of his first year accented the high rate of activity, the scope and interests of the planning and the doing, and the attention to personnel development throughout the system. The creation of the Kensington Elementary School was an early and central part of his programs. The image that arose had a number of aspects cutting across his personality, his perspective, and his administrative style. Such descriptors as imaginative educator, proactive, cosmopolitan, and practical reasoner captured the essence of the man. These elements were to remain throughout his tenure. Agency is a major concept in a theory of innovation. Now we return to the story of his next three years. Encased in that story is a further set of interpretations.

Year II: 1963–64

The Summer of 1963 seemed quiet. The board meetings were brief. The agenda items seemed a flow of unanimity that kept the District wheels turning. In August, the Board created the 'Citizens Advisory Committee of the Milford School District.' The committee was to be concerned with the 'building and educational needs' of the District and to have a membership of PTA and Mothers' Club presidents and other patrons after taking into consideration: socioeconomic level, geography, age, supporters and advocates of the public schools, parents and older residents. In keeping with the Superintendent's ability to capsule large issues in succinct statements, sometimes almost slogans, the agenda contained this brief paragraph:

> Citizenship participation has evolved slowly over the past generation and has been represented by a changing attitude on the part of educators, described as 'stay out — come and see — let's plan together.' The professional staff recognizes the tremendous potential in cooperative planning with patrons. (8/27/63)

At the Superintendent's request the Board unanimously voted to continue the relationship between the Architectual Design Institute (ADI) and to contribute

$2500 for that purpose. At that same meeting (August) the proposed Board Policy Book became a reality. The Inservice program (begun before Spanman's arrival) was to continue for a third year. The list of consultants contained the names of several nationally prominent educationists identified with the 'new elementary education' — individualized instruction, non gradedness, and team teaching.

For reasons not immediately apparent on the record, the Board reorganized itself, that is, changed officers, upon a unanimous series of votes. Mr. Ludwig became President and Mr. Baskin became Vice President. Following that, a resolution with several 'sweetness and light' 'whereases' concluded that the Board was the policy making body. The explicit wording was this:

> WHEREAS, The relationship between the Board of Education and the administrative staff of the Milford School District has been one of friendly good will and mutual respect, and
>
> WHEREAS, The Superintendent of Schools has been designated the responsibility for the execution of policies concerning the organization and administration, and
>
> WHEREAS, The Board of Education revised policies on August 27, 1963, clarifying the working relationship between the Board of Education and the administrative staff;
>
> THEREFORE BE IT RESOLVED, That the Board of Education reconfirm its interest to serve as the policy making body of the Milford School District and to delegate the execution of these policies to the administrative staff. (9/25/63)

The meeting adjourned shortly thereafter at 1:30 a.m. A strange item of human behavior? Were the 'rightful owners' trying to take back the store? Or, as several commentators told us in interviews, that the Superintendent presented the Board a 'me or him' choice between the Superintendent and the Board President because of the difficulties they had in working together. Mr. Wilkerson had been in the 4–2 minority opposing the hiring of Spanman. In a later interview, Spanman was to refer to this incident of change as equivalent to 'winning the battle and losing the war.' We will have more to say later on 'the politics of localism and proactive cosmopolitan leadership styles.' Manifestly, for the moment, a fragile quality seems to exist in the relationships among the incumbents, the Superintendent, the Board President, and the Board and their policy statements. More latently, a sturdy dynamic exists among such conceptions as politics, persuasion, power, policy, and the positions of school leadership.

At a 'lesser' or more mundane level, much of the year reads like the prior year. Spanman continued to receive invitations from diverse national groups to speak, to consult, or to join in as a member of a working conference. The Board continued to support this with time away from the District and, on occasion, expense money as well. Spanman was a busy, active, professional educator. Similarly, policy statements flowed out of subcommittees and typewriters continuously. 'The agenda was an inch thick at one Board meeting' recalled one staff member. The push for technology continued as various data processing systems, for example, IBM, were considered.

High school student scheduling was computerized through a contract with a local firm. Citizen involvement continued as well in multiple forms, most notably through the Citizens Advisory Committee. Discussions of future bond issues and tax levies continued.

In January of 1964, the Superintendent's agenda included two announcements conveying further the scope of his hopes for the District. First, the Dean of Education of City University, William Morrison, was to meet with District staff regarding a Milford — State Department — City University Program for Research and Development. He also raised a joint Summer program in nongraded curriculum and team teaching. The rationale was clear:

> School districts in America in the middle of the twentieth century no longer have adequate resources to appreciably change the behavior of teachers and students without the cooperation and wholesale involvement of other educational agencies, such as universities and state departments of education.
> ...develop closer working relationships between the various educational agencies in the fields of teacher recruitment, training, and research.
> The staff foresees university faculty members becoming involved with the School District and its problems. This involvement would be not only in a consulting capacity, but would include the development of curriculum materials for specific disciplines, and participation in the implementation and evaluation of projects.
> This item is for information. (1/25/64)

In a fundamental sense this was a major prelude to the Smith and Keith involvement and what was to culminate seven years later as *Anatomy of Educational Innovation* (1971). Spanman's net was adjustable.

The second item indicated a broadening of the kinds of relationships and a means for financing the activities. This item is reproduced *in toto:*

> XXII Proposal To Be Submitted To The Olds Foundation For A Financial Grant To Support A Comprehensive Project For Developing A Design For Learning.
> The administrative staff is convinced that the resources in the local school district are not fully adequate to reorganize content in the way that is necessary to prepare boys and girls for a living as well as to make a living.
> To date, the District has received three grants from the Architectual Design Institute, one grant from Technology, Inc., and the promise of several other grants from various sources. Included as Attachment II is a proposed project entitled, 'Comprehensive Project for Developing a Design for Learning.' It would be financed jointly by the Olds Foundation and the Milford School District. The duration of the project would be three years, starting July 1, 1964, and continuing through June 30, 1967.
> The Milford School District is concerned with a learning milieu in which the teacher and students 'find themselves.' This milieu includes

a) knowledge, b) the learner, c) the teacher, d) at a defined time, and e) a defined place or facility. It appears futile to believe that an appreciable alteration in one dimension, e.g., knowledge will not alter or effect change in other dimensions.

The proposed project would include a dynamic change in the learning milieu. It intends to develop a design for learning. The study will focus on the aspect of time and space, using knowledge as the constants; i.e., what time and space requirements are necessary to implement the desired knowledge.

Staff members have discussed the proposed project with officials of the Olds Foundation. A meeting is scheduled in February with Foundation officials at the AASA Convention in Atlantic City. (1/28/64)

To us, even two decades later, that appears as a powerful statement. First, a shift in goals is in place. Or, at least, an emphasis broader than an economic — earn a living — aspiration is being raised. This will require a reorganization of the content of schooling. Second, such a change will cost more than the District's local resources can provide. Third, some evidence appears that the District can compete for those resources necessary to move the chain of events along. Fourth, the conception of 'learning milieu' is based on a systemic view of interdependent elements. Fifth, the elements to be attacked directly, and here we seem to be back to the Kensington School, are its educational specifications and its physical structures built according to ideas and plans in the Specs. Sixth, the Superintendent's initiating, leading out quality is in evidence for the District has already been in touch with Foundation people. Finally, a clear statement of one kind of business transacted at national meetings appears. Spanman is an active participant in AASA.

Just as these plans were being developed, more local problems arose. The District voters defeated a million dollar bond issue and teacher's tax levy by roughly 1700 for to 2400 against. That's a long way from the necessary two-thirds majority required for new levies. Later, the Board split 5–1; Mr. Wilkerson, the former President, declining on the vote to resubmit. Two days later the Board met on a Saturday morning and reaffirmed its stand on pay for teachers and quality education. Then it indicated the consequences (threats?) if the 25 February submission was to fail. These included:

...1) assess a student instructional supply (fee) of $8.00 for senior high, $6.00 for junior high and $4.00 for elementary; 2) require payment of a secondary school textbook fee of $5.00 (grades 9, 10, 11, 12); 3) charge tuition for driver education instruction. $20.00 per student; and 4) reduce kindergarten program to one-half year.

It passed unanimously. Two former Board members, Edmond and Quigley, chaired the committee.

On 10 March 1964, within a month of these far reaching plans and hopes the District once again voted down the bond and tax proposals. They failed again to carry even a simple majority. The Board moved to implement its previously stated consequences. Only Mr. Wilkerson dissented.

On 24 March the week before the annual School Board elections, the current Board engaged in what had become a related sub-ritual. They voted a new three year contract to the Superintendent, 'at the same salary.' Here, too, Mr. Wilkerson dissented in a 5–1 vote.

Elementary school boundaries were in contention. Some children from a greater distance were being bussed from a dense neighborhood and children who were closer to Johnson School would have to walk to a farther elementary school. Further with increased building in their neighborhood, it was anticipated that:

> When it gets overcrowded at this point our children will then go through another redistricting program which will put them all back in the Johnson School from which they originally came. We protest this action before it gets started. (4/21/64)

The nature of neighborhoods, the issues of walking and bussing, and the policy of neighborhood schools has been with the District for a long time, arise from time to time, and will later become entangled with ethnic and racial changes in the School District. Conceptually these seem to be issues of political interest, conflict, and tentative resolution.

In May 1964, the Superintendent's passion for educating everyone and his passion for the novel and the creative appeared on the agenda as 'Item X, Tentative Instructional Meetings for 1964–65.' The item read this way:

> The staff, realizing its responsibilities for informing the patrons of the School District and members of the Board of Education of the nature and progress of the instructional program, plans to continue the series of monthly curriculum orientation meetings during the 1964–65 school year in accordance to Bylaw No. 9441 — Regular Meetings. The tentative program is as follows:
>
> September 8, 1964   Promising Practices in Elementary Education
> October 13, 1964   Promising Practices in Middle School
> November 10, 1964   Promising Practices in Senior High School
> January 12, 1965   New Methods to Organize Content
> February 9, 1965   New Methods of Organizing Pupils, Time, Space, and Teachers
> March 9, 1965   A Look at New Materials
> May 11, 1965   Plans for the Following Year

The energy, the staff organization, the planning abilities required for such 'simple' programs seems considerable.

So, Year II ended. Mr. Wilkerson, although no longer President of the Board remained in the critic's role and voted against several key items on the agenda. In this way he continued in the tradition of earlier incumbents we described as 'the strong Board member', individuals whose definitions of education differed from the then

Superintendent, Mr. McBride. Community resistance to tax increases remain. Spanman's cosmopolitanism, pursuit of resources, and stance as an imaginative educator continue. The origination of interaction and his proactive style continues to integrate the multiple aspects. The flow of activity continues unabated.

Year III of Spanman's Tenure: 1964–65

During the third year, all of the usual business continued and we omit most of it to concentrate on several special incidents.

Citizen Involvement: Law Suits, Committees, and Communities: The item in the Board minutes only hinted at the problem:

> Mr. Henderson moved that a special Board meeting be called for September 17, 1964, at 8 p.m., at the New Junior High School cafeteria, and invite the Registered Voters League of Milford and interested patrons for the purpose of informing the patrons of the District of Board actions and the reasons for them; to answer pertinent questions relative thereto; and to convey notice of the meeting to officers of the various organizations in the community. Mrs. Harcourt seconded the motion and it carried unanimously. (9/8/64)

Innocuous enough, but after reading five decades of meeting minutes, it sounded as though something were afoot.

The meeting was held. The Secretary read a letter from a Mr. Connor. 'Mr. Connor advised that no representatives of the people involved in the lawsuit against the Board would attend the meeting and gave reasons.' Questions and answers went on for two and a half hours and the meeting adjourned at 10:30 p.m.

On Tuesday 22 September, the Board acknowledged receipt of a 'Writ of Mandamus'. A copy was attached. The Superintendent and the Board were being sued because they were to provide 'free public schools', yet, they had instituted instructional fees of $4.00, $6.00, and $8.00 and book fees of $5.00, both of which were new to the District.[2] Secondly, though a teachers tax levy had failed, salaries were increased, and funds were taken from general sources into which the fees were being paid. The writ called this a 'subterfuge,' an action against the wishes of the voters. The Board's attorney filed a 'Motion to quash alternative writ of Mandamus' on two grounds. First, the 'alleged facts ... do not constitute sufficient facts.' And, secondly, that the assessment of fees '... is a discretionary action vested in respondents by law and is not subject to control by writ of mandamus.' The School lawyer submitted a ten page counter claim.

One of the ironies of school affairs, and a continuing difficult issue to conceptualize, is that no action is either simple of uniform even across definable subgroups. At the same time this group of patrons was bringing suit, another group of patrons, the Citizen's Advisory Committee was submitting its report from a year's activity.In the Superintendent's words, their brief was stated:

In establishing the committee, the Board indicated that the committee should have as its first responsibility a study of the building and educational needs of the School District, making reports as needed, including a final report to the Board of Education at the completion of the school year. (9/22/64)

The report came in at the time another part of the community was exploding in anger. The covering letter of the President of the Citizen's Advisory Committee noted the problem:

The Committee at the final meeting on September 14, 1964, adopted a resolution in which it stated that it believed it regrettable that the group which recently filed suit against the School Board did not bring the matter before the Citizen's Advisory Committee — a committee formed expressly to convey to the Board feelings and problems of the community regarding school matters. (8/14/64)

In short, the community was not 'all of a piece.' For all the actors in the system this posed an intriguing agenda of different but interrelated problems.

If that was not complication enough, that same evening the Board passed on procedures to implement a 'Professional Relations Committee.' This group, in time, would become the locus for issues in 'professional negotiations.' Policies and their bureaucratic structures seem to begin in one climate and to possess certain purposes and functions. Then, they, became actualized at later times and in very different climates and circumstances.

Policy #4161 provides for the establishment of a Professional Relations Committee for the purpose of discussion and reaching a mutually satisfactory agreement on the educational program, its improvement and development, salary, welfare provisions, working conditions, and other problems of mutual concern.

The following recommendations on procedures are submitted for approval of the Board:

1 The committee shall consist of six members: the Superintendent of Schools, two representatives designated by the Board of Education, and three representatives of the Community Teachers Association.
2 At the September meeting of each year the Committee shall elect its own chairman from among its membership, the chairman to serve for a period of one year
3 Teacher members of the Committee shall be released from school duties without loss of salary if and when Committee meetings are scheduled during the school day.
4 The Committee shall be empowered to appoint subcommittees for the purpose of studying matters of concern which may arise in the course of discussion, and of making recommendations to the Committee.
5 The Committee shall have available to it, provided by the Board of

Education, any clerical assistance necessary to the performance of its duties. (9/22/64)

The motion passed unanimously. As we read the item this is the formalization of a major shift in the arbitrariness of the power of the Board, which earlier we had called the 'Potency of the School Board'. It is a major innovation. The longer reach of this Committee will appear as our story of Milford continues to unfold.

In October 1964 the Board commended the Citizen's Advisory Committee and voted to extend its activities for another year.

A month later in what seemed an eminently sensible move, and one worthy of conceptualizing for its latent dimensions, the Board acted this way:

> Mrs. Harcourt moved that, inasmuch as there will be a long delay before the final decison in the test case concerning the assessment of fees, the Board of Education make available all books and materials needed in the various instructional programs to students who refused to pay the optional fee assessments, with the stipulation that at the time the court renders its decision upholding the authority of the Board of Education to assess optional book rental and supply fees, the students receiving the service without payment be required to pay the stipulated amounts immediately. (10/27/64)

The motion passed unanimously.

The significance of this seemed to be: 1) no child was to suffer, 2) the issue was changed from substantive differences to procedural differences — does the Board have the authority?, 3) The issue was relegated to a lower level of importance and saliency, $10–15.00 a youngster, more in keeping with its importance in the broader scheme of Board activities and Milford's education program. In the meantime the Board lawyer, Mr. Irby, continued to file appropriate memoranda, citing state law and legal precedent regarding the suit. The language of the statutes seemed to favour the Board, for example: '... the board of education *may* at its option also furnish all free text books ...' (10/28/81) The usual proviso was that the elementary schools should receive priority in any discretionary spending. Poor children also could be granted special status in provision of materials.

Meanwhile, another citizen group was raising money through voluntary contributions for mobile bleachers to be used at the high school and other schools. The $1500, plus $1000 from senior class donations and $500.00 from an 'activity account' put the $4000 goal in sight. A 'booster' group for athletic activities, especially at the high school, has been in Milford since the beginning.

The principle we seem to be reaching for is the old cliche 'you can't please all the people all the time.' The Superintendent and the Board presumably might: 1) take such conflict, partial disaffection, and parental support as part of the reality of schooling, 2) keep working at it — legally, in open discussions and hearings, and in their own decision making, 3) maintain some kind of gyroscope which blends general principles and values with 'the will of the people', 4) try to minimize such emotional reactions as anger, rage, and depression, 5) realize that the issues will pass and new ones will take their place, 6) only on rare occasions will the consequences be devastating — Board incumbents replaced, Superintendent fired. Such a social reality as this seems a given in Milford. Similar 'realities' must be present in other districts.

As we indicated also in our Chronicle of the Milford District, the communities involved in public schooling are neither singular nor simple. Milford is part of Midwest State. The Board members met with other board members of Suburban County over a set of 'legislative goals.' This year the items on the agenda included:

1 Removal of the present two-third's barrier restricting the passage of school operating levies...
2 Upgrading the State School Foundation Program Formula...
3 Reduction of the two-thirds majority on passing school bond issues...
4 Inclusion of kindergarten education in the Foundation program...
5 Amend existing statutes so that a tax rate would revert to previous rate in the event of the failure of a levy; not to one dollar, if defeated. (11/24/64)

A month later, it was indicated that group voted favorably on the recommendations. The essence of democracy, at least in schooling issues, is unending meetings, continuous attempts at persuasion among ever changing groups with different interests and agendas. The size and locale of the groups varies from small clusters of district patrons, to cross district elected representatives, to county programs,[3] to state legislatures and to state courts. To this point, minimal federal or national influences have appeared. The District has continuously opposed the idea of Federal Aid to Education, but equally consistently applied for any funds due it in current law.

On 26 January 1965, the Board passed unanimously a resolution to sign the 'Assurance of Compliance with the Civil Rights Act of 1964.' The key provision was:

...no person shall on the ground of race, color, or national origin, be excluded for participation in, be denied the benefits of, or be otherwise subjected to discrimination under any program or activity for which the School District receives federal assistance. (1/26/65)

The major program assistance at this time was NDEA money for upgrading programs in secience, mathematics and foreign language and aid to areas with large numbers of federal employees.

The inconsistency in the Board's position on Federal Aid seemed not to be missed among the members themselves. The depth of the feeling in the community was reflected in a motion in February. The Board split 2–4 on a motion to refuse all Federal aid:

Mr. Henderson moved that in recognition of the Federal Government's inability to meet its financial obligations, even with the excessive taxes already levied upon the people, the Board proposes to refuse all Federal Aid under Public Laws 815 and 874 and NDEA for the school year 1965–66, if the voters approve an incidental fund levy increase of seven cents to provide the funds presently budgeted and necessary. Further that this choice be given voters at the April 6, 1965 election. Mr. Tittle seconded the motion. (2/9/65)

Policy Codification.   As we have commented on numerous occasions, field work research methods require one to 'be around' or be in the setting a good deal. Such time involvement provokes a variety of interactions and observations of mundane activities. In the Summer of 1981, while reading Board minutes of the Spanman era, we shared a conference room with several employees who were updating the Milford Policy Handbooks. The large blue backed ring notebooks date from the Spanman era. The organizational structure of the books was set by him, his staff, and the Board. This appears as Figure 23. Many of the items still carry dates of 1963, 1964, and 1965. The substantive issues seem to be an amalgam of relevant groups inside and outside of the district and bureaucratic activities. The groups are obviously important community, Board, administrative, faculty and staff, and students. Individual schools represent the significant clustering of actors. Philosophy and goals, instruction, and business related to the major elements of organizational process.

Each policy was on a separate loose-leaf sheet in the book. Each sheet was formated as illustrated in Figure 24. Each policy was titled, numbered, and stated. References to appropriate state law were cited. Dates of adoption, effectiveness and amending were also included. The formating was a powerful, simple, unable innovation in itself.

The magnitude of that undertaking should have been obvious from the over-size bound volumes of Board minutes, even when split into Volume 1 and Volume 2 for each year. Similarly the size of the task should have been obvious from the month in and month out submission, discussion, and approval of section by section of policy which went on in those years. But it really was the appearance of a conference table stacked high with the three ringed notebooks which brought the significance of the codification task as well as its magnitude to salience or awareness. Through the years the evolving Policy Handbook has been another quasi stationary part of Milford's equilibrium. Spanman's 'innovation' settled an issue which had festered since the late 1940s and early 1950s, which was a major item in Mr. Lewis', the Board President, attack on Mr. McBride, and which almost got Mr. McBride fired in 1954.

The National Gamble In February of 1965, Spanman's cosmopolitan ambitions for Milford reached their zenith. With the cooperation and help of Dr. Jerl Cohen[4], the District Curriculum Director, he convened a nationally prestigious group of professional educators, foundation officials, and US Office of Education specialists. The Board officially sanctioned the meeting (although only a few days before the meeting was to occur) with this motion:

Figure 23: Structure of Milford's Policy Handbook

Numbering System	Topic
1000	Community
2000	Administration
3000	Business
4000	Personnel
5000	Students
6000	Instruction
7000	Individual School
8000	Philosophy
9000	Board of Education

Figure 24: Sample Page of Policy Handbook

Title:			NO.
			O
			F
			F
			I
			C
			I
			A
			L
Legal reference:			P
			O
			L
Policy Adopted:	Amended:		I
			C
Effective Date:	Page _____ of _____ Pages		Y
	Milford School District		

Mr. Baskin moved that the staff be authorized to continue to design a framework for a five year school improvement program designed to attract the interest of Foundation, National Education Association, and/or the US Office of Education, sufficient to provide a grant of one million dollars for the program.

The purpose of the program would be to provide for:

1 Better educational opportunities for boys and girls in Milford.
2 Professional growth and stimulation of personnel involved in curriculum study.
3 Better understanding of the nature of a comprehensive school district as a totality — its curriculum patterns, the administrative enterprise, community responsibility, and staff utilization.
4 The creation of a model demonstration school district for the nation, which will attract the interest and financial assistance of foundations, associations, and the US Office of Education.

Mrs. Harcourt seconded the motion and it carried unanimously. (2/23/65)

The Superintendent's agenda, as usual, elaborated on both the nature and rationale of the recommendation. Some nine 'prominent educators' were named as visitors who would 'consider the proposal developed by the staff. 'They represented prestigious universities on the west coast, the east coast, and the midwest as well as two nearby institutions. The Olds Foundation, NEA, and the US Office of Education were also in attendance.

The rationale indicated the scope and hope of Spanman and his associates:

> The program for curriculum reform in the School District involves a concerted attempt to develop a comprehensive curriculum design that involves the relevant components that exist in a school organization. The problem in the past has been that curriculum work has been patchwork with little thought given to the objectives of the organization nor the inextricable and complementary nature of the essential elements that exist to attain the objectives.
>
> The purpose of the symposium to be held on Thursday February 25, is to bring together selected authorities in curriculum, instruction, and the community with a view toward examining, discussing and questioning the conceptual model as a vehicle to be useful in delineating the objectives for education and defining the roles and responsibilities of all persons: learners, teachers, principals, the superintendent, the board of education, and the members of the community.
>
> A second task of the participants will be to identify the areas that should be studied in more detail and to discard those items that cannot or should not be studied at this time.
>
> An attempt has been made to touch upon the major components in the subject under consideration; however, there are doubtless some areas that were deleted that should have been considered. While some areas have been treated in more detail than others, this should not suggest that they are more complex nor more important.
>
> The projected time span of the proposed study is five years. The total amount of the tentative request from outside sources would be $1,000,000.00. (2/23/65)

His recommendations were included verbatim in the Board's action, as quoted earlier from the minutes.

Appended to the minutes, as usual, was a basic document prepared by Cohen and a consultant from Eastern University, who attended the conference. It included: 1) A cover letter to participants, 2) An overview, 3) Statement of problems (11), 4) Projected outcome, 5) Information about the Milford School District, 6) Projected Budget (approximately $200,000/year for five years), 7) Bibliography.

A brief summary set of interpretations by one of the participants (Smith, L.) gives an early perspective on the meeting itself:

> In short, it is very clear that many of the analyses we have been making of Kensington's aspirations, agendas, and problems have their counterparts in Milford's districtwide curriculum efforts.
>
> The high point of the district's curricular effort occurred in February

when representatives of private foundations and the United States Office of Education met with the Milford staff and the local and national consultants. Although many issues were discussed, the goal was curriculum reform; and although many examples of hopes and realities were provided, Kensington was the crown jewel.

The outcomes of curriculum reform were broad. Jerl Cohen's position paper prepared for the conference phrased them this way:

1 Better educational opportunity for boys and girls of Milford.
2 Professional growth and stimulation of personnel involved in curriculum study.
3 Better understanding of the nature of a comprehensive School District as a totality—its curriculum patterns, the administrative enterprise, community responsibility, and staff utilization.
4 The creation of a demonstration School District; not a lighthouse district in the traditional definition of the word where certain exciting innovations are being carried out with culturally advantaged children with educationally supportive parents; not a lighthouse in the sense that the 'truth' has been found, but a lighthouse in the sense that here is a typical district that is genuinely concerned about looking at curriculum and instruction in a meaningful way. The attitude would be for persons to come and observe, not the successes so much, but the types of problems that are encountered along the way and to observe the progress that is being made.
5 Serve as a 'seedbed' for theory building, a place for concept testing and empirical studies.

Eleven 'top priority problems were identified.' The stated objectives for public education in Milford, the social movements influencing curriculum, Kensington's role as a subculture in changing the entire district, the identification of district problems, the conflict resulting from curriculum reform, and the nature of the teacher role illustrate the tenor of the problems.

The conference chairman 'argued for building an integrated picture of district activities which then might be brought together for resources to implement the totality.' After a preliminary discussion they settled on using Kensington as a focus and as an illustration of the district's problems. The day replayed much of the content that we have raised elsewhere. In a sense the conference was caught in the three separate agendas of the three major figures of Milford. Cohen sought an overall umbrella or conception useful for rationalizing his activities. Spanman sought a structure for action—a means for reaching out into the district with Kensington as a model. Shelby sought pieces of Kensington that would be exportable.

Overall, approximately $200,000 a year for 5 years were the tangible goals. Neither that day nor later in the spring was the funding forthcoming. In retrospect, the failure in the Milford District's attempt for outside financial support of the curriculum project was most critical for Kensington as well as for the district in general. (Smith and Keith, 1971, pp. 296–7)

The gamble remained unsuccessful. Private funds were not forthcoming; funds from the National Elementary and Secondary Education Act were still a year or two away. Pushes from within the district and pulls from without were to fragment the small and fragile group clustered about Spanman.

Closing Out The Year. In retrospect, February was the year's high point. The March minutes indicate that the general thrust of the year continued. The Superintendent presented a 'this item is for information' statement entitled 'Summary of Curriculum Studies.' It carried a contrasting emphasis to the national gambit reported earlier. It seemed to carry a 'summing up' in a broader sense than that implied in the title. The Superintendent stated it in four short paragraphs:

> The decisive changes that are occurring in the structure of knowledge and the methods of learning demand that local school districts experiment and test the various methods of organization, of teaching, and of organizing content.
>
> Over one hundred projects have been instituted in the last two years in the School District. Seventy-seven are included in a summary sheet that is attached as Appendix 'D,' pages 1–11. The conduct of these projects is consistent with the administrator's philosophy that more and better education does not necessarily require more time—more teachers—or more money. Improvements can be made within the existing framework with a different and more effective use of time—teachers—money.
>
> Many projects have become a permanent part of the instructional program, such as team teaching in United States History at the Senior High School and block-of-time scheduling at the junior high schools. Some projects have been tested and found to be inappropriate for children in the District. Other projects will be encouraged for the entire School District during the coming school year, such as contemporary mathematics and non gradedness.
>
> Since curriculum studies begin at all times during the year, no statement is complete. However, the present summary includes all but the most recent. (3/23/65)

The format of the reporting seems simple, clear and informative:

Study or Program	*Grade Level*	*School*	*Comments and How It is Being Evaluated*

Although projects appear in every school in the District, Kensington led in number and size of efforts.

At the 6 April Board meeting, at 1 a.m. the unofficial election returns were received. One incumbent, Mr. Wilkerson, who had resigned as Board President, mid year, a year ago was re-elected. The second incumbent, Mr. Baskin, lost to Mr.

Figure 25: Innovative Projects in the Milford Schools

Edinburg	4
Field	4
Grant	3
Hillside	7
Johnson	2
Marquette	1
McBride	5
Midvale	2
Milford	2
Kensington	15
Williams	6
New Junior High	9
Old Junior High	7
Senior High	9

Reeves, a citizen active in school affairs who had run as a write-in candidate a few years before. The victory was clear cut. The winners each had a little over 4700 votes, the next high was 3700 and the losing incumbent, coming in fourth had 3200 votes. A fifth candidate drew 3600. Hindsight tells us clearly that the winds and tides were shifting. Foresight might have raised to the naive reader of Board minutes a series of questions:

1 The major opponent of the Superintendent wins handily, therefore ...?
2 A major supporter of the Superintendent loses badly, fourth in a five person race?
3 What's the philosophy of the new man?
4 Will the third place man try again? What's his point of view?

Partial answers appear in the tax levy which was also defeated resoundingly 3519 yeas, 6780 nays.

Further clarity in the meaning of the elections appeared two weeks later. For the first time, one of the Superintendent's recommendations did not receive Board approval. The item blended Spanman's national ambitions for the District, the place of Kensington in those plans, and his perspective on educational innovation:

Mr. Henderson moved that the Milford School District participate in the Southern State University Internship Program for the 1965–66 school year and that four interns (two/semester) be employed by the District to serve in the Kensington Elementary School at a salary of $1325 each per semester. Mrs. Harcourt seconded the motion and roll call vote was taken as follows

Mrs. Harcourt	yes
Mr. Reeves	no
Mr. Henderson	yes
Mr. Tittle	yes
Mr. Wilkerson	no
Mr. Ludwig	no (4/27/65)

The new member joined with the former Board president who had been squeezed out by the Superintendent. The current Board president, for this vote, joined the dissidents. The same group voted together to defeat a nominee for the District Insurance Advisory Commission. Was a coalition beginning?

Whether intentional or the chance juxtaposing of events the Superintendent's agenda contained, as Item XIV, a discussion of 'School Board — Administrator Relationship'. Most of his remarks were based on E.M. Tuttle's *School Board Leadership in America*. Additional references were to a publication by Arthur C. Croft Company and a monograph from the State Department on *Suggestions for Procedures for Midwest State Boards of Education*. Selected from Tuttle's statement were several basic principles, a dozen 'Legitimate Expectations of the Administrator by the Board,' and a dozen 'Legitimate Expectations of the Board by the Administration.' Spanman's neverending role of teacher/educator continued, in troubled times as well as good times.

Also on the agenda was a report by the Superintendent on President Johnson's signing of the Elementary and Secondary Education Act of 1965. Federal aid had arrived. Spanman indicated most of the money would go to schools with concentrations of low income pupils. Title III, on innovative local programs seemed the part most applicable to Milford. As part of his information to the Board he indicated the usual procedures after passing such a bill:

1   The funds must be appropriated by Congress.
2   The US Commissioner of Education must establish regulations concerning federal administration of the Act.
3   The State Department of Education must make application and submit state plans for the state administration of the Act.
4   The state application and state plan must be approved by the US Office of Education.
5   The local public school authorities must submit an application for a program or project, in accordance with provisions of the Act, to the State Department of Education for approval. (4/27/65)

In March, the Board unanimously adopted what seems an unusually worded resolution:

WHEREAS, the education of children is at stake in the Milford School District; and
WHEREAS, there is a critical need for a forty-two cent increase in the teachers levy to be levied for a two year period; and therefore,
Be it further RESOLVED that *every member of the Board will speak as he has voted in Board meetings and will not speak against any administrator, principal, teacher, member of the Board, or past actions of the Board, and will give whole hearted support to the passage of said teachers levy.* (Our italics) (5/11/65)

It seems hardly a statement to reassure a patron, or a superintendent, regarding the kind of principles enumerated from Tuttle's book a month before: 'There shall be a friendly good will and mutual respect between the Board and the administrator which makes possible complete frankness, confidence, and understanding concerning the conduct of the schools.' (4/27/65) Or, perhaps, an unreality exists in the professional literature on schooling.

The failure of earlier tax levies for salaries and the resubmission of a lesser levy to the community provoked a statement from the local CTA. A key paragraph suggests other facets in the continuing complications in the maintenance, improvement or reform of public education:

> It is the professional duty of the administration and the teaching staff to inform the people of the District of its educational needs. But it is not the duty of the administrators and the teachers to attempt to provide more educational services than the community is willing to pay for. To ask teachers to provide more services than the community is willing to finance is, in effect, asking the teachers to subsidize the education of the children of the District. It is both illogical and unreasonable for the administration and community to expect teachers to accept inadequate salaries in order that better and more complete educational services and facilities may be provided for a district which is unable or unwilling to pay for those services. *If the community is only able or willing to provide enough funds to maintain basic state requirements, that is all the Board of Education and the administration should attempt to provide.*
>
> *It is incumbent upon the Board of Education and the administration to progress at a slower pace and to take the community along, rather than to get so far ahead as to cause the community to refuse to support the program.* (Our italics) (5/11/65)

The 11 May Board meeting adjourned at 3:57 a.m.

Retrospective conversations and interviews with school personnel who were teachers at the time indicate that the content of the CTA's resolution was symbolic of a much wider range of dissatisfaction — inequities (favored status) between Kensington and other schools, a perceived lack of substance in the many extra teachers' meetings, and perhaps most of all the perceived disregard of salary schedules in hiring of many of the bright young Kensington teachers.

At the 25 May meeting a brief minute conveyed what might be called a conclusion about events in Milford: 'President Ludwig declared a 30 minute board recess at 8:30 p.m. in order to view a special local TV program entitled, 'Crises in the Milford Schools.' The Superintendent had taped an interview with one of the local television stations.

A special session Board meeting on 2 June didn't adjourn until 3:50 a.m. They had the task of waiting until after midnight for the unhappy news that the teachers' levy had failed once again. A motion was made and passed for a minimum $2.00 levy requiring a simple majority and another special election on 18 June.

Meanwhile, the push to finish the Policy Handbook continued through committee activities, initial presentation discussions, final editing and unanimous Board approval. In the 24 June meeting the Series 4000, Policies on Personnel were approved unanimously, excepting Policy #4141. The separate motion to approve #4141 was defeated 4–2. The Yeas included Henderson and Harcourt. The Nays were Wilkerson, Reeves, and Ludwig now joined by Tittle. The item in contention dealt with competitive conditions:

Temporary

A highly desirable incoming person who cannot be attracted by the salary available to him on a given step of the Teachers' Salary Guide may be paid a differential during his first few years of employment.

Permanent

A highly qualified person trained for a special field in which salaries are generally above those provided by the Teachers' Guide may be paid a differential while salaries in his field remain above the Guide. (6/24/65)

The Board returned to a uniform salary schedule.

A coalition of negative sentiment among staff, patrons, citizens toward Spanman and/or parts of his program now had received forceful spokesmen within the School Board.

Differentiated staffing received considerable debate in the 'Basis for Allotment of Teaching Positions.' Particularly questioned were two sentences from the general provisions:

In addition, a principal at his discretion and with the approval of the Superintendent may employ noncertificated personnel in lieu of certificated personnel. The number of noncertificated personnel. The number of noncertificated personnel shall be based on the average beginning salary of certificated personnel. (Policy #5826, June 1965)

The nay sayers were Wilkerson and Reeves.

The final item at that meeting, just before adjournment at 5:35 a.m. was a vote for a new three year contract for Dr. Spanman at a salary of $20,000/year. The 4–2 split remained on the lines of the previous votes. The minority included Wilkerson and Reeves.

After reviewing the progress of events in later Spring and early Summer, the special meeting of the Board on 6 July 1965 was almost anticlimatic. Superintendent Spanman had been invited to participate in a prestigious fellowship program and he requested a year's leave of absence. His letter followed the pattern of his agenda items: the opportunities, the purposes and rationale, the honor to the individual and to the organization, and the beneficial outcomes to both. The three purposes of the Fellowship capture both the flavor and flair:

1   To provide the experienced educator with an opportunity to leave the detail of local activities and problems for a year and come to see them within a broader context.

2   To bring fresh viewpoints to the senior staff of participating agencies and to establish a continuing relationship between the associations and future leaders of American education.

3   To return the participants of the program to their local communities with new techniques, workable solutions, and fresh perspective to offer to their work and their colleagues. (6/6/65).

203

The Board voted 4–2 to grant the leave; the nay sayers again were Wilkerson and Reeves. The item concluded with: 'Mr. Wilkerson requested that the minutes show that his reason for voting 'no' was that preferred the Superintendent's resignation rather than granting a leave of absence.' (6/6/65) With those wishes and sentiments, Dr. Spanman left the District temporarily. He was not to return.

The Final Year, IV: Acting Superintendent Alan Ranson

Apparently, the Assistant Superintendent for Business Affairs, Mr. Alan Ranson was felt to be the Superintendent's man. On the same split, 4–2 vote, he became Acting Superintendent, effective 11 September 1965. It seemed to be an issue of beliefs for Jerl Cohen became Assistant Superintendent for Instruction on a 4–2 vote, and Tom Mack, the Kensington Curriculum Materials Coordinator became an elementary principal, also on a 4–2 vote. In August Jerl Cohen resigned. He was replaced by Mr. Jim Luther, whose sabbatical leave to finish a PhD was deferred for a year.

The strand of localism, if it be that, was construed quite narrowly. A Central City committee working toward alternative tax structures for the metropolitan area was given a 3–2 (Wilkerson was absent due to illness) rejection. Their proposals for an income or sales tax, to relieve the strain on the local property tax, did not sit well with the Milford Board. The Yea votes came from Harcourt and Henderson, the core supporters of the now absent Steven Spanman. During the next few months letters from several Boards of Education in Suburban County were received supporting the task force's recommendations.

An informational item on the establishment of a county-wide vocational/technical school appeared. The Board took no action, but the citizenry of Suburban County was moving toward a solution of one of its longest standing secondary education problems, just a they had a few years earlier moved toward a Suburban County Solution of the special education problems.

The population crunch in Milford was now more at the Junior High School level. The Board voted unanimously three interrelated motions: '1) retain the K-6-3-3 concept 2) go on double sessions in the two junior high schools, 3) present a $1.8 million bond issue for junior and senior high classrooms. Building problems, that is the housing of students, occur in several forms — too many or too few, too many or too few at varying grade levels, too many or too few occurring sequentially, and too many or too few in different geographical areas of the district.

The Board received and read a letter from the Grand Knight of the local Knights of Columbus organization indicating its opposition to any new forms of school tax, income or sales: '. . . which do not allow distribution of such funds for the educational benefits of all children, regardless of school attended, whether public, private or parochial. . .' (12/22/65) The First Amendment and its interpretations by the courts and by subgroups of citizens also would not go away. Compromises were (are) difficult to achieve. The sentiments of pluralism are not always positive and mutually supportive. Both public school boards and parochial boards presumably live with resolutions which are less than optimal.

In late Winter and early Spring, a series of personnel dominoes fell. Mr. Shelby resigned as Principal of the Kensington School. Such a resignation, midsemester, is a rare event. Shortly thereafter the Board took action:

> Mr. Reeves moved that the Board of Education reassign Mr. Michael Edwards to the Kensington Elementary School as Principal, effective Wednesday, March 9, 1966. and that Dr. Ronald George be assigned as Principal of Field Elementary School until July 1, 1966, with a one month's extension of his contract period, effective Wednesday, March 9, 1966.

Mr. Wilkerson seconded the motion, it passed unanimously. The dissenting duo on the Board were now moving affirmatively and carrying the votes on the Board.

Concluding the Year: School Chaos, Superintendent Vulnerability, or Political Democracy?

Most times we have found it reasonably easy to sort the tangle of school events into themes, strands, and categories. Meanings in the perspectives of the key actors or in our own accumulating point of view seemed reasonably straightforward. The events of April and May, 1966 reflected so many endings and beginnings, so many isues and so many perplexing differences of opinion and shifting alliances that we finally settled for a general heading, 'School Chaos, Vulnerability, or Political Democracy?' Our first cut will be to establish a set of facts, reasonably agreed upon items. They seem to defy any simple patterning. Then we will try for several generalizations.

First, the Board met in regular and special session, five times each month, a total of ten meetings. For Milford this was a record. More meetings than at any time in the previous fifty years. The meaning is less clear.

Second, on the morning of 5 April the day of the school board elections, the Superintendent requested a release from his contract. The telegram appears as Figure 26, Mr. Henderson, one of Spanman's supporters, made the motion to accept the resignation. Mr. Reeves, one of his opponents, seconded the motion. The Board unanimously voted to accept the resignation.

Third, the Board usually stayed late and awaited the unofficial voting returns

Figure 26: Telegram from Superintendent

Martin Ludwig   1966 APR 5 a.m. 8:23

Have been reassigned to Division Director responsibility. Respectfully request release from contract today to continue in assignment. Opportunity to work with forward looking progressive board has been highlight of career. After visiting scores of boards across the nation in recent months am convinced yours ranks in top five per cent. You are to be commended for establishing and achieving high standards.

Respectfully,

Steven Spanman

---

on the night of the election. On this occasion they adjourned early — 9:45 p.m.

Fourth, a number of items were attended to, for example, the final bills to the architect and cabinetry contractor of the Kensington School were paid.

Fifth, Mr. Tittle resigned as Treasurer of the Board. Two days later, he ranked third in the group of seven in the Board election. Consequently, he lost his seat.

Sixth, the Board reconsidered an earlier, 16 March vote and accepted unanimously the resignation of the High School Principal, Joe James.

Two days later, on Thursday, 7 April, the Board received the official election returns. The President, Mr. Ludwig, had decided not to run again. Mr. Tittle, one of Spanman's supporters ran third in a seven person group. Mr. Tuley and Mr. Edmond were declared elected and were sworn in. In addition, the minimum teacher's levy, which required only simple majority, was declared passed.

Then, Mr. Henderson, also a key supporter of Dr. Spanman, read a short one line letter addressed to his colleagues on the Board: 'I herewith tender my resignation as Director and Secretary of the Milford School Board effective May 1, 1966.' (4/7/66) Immediatlely thereafter, Mrs. Harcourt's letter was read: '. . . informing the present and new members of the Board of Education that she had changed her decision to resign as a member of the Board and she would continue . . .' (4/7/66) Her letter is included as Figure 27. It captures some of the intensity of feeling existing in the Board, in the community, and among the school staff. In a retrospective comment, one long time member of the Milford School professional staff described her as 'in Spanman's pocket on any vote.'

Then the Board proceeded as usual to elect one of its members as President. The two members of the prior Board, Wilkerson and Reeves, who had voted together consistently in opposition to the Spanman program, were each nominated for President. The vote split 3–3. While no roll call is taken on these votes, a later motion to seek nominations for Vice President also resulted in a 3–3 tie. The nays were:

Harcourt
Reeves
Henderson

The ayes were:

Edmond
Wilkerson
Tuley

In effect, the two new members were supporting the originally sole opponent to Spanman. He had been Board President before and had resigned as President in an October showdown between himself and the Superintendent. The inference we might draw is that the two new members represented a strong conservative move in the community.

The Board went through five tie votes and finally agreed to meet the next evening, Friday, at 9:30 p.m. The Thursday night meeting adjourned at 12:15 a.m.

On Friday the 8th, the Board met at 9:30. A sixth vote was taken, the 3–3 tie remained. Discussion was called for. No discussion followed. A ten minute recess was called at 10:00 p.m. Executive session was declared at 10:10 p.m. Open session

Figure 27: A Board Member's Letter

April 7, 1966

To the present members and to the new members of the Board of Education in the Milford School District:

On April 5th, 1966, I indicated my resignation from the Board would be forthcoming in a matter of days. At this time I should like to state, for reasons contained in this letter, that I have changed my decision and shall remain a part of this Board of Education for the duration of my term, subject to the limits of my physical and mental strength.

First, because it is my sincere desire to continue to assist in providing the best education for all children.

Second, regardless of my personal feelings and attitudes, I shall continue to uphold within this School District the educational progress so clearly evident during the past four years.

Third, for the many people who have placed their confidence in me, I shall continue exerting every effort in taking the initiative to inform and alert all persons concerning, not only our schools but, all phases of education.

Fourth, because I believe in the leadership and integrity displayed by certain persons on this Board and in this School District, I feel obligated to fulfill my responsibility.

I should like to express my sincere appreciation to the personal courtesy shown to me by the members now leaving the Board and by the personnel who have left or shall be leaving the School District, also to those who, with an honest dedication toward the best education for all children, shall remain.

Upon due consideration it is against my better judgment to admit, for selfish reasons, that a discontinuation in my efforts to uphold the principles for which I believe, would constitute a personal satisfactory solution to anything.

Therefore, it is my decision to continue to be a member of the Board of Education in the School District of Milford.

Sincerely,

Harriet Harcourt

cc: All members of the Staff
    All teaching personnel

was reconvened at 10:40 p.m.: '. . . at which time both Mr. Wilkerson and Mr. Reeves withdrew their names for nomination of President of the Board of Education.' (4/8/66) From then on, the compromise which apparently had been agreed upon moved rapidly. A series of unanimous votes resulted in:

Mr. Edmond	President
Mrs. Harcourt	Vice President
Mr. Tuley	Treasurer
Mr. Reeves	Secretary

The positions were split between the factions. Each nomination was made by a member of the opposing faction. The meeting adjourned at 10:50 p.m.

On 20 April at 8:00 p.m., as agreed upon earlier, the Board met in special session to meet with the architects regarding additions to the Junior and Senior High Schools. New housing was required for the bulge in students now moving up the grades. The architects were from the local metropolitan area, rather than from out of state, as in the instance of Kensington. Plans were accepted, bids for equipment were to be sought. All votes were unanimous. The meeting adjourned at 11:00 p.m.

At the regular meeting on 26 April, Mr. Henderson's resignation was accepted, unanimously. It was dated May 1st. A dozen items of 'normal business' moved rapidly through a series of unanimous decisions. At 11:30, while in executive session, unanimity fell away over the issue of 'action on present administrators contracts.' The new conservative coalition wanted to table the issue until the 10 May meeting. The old 3–3 coalition appeared; the motion failed. Most of the votes were unanimous and favorable. Mrs. Harcourt voted against two elementary principals because of 'lack of cooperation in the educational program of the District.'

The appointments of Mr. Newton to continue as Junior High Principal and Mr. Overholt, a long term teacher and Assistant Principal at the High School, to become Senior High School Principal were stymied by 3–3 votes. The nays were from the new conservative coalition. Both were recommended by the Acting Superintendent, Mr. Ranson. Among the other positions open were Assistant Principals of each Junior High School and a new position as 'Coordinator of Governmental Programs and Adult Education.'

The Acting Superintendent presented letters from five citizens desiring consideration as a Board member to fill the unexpired term of Mr. Henderson. The Board met in special session on Saturday morning, 7 May at 9:30. Mrs Harcourt's nominee was defeated 2–3. Mr. Wilkerson's candidate, Mr. Greider, was elected on a 4–1 vote. Presumably Mr. Reeves rejoined the conservative coalition. The policy, based on State Law, that the Board replace its resigned member is another mechanism underlying the iron law of oligarchy.

On 10 May the Board held its regular meeting. The controversy regarding the appointments of principals for the Junior and Senior High Schools appeared in several items. A letter from a citizen, representing community feeling regarding the high school principalship, requested an appearance before the Board. Another citizen presented a petition containing 1156 signatures supporting Mr. Overholt for High School Principal. A petition signed by sixty-three of the High School teachers supported Mr. Overholt. The key paragraph in their petition stated:

> We have worked under his supervision this year and feel his leadership, administrative ability and integrity has been a great influence on the teaching staff at Milford High School. With his vast experience as Assistant Principal and supervisor of all the faculty and student body, he will give the leadership you most rightfully want at the Senior High School. (5/10/66)

The teachers at the Junior High School also rallied to the support of their Principal in a letter to the Board:

> We, the teachers of the Junior High School, have been informed that Mr. Newton, our Principal, was told that his contract has not been extended due to poor discipline in our building. We feel that discipline in our school is to be commended, especially under the crowded conditions.
>
> A majority of the teachers feel that Mr. Newton has been instrumental in promoting the pleasant atmosphere and high morale. Therefore, we find the report difficult to understand. (5/5/66)

These citizen and faculty petitions led the Board President, Mr. Edmond, to issue a formal statement:

> As President of the Milford School Board, my only interest is in the upgrading of our educational program so that the children of this district will receive the best possible education that we can provide within the limits of our budget.
>
> In voting on any issue I am not committed to anyone either on this Board or outside it. I will judge each issue on its merits. Where teachers and administrators have the educational qualifications for a position and have shown an active interest in the betterment of our schools and themselves by advanced study, self-improvement, and presenting themselves as persons dedicated to their profession by their speech and actions; these factors alone should be the only influence on the minds of the members sitting on this Board who have taken the oath to serve this district and represent everyone in it, whether they be in the minority or the majority. I do not approve of any expression by a Board member that would indicate representation of either a minority or a majority, as we on this Board are elected to represent the whole district and should be dedicated to the children striving for an education within it. (5/10/66)

Just before adjournment at 12:40 a.m., the Board agreed to meet on Saturday, 14 May, 'for the purpose of electing a Senior High School Principal.'

On Saturday morning, 14 May, in an hour and fifteen minute meeting, with a series of 4–2 votes, the new conservative coalition: 1) Voted not to make Mr. Overholt Principal of the High School but did make him Principal of the Junior High School on a two year contract, 2) Moved the Junior High Principal to the new post of Coordinator of Governmental Programs on a two year contract, 3) Elected Mr. Simons to a one year contract. His salary was indexed at 1.4, less than the 1.5 at the Junior High and the 1.45 for the Central Office post.

The regular meeting of Tuesday 24 May, was just that. Bills were paid, architectural plans moved forward, resolutions of appreciation for the recently departed Board members were made and passed, a contract was let for re-roofing one of the buildings, and so on. Three Assistant Principals were offered contracts. Late in the evening the President called for a special meeting three days later: '. . . for the purpose of interviewing candidates for the superintendency.' (5/24/66)

The *tenth* and last meeting of the busy two month period occurred Friday evening, 27 May, at 8:00 p.m. The Board had received applications from five individuals from outside the District. *None* of these made the short list to be interviewed. The four internal candidates were:

1 Mr. Ranson, currently Acting Superintendent
2 Mr. Eastman, long term teacher/administrator, formerly high school principal, currently central office administrative director of school organization

3   Mr. Eads, long term teacher/administrator, currently principal and director of maintenance
4   Dr. Ronald George, former teacher/CTA president, recently made elementary principal.

After a series of individual interviews and discussions, Mrs. Harcourt moved that Mr. Ranson be appointed. The motion lost 2–4. Then: 'Mr. Wilkerson moved that Dr. Ronald George be appointed Superintendent, effective July 1, 1966, for a period of one year at a salary of $16,750. Mr. Tuley seconded the motion.' (5/27/66) The motion carried 4–2. The new conservative coalition had started a new era, an era which lasts until today.

It seemed a far cry from the resolution four years before, that is: '... Ronald George, not be re-employed for the school year 1962–63, because of his contemptuous attitude toward Board members, his irrational behavior in public, and his totally unprofessional behavior ...' (4/10/62) The threads that hold social structures together and the slight if not chance events that determine large sequences of events are reflected in Mr. Wilkerson, a supporter of Mr. George in 1962, was the only Board member from the earlier time. He nominated George for Superintendent. Just a month before, Mr. Henderson had resigned from the Board. In 1972 he had voted to fire Mr. George.

Our story has come full circle. A highly critical Board had voted to fire Superintendent McBride in 1961. A large and bitter fight occurred. Ron George, a junior high social studies teacher and President of the CTA, backed McBride and brought an NEA committee into the District. This earned him the wrath of the innovative Board and almost cost him his job. These activities and interactions led to outside consultants, a more cosmopolitan short list and the hiring of Steven Spanman, Superintendent, 'a man who could talk the birds out of the trees.' The District was jolted differently, that is innovatively. To the majority it was a forward and better movement; to others it was ill advised. The community patrons were increasingly in the group perceiving the changes as 'ill advised.' The Board changed by votes and by resignations. The 4–2 majority eventually became a 2–4 minority. Is our episode one of school chaos, vulnerability, or political democracy?

A Tentative Summary and Conclusion

The movement for modernization which had begun in the Milford School Board in the fifties in the long tenure of Superintendent McBride overshot its mark in the reform movement of the sixties and the hiring of the radical educator Steven Spanman as Superintendent of Schools. He came to Milford as a man on the move with a concern for excellence in the education of the children of Milford. And for him excellence meant stong central office leadership from himself as superintendent, a radical child centered philosophy implemented with the latest educational technology both social and electronic. Individualized instruction, team teaching, and non-graded organization structures competed with overhead projectors, educational television and teaching machines. The centerpeice of all this was the innovative Kensington School, architecturally designed to accommodate the vision.

We have moved a long way away from the innovative Kensington Elementary School, our original starting point and our original problematic event. If 'agency' and 'politics' are a part of our current perspective on innovation, and they are, then Steven Spanman and his four years of tenure in the District provide vivid data on the meaning of the concepts. Mostly we have traced out the relationships between the Board and the Superintendent. Each reader will pick elements and events depending on his or her own interpretive agenda. We have only a few more general summary comments to make.

Whether one agrees or not with Spanman's agenda the vision and the scope of his aspirations are unquestionably large and far ranging. Most of this was laid out in the first year of his tenure as Superintendent. The district needed a new elementary school. This became one of the issues for the rethinking of the goals and the instrumentalities of education for the entire Milford School District. Outside consultants, visits to see new schools and the work of the architects, a set of *Educational Specifications* which elaborated the ideas into building realities, breaking and creating new personnel policies, recruiting staff on a national basis, all were part of the grand plan. The Kensington School opened in the 1964–65 school year. We recounted that story in great detail some years ago (Smith and Keith, 1971).

Within the district central office and the board room, perhaps the most fateful event, in the grand sense, was what we have called 'the national gamble.' Spanman and his key associates, Cohen and Shelby, wrote a five year proposal with a million dollar budget for the Olds Foundation, held a nationally oriented conference with representatives from government, private foundations, universities and research and development organizations in the winter of 1965, and tried to make the Milford School District and the Kensington School national models for the improvement of public education. Their hopes for an integrated approach to curriculum reform, for staff development, for administrative reorganization, and for community involvement were thwarted when funding was not forthcoming. They were a year or two ahead of President Johnson's broad and lavishly supported federal aid to education in the form of the Elementary and Secondary Education Act. Many of the proposals in the Milford and Kensington agenda were similar in intent to the content of several 'titles' in the federal program. Many of the Kensington faculty, after leaving Milford, would find 'homes' in one or another of those programs. Our *Educational Innovators: Then and Now* (1986) details much of that.

In the local Milford District, the array of innovative activities in curriculum, instruction, and staff reorganization in each of the schools and in the central office is remarkably large. Planned change can be a broad agenda. We recounted in some detail the development of a district policy handbook, an innovation of major importance, and one that was to outlast all of the others.

But if 'agency' was the hallmark of Superintendent Spanman, 'politics' was the hallmark of the Board of Education. And 'history', and the flow of events, leading up to the hiring of Spanman and to his departure and resignation four years later, was central to our interpretation of the context of innovation. The drama, both tragedy and comedy, was beyond anything we had imagined. The human condition in innovation and change in schooling is striking when examined in microscopic detail as we have tried to do here. But school dramas do not really end. They twist on through time in ever baffling ways. In Milford, the drama led to the long tenure of Ron George, the next Superintendent of schools.

Notes

1   We find ourselves reaching beyond the presented data for inferences related to other conversations, observations, and experiences. We insert them along the way to elaborate the evolving profile. In the methodology chapter we phrased this as triangulation. See also Smith and Kleine (1986).

2   The reader might note that free textbooks came into the District in the 1920s by Board action.

3   During this same period the district contracted with the County for 'Mental Health Services.'

4   Cohen's perspective and role appear in more detail in *Educational Innovators: Then and Now* (Smith, Kleine, Prunty, and Dwyer, 1986).

Chapter 8

The Georgian Period: Maintaining Small Town Values in a Complex Society

---

Introduction

The thesis we are proposing for the tenure of Milford's current Superintendent of schools, Ron George, is the educational difficulties, dilemmas, and visions of maintaining small town values, if not virtues, in a turbulent suburban community. As we present his story we find that his battle is not his alone, rather it is the story of the school board as well, and even more fundamentally it is a story of the Milford community. We believe that all this has much to say about the phenomenon of innovation in American education.

Prophetic, or happenstance, we are not sure, but several 'minor' items characterized the beginning of Ron George's tenure as Superintendent.

1   The Board interviewed only local, inside candidates, although five outsiders had applied.
2   Before appointing Ron George the Board had settled almost every major administrative appointment — principals and assistant principals and all central office personnel.
3   The Board offered him a one year contract instead of the usual three year contract.
4   And, finally, they paid him as the new Superintendent, $2250 less than his predecessor, an unusual event.

Now, the position of Superintendent, beyond whatever the personality, style, and aspirations of the incumbent, seemed to be 'hemmed in.' The new Board seems to have reordered the power relations between itself and the Superintendent. The Board seemed to be back in control. That seems a formidable set of givens.

A recurring generalization strikes one immediately on reading the 14 June minutes. Even though it's a special meeting, the Board attends to a large volume of usual business. A contract for constructing the high school cafeteria was awarded. And the major purpose of the special meeting was met. Redeemed Bonds and coupons were burned 'in the presence of two credible witnesses.' Contracts were approved for classrooms of exceptional children. Approval occurred for paying dues for Midwest State School Board Association. Authorization was granted to pay bills over the Summer. Bids were accepted for clocks at the Kensington and Midvale Schools. A $396,00 contract 'for exterminating services of all kitchen storerooms and warehouses in the District for the 1966–67 school year.' And on and on.

Symbolically, for our evolving political perspective on innovation and change, the new Board defeated, on a 4–2 vote, a $250.00 travel expenditure for the Principal of Kensington to attend a professional meeting to receive a national award for the Kensington Elementary School. The maker of the motion, Mrs. Harcourt, indicated that 'she plans to accept the award for the Kensington School, if possible, at her own expense' (6/14/66). The 'out's' were now the 'in's' and what was once good, desirable, and important was no longer so. Cosmopolitanism was one of those former 'goods.' Localism was now a virtue.

We seem to be seeing various minutes as 'symbolic' of the new Board and Superintendent. Perhaps it's just the contrast between George and Spanman, but . . . 'Mr. Tuley moved that Dr. George be allowed to attend the Midwest State Teachers' Association meeting November 3 and 4 *at his own expense*. Mr. Wilkerson seconded the motion and it carried unanimously.' (Ours italics) (10/11/66) Frugality and localism have returned — with a vengeance.

The District Saga in the Early Georgian Years: 1966–68

The First Year: A Different Kind of Beginning

The District, under the direction of its new Superintendent seemed to be characterized by 'normal business,' less turmoil, and smaller volume of reports, initiatives and expositions, and less time spent in meetings. The School Board meetings typically adjourned before midnight. The volume of explanation and 'paper' bound into the minutes decreased noticeably. Although the votes were sometimes split, 5–1 and occasionally 4–2, the coalition seemed gone. Rather, individual members were raising occasional objections to items they disapproved. Mostly, building additions were being built and day to day concerns were being handled with dispatch and unanimity.

In October the Assistant Superintendent Alan Ranson, the chief competitor for the Superintendency, who had been on leave, submitted his resignation, effective immediately. The Board granted it unanimously. He was joining the US Department of Education. Rumor had it that Spanman was instrumental in helping place him. This 'normal' ebb and flow of personnel seems critical for homogeneity and cohesiveness in a small group such as a central office staff. It suggests also that personnel changes and departures may be considerably less traumatic and actually better for the individual and the organization than is sometimes suggested.

In November 1966, the Board began what was to be a major set of substantive and procedural issues — discussions with the local CTA over salary issues:

> The Board discussed at some length the teachers' request for a four percent
> salary increase. It was the consensus of the Board that the District could not

afford a four percent salary increase at this time. The Board agreed that while they could not grant an increase at this time, they were sympathetic to an increase in salaries next year both in the beginning salary and the index. (11/19/66)

The Board asked the committee to calculate minimum and maximum schedules for different starting salaries and different indexes and to meet with them again a month later.

The meeting in December found the Board picking the lower starting level, $5500 rather than $5600 or $5700 but accepting the ten step scale and the new index. All this was contingent on passing the levy in February.

The Chairman of the CTA salary committee wrote the Board in January:

The Salary and Welfare Committee of the Milford Classroom Teachers' Association hereby expresses its appreciation for the cooperation extended by the Board of Education in the constructive discussions of teachers' benefits and the proposed teachers' Salary Index.

We express our sincere gratification that ours was the first and, to date, the only school district in which the School Board has given recognition to and invited representatives of the CTA to discuss their problems at a Board meeting.

We earnestly hope the Board will afford opportunity in the future to present more of our suggestions for proper consideration.

Respectively yours,
Mrs. Jill Wedgewood

Mixed in with the salary issue and special tax levy were several other issues. Patron concern erupted over community rumors that school boundaries would be shifted radically. The Board President acknowledged Mr. Tuley who issued a statement at the 24 January meeting that began this way:

Mr. Tuley stated that it had come to his attention that there was a rumor being spread that after the School Levy is passed, the complete school system will undergo a boundary change. Mr. Tuley said he knew nothing official other than the eleven principals are having their annual meeting to discuss school populations and that he wanted time now for Dr. George and Board members to express themselves and then open the meeting for public questions. (1/24/67)

The other comments indicate that a variety of suggestions and plans were under consideration and that all administrative suggestions would pass through the Board's usual review and action procedures.

The written statement of Mr. Tuley's, also enclosed with the minutes, was a bit hotter:

It has come to my attention during the week of a vicious and malicious (secret) rumor that definitely needs clarification if we are to pass the teachers' levy February 7th.

Through telephone calls and personal contacts, I have found out an official of our school system has stated ('This is secret but after the school levy is passed, the complete system will undergo a boundary change')

From experience, just using the word secret, and some action of past Boards, Paul Revere has delivered his 'secret' from border to border in our District.

Tonight will be the deciding night on will the school levy pass or fail . . .

Knowing nothing official — other than eleven (11) elementary principals are having their annual meeting to discuss school population, I want time now for Dr. George and all other Board members to express themselves, then open the meeting for public questions . . . (1/13/67)

Another Board member, Mr. Grider, in a longer statement also criticized the 'rumor monger.' Two paragraphs from his note raise the historical contextual issues that seem ever present:

That patrons believe this rumor and suspect the Board of deception indicates that there is still a residue of distrust against a previous board and administration, when half truths and rumor were frequently employed to delude the public. The present Board and administration have tried to be conscientious, straight-forward, and reasonable. We tried to provide transportation where a need existed, have eliminated the double sessions at the Junior High School, have worked with the CTA salary committee, and have listened sympathetically to the problems of parents and students.

That seems a potent criticism of the prior Board and administration and yields further insight on the particulars of the prior political action, from the perspective of the 'new Board.' It also indicates some of the particular substantive issues that split school communities. A later paragraph accents our evolving conceptions of board-administration relationships, from the perspective of the new group: 'This Board is not a puppet organization of 'yes-men' for any administrative official or committee. Our duty is to the patrons.' (1/24/67) If doubts existed on the nature and substance of the new Board-Administration relationships this kind of comment, addressed to a different issue, removes them one more time.

Also brewing in Suburban County were several larger petitions to consolidate some of the school districts into larger districts and a petition to consolidate all schools in Suburban County into a single district. The impetus at this time was financial equity. Suburban County had considerable variability in district tax bases and in tax rates. The poorest districts tended to have the highest rates.

Also in January, and this was earlier than usual, the Board on a 5–1 vote, offered Dr. George a three year contract with a $1000 raise, to $17,500. Mrs. Harcourt, the lone holdover from the Spanman coalition, voted 'No'.

The unofficial return on 7 February indicated the levy had failed. The Board moved unanimously to resubmit it on 17 March 1967. The official returns indicate it finally passed with a simple majority.

The April elections contained one more unusual item. School Board member Mr. Grider had indicated that he would be leaving the District in August to accept an out-of-town post. He accepted the position after the closing date for decisions to run for the Board, therefore it was too late for a candidate of similar persuasion to file. Consequently he decided to stay on the ballot. A group of citizens saw this as unethical. Their petition to the Board was rejected because the Board had no jurisdiction over the matter. The elections settled the issue, for Mr. Grider lost. The other incumbent, Mrs. Harcourt, the last of the Spanman coalition, also lost.

The community overwhelmingly rejected a small change in District boundaries 1090–4355. Citizens of Milford don't give away any of their territory.

A confrontation occurred with the part-time bus drivers, who thought they had been promised a $.50 increase but only received a $.25 increase per run. They indicated they would not drive the next day. Dr. George then responded: '. . . that it was their decision whether they drove the buses in the morning or not but any driver who refused to drive a bus Wednesday, April 12, 1967, would be dismissed.' (4/11/67) The Board went on record, unanimously, to support the Superintendent. The Board granted small increases to several other groups of non professional employees.

A special session was called for 27 April; the Board met with three state legislators, the striking and non-striking bus drivers, and some of the District patrons. The give and take found the Board's position essentially unchanged. The key statement was made by Mr. Edmond: 'Mr. Edmond said the Board had made its decision on what it felt it could do and he suggested to the drivers that anyone who wanted could fill out an application and when there was an opening he would be considered.' (4/27/67) Mr. Reeves indicated that the Board was concerned but that '. . . it could not give any of the non certificated people everything they wanted,' (4/27/67). One citizen, speaking from the audience, gave the Board 'a vote of confidence of the people of the District in the manner in which they handled the situation' (4/27/67).

The Board continued to vote for a conservative *status quo* state of affairs with an accompanying limit on spending:

> Mr. Edmond moved that the President vote against that portion of the League of Superintendents of Suburban County 1967–68 budget to hire an Executive Director and to maintain it on the same basis as has been done in the past. Mr. Wilkerson seconded the motion and it carried unanimously. (5/9/67)

The Board's fiscal concerns seemed to continue cutting in every direction, as one minute in June testifies: 'Mr. Edmond moved that the Board not renew its membership in Midwest State School Boards' Association for the 1967–68 school year due to an increase in dues. Mr. Eastland seconded the motion and it carried unanimously.' (6/16/67) Spanman's cosmopolitan thrust continued to succumb to a new Board's vision of frugal local public education.

The Board joined other districts in Suburban County in urging their legislators to vote against a teacher tenure bill. Among the parts of the bill about which dissatisfaction was expressed was:

1 inclusion of the Superintendent
2 one way protection for the teacher but not the district
3 program changes not recognized in reduction of faculty
4 retention only on a seniority basis
5 probation burden on the district to allege incompetency.

The public face of the legislator's perspective can be seen in a reply to the Milford Board:

> I will certainly give your views consideration, but as you know there are hundreds of boards in Midwest State and all other boards do not operate as your board has and all boards have not treated their teachers fairly. Suburban County is a peculiar situation in that a teacher can leave one district without selling his home. This is not true outstate. The matter will no doubt be very thoroughly discussed on the floor if the amended bill reaches the Senate. (6/30/67)

The Second Year: Routines Established

Dr. George's second year seemed to have fallen into an easy routine. In August the principalship problems had been solved and the teachers' salary concerns had been delayed until more information was known from the State Department. The Insurance Advisory Commission was functioning. Federal revenues included $473.00 for vocational education programs and $5019.00 for NDEA and Title III programs. The part-time bus drivers' wages were increased by $.25 for the morning run and $.25 for the afternoon run. Bids for junior and senior high towel and linen service were accepted as were bids for gasoline, for fuel oil, for uniforms, and for portable cafeteria tables. A contract for student teachers was signed with State Teachers College.

The regular once a month curriculum presentations to the Board continued, but they seemed more low key and often were presentations by central office personnel. The four inservice programs for the year, as presented in October, involved three textbook companies and their consultants in math, spelling, and English 'at no cost to the District.' The fourth was presented by the District math coordinator. A committee on Instructional Improvement was formed.

Dr. George's 'Agendas' for the Board were considerably briefer, partly in number of items, but mostly in the length of rationales and explanations accompanying each item. Most non business items were presented 'for discussion' or 'for information.' For a variety of reasons he was not leading out as Dr. Spanman had; the proactive style, as we called it, was gone. The Board seemed happy with all this for, on 24 October 1967, they voted unanimously to increase his salary to $18,750, retroactive to 1 July 1967.

Much of our narrative in Dr. George's first two years has broken out into many sub themes — teacher activism, financing of programs, the American dilemma, and so forth. In the Spring of 1968, we should note, meetings were being held regarding the possible statewide reorganization of the public school districts. The central issues were the elimination of small 100 pupil districts in outstate areas and reduction of the disparity in economic resources prevalent in the state. Suburban County could be affected by the latter moves.

In April the Board elections occurred. Mr. Wilkerson, a major controversial figure, opponent of Dr. Spanman and supporter of Dr. George, chose not to run. The other incumbent, Sherman Reeves, won handily. Mr. Wells joined the Board. Mr. Tuley was unanimously re-elected President, Mr. Eastland became Vice President. The Secretary and Treasurer posts remained the same. All votes were unanimous. It looked as though the conservative continuity would persist.

Conclusion of the Initial Years

As one reads the minutes and develops a narrative of Dr. George's first years, several close-to-the-data generalizations appear. 1) The Board has reasserted itself and taken back power which had escaped to Spanman, the earlier incumbent. 2) Frugality and localism vied with each other as to which was instrumental and which was master value. Sometimes they cut national and state ties to save money and sometimes they saved money to turn inward on themselves, their own problems, and their own resources. 3) While opposing state legislation for a teacher tenure law, the Board spent considerable time in good faith discussions, if not negotiations, and cooperative efforts with the local CTA. 4) School boundaries — between Milford and other districts and within Milford (elementary attendance areas) — remained nearly sacrosanct. When given a vote, the patrons wanted the *status quo*. What not given a vote they continued to protest vigorously. 5) Simmering, just off stage, about ready to return, is the American Dilemma. 6) Finally, we find the new Superintendent, for the moment, overshadowed by the Board, in tune with the conservative, frugal, localist sentiments, gradually learning his job and developing his style.

Superintendent George's 'Quiet' Middle Years: 1968–74

Introduction

To speak of 'quiet years' in the life of a Superintendent of schools may seem to reflect naivete if not a loss of contact with reality. But with our focus on 'innovation and change' in the district this was a time of quietness, stability, and gradual yet pervasive increase in ideological conservatism. The day to day business predominates, with a few exceptions. In August of 1968, the Board 'received' the Senior High Yearbook, paid the Summer bills, permitted the Jehovah's Witnesses the use of the Senior High Gymnasium and Cafeteria, arranged for the annual inspection of school buildings, awarded contracts for gasoline, oil and antifreeze, made arrangements with the Office of Civil Defense to store supplies at the Marquette School, bought ten sewing machines and cabinets for the New Junior High School, instructed the Attorney to prepare the papers for the bond issue, accepted the resignations of eight more teachers, elected 18 teachers, and continued the tax sheltered annuity program for a half dozen noncertificated and half dozen certificated personnel. The meeting adjourned at 11:42 p.m.

The Story Continues

Patrons, Poverty, and Other Problems.   In the Autumn of 1968, the first try at a bond issue failed the two-third's criterion, 2992 Yea versus 1821 Nay. Regarding the tax levy, the CTA Salary Committee met with the Board. The Board President asked: '. . . a member of the Committee to go over the District's books and see if they don't come up with the same figures as the Administrator. He said last year this was not done and they were always quoting different figures.' (10/15/68) The Board continued its very open and cooperative stance.

The North Central Association's secondary evaluation program came to the district in 1968–69 for the first time. This was the year of self study; next year would bring in a group of outside educators. On the Superintendent's recommendation, the Board approved the costs of the evaluation on 22 October. A month later, the Assistant Superintendent, the High School Principal, and the Chairman of the Steering Committee presented the issues briefly and engaged in a discussion on the evaluation format with the Board.

The Bond Issue for $1,800,000 was defeated a second time in December, 2168 to 1546. The Board voted unanimously to resubmit in January. Finally it passed 4295 versus 1849 on 28 January.

The lunch program returned in the form of a motion to: '. . . designate the Assistant Superintendent for Administration to determine which individual children are eligible for free or reduced price lunches under the established policy criteria.' (1/14/69) The Superintendent was the person to whom appeals would be made. According to the Superintendent's remarks, the 90th Congress was moving toward 'a more uniform national policy for evaluating need and protecting the identity of needy children' (1/14/69). The new regulations required written policies, clear indication of delegated authority, appeal procedures, and confidentiality procedures. The initial National School Lunch Act had been passed originally in 1946.

Also in February, the Board approved unanimously all the administrators' salaries and two-year contracts for the succeeding year. Dr. George received a new three-year contract at $2000 more than the highest paid Assistant Superintendent, $20295. In these trying financial times, Dr. George finally was catching up with his predecessor's salary.

In February 1969, the Board returned again to general financing of the District. Contingent on passing the levy, the minimum teachers' salaries would be increased $500.00 to a $6300 base. The Superintendent's Agenda contained these remarks:

The CTA Salary Negotiating Committee and the Board of Education Negotiating Committee have reviewed and discussed various proposals and counter proposals. In addition, the entire CTA, as well as the Board of Education, have considered various salary possibilities. At a meeting on February 11, 1969, the two committees reached an agreement. This agreement is to have a $6300 base with all other features of the salary schedule to remain the same. (1/25/69)

Curriculum issues arose in March 1969 in three separate items. The North Central Evaluation continued on schedule. The chairpersons of the Philosophy and Objectives Committee and the School and Community Committee met with the Board, along with Dr. Luther, the Assistant Superintendent, and Mr. Bakan, the High School Principal. The Board approved the District's participation in a Title III Social Studies Project. It approved a new high school course in Power Mechanics. A Title I Summer Program, with $14,617 from the State Department was underway. The regular elementary, secondary, and music Summer programs were continued.

The tax levy failed in March, 2382 versus 3157. The same levy was defeated again in April, 1964 versus 3166. Reports continued to circulate about groups across Midwest State trying to influence the legislature to change the two-third's requirement, to increase cigarette taxes for schools, and so forth (4/22/69). The levy failed again in May, 3382 versus 3105. Teacher CTA delegates were given released time to join other groups in Capitol City to meet with state legislators. The Board reactivated the Citizens' Advisory Committee of the District.

On 13 May 1969, overcrowding in one of the schools required youngsters from McBride School to be bussed to Johnson and Marquette. The parents' petition stated: '... that neither the best interest of the children involved nor of the community as a whole will be served by this decision.' (5/13/69) Changing school boundaries and moving children about never happens in Milford without complaints, petitions, and argument.[1]

At the same meeting, 13 May 1969, enumeration date were presented to the Board by the Superintendent. No minute was made over any discussion or action. In retrospect, it was an ominous sign of the demographic scythe which was to cut in reverse direction and become a part of the mid and late 1970s turmoil faced by the Superintendent, the Milford Board, and ultimately, the community. These data are in Figure 28.

In the midst of all the money problems, the Secretary and Treasurer of the Board in independent motions, again moved that they refuse compensation for their services. These amounts were $50 and $150 per year. This continued an earlier precedent. Board officers in Milford received no remuneration for their services.

On 10 June 1969 the levy was defeated once again, 4021 to 3021. That evening the Board voted unanimously to resubmit on 26 June at the same rate. Correspondence continued with State Representatives supporting increased state aid to schools. A variety of complications continued in the form of moves for tax equalization in Suburban County where the differences between the poorest districts and the wealthiest districts was substantial. Not so latent in the financial battles were

Figure 28: School Enumeration of Milford 1965 versus 1969

Age	1969	1965	Increase or Decrease
0	564	710	− 146
1	691	922	− 231
2	759	967	− 208
3	812	1,101	− 289
4	878	1,140	− 262
5	991	1,242	− 251
Total	4,695	6,082	−1,387
6	996	1,238	− 242
7	1,136	1,330	− 194
8	1,164	1,358	− 194
9	1,139	1,274	− 135
10	1,179	1,225	− 46
11	1,213	1,187	+ 26
12	1,237	1,188	+ 49
13	1,222	1,068	+ 154
14	1,098	916	+ 182
15	1,084	908	+ 176
16	1,069	885	+ 184
17	1,017	757	+ 260
18	811	774	+ 37
19	710	376	+ 334
Total	15,075	14,484	+ 591
Summary			
0–5	4,695	6,082	−1,387
6–19	15,075	14,484	+ 591
Total	19,770	20,566	− 796

proposals for varying kinds of consolidation of school districts. As we have indicated, this issue always brought out strong negative sentiments in parts of the larger suburban community. Further complications existed in opinion on the elimination of tax free regulations on municipal bonds. The Milford Board unanimously opposed 'the elimination of tax exemption on Municipal Bonds' (6/24/69). Also on 24 June the Board voted to proceed with next year's budget based on the total tax rate of $4.85.

On 26 June at a special session, the unofficial returns indicated the levy had failed once more:

> After a short discussion of the Teachers' Levy, it was the consensus of the Board that a decision not be made at this time and a meeting be held Tuesday, July 1, 1969, to discuss the Teachers' Levy with members of the Citizens' Advisory Committee, Mothers' Circles, PTAs, Ministers, City Officials, and any interested person of the District. (6/26/69)

In a sense, the State rescued the Milford District. The legislature passed the cigarette tax and the District would receive approximately $300,000.00, roughly the equivalent of the $.39 tax increase (from $2.50–$2.89 on the teachers' levy). The Board talked with the citizens' groups attending the meeting. Later, in executive session, the Board talked with the CTA representatives 'to discuss the teachers' viewpoint on the levy.' Shortly thereafter the Board voted to submit, on 17 July, the $2.50 levy which required only a simple majority.

From time to time, we have incorporated in our report total sets of minutes of particular meetings because they captured an image of educational life, community, policy, and administration in the Milford District. Such was the case of the Special Meeting on 17 July, to receive the unofficial election returns:

> Mr. Eastland read the unofficial election returns, which were 3813 for the levy and 908 against the levy.
>
> Dr. George informed the Board that a letter certifying the $4.46 tax rate for the 1969–70 year would be sent to the County Tax Commissioner's Office.
>
> Mr. Adams arrived at 8:12 p.m.
>
> Mr. Tuley moved that the administration be authorized to proceed with plans to have the Acme Electric Company complete electrical work on the new sports tower at the Senior High School, including a 1000 amp panel, for the bid price of $5966.00 and that plans be made for the Maintenance Department and the Dads' Club to proceed with erection of the tower. Mr. Wells seconded the motion and it carried unanimously.
>
> Dr. George read a letter from Mr. Billing at the County Audio-Visual Office inviting the Board and administration to preview the sex education films available from the County Audio-Visual Department. No action was taken regarding this request.
>
> A discussion of the type of sex education provided by the District ensued. The District doesn't have a K–12 sequential sex education program, and there are no plans, at this time, to institute such a program. The District, over the years, has incorporated sex education in the science and health departments and has cooperated with elementary Mothers' Circles in providing after school sessions in sex education with parental approval, for elementary children.
>
> Dr. George informed the Board that letters of appreciation for their roles in providing additional state funds were sent to State Senators and Representatives.
>
> There being no further business to come before the Board, Mr. Tuley moved that the meeting be adjourned. Mr. Wells seconded the motion and it carried unanimously. The President declared the meeting adjourned at 8:51 p.m. (7/17/69)

Money, athletics, sex, and politics, the staples of American life, or at least successful novels of American life, are indigenous to American Schools, or at least to Milford Schools, on this occasion. Small wonder that strong sentiments and intractable conflict run just below the surface of the Board's deliberations and central office administrative actions.

Perhaps also a less tongue-in-cheek summary comment might be made. In this first year of the 'quiet' middle period, the multitude of groups influencing the direction of the District in conjunction with the Board should be noted. The CTA Salary Committee was invited to inspect the financial records. The North Central Association came for the first time with its evaluative criteria for the High School. The patrons voted, and voted, and voted. The regional White House Conference was occurring. The participating citizens in the community were paying for the Adult Education Program. The Federal government was altering aspects of the school lunch program. Title I and Title III programs of ESEA arrived. The state legislature passed a cigarette tax for schools. A Citizens' Advisory Committee was reactivated. And lingering on the side lines, but beginning to appear were changes in demography — the shift in population of children in the community. Preschool, elementary, and secondary figures show the post war population wave was declining.

In November 1969, the North Central Evaluation proceeded and the Board received the High School self-study report and met with the Steering Committee. On 10 March the Board received the final report. Milford continued to become more and more a part of the national educational fabric.

The District also participated in an exchange student program at the High School level. Into such a curricular innovation comes on occasion, a touch of warmth: 'Dr. George read a thank you note to the Board from Miss Goteburg, a foreign exchange student from Scandinavia attending Senior High School, thanking the Board for the ski jacket the Board gave her for Christmas.' (1/13/70) We don't have data on the immediate consequences for Milford of such a program. When our thoughts run back to the origins of Milford High School in the late 1920s and early 1930s, the transformation seems incredible for the forty year period.

In an earlier discussion, we made the generalization that the schools gradually adopt the developing technology available in the larger community or environment. In this instance, increasing size and complexity of the District joined with availability. The Superintendent's agenda in January 1970 spoke to the issue of 'Budgetary and Payroll Accounting Equipment':

> In 1956, the School District purchased an NCR #31 bookkeeping machine. This machine was replaced by an NCR #33 in 1961. Both of these machines were primarily the same in operation and capacity. Our present machine has a nine total capacity. The vast increase in financial accounting and number of employees has made the present equipment rather inadequate.
>
> There has also been a continuing rate of deductions for employees due to additional taxes and fringe benefits, plus the continued changing of these deductions such as federal and state income tax, insurance, social security, and retirement plans. At the present, an employee could elect to have twenty deductions or entries on his check, depending on the type of position. (1/27/70)

After considering several plans, the Superintendent recommended and the Board approved unanimously: '... that the district purchase the Burroughs direct accounting computer, Style E4493, from Burroughs Corporation for $22,941, plus a programing change of $2391, or a total of $25,332.' (1/27/70)

Our more general experience in Milford suggests that the District lags behind most business organizations on the adoption of this technology. Xerox machines and word processors were slow in replacement of mimeograph machines and typewriters in the District offices.[2]

In February 1970, in what begins to look like an annual event now, the Board and the CTA Salary Committee proposals were up for discussion. The Board continues its tradition of meeting and talking with representatives of the Community Teachers Association, in spite of the frustrations connected with limited resources, due to an inability to convince the patrons to vote higher levies.

In February 1970, the Board voted the administrator's new two-year contract and the Superintendent a new three-year contract. They carried unanimously. Insofar as this is an important criterion of mutual satisfaction, the Board and the administration seemed to be working well together.

For those of us on university campuses in the late 1960s and early 1970s, when turmoil, conflict, and different perspectives occurred in high relief, the minimal problems in student activism in the elementary and secondary schools seems unreal. The Milford Board of Education seemed apart from most of this. In March 1970, a letter from a High School student was 'received' and became a part of the minutes. We present it as Figure 29. Its uniqueness, a single instance, speaks dramatically for the general state of the system.

At any given moment, discriminating between a one off occurrence and a straw-in-the-wind is a very difficult perceptual judgment. The sentiments driving this one high school senior will coalesce dramatically a year later.

If student Edward Connor's pleas for changing an aspect of the Milford School

---

Figure 29: Letter from a High School Senior

ATTENTION MILFORD SCHOOL BOARD

Do you know that you are operating in violation of the Constitution, not to mention several court decisions? Your prohibition of buttons, armbands, and insignias (such as ♀,⊕) is in clear violation of the First Amendment and several court cases: including Tinker versus Des Moines and Burnside versus Bryars. An additional interesting case in West Virginia versus Barnette. (For your full enlightenment obtain the Early September, 1969 copy of the Washington (DC) Free Press, 1522 Connecticut Avenue and turn to page 7.) Can an *American* school system operate that way? In the decision of Terminello versus Chicago the court gave this view of American rights; '... this sort of hazardous freedom and openness — that is the basis of our national strength and of the independence and vigor of Americans who grow up and live in this relatively permissive society.' You are doing a pretty poor job of educating your pupils for personal involvement in the democratic processes when you forbid students the most basic individual right — freedom of speech and expression. You had better wake up, Milford School Board, before someone besides the few politically aware students on your campuses recognize your repression of ideas dissimilar to your own.

Edward Connor
Milford Senior High

District were falling for the moment on deaf ears, the pleas of the teachers had fared better in the state legislature. On 7 April 1970: 'Mr. Irby, School Attorney, and the Board discussed the various aspects of the Teacher Tenure Law which becomes effective July 1, 1970.' Later in the evening: 'Mr. Tuley moved that the Board rescind Board Policy No. 4119.3 — Notification of Unsatisfactory Service — so it can be revised to comply with the Teacher Tenure Law. Mr. Wells seconded the motion and it carried unanimously.' (4/7/70) A major change in the ground rules of school governance had occurred. Presumably the Nussbaums of the world, if not having their retribution, now would have to be treated differently.

On 28 April, three members of Suburban County's drug abuse organization spoke to the Board. The Superintendent indicated they should make appointments with the junior high school principals. The smoking problem took on another aroma. Discipline issues now involved not only reasonably simple rights and wrongs of personal behavior and relationships among students. teachers, and administrators but also the larger community. Laws and penalties existed regarding controlled substances; public agencies at many levels, this time the County, representing different parts of the community were 'working' on the 'problems.' Milford's Board and administration were cooperating in those efforts.

Faculty and student rights intertwined regarding another brief minute in the Board record:

> Mr. Peter Alena, a faculty member of the Senior High School who had been reassigned to the Central Office, asked to speak to the Board in regard to his beard and why he was taken out of his classroom.
>
> The Board informed Mr. Alena there were other factors involved besides the beard, but, in regard to the beard, they felt that since there was a dress code at the Senior High School it was the responsibility of a teacher to set an example for the students and to teach the students the responsibility of adhering to rules and regulations even though they think they are wrong until such time as a rule may be changed by working through proper procedures. (4/28/70)

The complexities of individual rights, organizational demands, philosophies of change, multiple perspectives, and power (immediate and long term) were being operationalized.

The administrative action of Mr. Alena's reassignment provoked both a letter from a citizen who found the action 'absolutely incredible' and a more restrained letter from the President of the East Suburban County Ministerial Alliance whose members had heard the story on local TV. A paragraph from that letter raises another perspective:

> As Pastors we are concerned both for the rights of the individual and for quality education, concerns which we are certain you and the Board of Education share. To this end, we would appreciate a full appraisal at your

earliest convenience so we can assist in interpreting the District's policies
among our congregations. (4/24/70)

The local community has many subparts. They begin to stir at different times over
different issues.

Issues such as these are never simple and one dimensional. Some of the
complications appeared in a letter from Peter Alena to an assistant principal of the
high school, dated two months earlier, 24 February 1970:

> This is to inform you that I do not intend to return to Milford. At present
> my plans for next year are to continue in law school at City University, but
> in the day division. Currently I am enrolled in the night division, but I do
> not feel that I am giving either my position at Milford or law school the
> attention they deserve. I hope this early announcement will facilitate
> matters and aid you in your work. Also, at this time, I want to thank you
> for all the time and trouble you have spent in helping a freshman teacher
> adjust to a new experience. Be assured it has been greatly appreciated.
>
> Sincerely yours,
Peter Alena

Criss-crossing the rights issues are those of a beginning teacher, an individual still
making early career decisions, and a person trying out two demanding career
options at the same time.

What kind of a society do we want? What kind of schools as a part of that
society? Who is we — students, teachers, administrators, board, and citizens?
Analytically, these are ethical questions, socio-political questions, and organizational
questions. And perhaps that is what educational questions are — ultimately. For
those of us trained in value free educational science and research that seems an 'awe-
fully' large domain outside the usual scope of expertness.

But District business continued. The Spring 1970 tax levy met with defeat —
2292 for and 4363 against. 'Poverty' remained a major contextual given. The
housing report reflected several major items: the placement of kindergarten children
remained a problem for their numbers were always larger than the numbers in the
early grades because some children went from public kindergarten to parochial
elementary schools. Second, some schools were more crowded and others were
more empty. Third, the Suburban County Exceptional Children's Program rented
classrooms in local schools. Fourth, the continuous construction of apartment
complexes shifted populations in particular schools. Kensington was involved in
both the kindergarten issues (100 pupils) and the apartment complex issues (29
pupils).

On 23 June 1970, the Board voted to resubmit the $5.43 levy. They met with
the 'CTA Crisis Committee' and a group of patrons. They would decide in August
when to submit the levy and to reach a: '. . . decision as to when school would open
. . .' (6/23/70) The Suburban County Teachers' Association sent a letter in support
of the Milford Board's resubmission of the levy.

The year didn't really end. The calendar just ran out. And that may be important conceptionally. Some of us have a conception of educational time that has units of multiple lengths — a class period, a day, a week, a term, a semester, and a year. A concept such as the 'rhythm of the year' breaks down here. Some items clearly have a yearly pattern or regularity — for example, opening school, semester grades, holidays (especially for the younger children), hiring teachers, closing school. The Board is wrestling now with problems of a different scope, complexity, and a different kind of unit or interval.

A variety of summary statements about innovation and change in American Education might be made at the close of the 1970–71 school year, 'a year of trauma.' The financial guillotine hanging over the Board's head or the knife at one's throat reached its dramatic conclusion in the Autumn when five tax levies failed and the schools were closed from Thanksgiving to mid-December. Among other groups, the CTA actively participated in the discussions, the closed doors, and the aftermath of financial resolutions.

Hardly had that trauma been coped with and the Board ran headlong into a major confrontation with students at the Senior High School. The proposed revision of the dress code was moving too rapidly for the Board and not rapidly enough for the students. On 28 April some of the students stayed out of class, took to the roofs and disrupted the educational program.

Into these more dramatic events of stability and change in the District, appeared a very small item of a third force for change in the District. The minutes reported it this way:

> Since the District has an unsatisfactory rating in the area of pupil services on the elementary level, it was the consensus of the Board that the Administration start working to define the needs of the District, develop job descriptions, employ appropriate personnel, organize, communicate, implement, and work with the State Department of Education in formulating a program for the District. (6/22/71)

The Final Chapter in Milford's Story 1975–80

Introduction

Although we label this section 'the final chapter in Milford's story,' it is really our story which is ending, not Milford's. Briefly, we hope to bring the District story to the 1979–80 school year, the year we returned to Kensington for the intensive ethnography of the school and the year we interviewed most of the former faculty.[3] In this manner our historical context has evolved to the present day, a contemporaneous context for the Kensington School. The description and interpretation of the contemporaneous Kensington School now will have a contemporary district context and that context can be seen as having evolved out of a sixty-five year history of struggles to provide an education for the children of Milford.

Rather than detail events in a moment by moment, or minute by minute chronological style we opt to focus on several key issues. The Milford Community appears in demographic form as changing in multiple ways, and through the perspective of two key groups, the Citizens Advisory Committee and the District Housing Committee. Our second major strand involves 'the changing school board' which is consequence, correlate, and cause of the community change and school changes. It is perhaps 'the story' of this period in Milford. Finally, a half dozen major strands from our earlier history remain as important parts of Milford. Teacher activism reaches its apogee. Federal Programs continue to march through Milford. The American Dilemma takes on another major twist and turn. Through all this the curriculum, conditions of schooling, and student problems of discipline continue. Finally, there is 'business business.' A concluding image of the Board in June, 1980 completes our chronology and initial interpretation.

The Milford Community

Philosophic views vary regarding the school's relation to the community, for example, should the schools reflect the community or should the schools lead in changing the community? Years earlier, when the high school program was initiated year by year (1927–31) and when there was a question of its actual survival, one of the Board members at the time commented, 'the forward looking elements' prevailed. Perhaps 'forward looking' was easier to define and more easily agreed upon fifty years ago than today. Or perhaps the limited post World War I suburbanization, the streetcar transportation linkages, and the semi-rural townships and truck farms melded more easily with the new 'settlers.' Or perhaps times were stabler and the 'roaring twenties' had not roared through this part of America.

In the mid 1970s, Milford was a large working class/lower middle class suburban community beginning to be hit with major demographic changes — inflation, enrollment decline, increase in minority population, increased transiency, rise in single parent families, and a slight drop in overall socioeconomic status. In our view these portend complex school problems. The interplay of these changes and the actions and reactions of Milford's Board of Education and Administration, as schooling continues, maintains a drama of high significance.

To intellectually grapple with this we present a brief description of the community from a survey conducted for the High School North Central Evaluation, a description of 'problems' faced by the Board, and an account of two committees, the Housing Committee and the Citizens Committee, which the Board reactivated to help mediate the school-community relationship.

A Brief Demographic Description of Milford.   Images of communities arise in many ways. Mostly we have accented inferences from items in the Board minutes. Occasionally letters, news accounts, petitions, reports, and interview material have entered. Now, briefly, we excerpt several items responded to by 2200 households in the 1976 Northcentral Evaluation of the Milford Senior High School. It was presented then as a picture of the community. No comments appeared in the minutes that anyone thought it grossly distorted their view of the District.

Perhaps the central educational statistic is the educational level of the patrons. These were broken down by gender into the interesting labels of 'husband' and 'wife,' presumably because the questionnaires went to households:

	Husbands (per cent)	Wives (per cent)
Eighth grade or less	11%	7%
Some high school	17%	19%
High school graduate	38%	54%
Some college	22%	14%
College graduate	9%	5%
Advance college degree	3%	1%
	100%	100%

In short, a little more than a fourth did not finish high school. A few more of the women have high school certificates as their highest degree. Overall, less than ten per cent have college and post college degress, with the men slightly more apt to have done some post high school work. These data suggest a slice of middle America.

Three fourths of the men and women listed Midwest State as their place of birth. This kind of localism seems substantial. Perhaps even more significant is that ninety per cent of the respondents own their own homes, four per cent rent homes, and six per cent rent apartments. Their longevity in the community is varied. Under 'present address,' the figures indicate that a third had lived in the community more than sixteen years and another half have been residents for over seven years. Median income of males was $12–15,000; half of the women described themselves as housewives. Occupationally, a fourth of the men described themselves as professional or management, and another 50 per cent were clerical and sales, craftsmen and operatives.

Among a number of attitude and opinion items about the schools, we present several which seem to capture the overall perspective of the patrons. In regard to program emphasis and priorities, two questions seem significant:

	More Emphasis (per cent)	About the Same (per cent)	Less Emphasis (per cent)
To what extent do you think the high school should emphasize preparation for college?	41%	52%	7%
To what extent do you think the high school should emphasize preparation for a job?	67%	32%	1%

Milford is a worker's community. They want college preparation available, but they are keenly interested in having their sons and daughters prepared to enter the work force.

The role of the school in the community appears in several items. Two-thirds agree to 'the community is proud of this school' and three-fourths feel 'the school plays an important role in the life of the community.' The large majority approve of the school, but on another item more have doubts about the need for increased resources.

The patron views of Administration and Staff can be seen in the majority perceive Milford as 'responsive' to youngsters and parents; however, they remain, as always, more skeptical of the use of personnel and financial resources. In addition, several items seem perennial and important in the affairs of schooling at the classroom level: 60 per cent see the expectations of high school teachers as 'about right' and 60 per cent describe discipline the same way, and 60 per cent see the high school as 'good' or 'excellent.'

As we have indicated, the survey presents another kind of data on the nature of the Milford community and its views on education. No item in the minutes indicated anyone, Board members or Central Office Staff, was surprised by it. Nor were we. Milford became, post World War II, a suburban community of small homes built in tracts, often containing hundreds of units. Most of the people were born in Midwest State and moved out of Metropolitan City and from rural Midwest State into Milford in the fifties, sixties, and seventies.

Multiple Aspects of Community Change. The Autumn of the 1976–77 school year brought another change to the District minutes. The multiple and oft times negative aspects of community change found their way into the Board meetings in the frequency and kind of citizen's complaints, in the Districts multiple involvements with other community agencies and officials, and in the quality and frequency of discipline problems in the junior and senior high schools, and the severity of action taken to those problems. The items seemed to interlock and interconnect into a distinguishable pattern. They bring an 'alive' quality of individual patrons, staff, and students for comparison and contrast with the survey data just presented.

Some outspoken citizens have a reputation in the community and Mr. Ravarino's is no exception to that rule. He has frequently had something to say and often it was negative. This time he objected to 'motors running' in the Administration building over the weekends, to 'lights being left on in district buildings at night.' In addition, he indicated: '. . . people would not be interested in voting on a tax levy until they were shown something was being done about the permissiveness of the students in the District.' (8/24/76) His agenda had multiple items, but money and discipline seem not inappropriate labels for his concerns and threats as a label for his contemplated action.

The 'lights on' phenomenon was an attempt to help with a variety of crime problems in the District. The trade offs seemed to be the degree to which it was a deterrent to vandalism and theft versus the expense and cost of the electricity. The issue had come up at an earlier meeting and had stimulated the Superintendent to contact police chiefs in the three municipalities of the Milford School District. The Superintendent presented three letters, all in agreement, which he had received. One Chief put it this way in his letter:

> Light is a deterrent to Vandalism, Breaking and Entering, and Trespassing. It gives the Police Officer and interested citizens an opportunity to observe suspicious persons, and activities in and about our schools, as well as any other Public Buildings and Business places.
>
> Light makes the culprit think twice if there is a possibility that he may be seen, identified, and apprehended. (7/15/76)

Seemingly one makes a judgment that problems are in the offing. Action is taken, which carries costs. Citizens complain. Explanations, rationales, and alternatives are reconsidered.

At the Junior and Senior High Schools, discipline problems are taking on a different quality. They seem more serious, involve more people and are more complicated. We report *in toto* a few that capture that flavor:

> Mrs. Brown said her daughter Mabel was a student at New Junior High School and the girl who had the locker next to Mabel picked on her and she had to stand there until this girl opens her locker. Mrs. Brown said she told her to tell Dr. Leeper or Mr. Donovan (High School Administrators). She said she was picked on again that day and she told the secretary and the secretary told Mabel to tell her Counselor. Mrs. Brown said Mabel signed up to see the Counselor but as yet nothing had been done about the situation. Dr. Leeper assured Mrs. Brown something would be done.
>
> Dr. George had recommended that Mrs. Brown's son Kurt be expelled from school because of conduct prejudicial to good order, discipline, and danger to the life of another student.
>
> The incident started with a boy pushing Kurt up against a locker. Kurt did not report this to the Administrators and the next day Kurt brought a chain to school and came up behind the boy with no warning and hit the boy with the chain.
>
> Mrs. Brown said what Kurt had done was wrong but he needed to be in school and she didn't know what to do with him. She felt he needed a special school that could give him more time. She said Kurt's Juvenile Officer wanted to know what decision was made by the Board in regard to expelling Kurt.
>
> Dr. Leeper said Kurt had enrolled in May of this year and had been suspended once for skipping school. He said Mrs. Brown did not condone what Kurt had done and had been very cooperative.
>
> President Reeves said the Board and Administration would do anything they could to work with the authorities to help Kurt and Mrs. Brown would be informed of the decision of the Board. President Reeves thanked Mrs. Brown for coming to the meeting.

After a thorough discussion, Mr. Tuley moved that upon the recommendation of the Superintendent, Kurt Brown be expelled from the Milford Schools. Mr. Eastland seconded the motion. The motion carried unanimously. (9/14/76)

A mother has a daughter in the beginnings of difficulty and a son facing serious legal charges in the community and an expulsion from school. The problems requiring night lighting seem to appear during the day also.

In the very next item in the minutes of 14 September 1976, the Board took up another discipline case. This time, social issues entered in several ways:

Mrs. Angela Monticelli said on the second day of school, her daughter, a student at New Junior High School, was riding the school bus home and was attacked and beaten by a number of colored students on the bus. She said the bus driver stopped once but was told by one of the colored students to turn around and mind her own business and the driver did nothing to try and stop them. Mrs. Monticelli said they had to take her daughter to the hospital for treatment and showed the Board pictures of her daughter taken after the incident. She said the police were going to take action on the case. Mrs. Monticelli said her daughter could identify only one of the group and he was the one she thought hit her on the back of the head as she got off the bus. Mrs. Monticelli said she didn't feel the school had taken the right approach because some of the kids were suspended for only five days. However, she said her son Ed was suspended for five days for hitting the colored boy her daughter had identified and was put off the football team because he missed practice because of the suspension. Mrs. Monticelli said she didn't think this was fair because he was taking up for his sister and felt he should be allowed to play football.

Dr. Leeper said he spent two days trying to determine who did what. He said it is a problem to take one child's word against another one. Dr. Leeper said that there was one boy on the bus who added fuel to the fire by teasing Mrs. Monticelli's daughter and getting the other children riled up and he was given an indefinite suspension. He said he based the length of the suspensions for the other students on their honesty and truthfulness. He said if it had not been for that, he would not have known who did what.

In regard to Mrs. Monticelli's son Ed fighting, Dr. Leeper said he had talked to him the day before and told him not to do anything foolish as he would be suspended and probably be off the football team.

After a lengthy discussion between Mrs. Monticelli, the Board, and administration, President Reeves told Mrs. Monticelli she would be notified of the Board's decision and thanked her for coming to the meeting.

After further discussion, Mrs. Ostermann moved that Ed Monticelli be reinstated on the football team at New Junior High School. Mrs. LeDuc seconded the motion.

The motion carried 4–2. (9/14/76)

Once again families, brothers and sisters are involved. In addition, race is an issue. The school administrators, walking a narrow line on equity and long term trust, are too lenient for the parent who has come to the Board. The punishment of suspension apparently activates another rule: missing football practice, presumably for any reason except illness, means being dropped from the team. The Board, in a split decision, sympathizes with this particular parent this time.[4]

Shortly thereafter, the discipline issues wove back into earlier policy and into the community and citizen concern and action. It was now 2:20 a.m. at the same Board meeting:

> Each Board member was given a copy of the Discipline Resolution adopted by the Board of Education on March 11, 1975.[5] President Reeves appointed Mr. Eastland and Mr. Galper from the Board to work with a committee composed of Mr. Hellman, Chairman of the Discipline Subcommittee of the Citizens Advisory Committee, and someone he would pick, the Superintendent and one staff member to meet with representatives of the staff to discuss problems they have in the classroom and why there are some of the problems such as lack of enforcement of rules, etc. President Reeves said this would allow some means of commun-ication between the Board and teaching staff. (9/14/76)

Discipline issues continued to arise. One boy was expelled for threatening with an open knife and needing to be physically subdued by the principal and three teachers. Another student had to be restrained from hitting his opponent in a fight with a chair he had picked up. In our view the problems, as reported in the minutes and in conversations with District staff, have taken a major turn in severity and the Board was meeting the turn with a 'strong' or 'hard' line.

Besides increasing contact with such agencies and agents as police chiefs and juvenile court officials, the minutes report a long discussion with the Westside Youth Association. Several letters were attached related to these discussions. The issues carry the dilemmas of 'purposive social action' amidst social change. The minutes on 25 September 1976, begin with additional problems at New Junior High School. The Board commenced with the formal agenda.

> This item had been placed on the Agenda at the request of Mr. Ravarino as spokesman for a group of residents that reside in the area of New Junior High School. The residents objected to the use of the New Junior High School Athletic Fields by the Westside Youth Association and asked that the Board deny them the use of the field or they would start a door to door campaign to get the residents of the area to pay their taxes under protest.
>
> After a lengthy discussion, Mrs. Ostermann moved that the Board inform the WYA that they were considering not renewing their permit to use the District's athletic fields next year. Mr. Galper seconded the motion and it carried unanimously.
>
> President Reeves declared a ten minute recess at 10:30 p.m.

Two weeks later the issue returned for further discussion. One resident objected to traffic congestion, speeding, verbal abuse, and vandalism. He said: '. . . a large percentage of these people do not reside in the District and, therefore, are not taxpayers in this District.' (10/12/76) Further arguments indicated that the Suburban County Public Parks program was progressing and their property should be used. The Mayor of Marquette Township indicated he had been asked if the program violated a zoning ordinance. It did not. He urged the Board to put a fence between the school property and the residential property. Mr. Ravarino indicated he hadn't accused the Westside Youth Association of vandalism, '. . . but their activity brought undesirables into the area that were not residents of the district.'

The President of the Westside Youth Association, Mr. Schultz, wrote a long three-page letter responding to each of nine items about which complaints were lodged. He also met with the Board on 12 October 1976:

> Mr. Schultz said the WYA had used the facilities at New Junior High School since 1967 and believed their program had been beneficial to the youth of the local county area. He said their practice sessions were between 6:00 and 8:00 p.m. and they were off the field no later than 8:30 p.m. but the lights were always out by 8:15 p.m. Mr. Schultz said as far as litter, they police the area quite regularly. He said it was reported there were four burglaries in the area and in checking with the Marquette and Carleton Heights Police, there were two and one of them was on the other side of the highway and he did not feel it was done by boys age 7 to 13 years old. Mr. Schultz said the public address system is used only to tell parents who is doing what and is operated only at about 60 per cent of the capacity. He said as far as bringing in undesirables, he didn't know what they were talking about. He said they did have some boys from broken homes and they did take boys regardless of race, creed, or origin. Mr. Schultz said there wasn't any question they increased the traffic because they wanted the parents to bring the boys and take them home and encourage them to stay and see them play. Mr. Schultz said approximately 48 per cent of the families participating in the program are Milford taxpayers.

Mr. Schultz indicated that other land had been purchased and progress was under way on new fields. He wanted to leave open the possibility of using the fields if their new location was not ready. The Board responded:

> After a lengthy discussion of the situation, Mrs. Ostermann moved that if the Westside Youth Association requests the use of the New Junior High School fields next year, this be brought back to the attention of the Board to be involved in the decision making. (10/12/76)

The motion passed 5–1.

Seven months later, on 10 May 1977, the Board unanimously approved a request by the Youth Association to use the New Junior High fields from 5:30 to 8:30 p.m. week days and 10:00 a.m. to 8:30 p.m. Saturdays and Sundays. The fields in the new park were not ready as yet.

Our point is first, a simple one, when communities change, the schools, as part of the community, change also. Our point is a coupled one as well. The Board's efforts to steer its way through its never ending agenda of immediate practical problems seem really an effort at obtaining some kind of workable equilibrium among multiple values — economics, equity, education, not to mention basic health and safety. Sometimes it seems, 'education' becomes lost amidst the contention.

The Return of the Citizens Advisory Committee. Over the years, and particularly in times of stress and turbulence, the Milford Board has appointed and worked with an advisory committee of citizens. In August of 1975, the following minute was recorded:

> A discussion was held in regard to re-activating a Citizens Advisory Committee *since there has been some interest shown in the past few months.* (Our italics) It was the consensus of the Board that a committee of Board members be appointed to work with the Superintendent and his staff to formulate some plans and bring them back to the next Board meeting for further discussion. President Reeves appointed Messrs. Eastland, Galper, and Wells to be on the committee. (8/26/75)

We also include the verbatim minutes which indicate both some points of emphasis and the internal Board interaction over the proposal. As a consequence, one sees some of the people and issues in contention:

> Mr. Eastland, Chairman of the Board's Sub-Committee for the Citizens Advisory Committee, said the Committee met with Central Office Staff on September 2 and three basic types of Citizens Advisory Committees were discussed:
>
> 1 On-going District-wide Advisory Committee — subcommittees are assigned to areas of need.
> 2 Special Projects Citizens Committee — district-wide committees are formed to meet specific needs, i.e. housing, discipline, etc.
> 3 Citizens Advisory Committees — committees are formed to promote citizen input to the Board of Education. These committees are local in nature but have provisions for two-way communications between citizens and the Board of Education.
>
> Mr. Eastland said after a lengthy discussion, it was felt that parents are more likely to be interested in their local school problems than in District-wide problems. Therefore, it would be better to start at the local level with Citizens Committees in each of our twelve schools. These committees should have representation from school parent groups, other parents in the school, non-public school parents, and those without any school age children. No person interested in serving would be excluded.

In reading through the report and the minutes several items, inferences and hypotheses seem important: 1) The Board seems responsive to local patron interest and initiative. 2) Ambiguity remains over the concept of 'local'; this time school by school versus the district as a whole. 3) Committees almost always, and true in this instance, had some kind of administrative involvement. One might infer both legitimate help and/or keeping the committee from straying too far afield. 4) While representatives were selected to facilitate reporting back, the Board seemed always to welcome everyone if they wanted to attend. 5) A variety of reasonably standard gambits were tried for publicity and invitations to attend and to participate. 6) Historical references appeared, 'last time ...' as part of the pros and cons of alternatives. 7) Minority opinions (Mrs. LeDuc's) were presented but convincing one's peers is not easy, and in this instance did not occur.

The committees met in October at each school and submitted minutes of the meetings. The major result was small attendance, from three or four patrons to a dozen, averaging four or five. Among the citizens were some current and past Board members. Substantively the biggest recurring issue was apathy. Issues raised were taxes, levies, curriculum, discipline, programs for gifted, statewide tests, crossing guards, etc. In only one instance was 'human relations' raised.

In June 1976, the various Citizen Advisory Subcommittees reported. The 'Apathy Committee' reported a need for budget for publicity and a student handbook and that student projects be displayed in the District shopping centers. The Curriculum Committee urged greater parent involvement in counseling and program selection and that volunteer outside specialists be brought into the schools. The Discipline Committee recommended student ID cards to be worn on outside clothing, that unused classrooms be locked, that a human relations program be established, and a trial period for a smoking area be instituted, and that uniformity in discipline be stressed. The Board took the issues up one by one.

The Citizen Subcommittee on Discipline spent a day at the Senior High talking with teachers doing their prep periods about 'their main discipline problems.' The recurring items were: 1) marijuana, use, selling, and what to do about it; 2) class size; 3) differences in discipline among various buildings; and 4) need for ID badges.

A year later, in April of 1977, the Discipline Committee reported on 'fifteen meetings' with Administrators and teachers in the Junior and Senior High Schools to: '. . . listen and see what they had to say about discipline — good or bad and no attempt was made to influence their report.' (4/26/77)
Figure 30 contains the concerns.

Figure 30: Concerns Elicited by Discipline Subcommittee

Administrative Concerns	*Senior High Teacher's Concerns*
1 lack of respect for authority	1 student identification
2 smoking	2 teacher feedback on discipline referrals
3 marijuana	3 need of a central discipline authority
	4 smaller class size in basic courses
	5 absenteeism
	6 fence put up
	7 security personnel

The Committee was still working with the Junior High and Elementary School administration and staff.

The 'drug problem' was being handled with a letter to parents regarding the drug problem. The committee recommended that any student who had been suspended for a semester for drug use, transfer, or possession be required to have a minimum of five counseling sessions with an approved counselor before 'he' can return to school. The Board moved and unanimously approved the recommendation.

The Curriculum Subcommittee raised the idea of 'resource volunteer' citizens with special knowledge and expertise who might be helpful for curriculum enrichment, models, and awareness. In addition, the benefits of citizen 'ownership of schools', senior citizen activity and school-community relations seemed present also.

The Discipline Subcommittee continued its work with a gradual changeover of patron incumbents. Community meetings continued to be held, topics such as 'Juvenile Alcoholism' and the need for 'District-wide guidelines on disciplinary rules and regulations' were raised with key administrators, meetings were held with bus drivers regarding 'difficult runs' and 'chronic offenders.' (6/13/77)

In brief, during the period of population shifts and the rise of what the Board saw as major and serious disciplinary problems, a committee of Board members, citizens, and administrators were looking among themselves and to each other for definitions and solutions of problems. As we will see shortly, the Board had its own internal problems during this period. Because the central administration was aligned with one faction it too had problems. In these circumstances, the District, the schools, and the classrooms might also be viewed as having their problems.

The Reactivation of the Housing Committee. In response to the differential population shifts, the Housing Committee was reactivated in 1976–77. Kensington and Johnson Schools had picked up an extra room of pupils. Fifteen plans had been proposed by the Committee. Plan 11A was recommended: students from Kensington (twenty-three to Field and sixty-five to Midvale) and 103 from Johnson to McBride. The former are now being bussed and would continue to be. The latter are now being bussed and would now be able to walk.

Attendance areas and balance of pupil numbers remained a problem into 1979–80. The Board's procedures are caught in the brief minute:

> After a presentation by the Administration and a discussion of the recommendation, Mr. Reeves moved that seventeen (17) students be moved from the Johnson Elementary School to the McBride Elementary School. Mr. Tolman seconded the motion and it carried unanimously.

Later in the meeting, a representative of parents from another nearby subdivision wanted the Board to permit their children to be transferred. The stated grounds were safety in crossing a busy thoroughfare. The implicit grounds seemed racial: 'Mr. Falone said many parents were moving rather than send their children to Johnson School and asked that the Board reconsider letting these children go to McBride School.' At the time, Johnson School was ninety per cent Black and McBride was twenty-five per cent Black. The Board listened but took no action.

'Housing,' which pupils go to which school, is a never ending problem in a school district. As we have indicated elsewhere, the nature and intensity of the problem shifts from year to year and period to period. In the post World War II years, the population boom with its 'new school every year' as the dominant issue, became the defining criterion for the period. Now in the 1975 to the present period, the declining and shifting enrollments with its school closings and redrawing of boundaries dominate almost to becoming the defining criterion of the period. In 1975, as we reported, the Board closed two elementary schools, in 1979, an additional elementary school would be closed. In 1982, the Old Junior High School would be closed. The New Junior High would become a 7th and 8th grade center serving the entire District and the Milford Senior High School would become, once again, a four year school with grades 9–12.

While aspects of the story will continue to appear at several points, a few summary observations and interpretations seem warranted here. First, the problem is phrased as a technical problem rather than a political problem. Second, the Committee is staffed entirely by administrators, the Superintendent, the Assistant Superintendent for Elementary were *ex officio* and five principals with one principal chairing the group, were the regular members. Together these two events prevented, for better or worse, the opening for public participation and involvement the issues surrounding the changing racial composition of one side of the District and the reconsideration of the concept of neighborhood school in the light of the population changes.

The Introduction to the Housing Committee's report captures the basis and the tenor of our observations and interpretations;

> In September of 1976, in response to unforeseen and unpredictable enrollment changes at various schools in the District, the Elementary Housing Committee was reactivated.
>
> The primary reason for the reactivation of the Elementary Housing Committee was the influx of students at two of the district schools, Kensington and Johnson. Although the previous housing committee had done a commendable task in 1973–75, it was impossible at that time to predict the rapid changes that would take place in certain areas of the south side of the district, especially in the 1976–77 school year.[6] In a like manner, it appears almost equally impossible at this time to predict with accuracy changes which may take place in the various areas of the district, especially on the south side. However, relief for the two schools was obviously needed.
>
> After several preliminary discussions regarding the housing of elementary students, desirable programs, necessary facilities, and possible growth areas, it was decided that the Committee should address itself to the immediate problem at hand; that is, the relief of the overcrowded situation at Kensington and Midvale Schools. This relief was to be implemented for the 1977–78 school year. It was also decided to forward information and a recommendation to the Superintendent at the end of March or early April,

1977, so that a recommendation could subsequently be made to the Board.

Information for use by the Committee was gathered from the following sources:

Previous Housing Study

1973 Enumeration Census

Monthly Enrollment Reports

Elementary Principals

Various plans and possibilities for relief at the overcrowded schools were explored. These included:

No changes in any enrollment boundaries

Changing of boundaries among various schools

Change by grade level, 1–6

Kindergarten centers (busing)

Paired schools (primary and intermediate)

Middle schools

Changes by definable area (apartments, subdivisions, etc.)

After consideration of the various plans and possibilities, it was decided that the Committee would explore the changes of attendance areas necessary among the fewest number of schools possible in order to achieve the proper enrollment level for the areas affected. The basic attendance areas explored were: Kensington, McBride, Midvale, Field, and Johnson.

Presented hereafter are fifteen (15) possible plans for the consideration of the Board of Education. All the plans are feasible but several are more workable than others. The Elementary Housing Committee unanimously recommended Plan A-11 as the most feasible approach. In arriving at these many plans, the enrollment at the various schools as of the first month's attendance for the 1976–77 school year was used as the base line. (4/5/77)

The Board members and administration seemed to feel that consideration of housing as a political issue was a 'no win' situation. A number felt a law suit was likely regarding intradistrict racial balances, for the schools varied from almost 100 per cent White to almost 100 per cent Black. Such a legal definition of the problem never occurred.[7]

On 1 April 1980, the Housing Committee reported one more time. Among the items in paraphrased form were these:

1 In each of the last seven years the district had lost between 400 and 500 children.
2 Pupil/Teacher ratios of 25–1 elementary, 26–1 junior high and 27–1 senior high was a given.
3 '. . . the neighborhood school concept was maintained and attempts were made to reduce transportation expenses.'
4 A special board meeting on the issue and three patrons' meetings at three schools, north, central, and south, would be held in the schools. The report would be available at all the Milford schools for patron examination.

The report contained eleven options at the elementary level. Nine involved boundary changes and two involved school changes — Hillside Elementary or Milford Elementary. A five year secondary project called for closing the Old Junior High School and changing from a 6-3-3 structure to a 6-2-4 organization. The need for action was simple — declining enrollments and increasing expenses.

A petition appeared, which is not new to Milford, nor is the fact that it contained a sizable number of signatures, 425 this time. Further, the issues are as old as the District, opening and closing schools with shifts of pupils and impact on the neighborhood. The arguments have a heavy ring as well, although a couple of special elements appear for its Milford Village Elementary School, the oldest of the elementary schools. The petition appears as Figure 31.

On 23 April 1980, with the new Board in place (re-election by a wide margin of the two incumbents), a unanimous vote occurred on Option V-A. Hillside Elementary would be closed. Boundary changes in Option III-A passed unanimously also. Fifty-three pupils at Field would come to Kensington, nineteen pupils at Midvale would to Johnson.

Conclusion   Very quietly, the systemic perspective we have taken has arisen. The Milford community and its demographic characteristics and changes moves us into the arena of the Board. The Board's committees take on lives of their own, but only partially so, for quickly the central administration and its longer reach, the elementary principals, are involved.

It's the fascinating 'Board story' to which we turn now. As always, also, it's possible to talk about it in a self-contained way, which gives a focus, but it's equally obvious that it's intertwined with other actors, groups, events, and serials.

The Changing School Board

One of the most remarkable aspects of Milford, in our view, is that the Board is not under anyone's 'control', at least in any simple sense. The long history and final decision of Superintendent McBride, his conflict with several principals and several strong Board members seems to illustrate that. The shorter tenure of Dr. Spanman

Figure 31: Milford Village Elementary School Petition (425 signatures)

> We the people of Milford School District express our disapproval of closing Milford Village Elementary School at 8759 Pearl Drive for these reasons:
> 1 Milford Village is the only school in the Village (Edinburg has two). What about our neighborhood school?
> 2 It would take three buses if Milford Village School closes, only one if Hillside closes (additional expense).
> 3 Hillside would be easier to rent than Milford Village because it is a one-story building.
> 4 Hillside would be better for adult education classes because most adults drive and there is more parking space at Hillside.
> 5 Property values would decrease because of no neighborhood schools.
> 6 Milford Village Elementary was the first elementary school in this district.

carries a similar moral. Now, in 1974–75 and almost ten years into Dr. George's incumbency as Superintendent, a new name, that of Mrs. LeDuc, enters the record. In the Autumn she was part of the 'Concerned Parents' group trying to keep the Grant School open. She had helped solicit the 2000 signatures on the petition. In February, her name appeared a second time, in a letter announcing her candidacy for one of the Board of Education positions. On the same evening her name appeared for the third time: 'Mrs. LeDuc who had filed as a candidate for the Board asked if the Board had any response to the "Open Letter" to the Patrons and the Board from the Milford NEA which was in their publication "Accent" and would be in the local News.' (2/11/75) The Superintendent asked her if she had a copy. She said she did. He indicated a letter had been sent out. Only a little hindsight is needed to suggest that a faction of the concerned if not dissident community patrons might be aligning with a faction of the dissident teaching staff.

In April 1975, she won election to the Board by a wide margin. In the next two years, her story intertwined with the stories of two other individuals and became *the* story at the district level.

A further quality comes into the Citizen-Board-Administration interaction which suggests the political/personal/educational interests and issues at odds. In August 1975, another new name enters the record during the Patrons Participation part of the meeting:

> Mrs. Hilda Ostermann asked Dr. Eastman (Assistant Superintendent) if he had up-to-date figures on the assessed valuation of the District. When told that he did not, she asked if they would like the figure which she had secured from the County Assessors Office and when she was told yes, she reported that the assessed valuation of personal property for the School District for 1975–76 would be $15,897,510. Dr. Eastman responded that this was only part of the total assessed valuation and asked Mrs. Ostermann if she had figures on real estate, railroad and utilities, and merchants and manufacturers. Mrs. Ostermann said she did not. It was pointed out to her that the total assessed valuation projected for next year was $109,000,000 and that personal property valuation only made up a part of that total amount.
>
> In response to Mrs. Ostermann's statement that the district might have more money than they thought they would, Dr. Eastman pointed out that the District lost $800,000 in assessed valuation from October to December 1974. Therefore, it is difficult to indicate what the assessed valuation will be in 1975. (8/26/75)

Two weeks later, Mrs. Ostermann was back asking further questions about finances — paying bills before approval (for utilities), charges for use of school gymnasiums, and insurance. The insurance minute seems revealing:

> Mrs. Ostermann said she understood that part of the District's insurance coverage was dropped and was this because the District was a bad risk.

President Reeves said apparently the insurance company felt they could not make a profit but did not mean we were a bad risk. (9/9/75)

One doesn't get the feeling that there was much love lost here. A few minutes later, Mrs. Ostermann and Mr. Reeves were involved in another exchange which was recorded this way:

Mrs. Ostermann asked if a patron had a question regarding something in the Agenda and during Patrons Portion asked to be heard later in the meeting, and could they be heard. President Reeves said the Board would be happy to answer their questions during this open part of the meeting. He said normally the business portion of the meeting is not open to the audience unless there would be something that generated a lot of interest. (9/9/75)

These kinds of interactions, challenges if you like, continued on through the Autumn.

In mid-Winter, Mrs. Ostermann submitted her name for the April Board elections. In April 1976, in a six person race with two incumbents she came in second and became a member of the Milford Board of Education. The 5–1 Board had now become a 4–2 Board.

One of the dramatic aspects of the changing composition of the Board was the interpenetration and conversion of the Board versus teacher activism conflict into an *intra* Board conflict. A long interchange in the minutes in November 1975, after Mrs. LeDuc's election but before Mrs. Ostermann's, contained these excerpted and paraphrased items:

1 The Milford NEA was asking if money for raises could be found since State Aid had not materialized.
2 'President Reeves said the eight points were discussed at the salary committee and there was nothing new ...'
3 Mr. Eastland said there was one obvious place to get money and that was to go into balances and how far can you go into balances ... gambling ...

Then, significantly:

4 In response to Mrs. LeDuc's question as to whether a token raise of $100 couldn't be offered, President Reeves said for every $100 it would cost the District $70,000 and Dr. George said you would have to have money to meet the retirement costs and this would have to come out of the incidental fund.

Mrs. LeDuc then asked about the elimination of some programs. In rapid fire order:

5 Dr. George indicated Milford NEA had been asked by the Board about eliminating personnel but received no answer.

6   Dr. George indicated supplies had already been cut.
7   Assistant Superintendent, Dr. Eastman, indicated $18,000,000 of buildings had to be maintained.

Mrs. LeDuc said 'if we tighten our belts and go on an austerity campaign perhaps it could be done.' She was instructed once again:

8   Mr. Tuley said that the District was already on an austerity program.
9   Assistant Superintendent, Dr. Eastman said the District had been on the same levy for five years.
10 Mr. Reeves argued a tax increase was the only way. But this was caught in public sentiment over closing schools, etc.

Mrs. LeDuc came back one more time regarding 'better use of our money.' A Board member came back at her with:

11 The District is third from the bottom in assessed valuation and fourth from the top in salaries; better than its 'sister district.'

So, the Board majority and administration 'instructed' its new and dissident member.

But Mrs. LeDuc was neither docile nor easily deterred. She was the one on a 5-1 vote to rehire all administrators on two-year contracts. The no vote concerned declining enrollments, declining teaching staffs and no reduction in administrative staff: '. . . it will not look good to the public.' She could not convince her colleagues. She also was the only Board member to vote no on a new three-year contract for Superintendent George. No reason appeared in the minutes. Around the Central Office, the view was that 'she was out to get him.'

The Board continued all through 1975–76 with long involved discussions internally and with the teacher salary team regarding pay raises, budgeting and an increase in the tax levy.

In June 1976, after Mr. Wells' resignation the Board received two applications, one from Mr. Galper, the recently defeated incumbent, and one from Mrs. Nash. On a 3–2 vote, Mr. Galper returned to the Board. While the 'iron law of oligarchy' was eroding, efforts were being made to refurbish it. This interactional episode briefly but baldly indicates the workings of the social mechanisms underlying the principle.

In January 1977, two individuals filed for the April election to the Board: Mr. Reeves; Mrs. Saenger. Several other candidates filed shortly thereafter.

In February, on two votes to rehire all the principals on new two-year contracts and the Superintendent on a new three-year contract, the Board split 4–2. Mesdames LeDuc and Ostermann dissenting. The meeting adjourned at 2:05 a.m.

On 5 April 1977, Mr. Reeves (4807) and Mrs. Saenger (4348) were elected. Mr. Fern was a close third (4201). The Board was now split between three male 'old guard' members and three women 'progressives.' Superintendent George and the Central Office Staff continued to support and be supported by the three male, old guard members of the Board. The stage was set for a series of battles.

Those battles began four days later in special session on Saturday, April 9, at 8:00 a.m. when the Board began to organize itself through the election of officers. Mrs. Ostermann nominated Mrs. LeDuc for President. Mr. Eastland nominated Mr. Reeves. A secret ballot left the votes tied 3-3. The Board voted a second time, no change. Dr. George, who was chairing the meeting at the suggestion of Mr. Reeves, declared a ten minute recess for members to caucus and break the tie. After the recess, Mrs. Ostermann again nominated Mrs. LeDuc. Mr. Reeves withdrew his name and nominated Mr. Tuley.[8] Another secret ballot was taken. The tie, 3-3, vote remained. The Board requested Dr. George to contact the President of the Suburban County Board of Education to come and 'break the tie vote.' The Board recessed at 8:33 a.m. A short meeting.

A week later, Friday evening, 25 April at 7:30, a similar series of votes occurred and the County Board President voted. Mrs. LeDuc won 4–3 over Mr. Tuley. Mr. Tuley became Vice President by acclamation when Mrs. Ostermann refused the nomination placed by Mr. Tuley. The Secretary position was contested between the faction in the names of Mr. Eastland and Mrs. Ostermann. The vote went 4–3 for Mr. Eastland. Apparently the County Board President distributed the power. Next, Mr. Eastland nominated Mrs. Ostermann for Treasurer:

> There being no further nominations, Mr. Reeves moved that Mrs. Ostermann be declared Treasurer of the Board by acclamation. Mr. Tuley seconded the motion and it carried unanimously.
>
> The Board thanked Mr. Earle, the County Board President for coming the long distance to work with the Board (4/15/77)

The meeting adjourned at 7:42 p.m. A record for brevity.

The subsequent meetings are a mix of the 'new three' (our label) programming items, the 'old three' instructing them on the whys and wherefores of Board rules, regulations and constraints. For example, at a special session for discussion of a possible bond issue the old guard indicated that it was not possible to vote on having an 'internal audit' at this meeting. It could go on the agenda of the next 'regular meeting.' In addition, the minutes contained 3–3 votes on an October Bond issue versus a May Bond issue.

Board policy, and the racial issues we have called 'the American Dilemma' became entangled in the inexperience of the 'new three' and the infighting within the Board. The following appeared in the regular meeting of 26 April 1977:

> In response to President LeDuc's question as to whether there were any additions or corrections on the Agenda, Mrs. Saenger said the statement in Agenda Item XII — Integration of the District, stating she would have a presentation to make was in error and that no names should be put on an agenda item. Mrs. Ostermann said she did not have any presentation but did have some questions. Mr. Tuley said if a request is made for an item to be put on the agenda the name should be on it.
>
> Mr. Eastland said Board Policy No. 9230 stated the secretary will prepare the Agenda with the assistance of the Superintendent and with the

President's advice. He said he thought all items that are to go in the Agenda should be given to him to clear. He said he and the Superintendent make up the Agenda and the President can advise them. He said to tell the Superintendent to put all these items on the Agenda is not according to Board Policy and there was no way all these items could be handled in one meeting, particularly a business meeting.

President LeDuc said she had told Dr. George that Mrs. Saenger had asked for this to be on the Agenda but did not tell him she had a presentation.

Mr. Eastland said he felt anything of this importance should be studied and discussed by the Board before it was made public as *this item had caused pandemonium with rumors flying through the District.* (Our italics)

After further discussion, it was agreed that this item be removed from the Agenda. (4/26/77)

During the Patrons Participation, three citizens, two women and one man:

... spoke to the Board in regard to Agenda Item XII — Integration of the District, strongly voiced their objections to the fact that this had been brought to the public's attention and any idea of busing children to achieve integration. (4/26/77)

The complexities of social change appear when reform oriented, but inexperienced Board newcomers are up against highly experienced, wily conservative Board members. The complications are magnified in a community where a 'conservative' stance, especially on issues of race, budget, and educational basics, is not a dirty word but a mark of approbation. This is an image we continue to try to make clear.

Although most of the routine business went along 6–0, a few items were 4–2 with Mrs. Saenger splitting off from 'the ladies.' The 'progressive' label seems to fit the group. The 3–3 votes in May involved 1) support of students who wanted a smoking area at the High School and 2) support of the teachers, in this instance the removal of a letter of reprimand in a teacher's file for a comment to a parent that the parent 'could not get a fair hearing from the Board.' Liberalization of student rules and increasing the power of the teacher vis a vis Board and Administration were long term battles in Milford.

But in Milford, there are teachers and there are teachers. The teachers also split on a liberal–conservative dimension. 'The ladies' or one of them, the Board President, Mrs. LeDuc, got caught in turmoil while siding with one group to the consternation of the other group. Similarly, the patrons are split, although we have argued that the community at large tends toward the conservative. Mrs. LeDuc got caught here as well. Finally, from a political perspective, she made a serious tactical error in knowingly commenting negatively about the Milford Schools to a newspaper editor. Much of this was aired in the 14 June 1977, Board meeting. Several key minutes capture the flavor of the multiple divisions.

One group of teachers, under the impetus of Bill Perry, the teacher chairman of the Milford NEA Salary and Welfare committee continued to argue for the Board to negotiate with the teachers: '... the Board's present position to be an anachronism and to pursue such a course would do no more than create an anamorphosis.' (6/14/77) Distorted images, in part, lie in the eyes of the multiple beholders, so we would argue. Almost in response to our generalization, a second group of teachers entered a different perspective.

The second letter came from the principal and teachers (eighteen signatures) of the Midvale Elementary School:

> Mr. Eastland read a letter from the faculty of the Midvale School. The letter stated that they contend that Mrs. LeDuc, President of the Board of Education, had shown total disrespect and a lack of appreciation for the administrative and teaching staff of the School District by her comments in the *Village News* on June 1, 1977. The letter stated that in their opinion, Mrs. LeDuc had spoken as an unqualified representative of the District and does not portray the factual image of their professional services. The letter stated it was their utmost desire that she realign her actions in a more professional manner and allow more qualified spokesmen [sic] from the Board of Education or the Administrative staff to present factual District information. The letter asked a number of questions of Mrs. LeDuc: If Mrs. LeDuc contended she was there to serve various public groups' views then why reflect views that appear to be her own to the press; What evidence did she have to reflect discredit to the School District administration by implying dishonesty when every encumbrance for payment must be approved by the Board; How could she generalize about teacher absentee-ism; Asked that she clarify 'swift imaginative action'; The comment implying the need for alternative educational programs, did this not imply she wanted to expand programs rather than consolidate or enforce the present programs; As a 'para legal' how could she endorse a smoking area; Was she aware there has been a remedial reading program in the elementary schools for the past five years; And that they felt her statement about programs that are selected to make the work easier for the teachers, not to educate the children, was unwarranted. (6/14/77)

The two-page, single-space letter itself was more detailed, specific, and full of emotional outrage. In Milford, the airing of dirty linen, at best, is a complicated and subtle process conditioned by time, place, and circumstance. As the Board President and the leader of the teachers' faction in internal Board disputes, she found herself in a most precarious position with a group of elementary teachers and their principal.

Not only did the faculty of one school write in. The 'other' teacher organiza-tion, generally viewed as the more conservative group, has a letterhead, 'Midwest STA ... the professional way.' The Board minutes abbreviated their three para-graph letter into one paragraph:

> Mr. Eastland read a letter to President LeDuc from Dr. Jones Wales,[10] President of the Milford CTA. Dr. Wales said the executive Board would like to express their disappointment with Mrs. LeDuc's recent interview

published in the *Village News*. His letter stated that there seemed to be nothing positive in her views of the Milford School District and the comments were untimely and inappropriate as the same issue carried the advertisement supporting a bond issue sorely needed at this time. Dr. Wales' letter said they felt her letter had neither served the best interest of the School District nor the best interest of the students. (6/14/77)

A reporter from the Village News answered questions and indicated that the paper would not print a retraction because it was a fair and accurate presentation of Mrs. LeDuc's stated views.

That same evening, other parents were writing and commenting on upgrading the tennis program at the High School and petitioning (twenty-six signatures) the Board not to permit smoking on school property. The issues come rapidly, don't stop, and make a variegated package.

The 'outside study gambit' reappeared in the Milford Board meetings in the early Summer of 1977. Essentially this involves bringing some outside group to look into District affairs. Our report of the early history of Milford indicates this was an important tactic used by Board Presidents in fights with Mr. McBride, an earlier Superintendent. In the present instance, the initial thrust was for an 'internal audit.' This was enlarged to an 'Educational Management Study' and then expanded to include 'all paid employees of the School District.' The final vote was to secure competitive bids from at least two other firms ($10,000 was the preliminary estimate) and *not* at this time to actually have the Study. That vote was to come later. The discussion was long and the meeting adjourned at 12:50 a.m.

The issue carried over into the 28 June 1977 meeting. More letters and more arguments pro and con on Mrs. LeDuc's actions and the behavior of the patrons at the previous meeting were heard. Mr. Earle, President of the County Board of Education, voted 'no' on the motion to have a trial smoking area at the High School.[10] He indicated he could not vote on the letter in the teacher's file because the parent had not been asked to a hearing and he (Mr. Earle) could not vote on 'hearsay.' The third vote, on the Educational Management Study, was disallowed because it had not yet come up for a formal vote — only a 4–2 vote to have bids. The twenty-three item agenda meeting lasted until 3:20 a.m. Physical stamina joins experience and manoeuvring as requisites for Board members during periods of sharp and evenly divided political and educational conflict of interests and perspectives.

Three months later, 13 September 1977, the Board voted 3–2 (Mr. Tuley was absent) to let a $13,000 contract for the Educational Management Study. The motion failed because State Law requires a majority of the total Board for letting contracts. Patrons spoke pro and con on whether it was needed or was a waste. A month later, a Mothers' Circle Council letter was read. They *unanimously* disapproved of spending the money for the study. The Council involves representatives from Mothers' Circles at all the schools. In Milford, and probably in most districts, when one speaks of 'grass root opinion', one cannot get more basic than this.

Figure 32: Tie Votes in the 1977 Board Minutes

President	9 April 1977
Secretary	9 April 1977
Smoking area in high school	24 May 1977
Letter of reprimand in teacher's file	24 May 1977
Letter of reprimand but without 'breach of contract' phrase	24 May 1977
Resume Salary Discussions with NEA Salary and Welfare Committee	14 June 1977
Smoking in high school	14 June 1977
Dr. Eastman as Board Representative to Salary Discussions	11 October 1977
Mr. Gillespie and Mr. Ritter as Board Representatives to Salary Discussions	11 October 1977

Also that Autumn, Mrs. LeDuc voted no on a 5–1 split regarding a bond issue. She rejected the urging of her female Board colleagues and the citizen chairman of the bond campaign to make it unanimous. (10/11/77)

In November 1977, the tie vote on the Board representative to the Salary Discussions was broken by Mr. Earle, County Board President. He supported Mr. Gillespie, Assistant Superintendent of Elementary instead of Dr. Eastman, Assistant Superintendent of Secondary. The former was the choice of the Superintendent, backed by the three male members of the Board.

On the same evening, shortly after this tie vote on the Salary Representative, the assault on the District Policy and its control by 'the ladies' or 'the progressives', or the 'new reformers' was all over. The minutes read this way:

> Mr. Eastland (Board Secretary) read a letter to the Board from Mrs. Saenger. Mrs. Saenger said she was submitting her resignation as a director and member of the Board of Education as of the close of the November 8, 1977, meeting because she would be moving from the District and would no longer be able to serve in this capacity. She said she deeply regretted that she could not fulfill her three year term. Mrs. Saenger said this had been a unique experience for her and she was proud to have served the School District in this capacity. Mrs. Saenger extended her best wishes to the Board in their future endeavors.
>
> President LeDuc told Mrs. Saenger that it was with deep regret that her resignation was accepted. (11/8/77)

That finished this most recent phase of conflict in Milford School District.

It seems helpful to summarize the issues which went to 3–3 votes in the District between 9 April and 11 October 1977. Figure 32 contains these.

In sum, the issues were over control of the Board, relations with the teachers' groups, and more liberal student rules.

Almost by way of summary, we have tried to capture the events surrounding the Board's "return to normalcy" in pictorial form, Figure 33.

In real life, stories always have epilogues. Such is the case of our split vote. The vote on replacing Mrs. Saenger split on the same lines, 3–2. The new member voted with the conservaties. Late Winter and early Spring was full of 4–2 votes — pay raises

Figure 33: Dynamics of Board's Return to 'Normalcy' (1977)

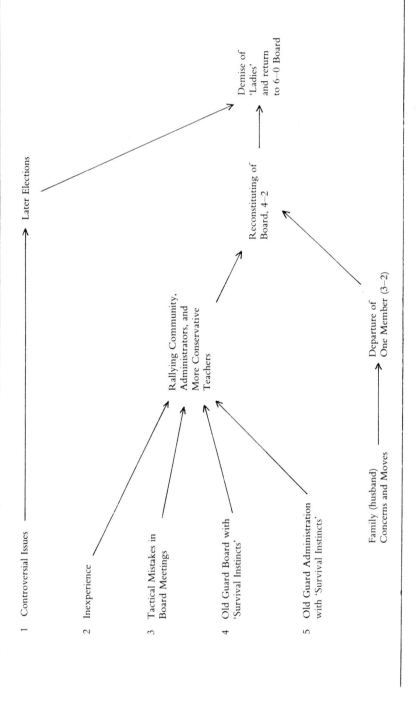

1 Controversial Issues ─────────────→ Later Elections

2 Inexperience

3 Tactical Mistakes in
Board Meetings

Rallying Community,
Administrators, and
More Conservative
Teachers

4 Old Guard Board with
'Survival Instincts'

5 Old Guard Administration
with 'Survival Instincts'

Reconstituting of
Board, 4–2

Demise of
'Ladies',
and return
to 6–0 Board

Family (husband) ─────────────→ Departure of
Concerns and Moves   One Member (3–2)

for teachers, resolutions of extra duty pay, accepting NEA teacher package on salary grievance policy, and RIF policy.

Purchase of a computerized accounting equipment system, and software were 4–2 also. Dates for making up Snow Days were in contention. 20 February became a regular school day, 4–2, as did three days originally scheduled for 'Easter Vacation' (29, 30, and 31 March). Extensions of administrator contracts for two and three years were approved, 4–2. And finally, no Board member was to go to the school lawyer without Board approval or through the Superintendent's office; again the vote was 4–2. Eighteen teachers were placed on leave of absence with 4–2 votes.

In April 1978, the denouement continued — by another third, Mr. Tuley won re-election with 2715 votes. Mrs. LeDuc lost to Mr. Tolman by 14 votes, 2387 to 2373. Mr. Fern beat Mr. Heinrich for a two year term, 3021 to 1755. Mrs. Ostermann now was a lone dissenter in a number of subsequent votes in the late Spring of 1978.

The degree of heat in the interpersonal relations between Board members doesn't wane easily and readily. Mrs. LeDuc spoke as a patron at the 25 April meeting after her failure to win at the polls;

> Mrs. LeDuc spoke to the Board in regard to the family that took their children out of school because of poor eduction, the incompetency of administrators, accused Dr. George of lying to the Board, and accused Mrs. Sandran, teacher at Williams School, of harassing and pumping her son on personal family matters and that several parents have had trouble with her for years. (4/25/78)

But her day, for better or worse for the Milford District, was over. And so was the 'progressive' or 'reform' movement.[11] Later ripples, cutting across the conservative tide, appear in stories we have attached to other themes. But Milford remains firmly, and in the eyes of Board and Administration, openly and proudly conservative in these generally turbulent times.

A Final Scene

Movies often end with the hero and heroine walking along a dusty road, up the hill, toward a summer sunset. Research reports often finish with broadly drawn conclusions and utopian recommendations. Accounts of School Board deliberations and schooling at the District level seem more like old soldiers — retaining their integrity as they fade away. It's hard to know who the heroes and heroines are, and sunrises and sunsets keep recurring and recurring and recurring. In May and June 1980, a final set of images, a last scene as it were, occurs as several themes pop out again in slightly new garments.

Gordian knots come in all shapes and sizes in the public schools. A short paragraph captures one worthy of Gordius and Alexander the Great:

> Mr. Eastland read a letter from Mrs. Bobbe Berra expressing her concern and displeasure on the Title I Program. She said her son attends Catholic

School and needed to go to Summer School. She said she proceeded to call the Milford District for information and was told that her son was not eligible to attend Summer School because he did not live in one of the specified areas. She said she understood that lower income families and neighborhoods need help and the fact that government money was available to help them was fine but what about her son? She said he needs help too and she did not think it was fair that middle income families were disregarded. She said she was sure that her son was not the only child in the District that needs the benefits of a Summer School Program.[13] She said the fact that she had to turn to a neighboring school district for help was unfair. She said she thanked the Board for reading the letter and she felt she had to let someone know how she felt. (5/27/80)

At the same meeting in late May, the Board accepted the resignations of a half dozen teachers, not a large number for a District as large as Milford. The significant aspects were several fold. All but one had more than ten years experience. The response of four, 'signed with another district' was unusual; personal reasons and family reasons cover a multitude of problems. Three were New Junior High School math and science teachers. Five of the six were men. Staff accounts accented 'They were among the best teachers.' and 'They had had enough and were going to districts with less problems.'

In June 1980, four Board meetings were held, two special and two regular. The special session on 3 June reported the unofficial returns on the tax levy: 'Yes 1953 No 3143' The later meetings indicated some of the reasons, as perceived by patrons in the Patrons Participation part of the Board meetings. We list them in paraphrased form: 1) retired people, 2) should cut some administrators, 3) teachers and parents should have more input, 4) not enough information gotten out, 5) need for a door-to-door campaign, 6) the desegregation case in Big City not helping situation, 7) youth group in one church 'came on a little too strong,' 8) the teachers had signed a contract yet were threatening a strike. Tax levies have come and gone. In recent years, passage has been very difficult for all kinds of reasons, many of which appeared in the paraphrased list. The not so latent impact of demographic shifts appear: aging population, decreased number of pupils, changing populations, and turmoil over changing youth, teacher activism, and imminent court action regarding desegregation.

At the 10 June meeting, the Assistant Superintendent, Dr. Luther, reported on the results of the recently established state-wide Basic Skills Test (BST). The results were not encouraging:

	1978 (per cent)	1979 (per cent)	1980 (per cent)
Reading	86.8%	87.9%	87.8%
Mathematics	—	67.2%	62.4%
Social Studies	73.7%	—	53.8%

In his words, reading 'remained constant,' math 'showed a drop,' and social studies 'was very weak.' The Board had a question and answer period and thanked him for the presentation. On the surface, elementary curriculum has become basic skills. Such an approach would not offend many of the patrons and the staff. For a community proud of its schools, the 'low' percentages were disturbing.

At the 17 June meeting, the metropolitan desegregation issues reappeared. Milford continued to believe it had not been a part of Metropolitan City's problems and hence did not believe it should be a part of the solution:

> The Board discussed the letter of Dr. Adams (Midwest State Superintendent) of June 11, 1980. Dr. George reported that Mr. Pierce (School Lawyer) advised that some one should go to the meeting of June 18 and listen to what was presented but not participate in any of the discussion. If the question of naming another attorney should come up, they should merely say that the District's attorney was unable to accompany them to the meeting. There was some discussion as to securing another attorney to represent the School District and a number of names were discussed. The administrators were directed to contact Mr. Pierce in regard to securing another attorney. (6/17/80)

A week later, the Board accepted the resignation and retained Mr. O'Brien at the same fee for the next six months.

The battle is joined. From the Board and central administration's position, Milford did not contribute to the segregation of Metropolitan City and hence should not be compelled to be a part of the solution to the City's problems. Further, as the Board members see it, the solution of mandatory Metropolitan Desegregation with its massive transportation and financial costs and complications in 'a solution that has not worked anywhere in the United States. It would pull Milford down while not improving Metropolitan City,' as the Board perceives it.

Among a number of issues — tax levies, basic skills test scores, and desegregation remain major agenda items for the Board, for Milford. And, it goes without saying, for other local and state communities, and the national community as well.

Conclusion

We have labeled this chapter, 'Maintaining small town values in a complex society,' for we have an image of a different kind of tension in Milford from the kind that prevailed in the Spanman era. And we beleve that this new tension provides a very different kind of context for educational innovation than that which prevailed in the recent earlier years. At a minimum, any individual agent, be he or she a superintendent, principal, or teacher, has a very different probability of success in calling for or implementing any new educational idea.

We do not think it is stereotypic to speak of Milford in terms of small town virtues. Frugality, conservatism, localism, taking care of oneself, and individualism, all seem to run through the school board minutes and our conversations with staff and community members. Passing tax and bond levies was very difficult and years of lack of success were the norm. Without resources, changes of any kind that cost money were difficult if not impossible. The community, the school board and the superintendent were all of a piece in this regard, for most of the period. The male conservatives won out over the female liberals, the non certificated personnel unions and teacher organizations, and the liberal cosmopolitans in most instances. Dress codes, discipline, and conformity to local community standards of right and wrong were part of the high school world. Localism, the taking care of oneself without, or with a minimum, of state or national help in the form of laws, rulings, or consultants was the preferred mode of existence by the majority of the community. Majority rule prevailed.

Issues of more currency in the national community — teacher tenure laws, negotiations and collective bargaining, civil rights of minorities, concerns over and priorities of equity as values — tended to receive less attention and less support in Milford. Milford took a particular side in the 'big' debates of the last twenty years. It was an increasingly conservative stance. We spoke of it as maintaining small town values in complex society.

Notes

1 The most vivid account of parental concern over school boundaries appears in our discussion of neighborhood schools in Book II: *The Fate of an Innovative School*. (1987).
2 In contrast, former Superintendent Spanman, now a Professor of Education, remains surrounded by technology. He has his personal Apple computer in his office. See Book I for an extended account of the consistency in his orientation.
3 These are Books I and II, *Educational Innovation : Then.and Now* (1986) and *The Fate of an Innovative School: Kensington's First Fifteen Years* (1987).
4 Two weeks later, Mrs. Monticelli was back regarding District payment of hospital bills for her daughter. 'President Reeves said Mrs. Monticelli and the Board had almost a three hour discussion on this situation in executive session last Board meeting and Mrs. Monticelli knew what action had been taken.' (9/28/76)
5 That policy appeared and reappeared in the minutes, for example, in the 11/25/75 minutes it was restated:

> '. . . no staff member should be subject to any physical abuse by any student. Such behavior will be dealt with to the fullest extent of the disciplinary powers of the School District.' Suspension and expulsions

Suspension and expulsions were the far reaches of that power. The decisions were almost always unanimous.
6 One of these was the almost complete changeover of Kennerly Heights from White to Black in a little over a year. A fuller discussion of this part of Kensington's history appears in Book II, *The Fate of an Innovative School* (1987).
7 A Title IX investigation over minority hiring of teachers and administrators did occur. For a three year period, Milford's plans and practices were reviewed. At the close of the period, compliance was indicated.
8 In earlier years, this ploy worked when both nominees withdrew and the factions, less severely in conflict could agree on a third party.

9 'The ladies' was a label used by some of the district. 'Progressive' was our interpretive label.

10 Two years later, Dr. Wales, a junior high school math teacher, will become principal of the Kensington Elementary School upon the early retirement of Mr. Hawkins. Some would argue that choosing sides, taking a stand, or having a clear professional position does make a difference.

11 That vote settled the issue to the present day. Milford High does not have a smoking area.

12 Mrs. Ostermann lost her seat the following year.

13 The regular summer elementary program had been dropped a year before because of declining demand.

Section Five
Concluding Contextual Themes in Innovation and Change in Schooling

Chapter 9

A Systemic and Historical Perspective on Innovation[1]

Introduction

In the preface and the first chapter of this book we set two common sense questions. One of these was why had the Kensington School been built in the Milford District in the first place? Secondly, we wondered why it had been built at this particular time? Now, after our long historical accounts, the simple answers seem to be that McBride's long tenure as Superintendent got caught up in a wave of modernization from strong leaders in the community. The resolution of the conflict that arose seemed to overshoot its mark. As he was ousted in what we called 'the tangle of administrative succession,' the Board seemed to go well beyond its community mandate and to have hired a young imaginative Superintendent, Spanman, who took the district beyond where most of the community wanted to go. But in his four year tenure Spanman was both active enough and around long enough to have had several long term impacts on the district. One of these was the creation of the innovative, radical, child-centered Kensington School. Lurking within these simple questions and answers, are a number of important issues in the conceptualization of innovation. It is to these we now turn in this final interpretive section.

This monograph has had two major intellectual objectives. Initially, it was to provide an historical context which would increase our understandng of educational innovation, as exemplified in the initiation of the innovative Kensington Elementary School. That remains a central purpose. The second purpose arose from carrying out that effort. As we inquired into this context, the story of the Milford District became fascinating in its own right. The data, especially the School Board Minutes, were so potent in both their effects on us as researchers and on what they seemed to say about the problem of school change, that they forced a reconceptualization of the original project, 'Kensington revisited: a fifteen year follow-up of an innovative elementary school and its faculty.' The overarching idea, 'Innovation and change in American education,' arose as a theme around which the many pieces might be integrated. The blending of historical methods with more contemporaneous social science methods became a reality, a problem, and an agenda. The Milford School District has changed in many ways since 1915, for a number of reasons, and with complicated interactive effects. In our view, now, anyone who attempts to talk about school innovation ahistorically, without an understanding of the kind that an historical case such as the Milford chronicle gives, is seriously limiting their perspective. Such an accusing finger points first at ourselves and our original study, *Anatomy of an Educational Innovation* (Smith and Keith, 1971).

Another way of speaking to the issues in this concluding section on 'contextual themes' is to ask ourselves what we have learned about the history of innovation and schooling in the Milford School District that students of educational history don't know. For instance, do we know anything that David Tyack and Elizabeth Hansot in their book, *Managers of Virtue: Public School Leadership in America, 1820–1980* (1982) don't know. In part we will engage these authors in a conversation as their insights are run against our data and ideas, and our insights are run against their data and ideas. Such a give and take should increase our understanding and perhaps more general understanding.

One place to start blends issues of content with issues of research strategy. In *Managers of Virtue*, Tyack and Hansot distinguish their effort from Cremin's earlier historical work in that Cremin took a broad cultural view of education while they concentrated on 'public schooling,' more formal or institutionalized education. We have elected to narrow this focus one step further and have concentrated on a single school district. In addition we have tried to keep the concept of 'innovation' continually in mind as we looked at the issues of change over the sixty-five years of District history. Such a case study gives its own kind of integrity to the perspective, even as it sacrifices other possibilities of integration such as those sought by Cremin and Tyack and Hansot. Our conception of 'context' seems tighter and closer to particular events because of this. In their 'afterward' they use the conception of leadership to illustrate their point: 'Indeed, leadership is so dependent on context that it cannot be understood apart from time and place' (p. 265). Milford's Superintendents,: Briggs, Grey, McBride, Spanman, and George were particular individuals working in Milford at particular times as we have tried to show in considerable detail. To know them and to understand 'innovation and change in schooling' one has to know their Boards of Education, their communities and their times. Our narrative has done this.

As Tyack and Hansot continue their discussion they comment: 'Above all, we think it is useful to question the search for universal and eternal generalizations and instead to pay attention to the changing context of ideas, interests, and political and economic structures within which educational leaders have operated' (p. 265). In a sense, we, too, have struggled with the degree to which social science and educational generalizations are time and context free. For us, our very subtitle, 'History, politics and agency,' is in itself a major generalization about the nature of innovation and change in schooling. Our conceptualizations are not nomothetic-deductive structures or 'theoretical palaces.' Rather, they are tools or instruments for thinking about the problems at hand, in this instance, innovation and change. They seem generalizable enough and powerful enough to look at innovation in other settings far removed from Milford. In this sense, we lean toward a more analytical/theoretical interpretation than do Tyack and Hansot.

The Longitudinal Nested Systems Model

Multiple Actors and Processes: A Systemic Perspective

Our 'brilliant' analytic generalizations and interpretations seem to keep appearing as truisms. A systemic view of change in schooling is simple: at one time or another the education of Milford's children changed because of action taken by almost every part of the system. Student protest — and a law suit — altered the dress code. Teacher demands regarding salary, welfare and working conditions gradually shifted Board policy and action. Principals at times were in severe conflict with the Superintendents, and, at other times, they wrote 'institutional plans' which shaped school programs and organizational structures, at least for a while. On other, and many, occasions, Superintendents had their way and the school system changed or changes were resisted — McBride did not want the union in Milford and Nussbaum was on his way. Finally, and perhaps most importantly, the Board 'moved, seconded, and passed' item after item. A high school was opened in the late 1920s, new schools were built, and others were closed. The high school curriculum went from four units in 1927 to over a hundred in 1980.

A major part of our story has indicated that actors and groups of actors outside the Milford District have been major agents of innovation and change in Milford. Local, state, and national governments in their legislative, executive, and judicial branches have each had their say at different times and places on different events.

Individuals and groups from professional educational organizations and from colleges and universities and private foundations, whether in the form of investigating committees, research and development surveys and investigations or consultants have had profound effect on Milford. Neither the buildings that were built nor the personnel who staff them have been left untouched.

Throughout our account, the people who make up the community have been clustered and categorized by various labels and concepts which we generally have called demographic influences. The very number of families and children has changed dramatically over the years. The religious and racial composition of the community, the socioeconomic status of the families, and such items as their transiency have exerted dramatic effects.

In our attempts to pattern the influences toward modernization in the McBride period we eventually found ourselves clustering events into different loci of influence and agency. During his long twenty-seven years as Superintendent, it seemed as though innovation was arising from different points at different times — individual teachers, multiple teachers organizations, principals, the board, outside professional consultants, the local community, and eventually the national government, both in the legislature and the courts. We found McBride himself to be only one of the agents for innovation. As we moved back and forth between and among the other Superintendents and the events in their tenure we were moved another step toward what we are now calling a longitudinal nested systems model of innovation and change.

In addition we seem to be presenting a more analytical view of 'the times.' One needs a way of stating the nature of an actor's world as he or she contemplates innovation. In the Briggs period, or in the McBride era, or in the Spanman interlude, or in the Georgian period, the 'times' were different, that is the demography was different, the national or state laws were different, the community was different, or the Board was different. The constellation or pattern of the elements meant that some things would be easy to accomplish and some things would be difficult in these different times.

In summary, agency and context intermixed over time. Innovation took on both a dynamic and a politically interactive quality. That is what we keep trying to capture in our theoretical net. Increasingly, that net seems a more and more powerful way of thinking and talking about innovation in schooling.

Beyond the analysis of the school district into a series of discernible parts, clusters of actors, all of whom at one time or another brought about change in the district, a systemic analysis would suggest multiple processes of change. In Figure 34 we have quickly listed 'a rag bag of social processes.'

Such a collection seems to raise several key hunches. First, innovation and change must be relocated in the core of the human condition, the processes involved as people go about solving their problems, carrying on with their lives. Second, anything less is to return to overly simple accounts of the reality. Third, some clustering of processes, ordering them in terms of prevalence and importance, and beginning to move intellectually, both analytically and synthetically, seems important. These ideas move us close to the position taken by House (1974) in his *The Politics of Educational Innovation*. To take an illustration or two from the many in his book, for instance, 'the primacy of personal contact,' we can see some of the parallels and contrasts. He comments, 'In this book personal contact is seen as a basic element

Figure 34: A Rag Bag List of Social Processes In Innovation and Change

individual initiative
conflict
negotiation
bargaining
cooperation
voting
compromising
pressure groups
squeaky wheels
discussion
debate
legal advice
spying
open hearings
outside experts
threats
planning
borrowing of ideas
accidents
resignations
strikes
practical reasoning

of educational change. Inducing change in the behavior of a number of persons requires, in effect, establishing a new social system' (1974, p. 9). Later, 'advocacy' becomes a specific illustration of the kind of personal contact he means. And still later, he presents a model of the progress of advocacy which we have reproduced as Figure 35. Such a model is not alien to the approach we are moving toward. We would note that the overall language is close to common sense. In our view that is a virtue, that is, it has some major strengths. On the right hand side of the figure, the concepts of decay and rejuvenation seem to imply an overall organic or natural history metaphor. In our view of the early years of the Milford District we saw the district 'evolving.' The introduction of 'careers' and 'sponsorship' as variables also seem potent. Those conceptions guided a large part of the analysis and interpretation of our *Educational Innovators: Then and Now* (1986).

The contrasts with House's position will unfold as we continue to develop what we call our 'longitudinal nested systems model of innovation and change.' In brief, we have a strong commitment that one appropriate and major level of analysis of innovation is 'interactional.' Beyond personal contact as a single concept, there is a social psychological or social interactional level of analysis which lies between psychological theories of the individual and social theories of the state or of social movements. We believe that is an important focus for practitioners and the trainers of educational practitioners. Again and again we return to the interactions of individuals as the 'mediators' or 'mechanisms' of innovation. Initially we found such a perspective in the work of George Homans' *The Human Group* (1950). Increasingly, over the years we have tried to restate that position from a more interpretive or symbolic interactionist perspective rather than Homans' more social behavioristic position. In addition, we have tried increasingly to formulate the data and arguments in the language of an educational theory, rather than the language of applied social science. Finally, the role of historical data and analysis, that is, the longitudinal or diachronic, has become important for our point of view.

This collection of multiple actors in the Milford drama and the multiple processes of change seems to move us well beyond what Tyack and Hansot have called 'simple celebration or recrimination' and to set the stage for one of their major hopes for historical research in education. 'A history of public-school leadership that is simply a tale of injustice and elite imposition and not also a story of generous ideals and common effort lacks the complexity and texture of actuality.' (p. 11). But even this more 'balanced' view of theirs is a far cry from the day to day, and year by year view we have tried to provide on the road to both complexity and texture. Common sense accounts and theoretical concepts merge in our construction of the worlds of schooling in Milford.

The Longitudinal or Historical Perspective

Through the six to seven decades covered by this chronicle, the Milford District changed. The elements were both large and small. The governance structure shifted from a three director district to a six director district in 1925. In 1931, elementary

Figure 35: Advocacy and the Process of Innovation (After House, 1974, p. 54)

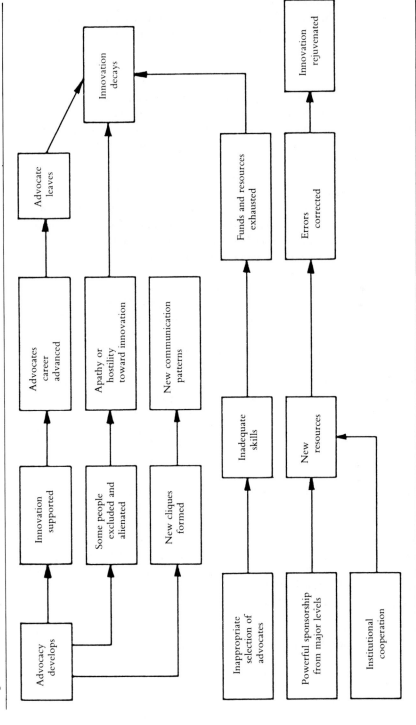

school programs had been expanded to include a four year secondary school and the District graduated its first high school class, a tradition that has continued now for over fifty years. In 1949, the District expanded by fifty per cent when it annexed and consolidated with the Marquette District. The school as an organization found itself bigger, with new positions, and with a flow of incumbents over the years. Specialization and organizational charts appeared. Budgets and accounting procedures arrived. Policies and procedures were formalized. Conflict was never far from the surface as individuals and groups contended over the direction and nature of education and schooling in Milford. With details far too numerous to summarize the small stories accumulate of school boundaries, of pupil discipline, of gradual increments in program, perhaps exemplified best in buying bats and balls, reading books, sousaphones and finally libraries, shops, and language laboratories.

From the long, historical or longitudinal perspective the concept of eductional innovation, as 'deliberate planned change for the better,' began to lose its sharpness and its potency as an educational concept. It did not sound so right for it implied an orderliness, a rationality, a clockwork quality which seemed by-the-mark in Milford.

Now we propose briefly to focus more directly on the Kensington School, to play back on our original study of Kensington and Milford, and to generalize from our history toward a way of looking at innovation and change.

The Early View of Kensington

Only on rare occasions are social scientists and educators able to make predictions and then check them out many years later. We are fortunate to have that opportunity. Over fifteen years ago we studied the first year in the life of Kensington, an innovative elementary school (Smith and Keith, 1971). The school building was new, with exciting architecture, and open space. A faculty had been brought together from all parts of the country. The approach to curriculum, instruction, grouping, and administration was new, different, non-traditional. A number of events and conditions we observed then led us to forecast changes for Kensington in the years ahead. In Figure 36, from the original study, we saw incongruities between the community's vision of schools and Kensington's innovativeness. This disharmony meant increased external pressure for both the Kensington School and the Milford District Central Administration. As we begin to see personnel and policy changes, the handwriting on the wall seemed to read: 'reversion to the old Milford type.'

Fifteen years later, we found our prediction to be true, but overshadowed by what we found the 'new Kensington' to be. Some of our initial observations on returning included:

1   The school now had its fourth principal.
2   While none of the original faculty is currently teaching at Kensington, a core group of a half dozen has been here for twelve to thirteen years.

Figure 36: The Social Context of Kensington's Administrative Change (from Smith and Keith, 1971. p. 16)

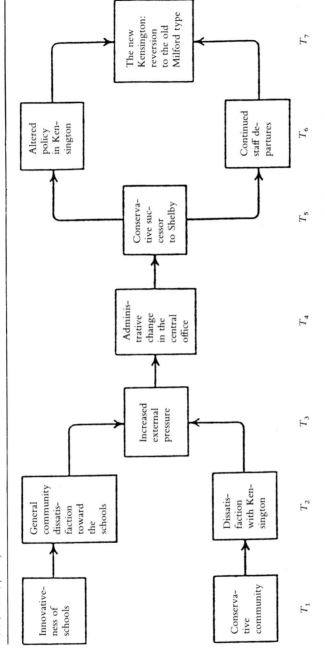

3 The physical plant has changed: the outdoor play shelter has been enclosed and made into a multi-purpose room, several walls have been built between instructional areas, and barbed wire is strung on the perimeter of the roof.
4 Approximately 60 per cent of the pupil population is now Black in contrast to the previous 100 per cent White.
5 The school is graded and teachers and children are identified by grade levels rather than the broad non-graded divisions (Basic Skills, Transition and Independent Study Division).
6 Textbooks and dittoed worksheets are now widely used as instructional materials.
7 A special education program for learning disabilities occupies a teacher, a room and several dozen children.
8 Corporal punishment is now part of a set of multiple approaches to discipline.[2]

In short, our checking on a simple prediction made 'unwittingly' years ago, ensnared us in some of the most complex and exciting current issues in educational and social science thought.

When we now ask when, how, and why these changes have come about we find a series of events, some fortuitous, others the result of decisions of men and women, related to changes in the Milford District, the county, the state, and the nation. Furthermore, we find that many of these changes are not Milford or Kensington innovations, that is, planned, creative changes initiated by the District or the School. Rather, they are reactions and responses to factors originating in these multiple, external contexts. As we sought to explain the changes in the School, we found ourselves drawn back in time and into more distant places. Kensington School's immediate geographical and social context is the Milford School District. It was not surprising to see both the School and the District to have interdependent histories. As we began exploring these histories, we found plots and themes that enmeshed with even more far-ranging contexts. It was as if Kensington's history was circumscribed by Milford's, and these two in ever widening temporal and spatial milieus. When we first conceived of returning to Kensington School, its fifteen year history seemed to define our task. We found that we could not explain the changes in this once innovative school with such a narrow conception. Our notion of 'Longitudinal Nested Systems' is an effort to come to grips with the role of these interdependent contexts in shaping the school we found on our return visit. We have displayed this model in Figure 37, which is a simple grid with systems nested on the ordinate and the time line of the abscissa. What is missing are only the concrete events in the Milford and Kensington story.

Our conception of longitudinal nested systems is really an extension of our efforts to account for policy and curricular efforts from several intensive inquiries in classrooms, schools, districts, and government agencies (Dwyer, 1981; Prunty, 1981; Smith and Geoffrey, 1968; Smith and Pohland, 1974; Smith and Dwyer, 1979; Smith, 1977; Smith, In Process). In fact, the rudiments of our model were presaged in our first study of Kensington when we noted:

Figure 37: The Longitudinal Nested Systems Model

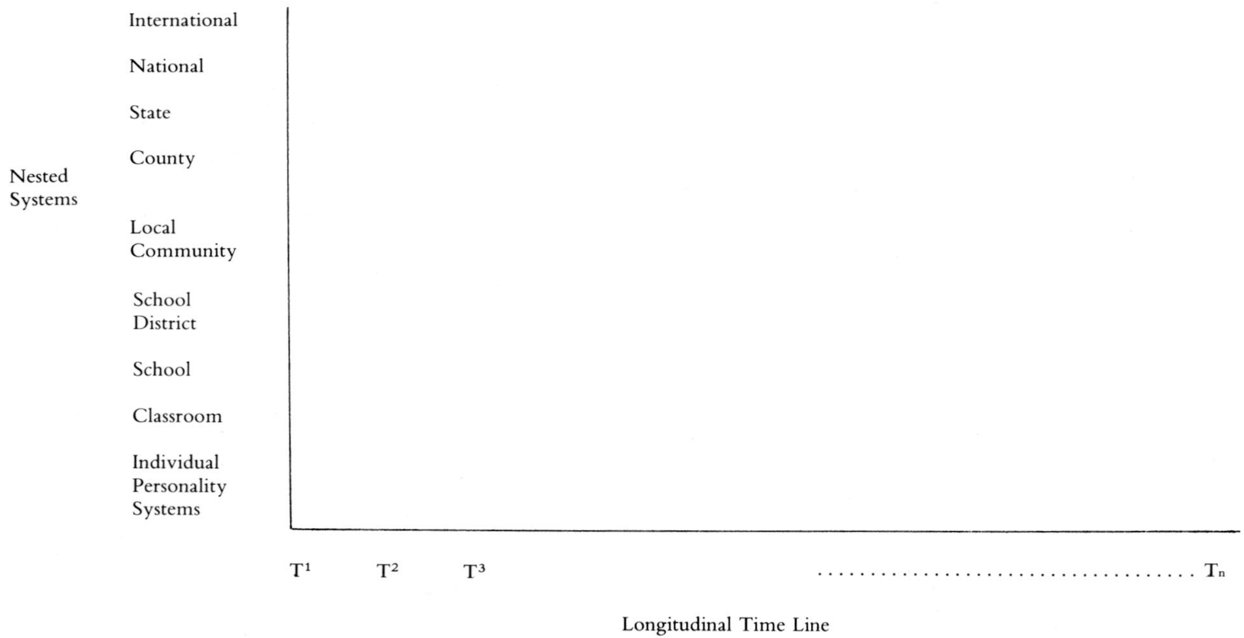

International

National

State

County

Nested
Systems

Local
Community

School
District

School

Classroom

Individual
Personality
Systems

T^1 T^2 T^3 . . . . T_n

Longitudinal Time Line

At a very concrete level, one of the most striking generalizations is that the social environment has a number of discriminable parts. Each of these parts is a miniature social system in itself. These systems have interdependencies among themselves as well as with Kensington. (1971, p. 121)

Fleshing Out the Model

We have presented an initial set of predictions overlaid on our earlier long chronicle of community, district, county, state, national, and even international events. We also presented in skeletal form our Longitudinal Nested Systems Model. We indicated that our conception formed around two dimensions, time, and space. We are now ready to flesh out that earlier conception with some specific events in Milford's and Kensington's history, demonstrating the use of the model and discussing its contributions to the study of change and innovation. We also believe this approach extends the analysis of social systems in education. As such it represents a fresh look at an often underemphasized or overlooked point. Some years ago, Homans simply but aptly stated the importance of such holistic views of interdependent systems:

By studying any state of affairs as a whole, as the sum of its parts and something more, we are often able to understand it in a way we could not otherwise have done. This is a commonplace, but like many commonplaces is important and often forgotten.

Perhaps it is pretentious to say that an attempt will be made to describe the social order as a whole. All that these words mean is an attempt will be made to consider not simply a few of the important aspects of society but rather as many as possible. the list cannot in fact be complete, partly because the records ... are necessarily fragmentary and one-sided, and partly because different generations of scholars see with different eyes: the men of the present day cannot tell what the future will find they have overlooked. (Homans, 1941, p. 4)

The general model we presented in the introduction was a simple grid. The nested systems were arranged hierarchically on the ordinate; the time line was constructed on the abscissa. The generic quality of the model is suggested by the possibility of inserting any set of nested systems on the vertical axis and any time line on the horizontal. In Figure 38 we insert the systems we have seen as relevant to Kensington and Milford, and a time line from about 1910 when the first records of Milford appear. Into this, we place some of the items and events from the stories we have told in our narrative. Simply, we are capturing instances of innovation and change, putting them into categories which are more general and abstract, and then arranging them to demonstrate their temporal relations. We contend that each such conceptual act adds clarity and depth to the Kensington story and improves our ability to think about our original problem — what happened at Kensington? The process has not only been enlightening in this respect but has expanded the initial conceptualization of the study by suggesting further fruitful avenues of inquiry. For

Figure 38: Selected Events and School Personnel Arrayed on The Longitudinal Nested Systems Model

	1910	1920	1930	1940	1950	1960	1970	1980
International				World War II (1935–45)	Sputnik (1957)		Vietnam War	
National (USA)				Post World War II Baby Boom (1945)	Supreme Court Desegregation Decision (1954)	NEA Intervention in District (1962)		Equal Education for Handicapped PL94–142 passed (1975)
State (Midwest)				State Law for School Reorganization (1948)				Statewide Basic Achievement Testing (1978)
County (Suburban)				Reorganization Suburban County Districts (1949–52)		County Services for Exceptional Children (1962)		CSES Involvement in Kensington (1978)
Local Community (Several Municipalities)						1) Population Shifts, 2) Land Development 3) Extensive Building of Apartments	1) Community Receipt of Federal Housing Support 2) Population Shifts (1975)	
School District (Milford)		Six Director Board (1925)	First Superintendent Appointed: Briggs (1928–30) / Grey's Superintendency (1930–35)	McBride's Superintendency (1935–62) / Marquette District Annexed (1949)	Massive School Construction: 10 Buildings (1952–64)	Spanman's Superintendency (1962–66)	George's Superintendency (1966–)	
School (Kensington)	One Room School (1910)					Shelby (1964–66) / Edwards (1966–76)		Wales (1979–)
Classroom						Building Walls (1966–)		
Individual Personality Systems						Charismatic Personalities (Spanman, Edwards)		

example, as we view the Milford District story as an important influence on Kensington events, that story becomes significant in its own right. As we indicated, one of our guiding questions was not only 'How and why did this school change from 1964 to 1979?' but also 'why did the Kensington School appear at all in the Milford School District?'

In our first look at the Kensington School in 1964 (Smith and Keith, 1971) we focused primarily on the School itself, limiting our comments about innovation and change to people and events connected directly with the School. Analysis of the community, parents, and district administrators was undertaken almost entirely from observations at the School or in meetings that intimately concerned the setting. Today, we find that perspective insufficient to explain how Kensington has changed. This fact alone speaks to the increasing complexity of the setting and the methodology needed to understand it. Any issue we would begin to examine — administrative succession, discipline, curriculum, racial change, etc. — carried us into ever wider circles of inquiry.

The multiple categories of antecedents for the changes at Kensington most easily fell along geographical, political and organizational lines: international, national, state, county, community, district, and school. In part, this captured the spread of the nested systems, but the narrative also indicates that we found much of the interaction between the systems to be typified by conflict, politics, and legal constraints. Each theme and strand we pursued developed as a twisted blend of these multiple systems. Those events that represented innovations: intentional, planned, creative alternatives, soon were entangled in other kinds of change growing out of personal and political interests, activities of other organizations and forces emanating from larger systems.

A further look at one theme, the significance of racial change at Kensington, will illustrate these points. From 1964 to 1979, Kensington shifted from 100 per cent White to sixty per cent Black enrollment. One of the most dramatic changes in the Kensington School revolved around a series of 'nested' national, state, and local events. As we indicated, education of students in Midwest State was segregated legally by race until 1954 when the Brown vs. Topeka Supreme Court decision was handed down. Following that was a ruling by Midwest State and a decision by the Milford School Board. The latter was phrased quite explicitly as noted in the *Milford School Community Bulletin*:

> Segregation to end in Milford Schools September 1, 1955.
>
> After a ruling from the Midwest State Attorney General and a ruling from the State Department of Education at Capitol City, the Board of Education of the School District of Milford *has decided* (our italics) that segregation in the Milford School District will end on September 1, 1955.
>
> The status of our schools will remain the same as in the past until September 1, 1955. (Board Minutes, 1954)

In a larger sense, the court decision and the multiple interrelated events of the deteriorating central city, problems in federally subsidized housing, and public attitudes toward education, school integration and neighborhood schools led to the large demographic population shifts of the mid 1970s.[3] These, in turn, changed the Kensington School from a school with just a few isolated non-Caucasian youngsters to a school that is now approximately sixty per cent Black. The cultural, social, educational impact of that shift in population is dramatic.

We find a host of observations captured in the tangled impact: 1) The community consists of predominantly White neighborhoods, some integrated neighborhoods and a few predominantly minority neighborhoods; 2) Over the years, there were several instances of school boundary changes in the District to balance pupil numbers. Despite those changes, one set of schools in the District remained mostly White, while others became sixty per cent to ninety per cent Black; 3) There has never been a Black person on the Milford Board of Education. In a recent election two Blacks ran for the Board. Both were overwhelmingly defeated; 4) District wide, there is one Black administrator, an assistant principal; 5) the Kensington School, in 1979–80, had two Blacks, one counselor and one teacher, on the professional staff. The teacher was moved to another school the following year because of recency of tenure and declining enrollments; 6) District policy has consistently followed a neighborhood school concept; 7) Kensington staff responded, in part, to their changing student population with more walls, more traditional curriculum and instructional styles, and tighter discipline; 8) Regarding the variety of emotional response to changes in racial composition, one commentator described Kensington positively as 'sunkissed,' a change for the better. The feeling of another was expressed by analogy to Kubler-Ross' (1979) analysis of death and dying: Kensington went through stages of denial, anger, bargaining, depression, acceptance and hope. For better or worse, we find these powerful metaphors. The phenomenon is not one taken lightly. In short, state and federal steps taken to integrate schools are in opposition to local housing patterns, and continuing locally elected conservative Boards, and less of a priority than a number of educational policies regarding school organization and personnel.

The example of antecedents related to the racial changes at Kensington is only one of a more complex set. It is joined, as told in the narrative, with other strands such as inflation, PL 92–142, the 'back-to-basics' movement, and state guidelines and local concerns over discipline. One more illustrative theme deepens our view of this tangle of strands. Our descriptive stories hinted at the checkered history of discipline in the District and at the Kensington School. Some of the very earliest items in the Board minutes were actions taken regarding pupil misbehavior. Concerns over corporal punishment occurred early and the Board articulated in 1925 a 'no corporal punishment policy' and argued for school suspensions in serious cases and a hearing before the Board. Over the years that policy was lost, new views appeared, and the District has wrestled long and hard with what is, in our view, a very complex and difficult practical problem. The initial Kensington policy articulated by Shelby, in its list of 'from-to' aspects of its formal doctrine was an attempt to move from 'external discipline, external motivation, restricting pupil interaction, and the teacher as a controller of pupils to self-discipline, self-motivation, encouraging pupil interaction and teacher as organizer for learning.' and we have noted that Dr. George's initial mandate from the Board and his own predispositions and attitudes lay in the need for discipline and control as a pre-condition for pupil learning. Our narrative indicated the flow from Edwards to Hawkins to Wales in point of view.

In the Spring of 1980, the continuing concern over discipline was reflected in Kensington policies of paddling, detention and suspension devised by the staff and Principal. These have been supported by the Central Office. Discipline was an issue in the recent Board elections. One incumbent Board member was described in a news account:

> He said he had focused most of his campaign on quality education and discipline within the school system. 'I just believe in discipline,' he said. 'I think there has to be a re-emphasis on discipline in order to keep quality education.' (PD, 1980)

The incumbent was returned to the Board with over 5000 votes. The losing members garnered less than a thousand votes, less than one sixth of the total. While a number of other issues were critically involved in the election, the point we would make here is the congruence in action across the classroom system, the building system, the multiple aspects of the District as a system, and finally to the Milford patrons' views represented in the annual school elections. We recognize that changes in discipline are but one of the differences we found at Kensington fifteen years later. Again, our model helps to simplify the picture of the accumulating effects of actions from the nested systems. By examining the specific events recorded in the model in Figure 37. we can develop a more abstract version, Figure 38, which illustrates more general classes of actions or antecedents and a general flow of consequences from events in the world, nation, and state to community responses, to district, and to school.

In effect, we are back to Figure 36 and the prediction from fifteen years ago, 'The new Kensington: reversion to the old Milford type' (1971, p. 16). Now also we can examine Figure 39 and see what we have learned. The first conclusion is that Milford has changed and the return to the 'old Milford type' is vastly more complicated than the label would indicate. Michael Edwards, Kensington's second principal, did, in part, take Kensington that way, but he, too, was a maverick in Milford and was responsive to many of the original ideals of Kensington. Second, events in the larger systems, in which Kensington is nested, have their own integrity and dynamic, for example, 1954 was a major year. The consequences have been felt only in the last half dozen years. Finally, and most particularly in the school the 'effects' seem much more interactive than linear. Demographic changes flow in and out of perceptual changes which in turn flow back and forth from curricular and instructional changes as the various classes of actors in the school, principals, teachers, and children interact over the years.

With this deepened view of the re-establishment of the 'old Milford type' at Kensington and with a more intensive view of the Milford School District qua district and its history since the turn of the century we are tempted to venture a further prediction. From even before Mrs. Briggs, the first Superintendent, when an early attempt to establish a high school failed because of lack of awareness of state regulations, to her difficulties in a tax levy being rescinded because it conflicted with

Figure 39: A Longitudinal Nested Systems Portrayal of the Changes in the Kensington School

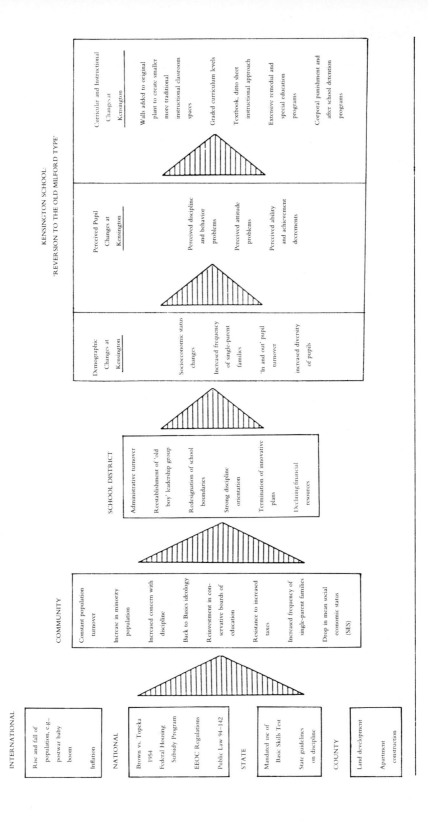

KENSINGTON SCHOOL:
'REVERSION TO THE OLD MILFORD TYPE'

INTERNATIONAL

Rise and fall of
population, e.g.,
postwar baby
boom

Inflation

NATIONAL

Brown vs. Topeka
1954

Federal Housing
Subsidy Program

EEOC Regulations

Public Law 94–142

STATE

Mandated use of
Basic Skills Test

State guidelines
on discipline

COUNTY

Land development

Apartment
construction

COMMUNITY

Constant population
turnover

Increase in minority
population

Increased concern with
discipline

Back to Basics ideology

Reinvestment in con-
servative boards of
education

Resistance to increased
taxes

Increased frequency of
single-parent families

Drop in mean social
economic status
(SES)

SCHOOL DISTRICT

Administrative turnover

Reestablishment of 'old
boy' leadership group

Redesignation of school
boundaries

Strong discipline
orientation

Termination of innovative
plans

Declining financial
resources

Demographic
Changes at
Kensington

Socioeconomic status
changes

Increased frequency
of single-parent
families

'In and out' pupil
turnover

increased diversity
of pupils

Perceived Pupil
Changes at
Kensington

Perceived discipline
and behavior
problems

Perceived attitude
problems

Perceived ability
and achievement
decrements

Curricular and Instructional
Changes at
Kensington

Walls added to original
plant to create smaller
more traditional
instructional classroom
spaces

Graded curriculum levels

Textbook, ditto sheet
instructional approach

Extensive remedial and
special education
programs

Corporal punishment and
after school detention
programs

state rules, we find a lack of understanding of problems and concerns with state and federal involvement in education in Milford. The gradual acceptance of federal monies and federal regulations for buildings and school lunches appear in our longer account of the 1930s and 1940s. Today, the concerns in civil rights regarding women, handicapped, and minority education within and between school districts, in federal monies for programs, and in multiple federal regulations are very much a part of the School District. Milford, the community, the board, the administration, seems on a collision course with state and federal regulations. These events seem also to be increasingly a part of state and national politics in the current (1980) elections. Candidates are making issues and taking stands about bussing, decentralization of low income housing, and amount and kind of federal spending. Perhaps we shall have another opportunity to check our prediction. If so, part of the 'next' Kensington story may be a tale of a district and the courts, local control versus state control versus federal control of education.

Contributions of the Model

The Significance

We emphasize that the longitudinal nested systems model is a tool of inquiry and analysis. It offers a structure which helps us think through our data and a format in which our data can be arrayed for analysis. This perspective has implications for both the meta-theoretical and the theoretical levels of analysis. For example, it argues implicitly for a contextualist root metaphor rather than a formistic, mechanistic or organic one (Pepper, 1942; Sarbin, 1977). Theoretically, it seems open to varied substantive theories, for example — organizational, political or cultural. In this regard, as the Kensington and Milford stories unfolded and the longitudinal nested systems model arose, it provided an important understanding for another set of ideas which was dimly perceived in the initial proposal: 'Cultural, organizational and social psychological change theories: an educational test case.' A competing theories notion struck us as a fruitful future effort. What would result if we attempted to compare, to contrast, even to synthesize or extend various theories of change in light of the model? Visions of recent attempts at synthesis by House (1979) on innovation theory and Allison (1971) on policy theory danced through our heads. That agenda both entices and overwhelms us. For now we are satisfied to speculate about these possibilities and postpone the systematic effort and report on its outcome in future publications.

Further, the model helps locate our approach in relation to other social science studies of change and innovation in education.[4] *First*, we find ourselves examining increasingly long periods of time for relevant information in our inquiries. This differs from the snap shot variety of study which examines a brief, specific period. *Second*, our perspective involves a holistic view of events; we contend that one cannot understand an innovation or change in a system without considering the larger system of which it is a part. *Third*, our model makes explicit a hierarchical arrangement among the rested systems. It highlights the direct and indirect 'controls' one system may impose on another. *Fourth*, the longitudinal nested systems notion allows one to focus on parameters or 'givens' of the field of action set by one system upon another. *Fifth*, it assumes some autonomy both analytically and practically for each system. Perhaps less than some educational theorists imply and more than some educational practitioners perceive. *Sixth*, it builds upon a psychology of individual actors and their interactions, involved in events or scenes, that cumulate into meaningful structures resembling plots in drama and literature (Kelly, 1955 and Sarbin, 1977). *Seventh*, it includes a respect for the chance event, the fortuitous, the serendipic which nature forces upon us in the form of health or illness, death, and luck or natural disaster. And, finally, *eighth*, our conception aligns closely with the perspective of some historians, but we differ from them too, in that our longitudinal approach carries the time line to the present, the realm of contemporary events.

Our orientation leans us in the direction of storytelling as an important element in explanation of change and innovation. Yet, we cannot relinquish the value of more abstract, conceptual forms of analysis. As such, we place ourselves in a debate commonly waged among historians, that is, how to best contribute to cumulative knowledge. Hexter (1971) described this diatribe as 'storytelling' versus 'scientific explanation':

> Historical stories are quite unlike scientific explanation sketches. The latter are *thin*; they have to be filled out with missing words and sentences formulating the missing implied laws and boundary conditions. But although historical stories omit a good many laws and conditions, too, and although some laws are rather hard to find even when one looks for them, those stories are not thin; by scientific standards they are often fat, egregiously obese, stuffed with unessential words quite useless for the purpose of adequate and satisfactory explanation. (Hexter, 1971, p. 151)

Although the Longitudinal Nested Systems Model will not resolve the debate, it keeps us moving by providing a working solution to, if not compromise between, 'storytelling' as explanation and 'scientific explanation' and a way to begin to integrate more abstract concepts and theoretical generalizations into thinking about innovation and change in education. It leads easily into what Hexter (1971) calls 'processive explanation,' a kind of explanation that involves knowing an historical outcome and selecting from an infinite number of 'true facts' those necessary to account for the outcome.

Further, we feel that the model takes vignettes such as the potent ones of Tyack and Hansot and puts them into an even more powerful context. They comment regarding demographic changes and administrator action in New York City:

> In fifteen years the number of students swelled by 60 per cent. Beset by scanty financing and conflicting political pressures, Maxwell nonetheless tried to expand and systematize what he regarded as a chaotic collection of schools. He created a whole new range of services: special classes for the handicapped, school lunch programs, medical inspections, vocational training, vacation schools, and rooftop playgrounds for children (1982, p. 106).

As part of a longitudinal nested systems model of innovation, the demography of the early twentieth-century fueling innovation in New York City parallels the demography and innovation of Milford throughout the twentieth century. Our analysis raises questions of state laws, of school board deliberations, of particular schools and classrooms. The language of practical problems and common sense seemed more critical in Milford than 'the language of science and business efficiency' used by Tyack and Hansot.

More generally, though tentatively, we feel that our model may aid discussion of the place of values in educational thought (O'Connor, 1973; Hirst, 1973). We believe that that is at the heart of what is sometimes called practical reasoning (Schwab, 1969; Reid, 1978; Smith, 1987). We believe one's viewpoint on the role of values in inquiry and policy-making has major consequences for the models one builds in education and the practical decisions that must be made. We would argue that the Milford District was 'caught' in its history in a variety of ways. We would also add that the District has forgotten some of its history. That lineage with the past could become an illuminative part of District discussion and debate, curriculum and teaching, and a new perspective on old problems. In that light, our model becomes one contribution into the 'what-does-one-do-now' agenda of patrons, parents, pupils, teachers, administrators, and board members. We believe educational research and theory must deal with the questions of values and assist the practitioners through their quandaries. We see some of that begun in Fein (1971), Gittell *et al.* (1973), Rokeach (1975), and Peshkin (1978). The imperative in this area stems from wrenching issues in conflict today, to wit: the inherent conflict between such stances as 'fraternity/community/neighborhood schools', 'equality/justice/affirmative action/desegration,' or 'liberty/freedom/individualism/local control.'[5] We have seen such divergent values in conflict at Kensington School and the Milford District. We know they are at issue elsewhere too.

The Play of Power and The Longitudinal Nested Systems Model

In a recent revision of his book *The Policy Making Process*, Lindblom (1980) makes several distinctions which seem very important for understanding the Milford School District as an exemplar of innovation and change in American education. First, he targets the domain of policy making as:

> ... an extremely complex process without beginning or end and whose boundaries remain most uncertain. Somehow a complex set of forces together produces effects called 'policies,' ... to understand policy making one must understand all of political life. (1980, p. 5)

Policies are those 'settled courses adopted and followed by governments, institutions' or other groups, according to Webster. Innovations as creative planned changes seem similar in kind. The gradual evolution of Milford's School system seem well within the label of a 'complex process without beginning or end.' At times, for purposes of description and analysis, we have broken into the unending stream.

A second distinction of Lindblom's focuses on the criteria for judging public policy making. In a democratic national state and the communities within such a political structure, efficacy in solving problems and responsiveness to popular control are the twin standards. Neither is simple to apply in any particular situation. Efficacy lies in the eyes of multiple beholders, at least to some degree. Popular control varies in and among issues and subsystems involved. With the clockwork regularity of April school board elections, incumbents fell out of favor and were challenged at critical times. The 'good guys' and the 'bad guys' involved different factions in the community and they came and went. Internal to the organization, different levels of administrators, teachers, and parents found that their ability to influence policy shifted across times, places, and issues.

A third item in Lindblom's discussion of policy making is the distinction between the intellectual aspects of policy making, what he calls information and analysis, and the social or interactive aspects of policy making, what he calls the 'play of power.' Our description and analysis has accented both. But it is to the play of power we want to turn for a final comment. It provides a dynamic quality to our longitudinal nested systems model. Lindblom sets the stage this way:

> Because in the real world, analysis is not conclusive, in order to set policy, people interact to exercise, influence, control or power over each other. . . .
> The political interactions through which people control each other we shall call the play of power. (p. 43)

The metaphor is a game, a game with rules, with players of varied abilities, interests and resources and with outcomes in the form of policies.

As we have commented at several points, reading school board minutes is not only 'experience' or 'an experience' but at times it seems to approach being a 'memorable experience'. The events, capsuled in the brief minutes, pound incessantly at one as though standing under a not so slightly cascading waterfall. In the multiple strand of events of Mr. McBride's later years, our stories have accented changes and attempted changes in multiple aspects of the district.

From the several stories, the beginnings of a model of domains of activity or events and levels of system, can be interrelated with kind of parent or citizen's activity. The battle over elementary school boundaries seems to have been fought through meetings and petitions of a specific neighborhood interest group. The battle over the superintendency was fought and resolved through campaigns, community action, and ultimately the election of and/or defeat of particular Board members. McBride's people got elected. Mr. Lewis and Mr. Krist were defeated; the 4–2 Board became a 2–4 Board. That classroom events were being resolved in conferences of parents, teachers, and principals is supported by other data (for example, see *Anatomy of Educational Innovation*, 1971, and *The Fate of an Innovative School*, 1987).

While at one level this is all simple and obvious, at another level it suggests the need, when talking of eductional innovation and change, not to ramble about generally. Rather one needs to accent the level of the system (and the domain of activity) one seeks to change and to consider the modal modes of influence that may be grounded in practicalities, mores, or in legal precedents and structures. This seems a particular cut into the general concept, play of power.

The generalization of our point is that each level of the system has its own modal way in which influence, power and control are exerted and that each system 'nests' within a larger system. The larger system exercises more direct influence on the smaller one and mediates influence from still larger systems. Along the way, a variety of checks occur. Often, in the final analysis, constitutions and bills of rights set limits and rules, and one person one vote interactions, the smallest system exerts controls on every other level.

We contend that our view of Milford over the years and the longitudinal nested systems model which seeks to generalize the view is both a necessary and powerful vantage point for anyone addressing the problems of innovation and change in schooling.

The Policy Handbook: The Model and Another Illustration

Our monograph is full of illustrations, yet we cannot resist one more as a concluding item regarding the perspective we are trying to build. Of all the innovations introduced by Dr. Spanman as Superintendent, the one that has lasted the longest and been the most highly regarded, is the Policy Handbook. It seemed to have several critical features: 1) Wide scope, 2) A logical structure of categories, subcategories, and specific items, 3) An integration both generally and specifically with State Laws, 4) A coding or indexing of items permitting easy access, 5) A one item per page looseleaf format which permitted easy change and replacement, 6) It seemed useful to everyone — Board, Central Office Staff, teachers, parents, lawyers, etc. — in the District, especially when conflicts arose.

In a preliminary way, Figure 40 indicates the context of the Development of the Policy Handbook. A number of state statutes constrain local school districts. Milford has had a history of uncodified or partially codified policies. During the early 1960s, under Spanman's initiative, the Central Office Staff, with Board discussions and consensus, worked toward a codification of policies. Subsequent to these efforts, the Board approved formally, each item in the Blue Policy Book. From that point it became the baseline for innovation and change in the District. In later discussion in Board minutes the Policy Handbook 'as Baseline' returned in several quotes. Figure 41 lays out those elements. An appropriate metaphor might be a view of the Blue Book as the Board's gyroscope.

To elaborate the point we emphasize here that the innovation brought about the clear formalization and specification of policies and then interlocked with all sorts of later changes and attempts to change. In 1975, such diverse items as procedures for reduction in the force of teachers and the policy on 'married students' were raised, considered, and in the latter case, revised around a specific problem faced by the Board.

But the most fascinating part of the story of Milford's Policy Handbook as it

278

Figure 40: A Preliminary View of the Policy Handbook as an Innovation

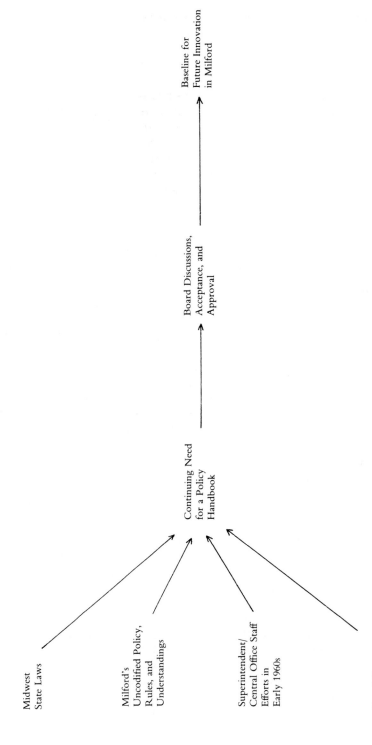

Midwest
State Laws

Milford's
Uncodified Policy,
Rules, and
Understandings

Continuing Need
for a Policy
Handbook

Board Discussions,
Acceptance, and
Approval

Baseline for
Future Innovation
in Milford

Superintendent/
Central Office Staff
Efforts in
Early 1960s

Board Consensus

Figure 41: A More Analytic View of the Functions and Consequences of the Policy Handbook

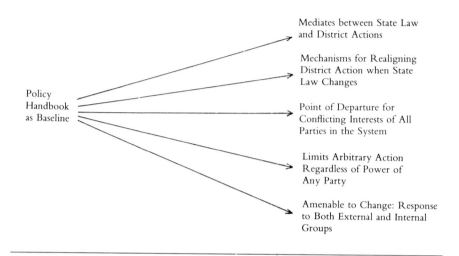

pertains to a systemic view of innovation and change resides in the more detailed story of its antecedents. Figure 42 contains this analysis.

Briefly it amounts to three coalescing strands. Southern City, Spanman's prior school system, had been wrestling with similar policy codification problems. Two educationists, Davies and Brickell, had a long research serial on school boards dating back to the late 1940s and early 1950s (Davies and Hosler, 1949, Davies and Prestwood, 1951), which culminated in a policy handbook sold commercially. Southern City bought the system while Spanman was an administrator there. Milford, as we have indicated, had its own history of policy codification problems. These three strands came together when Spanman became Superintendent in Milford. The Milford scheme became conceptually a simple revision of Southern City's Book, although practically it required an immense amount of work to fit it to the local Milford situation.

Conclusion

For a century, anthropologists, among other social scientists, have argued the dilemma of the relative importance of diachronic or historical analysis versus synchronic or contemporaneous analysis. In studying primitive cultures the fear of the diachronic was that they would result in a 'speculative' non data based history, because of the limited records available. Some students of anthropological history, theory and methods, for example, Kuper (1983) argue that field work of the Malinowski variety leads one to more contemporaneous analysis. By looking at

Figure 42: Origins of Milford's Policy Handbook

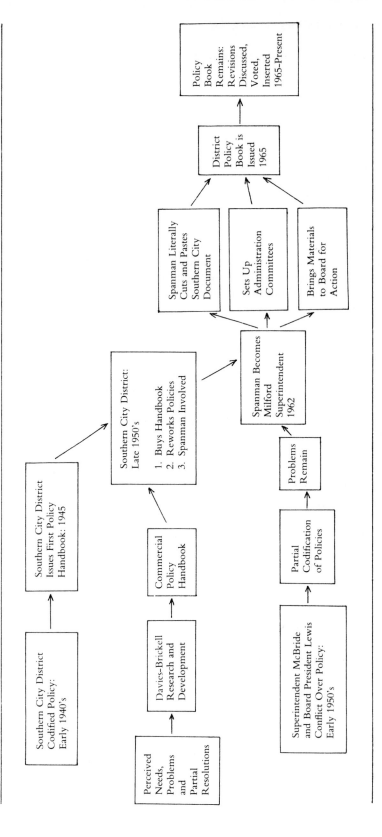

schooling as open systems over time, in terms of a longitudinal nested systems model, we have provided a format for resolving the dilemma.

Educationists, as we have presented them, in the limited sample of Tyack and Hansot and House, and in the limited and sketchy illustrations of what are truly major efforts, tend to be historians or contemporaneous social scientists. The former tend toward narrative orientations with less concern for formalizing their theoretical insights. The latter tend to be more applied social scientists — organizational theorists and sociologists — with less concern for the history of their substantive concerns. We are arguing for the importance of more intimate contact between the two.

Our presentation of the Milford School District over some half dozen decades, through some five school superintendents, with a focus on educational innovation in general and on the Kensington School in particular, is a potent illustration of the model and its ramifications. As the titles of our sections and chapters indicate we raise the particular problem of the early origins and evolution of schooling and a concern for its conceptualization as innovation. At times we felt like natural historians, doing what Darwin did on the Beagle and what Tocqueville did in his travels through America. McBride's tenure as Superintendent, the longer rhythms of stability and change, gave us a view of modernization as innovation. Finally we returned to 'radicalism and conservatism: the high drama of innovation' in the Spanman and the Georgian years. Each of those times gave us a chance to look at the system with its contemporaneous interconnections and its antecedents and consequences. The political processes and the play of power were intrinsic to that analysis.

Beyond the particular substantive findings about the Milford School District and the beginning interpretations and generalizations, the historical view, at least as we raise it provides another outcome. In seeing the Milford District near its beginnings and when it was quite small, brought issues of school structure and process into bold relief. Governance, administration, curriculum, and teaching were so visable and obvious that one could almost see, feel and touch them without screens of rhetoric or bureaeucracy lying between. This seemed particularly illuminating for our concern for educational innovation. The building of new schools, the creation of new positions and roles, the development of policy were all 'innovations,' specific planned improvements. Later complications in the processes and principles, seemed just that, complications. The underlying phenomena of innovation remained. Finally, even though using the 'systems' label, we feel that we have opened the way for a major reconstrual of the way educational theorists, particularly those in educational administration, talk about schooling. This reconstrual toward a contextualist root metaphor weaves into the next chapter of the overall conclusions and implications.

Notes

1   We vacillate in the use of historical, diachronic, and longitudinal as the term to encompass the 'over time' aspect of our thinking. Historical is the broadest label and the

one closest to common sense usage. Diachronic belongs to anthropology. It is contrasted with synchronic, an analysis of structures and functions independent of time. Anthropologists since Malinowski and Radcliffe-Brown have focused on the synchronic. Longitudinal has a long history in developmental psychology. To us it connoted also an integrity of a phenomenon over time. In this instance, our focus was on a school district.

2   These items are traced in detail in *The Fate of an Innovative School: Kensington's First Fifteen Years*, (Smith, Prunty, Dwyer, and Kleine, 1987).

3   Similarly, the postwar baby boom, new housing, and jobs in decentralized industry contributed to the expansion of the Milford District from three schools to fourteen between 1950 and 1964.

4   Our investigation, *Federal Policy in Action: A Case Study of an Urban Education Project* (Smith and Dwyer, 1980) is a 'history and analysis' also. It anticipates many of these ideas.

5   Whether the values and issues cluster in these ways seems an important analytical and empirical problem in its own right.

Chapter 10

Innovation and Educational Administration: The Metatheoretical Perspective

Introduction

Rethinking one's scientific and practical action assumptions is a fundamental problem in the nature of cognition and personal constructs. We seem to have been at this since the mid 1960s when we began what became *The Complexities of an Urban Classroom* (Smith and Geoffrey, 1968), the first of our participant observation or ethnographic case studies. Along the way, each of us has been involved in a series of interrelated projects.[1] The intellectual string on these issues continued to be pulled as we read educational administration monographs and articles by Griffiths (1966, 1977, 1979), Greenfield (1973, 1978), Bates (1981) and others. Now our task seems to be to move away from Kensington and Milford to more 'experience distant' conceptions, as Geertz (1983) uses the term, and ask ourselves, what does all this mean for social scientists and educationists, our principal audiences. Within these groups it is probably educational administrators and organizational theorists who are the focal groups. Our literature search turned up a half dozen key articles, monographs, and books which became foci or theses upon which we clarify and present our own perspective.

Personality, Cognition and Social Interaction in Innovation

When one sits in the quietude of one's office at the University or even in the conference room space off the main flow of action in the Milford Central Office, the differences in the scholarly contemplative university life and the hectic life of Board member as policy maker or Superintendent as administrator come vividly to mind. At several points, and for different purposes, we have contrasted the Superintendency and the Board. Here we raise and accent several important similarities. In retrospect our generalizations seem terribly obvious and simple. We have been struck however that our reading in the literature of social science and education and our conversations with colleagues have not raised the items in our consciousness to the degree we now perceive them and to the importance we now attach to them. So much for learning to appreciate something.

We have labeled this section: 'personality, cognition, and social interaction in innovation.' The discussion continues to elaborate our interactional perspective. We are concerned with what people say and do with each other, how they think about and interpret the educational world around them, and how all this bears upon their more general dispositions. For individuals interested in innovation and change at the practical level of schooling, this seems an appropriate level of analysis. A half dozen subissues arise in our data and interpretations.

Ill Defined and Entangled Problems

Insights come from many sources. In a series of discussions with Professor David Gordon of Ben Gurion University, Beersheva, Israel, he put us on to Reitman's (1965) concept of ill defined problems. Ill defined problems, often those involved in creativity, have no well accepted criterion or set of criteria which enable one to decide when the problem has been resolved. Reitman's analytical illustration is a case study in music, a composer creating a fugue, or as he delightfully calls it, 'the autobiography of a fugue.' In the protocol reporting on the activity comments appear such as 'theme,' 'countersubject,' 'pianistic,' 'the proper consistency of tension,' and 'Yes, that will probably work.' In Reitman's analysis he speaks of 'constraints upon the problem solution,' 'open constraint,' 'the sequence of transformations,' 'constant proliferation,' 'abstract new transformational formulas,' 'particularization of components,' 'conventions,' and so forth. We are reminded both methodologically and substantively of Beittel's *Alternatives for Art Education Research* (1973). He extends the importance of both the artistic and the aesthetic metaphor and the utility of the conception of ill defined problems. It is our contention that most social problems, problems involving people, are ill defined problems in this sense and that many if not most of the more technical or technological systems developed for problem solving do not work in the more classical or traditional sense as Boards and Superintendents try to solve these problems.

Another obvious truism, perhaps, is that the practical problems faced by leaders of all kinds — Board Presidents, Superintendents, CTA Presidents come in almost hopelessly mixed tangles and snarls. As true as that seems, it also seems that little attention has been devoted to the intellectual action, and political efforts needed to cope with such mixed issues. For instance, as our narrative indicated, the Autumn of 1974 illustrates our point beautifully. These strands seem involved: 1) School enrollments were declining, a Housing Committee was developing an analysis and set of proposals regarding school closings. 2) The Milford State Educational Association was stirring much more actively. They continued the press for an outside NEA professional consultant/negotiator to meet with them and with the Board. 3) The community had not passed higher tax levies or board levies in a decade, in spite of yeoman efforts by a variety of professional and lay groups. 4) A

'Concerned Citizens' group had collected 2100 signatures on a petition to keep the Grant School open. And 5) One of the leaders of the Concerned Citizens' group later became a successful candidate for the Board and was viewed also as a 'teachers' candidate.' The intellectual and political problems can be seen in each group having a leader, some elected, some appointed. The agendas and strategies of the different groups sometimes and on some issues overlapped with one or another of the groups. Our question is — how does one begin to think about such a mixture?

An earlier analysis of 'problem' in the context of field study research and the 'problems' it tackles led us toward the complicated conception that we present as Figure 43. Essentially we argued that a problem involves a present state, a preferred state, and a gap between the two. Further, we argued each of those has a structure, an historical context and a contemporaneous context.[2] The conceptualization of each of these can occur from multiple perspectives at multiple levels of abstraction. The resolutions, in turn, can be cast in varied forms: data, narrative, theory, and metatheory.

At other points in this monograph we have alluded to the wealth of problems contained in the 'preferred' category. Values and 'oughts' have once again permeated the structure of the 'is' language. Our systemic theory suggests that different individuals and subgroups might hold very different views of each of these elements; our data clearly support the conjecture.

We are now making two further points. First, most schooling issues faced by the board and administrative staff are 'ill defined problems,' that is, there is no clear criterion for the acceptability of a solution. Second, each problem is 'almost hopelessly' entangled with other problems. This entanglement creates further problems, 'meta problems,' in deciding on agendas and priorities in order to cut in on the tangle. Even some of the most interesting practical problem solving research pales in the heat of such difficulties (Bloom and Broder, 1950; Maier, 1963; Maier, *et al.*, 1957).

For us, one of the major outcomes of this study regarding problems and problem solving, is the image of Superintendent Spanman's use of practical reasoning in the service of innovation. The mode of thought which captured our attention appeared in several places in the agendas of Superintendent Spanman. Usually they were phrased in the form of several steps. 'What are we doing now?' in one or another curricular area, administrative practice, or organizational structure. This tended to be the first step. It seemed to provoke an array of comments or reactions with a mixed descriptive and analytical focus, with a mixed common sense and theoretical language, and with a mixed pro and con evaluative stance. The keepers of the political *status quo* were able to speak in detail to their point of view. Similarly the advocates of change were able to begin to talk about the issues from their point of view. The second step, 'What problems are we having?' tilted the balance and gave the reform oriented people their say. At this point two kinds of differences in values and preferred states arose. The 'is' and 'ought' differences appeared in the discussion. Also, the subgroup differences in values, preferred states, and 'oughts' appeared. Then the political process began in earnest as individuals and subgroups argued and attempted to persuade. Into these discussions came the third

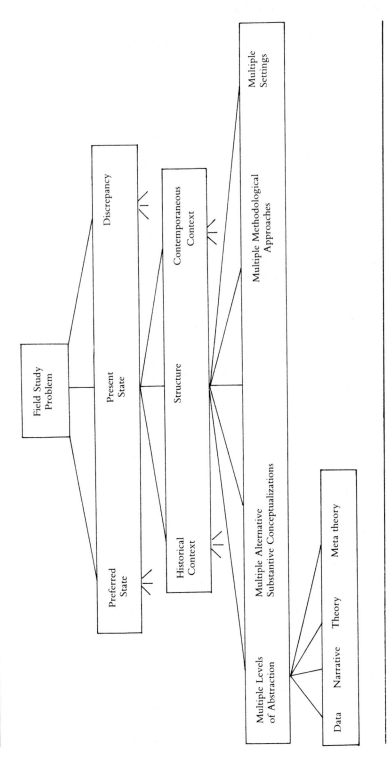

Figure 43: The Field Study Problem as a Concatenation of Elements (Smith. 1981. p. 94)

step, 'What promising practices and programs' are available to merge the present states and the preferred states. Creativity appeared in the form of innovations more generally available in the literature and the educational culture. Local ideas and creative possibilities also were spun out. In an earlier chapter we listed a table of numbers of innovations by school that occurred during one year of Spanman's tenure. The district was alive with new alternatives in curriculum, teaching, staffing, and organizational structures. The final step involved 'Actions to be taken and problems with implementation.' Always on Spanman's agendas and in his discussions with the Board and with the administrative staff was a call and move to action based on one's best thought. This kind of thinking mixed with his 'shaker and mover' disposition and style.

Spanman's intellectual house was not only always in order but usually two steps ahead of everyone else's agenda. His goals and priorities, phrased in several levels of both abstractness and concreteness, his reasons, his view of difficulties, his understanding of time, place and circumstances, and his search for imaginative options were always followed by an action recommendation. He had a fascinating way of dealing with entangled and ill defined problems.

The Unpredictable and Often Uncontrollable Environment

In our reading of Board minutes and other documents, and in our conversations and interviews with Milford personnel we came away with a concept, the unpredictable environment. We believe it's important in the analysis and conceptualization of district organization and administration. While we use the label 'unpredictable,' our mode of thought tends to be probabilistic rather than categorical and we implicitly think in terms of 'degree of unpredictableness.' That is, some events seem totally unpredictable, some seem improbable, others are probable, some are good bets, and others, local taxes and April Board elections, are dead certain.

For instance on the unpredictable end, reading along in the minutes of 1938, we came to a notice of a Special Board Meeting called for 9 March 1938. With no introduction, the first item stated:

> Mr. McBride reported he had a call from Mr. Dudley who is in the lumber business. If possible, Mr. Dudley would like us to buy the lumber from him. Mr. Sherman also called, saying he would like to put in a bid on rebuilding the school. (3/9/38)

It was two sets of minutes later before the phrase 'after the fire' appeared. Obviously some kind of 'natural disaster' had occurred and the Board was mobilizing to take action to cope with the event. Over the years, two major fires occurred, this one in 1938 at Clear Valley School which was now the junior and senior high school and in 1955, when the Marquette School burned down.

A natural disaster seems to be an abrupt change, a crisis, caused by 'an act of

God,' by natural, or by accidental events rather than intended social action. Failures in bond issues on tax levies might be seen as purposive crises. Theoretically, one line of analysis might be about 'crises in general' and another line of analysis might be the distinction between natural and man made disasters or crises. As unpredictable events they create problems for Boards and Superintendents.

The point however, is that no matter how hard one tries, limits exist on how much of the environment one can predict and control as Board President, Board Member, or Superintendent, not to mention as principal or teacher. Individuals and groups vary in their desires and interests in effecting change, in innovation. Similarly they vary in their foresight and prudence. Also, they vary in their social and political skills of persuasion, bringing their colleagues along, and working out majority agreements. And these are important differences. But beyond that, the physical and social world remains, in part, both unpredictable and intractable. And that's a major policy and administrative problem.

Resources and Costs

Throughout our report, resources and their related stories have been close to our consciousness, a concept not far from our thinking. A theory of educational innovation and change cannot do without it. Sometimes it's a given — a difficult to alter element in the system. Other times it's problematic when community hopes are high and tax levies and bond issues can be passed with some planning, some patron involvement, and some effort. Other times it's a vague possibility perceived on the horizon and successful only through entrepreneurial efforts. Though we do not have comparative data from other districts, McBride's efforts from the 1930s and 1940s in obtaining Federal Funds seemed to have been very successful. Later, Spanman's bid for substantial resources from the Olds Foundation failed. In a sense, he never recovered the initiative he had underway.

In 1956, when we first saw the Board's analysis of the cost of its elementary buildings and the analytical power of simple arithmetic in reducing building costs to costs per room, and room costs to costs per square foot, we were struck by a difference. No longer was there a simple 'We need a new school. It will cost X. Our bonding indebtedness is Y. We'll need a bond issue of size Z.' Now the resources needed would meet a criterion of costs from building to building. In Milford's case in 1956, the figures ranged from $9.40 per square foot for Grant School to $15.80 per square foot for Johnson School. That's a large difference. Justifying such difference on educational grounds became a major agenda item for a Superintendent and a Board, as Spanman would find in the early sixties with the innovative Kensington School.

Finally resources and costs interrelate as antecedent and consequence, as opportunity and constraint, in the tangle of the unpredictable and turbulent environment on the one hand and problem solving and coping by the Board on the other hand.

The Press and Priority of Immediate Problems

As the Milford chronicle has indicated, the social environment seemed to have its own dynamic, operating, in part, under control of forces and events outside the district. The turbulence, as some social scientists (Emery and Trist, 1975) have described it, created a press and a set of priorities for the Board and the administration. In the 1920s and 1930s items such as population growth, the rural to suburban shift, citizens' desires for a high school, the changing technology in the community (for example, electricity, gas, roads, phones), the national depression and World War II seemed to dictate the Board's agenda and priorities. After World War II, county and state redistricting set the stage for mergers and resistance to mergers, population explosions turned farmland into subdivisions and forced property trading and buying, legal condemnations or threats of condemnation, and all the problems, excitement and details of constructing buildings occurred.

The point we are making is simple. Much of the setting of priorities, which can be a difficult intellectual task, is settled by the press of outside forces which moves citizens, board members and school administrators into simple agreement — a crisis exists, we have several hundred students, and new schools need to be built. The press and prior experience with America's expanding population crowd out all thought that some day the bulge of the population explosion will pass and that too many permanent schools might exist. Time and again this seemed to be the way things went in the district.

The Ebb and Flow of Conflict

In following Mr. McBride's long tenure, not to mention Briggs' and Spanman's brief tenure, we came to a way of perceiving and organizing our perceptions of the Superintendency. We called it the ebb and flow of conflict. It seems important for a theory of innovation and change. Once again we feel the need for comparative data, but our guess is that McBride's involvement in conflict is not atypical. He fought with individual teachers, with his high school principals, and with assorted individuals and clusters of Board members. Stories at each of these levels have been recounted in some detail. The point we are making here is that each had significant bearing on innovation and change in the district. Any innovation, such as changes in teacher control of policy, will be supported or resisted in a variety of ways. The Nussbaum case highlighted McBride's resistance to teacher unionization. Similar sentiments were found in the high school principal and the central office administrators. The results appeared as pressures applied to various critical points in the system, for example, neutralizing the Community Teachers Association, the firing of the teacher, and the long battle in the courts. Each action or reaction has such a context.

A critical part of the generalization on ebb and flow of conflict lies in the periodicity of quietude and intense confrontation. On occasion, as in the twenties and forties, the district was quite calm. Anyone observing at that time would have a very different picture than in the early fifties and early sixties when Board Presidents Lewis and Tompkins were locked in powerful struggles with McBride. Seen from this longer perspective, the functions and dysfunctions of social conflict take on a different perspective. The 'good guys' and the 'bad guys,' the heroes and the villains are neither so easy to identify nor are the labels so unambiguously applied. Policy making and administration became inextricably linked to these periods of ebb and flow.

The conflicts were far from inconsequential. People lost jobs. Programs appeared or ceased. Parents were pleased or seethed. Children went to a particular school and received particular kinds of instruction or went to another school with other teachers. Programs existed or they did not.

One of the strangest aspects of this ebb and flow of conflict is that most of the other business of schooling seems to go along normally. The Board decides on large numbers of issues — buildings, maintenance, curriculum, etc. The day to day administration of the district and the individual schools continues. Teachers meet their classes. Instruction and learning continue. The conflict seems to be restricted to particular individuals and/or to particular issues. The broader structures — organizational, administrative, instructional — remain in place and the activities they encompass continue. But modifications gradually creep in, as we have shown time and again.

In short, a potpourri of concepts which includes 'nested systems,' 'politics' and 'ill defined and entangled social problems,' almost by definition is a prelude to a concept of innovation. In our view, and as we elaborated more intensively in our discussion of religion and school reform in *Educational Innovators: Then and Now* (Smith, Kleine, Prunty and Dwyer, 1986), one of the most important legacies of many religions is the pervasive belief about a utopian 'one right way,' as one of our teachers labeled it. Along with educational historians such as Cremin (1980) and Tyack (1974) we feel such a view has been a large part of American education for the past two centuries. Also, we see it as being a major factor in Western civilization as well as American society. One of the consequences of such a view is seeing conflict, disagreement, and debate only as a temporary instrumental problem, one which can be resolved when everyone 'understands' or 'knows the facts.' In our view, when important interests, sentiments, and values are in conflict they are not resolved so easily.

A contrasting perspective and one more in accord with our data and interpretation is Wirt and Kirst's (1982) concept of turbulence — conflict which has breadth in scope and depth in crucial issues. Their model for turbulent school politics as conflict is presented as Figure 44. Their 'core constituencies' are our relevant subgroups and individuals. Their issue demands tend to be more general and abstract phrasings of our issues, with reference to a particular subgroup. While the Milford parents are interested in shared control, so is everyone else in the system; teacher power seems an identical concept with a different label. But in Milford the parents are mostly involved with school boundary lines, opening and closing schools, occasional transfers of principals and firing of a teacher, and more recently discipline in the junior and senior high schools — smoking, controlled substances and violence. Teachers in

Figure 44: A Model of Turbulent School Politics (Wirt and Kirst, 1982, p. 9)

Core Constituency	Issue Demands	Intervening Variables	Demand Targets		Administrator

Parents → Shared control
Taxpayers → Finance reform
Minorities → Desegregation
Teachers → Teacher power
Students → Rights
Federal-state agents → Mandates

Community structure

Interaction of demands

Board

Interaction

Superintendent
Central office
Principal

Altered authority

Extracommunity stimuli
New Concepts
Crystallizing events
National media

Extracommunity constraints
State: courts, legislative agencies
Federal: congress, courts, agencies
Professional norms

turn are concerned about their jobs, salaries, working conditions (mostly curriculum and classroom autonomy). In Milford, a major split exists, as exemplified in the Midwest State Teachers Association and the Milford NEA organizations regarding teacher power. Conflict within subgroups or core constituencies continually complicated our case.

As powerful as we believe the conception of Wirt and Kirst is, we find ourselves taking issue. This seems to be at several levels. First, the model does enable us to pinpoint and highlight specific issues in the Milford story. Any model or theory which stimulates dialogue is meeting one of its most important purposes. Second, Wirt and Kirst have deliberately accented current issues and trends. We have deliberately tried to trace the ebb and flow of issues over a sixty-five year history. Third, we have accented a single case, the Milford School District, while they have opted for a broader set of national data. Fourth, their 'extracommunity stimuli and constraints' seem important but do not rest easy in their model, as we read it. Fifth, the linearity of the model moving toward the 'demand targets' of Board and administrator poses all of the difficulties of trying to represent an interactive system. Further, in the particular instance the model ignores some of the most important kinds of conflict that existed in Milford, that between the Board of the Superintendent, as our story of the 'tangle of administrative succession' indicated. Finally, we would accent a Brunerian (1966) kind of notion regarding the various formats for presenting one's ideas. The 'iconic' models, which we, too, have favored over the years, have certain strengths and weaknesses as do the more concrete 'enactive' and the more verbal 'symbolic' modes of representation. Our criticism is as much of ourselves as them.

For the moment, we select and focus only on one class of actors, the Superintendents. One of the most fundamental generalizations we have about the Superintendency, after examining five Superintendents, is 'living with conflict.' Except for Grey (who died after five years in office) every other Superintendent, Briggs, McBride, Spanman, and George lived with it — sometimes sporadically, sometimes constantly, and usually traumatically. That now seems so simple and so obvious.

The implications seem a bit less obvious. What does the phenomenon of conflict mean for selection of Superintendents? And what does it mean for questions such as how realistic are self selections of teachers who want to become principals and principals who want to become central office staff and central office staff who want to become Superintendents? What are the implications for educational training programs for administrators? What do the 'administrator' text books say about conflict — its antecedents, its nature, its consequences, its resolutions? How are administration courses taught? What can be learned from lectures, discussions, simulations, role playing, internships? Are there aptitude-treatment interactions? What kind of research and theory exists to inform this part of practice? Who is doing the imaginative inquiry and thinking in this area? Is it possible to codify such knowledge? And even if it is — is it useful knowledge? And especially for us here, what does it mean for educational innovation?

Beyond the stories of Briggs, Grey, McBride, Spanman, and George, what is the experience of other Superintendents in other districts? To what degree is Milford unique? To what degree are school districts, school districts, school districts? What are the multiple strategies and tactics used by Superintendents as they thread their way through the complications and complexities of such a position? What support groups, roles, and individuals exist? Do other Superintendents have a School Board president who is sympatico, who drops in for a cup of coffee and a chat a couple of times a week as did Mr. Reeves, in Superintendent George's later years? Do some find solace and help in local peer groups of Superintendents? Does AASA play a role for others? Or, are the issues of social conflict better conceptualized as individual 'stress'? And what of the array of mechanisms — family, church, clubs, hobbies, travel, and exercise as the preferred modes?

Although we are by no means experts in any of these areas, we have run into serious conflict in earlier studies of educational organizations. The most dramatic instance was in our *Federal Policy in Action* study (Smith and Dwyer, 1980). Our interpretation and model building from Anderson's (1937) work on these processes was stated this way:

> The most general theoretical statement of Anderson's, and a minimally cited one at that, was the 1937 work with kindergarten children. We have abstracted the theory into Figure 45. The chain of concepts begins with differences among individuals in their needs, abilities and goals, producing conflict and incompatible actions. He argues that group members and leaders, teachers in his analysis, typically respond dominatively or integratively toward the conflict. He separates out compromising as a separate alternative. To the dominative reaction, higher frequences of submission or resistance follow. Integrative reactions, seeking common purposes, produces higher frequences of creativity, spontaneity, and growth. Compromise does not remove the differences, although, we would add, it frequently allows other task activities to occur. Other times it creates more problems. (Smith and Dwyer, pp. 358–9)

Figure 45: Anderson's Early Theory of Conflict (1937)

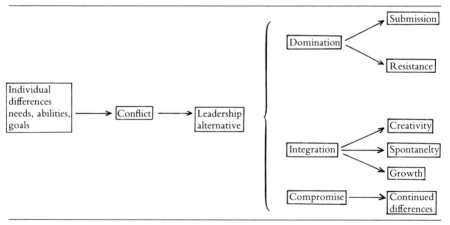

In almost every story of conflict we have told, the main issue was encumbered with subsidiary and/or unrelated issues. In the struggle regarding the tax levy in 1970, the point was made vividly with: 1) the problems at Edinburg School — the streets jammed with parents' cars, faculty cars, and muddy fields if not parking lots; 2) Parents of children attending parochial schools were doubly or triply offended by their work routines being interrupted, possible difficulties regarding public safety, and having to pay for and support the inconveniences besides; 3) Similarly, adolescent teen town, drinking and peace disturbance overlapped the tax levy problems as well. How does one, as a Board member, keep from getting angry, show concern to citizens with presumably justified complaints, help solve the problems and yet not get deflected from the major issue at hand, and get the levy passed so that the schools could stay open?

The Milford Board and Superintendent coped in a multitude of ways. Frequently, the Board and Superintendent called on relevant outside groups and individuals. Often this was with varying but limited success. One request of twenty-five mayors and aldermen and other elected officials received a response from only three. On another occasion, the State Representative from the area was influenced to talk with the Governor who in turn was helpful, in affecting a short term reprieve, with an advance payment of $300,000 of State aid.

The Board frequently broke problems into pieces or chunks which involved different time units: immediate or short term, intermediate, and long term solutions.

Perhaps, in this concern for conflict among individuals and groups with legitimate interests and in the Board and Superintendent's wrestling with the problems, the political perspective which we have been fumbling towards comes more clearly into focus. Community leaders, church leaders, and elected representatives are called on for help. Presumably one's success in this depends upon a history of nurtured relationships, rather than one off attempts. The individuals who are woven into that community fabric and who stand well with their peers seem much more likely to achieve some of the desirable consequences. Presumably there are costs to such relationships. The others make demands on you as well. Some of your freedom for autonomous action gets lost in this kind of give and take, of helping and being helped. Social exchange exists in multiple forms.

If we ask about social conflict and innovation and change, we find ourselves broadening Coser's (1952) conception of the functions of social conflict. Innovation and change are antecedents as well as consequences. A systemic view accents, for us, a broader skein of interrelationships. Integrative solutions are difficult and rare.

After the Fact Administrative Changes

In pursuing our thesis on innovation and change, we have moved to a complex political-cultural stance. One piece of this appeared in Mr. McBride's behavior, which we have called 'after-the-fact-administrative-changes.' McBride had been under attack in the early 1950s by the Board President, Mr. Lewis, and several members of the Board for a variety of issues — lack of clarity in administrative organization and duties, school dropouts, high school counseling and guidance programs, and follow-up of students. While McBride argued consistently against the charges when the political fight was on, *after* he won the battle he moved to tidy up district affairs, on the very items for which he had been criticized. In the Spring of 1955, the minutes are full of organization charts, realignment of administrative positions and spelling out of duties. We have sketched the flow of these events in Figure 46.

The reality of the phenomenon does not seem open to question. The meaning and dynamics of the event might raise a number of interpretations. McBride was a proud man. He ran the district internally as an autocrat, mostly benevolently. In the community he was a hard working and well liked local official and informal politician. When the events moved too fast and outran him or when he underestimated Mr. Lewis he got caught. He recouped politically by rallying a faction of the community and regained a majority on the Board. *Then*, he attended directly to the internal problems. To a degree, the arenas of activity are independent, but, to a degree, they are not. The beginnings and endings of problems and resolutions are very difficult to define.

Common Sense Modes of Thought

In recent years, we have become enamoured of common sense thought in its multiple forms (Smith, Dwyer, and Prunty, 1981). In that essay review we looked at Lindblom and Cohen's (1980) position on usable knowledge and professional social inquiry. We blended it with McDonald's (1977) position on social roles in evaluation — democratic, autocratic and bureaucratic. We added aspects of our own perspective. Yet we remain with the belief that the surface has only been scratched regarding common sense modes of thought. In a few paragraphs, we suggest some observations, arising from our data, to indicate where that analysis might go. In brief we are reflecting on the ways the district personnel think about problems, how it goes about problem solving.

Periodically, we were overwhelmed by the variety of issues the Superintendent and Board confronted on any one evening. On occasion we backed off and listed the items. The generalist-specialist dimension immediately came to mind, with the immediate evaluation, it's impossible to know well all one needs to know. One must

Figure 46: The Political and Cultural Antecedents of Change: After the Fact Administrative Changes

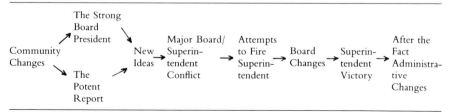

be a jack-of-all-trades, with the corollary, master of none. We were reminded of medical general practitioners and the use of medical specialists. We wondered if the analogy held for professional education. We kept coming back to phrases such as 'conventional wisdom' and 'common sense thought.' We seemed to be seeing synthetic skills pushing toward a general point of view rather than more specialized analytical skills. We continued to wonder about the nature of training and experience, necessary and desirable for a Superintendent or a Board member.

Throughout the chronicle and in several analytical sections we have commented not only on the variety of problems, their origins in an unpredictable and often turbulent environment, and the rapidity or pace with which they flow on to the Board and the Administrative Staff. The latter are caught always with too little time for detailed specialized reflection.

We ran into a number of items that seemed clustered into a category which we called 'interdistrict comparisons as inquiry.' One of the changes over the years was the district awareness of 'how it's done elsewhere.' New building designs, birthday cut-offs for kindergarten attendance, and teacher salary schedules, among other items, were brought into comparative focus. At times the Board, through the efforts of district administrators, sent off questionnaires or made telephone surveys of practices in other parts of Suburban County. In still later years, groups such as the CTA, initiated similar activities and fed results to the Board.

A key item in such comparative inquiry is the manner in which it handles the problem of justice or fairness in practical problem solving. Most scientific modes of problem solving do not cope easily or well with the kinds of ethical or value issues that 'fairness' poses.[3] Assessments of how things are done in neighboring districts, especially subsets of neighboring districts which are alike in size, resources, socioeconomic status of patrons becomes a very powerful argument for equity and justice. On some absolute standards one may not be very well off, but if people in like circumstances are no better off, the resolution can't be all bad, so would seem to be the logic of the argument.

If one pins one's faith on the abilities of semi independent clusters of citizens to explore common problems, define and redefine the central or relevant issues, to be aware through idiosyncratic experiential and educational backgrounds, varied simple and complex work situations, and through exposure to multiple local and national media of alternatives, and to be able to develop plans and reach decisions, then the potency of interdistrict comparisons looms large. One might eulogize the educated common sense and the power of free and open communication and debate.

These issues might be construed into a pattern of 'Board and administrative policy making and problem solving.' Figure 47 represents such a construal.

Blending Politics, Common Sense and Scientific Educational Research

But more formal social science inquiry was not totally denied or missing in Milford. Currently, as we have indicated, considerable controversy exists over the nature and

Figure 47: Board and Administrative Policy Making and Problem Solving

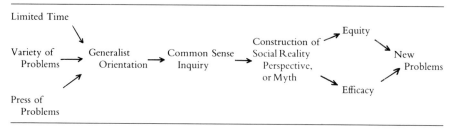

role of 'Professional Social Inquiry.' PSI, as Lindblom and Cohen (1970) call it, in the formation of public policy. While we were thinking about some of these issues (Smith, Dwyer and Prunty, 1981), one of the most dramatic stories in the Milford Chronicle arose. The State University Survey, which might be seen as applied educational research, became a major item in the struggle between Mr. Lewis, the Board President, and Mr. McBride, the Superintendent. The incident was a far cry from Lindblom and Cohen's lament: 'In public policy making, many suppliers and users of social research are dissatisfied, the former because they are not listened to, the latter because they do not hear much they want to listen to.' (1977, p. 1) The most intriguing comment for our thesis regarding innovation and change in schooling is the complexity of the impact of the research. By this we mean several things. First it had dramatic short term effects, as in the controversy and near firing of McBride. Second, the research report was political in origin, in interpretation, and in use. It illustrated and enhanced the conflict between Lewis and McBride, it stirred considerable controversy in the community, and it preceded the dramatic defeat of Lewis in the Board elections. Third, it became almost an agenda for Mr. McBride's actions to change the district over the next few years.

School surveys are only one kind of educational research, and this particular survey had its own idiosyncracies as we reported. But it produced a kind of 'criticized knowledge,' a step beyond the 'uncriticized knowledge' of common sense (Pepper, 1942). It was carried out by an outsider whose considerable experience in such work provided a number of comparisons. The outsider attempted to be objective (and unbiased) in soliciting data from many parts of the community on a wide range of relevant issues. The biases, or the perspective of the outsider, reflected the conventional wisdom of the professional education community. That's a powerful and persuasive set of conditions surrounding any argument introduced into a political controversy.

Obviously we are not arguing here that this is the only role for educational research in innovation and change nor that it is the best role. Rather for the moment we are content to state that this is one interpretation of how Professional Social Inquiry (PSI) intertwined in the evolution of the Milford District. Equally gripping are other variants of inquiry which occurred. The investigation by City University for District Consolidation appeared just as our initial story was ending. Only time will tell if it will be one of those items that comes and goes and leaves negligible impact. Contrasted with that, was the survey by the architectual firm of Lloyd,

Lloyd and Murphy which contradicted parts of the Central State Survey, and which led ultimately to building the award winning new high school. And then, too, there were the NEA consultants of the McBride era who came in, 'informally' in the Board's view, but at the behest of the CTA. They did their inquiry, essentially interviews, group meetings, and document reading (the Board minutes) issued a report and provided the Board and the Superintendent with a way out, both a face saving way out and a set of procedural mechanisms to move on with the selection of a new Superintendent. But, as in all purposive action, the seeds for later problems were sown.

'Intellectual Turmoil in Educational Administration'

Thesis

We put our subheading in quotes because it is the title of a recent article by Griffiths (1979).[4] He presents a half dozen criticisms of organizational theory: 1) the need to demystify organizations, that is, formal goals may be minimally important; 2) the place of women, race, and unions in schools has been unexplained by organizational theory; 3) external events, the environment, are more important in schooling than most theories entertain; 4) that universality of organizational theory is a myth and one needs more restricted theories; 5) most organizational theory takes a monopolistic/capitalist world as a given; the neo–Marxists argue alternatives; and 6) the epistemological basis of most theory is positivistic which is now being questioned on many fronts. In our view, Griffiths is fumbling toward a new intellectual synthesis, perspective, or paradigm. It is an excruciatingly difficult task, as he says: 'I approach this task with a certain sadness, because it is not possible to do the job without challenging virtually all the premises that I have accepted during my career.' (1979, p. 44).

For a way out, Griffith proposes several new steps for the field of educational administration. First, he indicates attention must be paid to the epistemological issues. Implicitly in agreement with him, our discussion here has been prefatory, our major attack on that occurs elsewhere (Smith, 1979, Smith *et al.*, 1984). Suffice it to say that our overlapping methods of history, life history, ethnography, and return to an educational community studied fifteen years before represents a major thrust, reanalysis, and synthesis of the usual social science methodologies in studying eductional events, including innovation and change in educational organizations.

Griffith's second step is a concern for 'restricted theories,' what others have called middle range and miniature theories, rather than a 'general theory.' We have long been in pursuit of a theory of eduction. Our special view is that the nesting of metatheory, formal theory, and substantive theories (miniature, middle range, and grand) as well as descriptive narratives, themes, vignettes, and episodes turns this issue on its head, and is a viable integrative framework. Another way of saying this is that the concept, 'theory' is a much more complex set of ideas than most educationists have realized or entertained. Merton (1957), Mills (1959), Glaser and

Strauss (1967), Smith, Dwyer, and Prunty (1981), and Zetterberg (1965) all suggest images of theory and its problems which seem more promising than Griffith's 'restricted theories.'

His third and fourth steps involve specifying the piece of theory being attacked, what needs saving, and what needs replacing in the sifting of past efforts. In this summary and conclusion section, we targeted a half dozen specific topics, as earlier our narrative and commentary has done. As we tried to make sense of these topics, themes, and positions we believe we analyzed, subsumed, and eventually synthesized them into our position. Briefly, our agenda is empirical data in support of potent stories, concepts, theories, and metaphors.

His fifth point asks for more complex theories instead of oversimplifications. This has never seemed a problem for us. Our special view here is that each concept, proposition, or miniature theory is always grounded in a detailed case study. The nuances of the case, its particularity and its complexity, must always be preserved and presented. The ideas, the interpretation, the abstractions need to have both elegance (simplicity) and potency (make a difference) in helping one to understand the case at hand and be useful in the beginning to solve problems in the next case (or practical situation) encountered. The transfer of training issue, while hoary in eductional thought, we believe is ripe for reanalysis and reinterpretation.[5]

Griffiths' final step, 'rationalize or otherwise dispose of the criticisms' seems a simple argument, in spite of his points in steps two, three, and four. It seems an argument for a better general theory, at least of educational organizations called schools or school districts. One always thinks one has a leg up on this or one shouldn't be writing and publishing. New critics will test how well we do here.

In our more grandiose moments we believe that implicitly we have been working through the Griffiths hypotheses on intellectual turmoil in administrative and organizational theory. We believe our study of the Kensington School encased in the historical and contemporaneous context of the Milford School District and focusing on the theories of innovation and change offers the possibility for the kind of paradigmatic resolution which Griffith desires.

Antithesis: Greenfield's Critique of Administrative Theory[6]

When we first encountered Greenfield's 1975 paper, 'Organizations as social inventions: rethinking assumptions about change' we were stimulated all through it, cheering part of the time and ultimately saying mostly — 'Yes, but . . .' For our purposes now, we respond by taking a number of his points, giving an agreeing 'yes,' and indicating our reservation.

1   It is possible to see organizations as created by people, often some other people — citizens or boards of education; and often according to certain rules or laws, for example, state constitution or state department of education edicts and yet as a real object in the world.

2   Once created one can deal with the organization proactively or reactively (for example, Spanman versus George).

3   Seeing the organization as an object is not to deny that multiple individuals and subgroups perceive 'it' differently or that one group's image of the organization may be dominant.

4   Nor do we deny that this dominant image may define some goals and subgoals or may be in conflict with other images (for example, back to basics, discipline as a prerequisite for learning, the high school should serve both college preparation and immediate work force employability).

5   Different concepts used in thinking about schools may be meaningful to varying groups. For example, to the participants, what Geertz (1975) calls 'experience near' concepts are more important. Others may be more meaningful to the observer/analyst and his community, what Geertz calls 'experience distant concepts.' In our view, if the latter have potency they may become part of the conventional wisdom or common sense of a later era as Toulmin (1972) suggests.

6   Greenfield proposes 'In organizations, the transforming mechanism lies within individuals.' Others, who share some of the perspective (Becker, 1970) would argue the 'mechanism' lies in actions and interactions. Still others see potency in adjustive conditions (Blau, 1956, and Etzioni, 1966).

7   Greenfield seems to argue that organizations are an invented social reality which hold for a time and are then vulnerable to redefinition through changing demands and beliefs among people. Again, 'yes, but ...' Some aspects of the school as an organization in Milford have lasted a long time. The annual inspection of schools is a simple illustration. It has occurred for the sixty-five years if recorded history of Milford. Such activity is based on a state law, which can be changed. The law isn't immutable, but it's been around a long time.

8   Generalizations in any 'science' vary in their generality and durability, whether they be from an inner human perspective or an outer perspective. (Meehl, 1954, 1973).

9   We share a part of his belief about being prescriptive about schools; that it is a more complex activity than many 'organizational doctors' appreciate. The 'good guys' and the 'bad guys' in Milford are not obvious to everyone.

10   At points (p. 562) he seems to be arguing against a large and varied cast of educational theorists, in our words, 'organizational sinners' — grand theorists, O.D. types, revisionists, and these single view types who support 'the one right way'. We, too, have problems with each of these groups.

11   He argues for an historical and comparative perspective trying to understand schools for their own sakes. And we agree. Hymes (1980) makes an interestingly similar point regarding educational ethnology.[7]

And, among a number of other themes, we pick one final methodological item which we believe accents a perspective central to our effort;

12   'In abandoning received theories about organizations in general and about schools in particular, we will have to look to a new kind of research — one

that builds theory from the data rather than one that selects data to confirm theories developed apart from the data. The requirement directs us to theory from observations in specific organizations; it directs us as well to understanding the actions, purposes, and experiences of organizational members in terms that make sense to them.' (pp. 563–4)

Stated alternatively, we believe we have a problem(s), several sets of data, and multiple perspectives, interpretations, abstractions, and theories that meet the spirit of many of Greenfield's aspirations when he stated in a later essay:

Accepting organizations as invented social reality requires: 1) that theorists give up the search for the one best, single representation of social reality, 2) ... describe the process people use in construing reality, 3) ... be that reality with all the possibilities that the human mind reads into experience, 4) ... theories not be seen as supreme or as the best estimate of truth even for short periods of time, 5) ... should show the same variety, inconsistency and complexity of reality itself, 6) ... visions of the world that people act out, 7) ... 'verification' of theory becomes as much a moral judgment as an empirical science. (Greenfield, 1978, p. 12)

And so we have this monograph: *Innovation and Change in Schooling: History, Politics and Agency.* And we have our trilogy: *Anatomy of Educational Innovational: A Mid to Long Term Re-study and Reconstrual*

Conclusion: A Metatheoretical Perspective

Over the years, it has frequently been our experience to pose problems, to make decisions, to do common sense things procedurally, and even to adopt tentative theoretical perspectives which later turn out to be better and more important than we realized at the time. Our tacit knowledge and understanding kept running ahead of our more formal knowledge and understanding. This is an interesting and important issue in any craft or set of practical activities. Our most formal attempt to deal with one part of such an evolving position appears in Smith (1981).

Beginning A Synthesis: An Earlier Position from Sociology

In an important sense, our entire trilogy. *Anatomy of Educational Innovation: A Mid to Long Term Re-study and Reconstrual,* can be taken as a synthesis of educational administration theorists such as Griffiths and Greenfield, or, more grandiosely, a subsumption of their position, arguments, and debate into our position. Here we point to a very brief but elegantly stated sociological position which has served as a major guideline for us. In his three page preface to *Sociological Work* (1970), Howard Becker made these assertions:

1 I conceive of society as collective action ...

2   ... and sociology as the study and the forms of collective action.
3   When you think of society as collective action, you know that any talk
    of structures or factors in the end refer to some notion of people doing
    things together, which is what sociology studies.
4   If you see society as people doing things together, then you see the
    necessity of studying social life at first hand ... lengthy periods of
    participant observation ... detailed unstructured interviewing.
5   If you study collective action, you cannot avoid the knowledge that
    everything — every person, every group, every action, every event —
    has a history.
6   ... leads inevitably to a conception of process.
7   Likewise, you cannot avoid the knowledge that events are transactional
    or interactional, that you understand what one person does by knowing
    the network of interaction he operates in ...

and

8   I have tried in my own work to take those ideas seriously, accepting and
    following through on their implications even when that requires doing
    violence to accepted notions of how the world is or how sociologists
    ought to study it. (1970, pp. V and VI)

That stands as a prior and major metatheoretical stance which we find now
congruent with our attempts to look at the Kensington School and the Milford
School District.[8]

The Board Minutes

This time it was the discovery of the School Board minutes. We became obsessed
with them, couldn't let them go, couldn't figure out how to handle them quickly
and easily, yet couldn't understand why we were intrigued. Now, near the end of
the exercise, a number of items come to mind. Metatheoretically, they; 1) involved a
new data source or data category; 2) upset the pattern or structure of our thoughts
about schooling; 3) moved us beyond our 'normal science' and presaged a
paradigmatic shift; 4) generated excitement and disquietude; and 5) demanded the
best of our creativity. In any research, that's a happy set of circumstances.[9]

Substantively the minutes forced upon us: an historical view — 'You've
discovered history' as one commented; a view of social events as the products of
individual and group decision, especially the 'moved, seconded, and passed' actions
of the Board; dimensions of political interest and social conflict; the roots of
rural/small town American Democracy; the evolution of a school district from a
small, two teacher, three director school and district into a large, 10,000 pupil, 13
school, complex, suburban district. While on the surface all that may not seem
revolutionary, it did carry that kind of impact for us.

Although we certainly did not approach the records carte blanche, our
admonitions were procedural — to look at the specific, the concrete, the mundane

(Homans, 1950), to try to get the story straight (Scriven, 1959, 1972; Hexter, 1971), and to take the position of the 'natives' and look to their meanings (Malinowski, 1922; Geertz, 1973). In addition, we had the powerful organizing devices of: 1) the original study and book, *Anatomy of Educational Innovation*; 2) the questions from the current research proposal, 'What had happened to the Kensington School? and Why?'; 3) the evolving question, 'Why had they built the school in the first place?', and 4) the shifting theme toward 'Innovation and Change in American Education.' Research serials, as well as artistic serials (Beittel, 1973; Smith, 1979), impose their own dynamics on problems and actions.

Contrasts: Zeigler and Goldhammer

A second kind of serendipity also seemed to be in the offing. In field work, at least as we practice it, the intensive literature search comes relatively late in the inquiry process. We often use it to help see our data and ideas in a broader, intellectual setting. We try to generalize our findings. We have seen this intellectual activity as the relation of the particular instance to a larger, more general, more abstract class of events (Smith, 1979; Diesing, 1971)[10] This becomes a practical task when one views conclusion sections as offering the analyst and interpreter a variety of intellectual options. One can summarize and finish with a general moral. Or one can find an analogy or metaphor which captures what one has been trying to say more explicitly all along. Further one might highlight a few of the high priority items, shucking them of encumbering detail and less significant ideas. Also one might aspire to a more abstract reconstrual or reconceptualization of the domain under analysis.

Among the spate of books in the general domain of the superintendency, school organization, and politics — if not innovation — is Zeigler, Kehoe and Reisman's (1985) exciting and provocative *City Managers and School Superintendents: Response to Community Conflict*. The dialogue between their work and ours seems instructive about the issues of 'history, agency, and politics.' In their introduction they state several important assumptions to their work. They believe, as do we, that the school district is an important 'primary governmental unit' or level of analysis. They view, as do we, that a comparative mode of analysis is important. They contrast school Superintendents with city managers and we contrast Superintendents at different points in time, but in the same district. Some significant pluses and minuses occur with each approach. Their research methods rely most heavily on interviews, questionnaires, and two scales (professionalism and leadership.) Our methods blend formal records of Superintendent agendas and Board minutes, open ended interviews, and direct observations of meetings and activities. They tend to accent the contemporaneous, while we accent the historical as well. Their focus is on conflict management while ours is on innovation and change, with conflict an important variable in understanding the innovations and changes.

Much of their argument rests on the dilemma or tension between the neutral, expert, technical knowledge of the professional bureaucrat and the need to be responsive to the pluralistic political demands of the community. In the course of specifying their view of the similarities and the differences between the school superintendents and the city managers, they seem to us to move toward almost a strawman view of the superintendency, at least as we perceive it in the Milford School District. For instance they speak of education as being 'a single service,' at least in contrast to the city manager's job. Perhaps so, but our view of the superintendency, especially in contrast to the university professorship, is that of the generalist. The array of tasks and the array of knowledge demands seem very broad in our accounts of Briggs, Grey, McBride, Spanman, and George. As those demands stretched at times, these individuals were in conflict, to the point of losing their jobs.

In their discussion of 'the dangers of evangelism,' Zeigler *et al* make several comments pertinent to the superintendency and innovation. First they state, 'Not only do schools embrace the goals of the reform movement with more vigor that do cities, they also are more responsive to technologies and fads, as long as they are presented as being the product of professionally generated, technologically so-phisticated processes' (pp. 6–7). The contrast between Spanman and George is so great on this item that one could argue that the 'within group variance' is greater than the 'between group variance.' There are superintendents and superintendents. Zeigler, Kehoe, and Reisman's next statement brings a similar reaction from us. 'Today's expertise is less an expertise of scientific management than a more generalized commitment to the notion that innovations, created professionally are preferable to responsive policies based on the values of local consumers of education' (p. 7). Once again this does not capture the flavor of the complexity of what Spanman was trying to do as he mixed national and local initiatives in his innovative program. Nor does it capture the difference between Spanman and George, for the latter was highly responsive to his local board and community. His 'localism' as we phrased it, denies their whole point. Even the particular illustrations they use, team teaching, organizational development, and individualized instruction were at the heart of Spanman's approach, to be fostered, and at the heart of George's approach, to be eradicated. Agreements on 'public interests' had their ups and downs throughout Milford's history. Early on, phrases appeared like 'the forward looking elements of the community won out.' Later, in such stories as 'the tangle of administrative succession' the public interest as a unidimensional phenomenon was nowhere to be found.

Zeigler, Kehoe, and Reisman talk about the more intimate connection of one's educational training being more tightly linked to the performance in the superinten-dency position than in the position of city manager. Although we know little of the city manager's role, the importance of the training programs for the superintendents who held the position in Milford over the years seemed far less significant to us as observers than our reading of Zeigler, *et al*. McBride, Spanman, and George all seemed to operate out of educational convictions on the one hand, but convictions that seemed more an outgrowth of their experience than their training. But even more critically, in what we have called 'the play of power' we found each to be consummate politicians working off a base of their own personalities and personal styles with roots far deeper than their preservice or PhD training program. One of the major generalizations we made for innovative teachers teaching and for principals principaling, as well as for superintendents administering, in *Educational Innovators: Then and Now*, (Book I), and in *The Fate of an Innovative School: The History and Present Status of the Kensington School*, (Book II), is that the roots of their actions lie very deep in the personalities of themselves as individuals. In those accounts we raised a number of questions on the selection as well as the preservice and inservice training on the careers of school personnel.

Our extended illustrations of conflict and the contexts of the conflict over the years have a complexity, or as we were prone to phrase it, a systemic quality, that a label such as 'conflict management' seems a bit too technical and too simple. McBride in his fights with his principals and in his two lengthy confrontations with his boards of education seems in another world. 'Superintendents believe that there are two options available to a Board: to trust them or to fire them. Compromise, in which the administrator adjusts his or her recommendtion or perhaps abandons the less acceptable ones, is not considered "professional" to Superintendents' (p. 49). The machinations of McBride, the dash of Spanman, and the informal coffee drinking, dialogue, and mutual adjustment of George and his President Reeves, all have a quality far from our reading of Zeigler *et al*.

In their final chapter, on 'future trends' and 'what we have learned,' Zeigler *et al*. pinpoint the contradiction that on the one hand Superintendents dominate lay Boards and that on the other hand Superintendents are beleaguered. Part of their analysis suggests that Superintendents 'have been relatively sheltered from conflict until fairly recently' (p. 158). This was not true in the late 1920s of Milford's first Superintendent, Mrs Briggs, nor was it true of those who followed her on through the seventies and into the eighties. 'Heroes' and 'heralds' does not handle the beleaguerment, for us, as well as personality dispositions in interaction with the particular situations. The Milford data do not support 'the thesis that educational policy making is dominated by the professional, even when the lay public is formally involved' (p. 165). The longer view of who was there before and who came afterward, as in the sequence from McBride to Spanman to George, suggests that the community worked its will in tangled ways. In Milford, it is not necessary 'to reestablish school boards as a viable and responsive institution' (p. 168) vis a vis the Superintendent. The key issue seems to be in the responsiveness to the growing pluralism of the Milford community.

Next, we found ourselves stunned in reading Keith Goldhammer's provocative little book, *The School Board* (1964). We remarked to ourselves that our account of Milford's recent history, heavily an account of the Board and Superintendents was quite different. In trying to isolate those differences we generated a list of a baker's dozen items. And, as we looked at that list, we felt that our tacit knowledge had been running well out ahead of our formalized knowledge — we knew better than we realized, a not unusual phenomenon in this kind of research, as we have said. Consequently, we present Figures 48 and 49. The first is Goldhammer's Table of Contents. The second is our list. Then we explicate briefly each of the items on his list and on our list.

Goldhammer's book is very different than ours in scope, purpose, style, and form. In Griffiths' forword, as content editor, he comments, 'This is an outstanding

Figure 48: Chapter Titles From Goldhammer's 'The School Board' (1964)

1   The Historical and Legal Foundations of the American School board
2   School Board and Community Relationships
3   School Board and Superintendent Relationships
4   The School Board and the Social Structure of the Schools
5   How School Boards Conduct Their Business: The Decision Making Process
6   The School Board Member
7   The Future of the American School Board

Figure 49: Contrasts with Goldhammer: Toward a New Perspective

1   full of people with interests, motives and sentiments
2   who are making choices and decisions
3   which lead to actions and interactions
4   which are in a context — historical and contemporaneous
5   which gives a dynamic or processual quality
6   as a case it is interrelated and systemic
7   substantive focus is on innovation and change
8   blends/mixes/integrates the specific/concrete/particular and the general/abstract/universal
9   focuses on the 'real,' the 'is' rather than an external 'ideal,' on the 'ought,' or the prescriptive
10 part of the real is the 'multiple ideals of the several actors and subgroups out there'
11 those ideals are often in conflict and are resolved by a variety of social/political processes
12 eventually all individuals and subgroups make up their own minds
13 ultimately integrates is/ought dichotomies in an R. N. Hare (1952) type configurated decision
    of principle
14 as personal experiences cumulate (and case studies are surrogates for those) one builds toward
    one's own syntheses of decisions of principles

book on the work, purpose, and functions of school boards. Although there are several books in the field, this one stands alone in that it has a solid research base' (1964, p. vii). This immediately sets a concern for us, for we have cited a 'later' Griffiths who has recanted from much of what he perceived to be the 'theory movement' in educational administration. Does this now apply to forewords like this and books like Goldhammer's *The School Board*? The sociology of science, as applied to educational administration, if not social science in general, is a context which now whets our appetite.

We found Goldhammer's first chapter on 'historical and legal foundations' filling gaps in our knowledge. As he writes of the 'origin of the American School Board' he argues that communities all over America, places like Milford we believe, obtained their initial form as replicas of innovations, social inventions, of New Englanders from the mid seventeenth century through the eighteenth century. Originally the colonies and later the states required towns to establish and maintain schools. As Goldhammer phrases it,

'The local school district and the local school board were ready-made devices for constituting educational authorities to attend to the state's responsibility for the education of its children in each remote hamlet as well as in its metropolitan centers' (p. 4.)

Our early discussion of the origins of the Milford District assumed some such prior set of conditions. For our purposes he presents an important lesson, school districts and their Boards of govenance are intimately tied into the constitutional and legal structures of the individual states. That seems to us now to be an extraordinarily important point for all social scientists to recognize and to emphasize.

In the next several chapters, on the School Board's relationships to the community, to the Superintendent, and to the social structure of the schools themselves, Goldhammer presents essentially a structural-functionalist analysis of the Board. By implication, so we would argue, he also presents a technological, almost managerial, point of view. Further, one might argue it has a positivistic flavor to its metatheory or root metaphor. As these implications are drawn, we find ourselves parting company with his analysis. It seems here that the later Griffiths (1979) might also reconsider his prefatory remarks.

As we told our stories of Superintendent Briggs and her problems with her board and our stories of McBride and his conflicts with his high school principals (for example, Hightower), and with his potent School Board presidents (for example, Lewis and Tompkins), we moved toward a more contextualist root metaphor (Pepper, 1942) or a dramaturgical model with actions, events and emplotment (Sarbin, 1977). It wasn't that Goldhammer was reporting facts and concepts that were 'false' but rather that the very form of thought, the metaphor, missed an important kind of reality. For example, the discussion of 'School Board members' concepts of the Superintendent's roles' raised those of executive secretary, educational leader, business manager, community leader, and intermediary between Board and staff (pp. 42–46). While one can't quarrel with this at one level, this 'structural' view loses the dynamic or processual quality of people acting and interacting, in conflict and collaboration, at particular times and places, over particular issues and events. To us this is a major loss. Later, in his discussion of 'the emergence and resolution of conflict' (pp. 67–69), he raises ideas such as 'serious consequences for the effectiveness of school operations,' 'How, then, can conflict be avoided . . .' and 'Above all, experience shows that school board members, administrators, teachers, and other school employees must seek to develop a team spirit in which each participant recognize the contributions being made by other participants and the mutuality of interests involved.' Our view of Milford's history is that there were important differences in the nature of goals and objectives in the education of the children of the community and of the kind of individuals and community desired by the various actors and subgroups in the community. These were important. They were being resolved by political and organizational action at multiple levels. These were the important events in our eyes as we observed, interpreted, analyzed, and evaluated our data, and developed the beginnings of a theory. They do not appear in *The School Board*.

Finally, we would note that the account of decision making (pp. 80–3) and 'serving the public interest' (pp. 99–103) implies a rational actor perspective that many students of policy making (for example, Allison, 1971, and Lindblom, 1969 and 1980) are now reconstruing. Issues in the 'combining of local control and local responsibility' set the stage for some of our interpretations in our final chapter.

Obviously, our intent is not to disparage Goldhammer's work, which is provocative in its brevity and clarity, but also obviously, we believe we have come out of our experience with a point of view that is quite different. We believe our point of view is not simply different in the sense of a substantive middle range theory of school boards, but that it possesses an integrated view of schooling across several levels of analysis. For instance, our perspective encompasses the kinds of data one collects when one thinks about schools, the kinds of methods and procedures linked to those data, the kinds of accounts one renders of those phenomena — both common sense and technical, the kinds of concepts, propositions, principles, and generalizations one uses in one's thinking, and finally a root metaphor, a world view or metatheoretical perspective that is consonant with the other levels of analysis and synthesis. We believe this perspective to be the most fundamental intellectual achievement of this part of our research.

For now, we have used Goldhammer as a means of articulating our perspective, essentially at the level of assumption behind the kinds of data we gathered and the kinds of substantive ideas and theory we will pose shortly. This is basically our conception of metatheory. To be more specific, the first six items in Figure 49 indicate we are making statements consonant with Pepper's (1942) contextualist world view and with Burke's (1945) dramaturgical model. Substantively we feel it puts us into the psychology of personal constructs of George Kelly (1955) and the dramaturgical sociology of Goffman (1959) as these have been brought together by · Sarbin (1977) with the 'emplotment metaphor.' In education, such symbolic interactionists as Delamont (1976) and Hargreaves (1975) have a similar view.

Items 4, 5, and 6 suggest an historical framework and a systemic framework. In an earlier chapter on our findings, we used the term 'longitudinal nested systems model' to capture our meaning. For clarity, we would note that the system's idea, for us, is not the closed, convergent, mechanical model of the operations analysts but rather the open, divergent, holistic idea suggested by the constructionists, the aestheticians and artists, and some systems theorists.

Item 7, innovation and change, is partly our attempt to deal with the initial substantive problem at hand, but also to capture planned or intentional action on the one hand and the larger category of unplanned alterations as well. In our view, these two concepts have been separated and kept too far apart.

Item 8 attempts to dissolve one of the major dichotomies of the logical positivists (Joergensen, 1951), the split between the operational, data language, and the theoretical, conceptual language in favor of a more configurational concatenated or patterned account of events. This implies a shift in the concept of explanation from a covering law model (deductive nomothetic or inductive statistical) to a pattern model (Hempel, 1965; Kaplan, 1964; Diesing, 1971).

Item 9 tries to focus on two points. This first is an attempt to be wary of judging individuals and groups, particularly from an earlier time and place, against a latter day set of standards, ideals, or idealogy. The second aspect of Item 9 blends with 10–13 and attempts to take a position on the is/ought dichotomy of Hume, its extension by the positivists of the early twentieth century; and its part of the dominant ideology of American educational researchers (for example, Campbell and Stanley, 1963) if not more world wide social science.

Item 13 is fundamentally an acceptance of R.M. Hare's (1952) decision of principle. When everything has been said, which is the extended account of all the items, then one has to decide how one wants to live — and then do it. That's our understanding of his decision of principle. Finally, Item 14 individualizes and personalizes that.

As one traces out one's assumptions and the roots of the assumptions, an awesome intellectual agenda is created. While this came to focus as we read Goldhammer's book, it obviously had been brewing for some time. Equally obviously, it is a long way from being finished. For us, though, it sketches the level and kind of issues we believe are at stake at this point in our work and in our interpretation of where educational thought in innovation, administration, and schooling, should be moving. This is our meaning of a metatheoretical perspective.

Notes

1   See the bibliography separately and together under Smith, Prunty, Dwyer, and Kleine.
2   These items have influenced the nature, conceptualization, research strategy and interpretation of 'Kensington Revisited' project.
3   N.R.F. Maier and his associates (Maier, *et al.*, 1957) make a strong case for multiple role playing and decision making groups as an alternative strategy. They distinguish between quality of solutions and acceptance of solutions. Their approach, so they argue, comes out 'high-high' on the two criteria.
4   In a sense this is a bit unfair to T.B. Greenfield who started the argument with Griffiths, whose position is closer to our own, and whose thinking helped clarify our own as well.
5   As sometime educational psychologists (Smith and Kleine) with roots in Thorndike and Woodward (1901), this one has nettled for a long time.
6   The two main sources we have relied on are the (1975 and 1978) papers.
7   We develop Hymes' argument in detail in Book II of our triology *The Fate of an Innovative School*. (Smith, L. *et al.*, 1987)
8   Elsewhere, (Smith *et al.*, 1984), we extended this position, and ours by reference to C. Wright Mills' provocative little book, *The Sociological Imagination* (1959).
9   On the negative side, it has been pointed out to us by a number of colleagues, and we realize as well, that the minutes have weaknesses also. We speak to those issues and the ways we have tried to compensate for the weaknesses in the Methodology chapter.
10   Diesing (1971) goes so far as to state this activity as 'the' problem of case study research. A century and a half ago, Tocqueville (1969 Edition) spoke eloquently to the same point.

Chapter 11

The Many Faces of Democracy in Innovation and Schooling

Introduction

Among the many things this study did not start out to be was a political science investigation. An essay on democracy was perhaps as far afield as any aim that might have been on our minds. The issues, the data, the evolving interpretation dragged us in this direction. A half dozen subissues seem knitted together here. The political context of schooling has major significance for innovation and change, significance far beyond our initial appreciation. National and state problems and purposes have vied longer and more intimately with local problems than we had at first realized or understood. The nature and importance of responsiveness of the schools to the wishes of the community has a subtlety, a complexity, and a scope which we found to be startling if not overwhelming. Finally we learned what 'voting' was all about; our high school civics teachers can finally rest in peace.

The Political Context of Schooling

Several key items are involved in our meaning and use of the term political. First, different interests of different subgroups in the community and in the school organization exist. Second, different perspectives, beliefs or cognitions exist about the structures, processes and outcomes of schooling. Third, these differences in interests and perspectives meet and frequently collide in the form of social conflict. Fourth, a variety of structures and processes exist to channel, work through, and resolve the conflicts. Social scientific labels and clichés like 'conflict resolution' seem too simple for the reality. Citizens talk, organize and present to the Board. At times, candidates for the Board engage in hotly contested campaigns and elections. Within the Board, disagreements are talked about, argued over, and voted upon. Strong personalities come into play as do potent reports and consultants. The reports and consultants seem to have their latent as well as manifest uses by all sorts of people. Fifth, no position nor subgroup in the organization escapes these political events, as we saw in Board-Superintendent, Superintendent-Principal, Teacher-Board, and CTA and Union-Superintendent relationships.

For many years the word 'politics' has been anathema to many professional educators and citizens. Three decades ago, in a trenchant essay, Thomas Eliot (1959) made this comment:

> Surely it is high time to stop being frightened by a word. Politics includes the making of governmental decisions, and the effort or struggle to gain or keep the power to make these decisions. Public schools are part of government. They are political entities. They are a fit subject for study by political scientists. (1959, p. 1035)

Sixty-five years of Board minutes, agendas, letters, and reports seem to say 'amen' to Eliot's admonition. He ties this view to the larger moral and ethical base of liberal democracy:

> If all the significant political factors are revealed, the people can more rationally and effectively control the governmental process. Such at least must be the faith of the political scientist who, devoted to the search for truth, believes that 'what can be' is not less the truth than 'what is.' (p. 1036)

If one takes this stance then immediately one finds, as we did, that relevant individuals and groups — Mothers' Circle, Milford NEA, Boards and Board factions, Superintendents, Central Office Administrators, Principals, Community Athletic Associations, Juvenile Courts, Mayors and State Representatives, District Judges — are all in the activity of schooling. Secondly, if one adds a value premise regarding democratic government, as we would, then, the politics of education ought to be an important domain of activity.[1]

Our interlocked story, 'The tangle of administrative succession,' of Superintendent McBride's departure, Superintendent Spanman's arrival, controversial four years, and departure, and Superintendent George's arrival (and his fifteen years' tenure) can be seen as a set of political events in which the citizens of Milford were deciding on the kind of education they wanted for their children and youth. Beyond the emotional labeling of 'good guys and bad guys,' fundamental issues were at stake: localism versus nationalism, traditional curriculum versus individualized curriculum, pupil conformity versus individual freedom for pupils. In our view, well informed and well intentioned citizens could legitimately come down on either side of those issues as they relate to preferred ways of living. And, in Milford, citizens did come down on different sides. And, as some of our quotes from Board minutes and letters to the Board indicate, it was often with strong or poignant emotion as factions won and lost and as policies remained the same or changed.

In Eliot's view — politics — who gets what, when and where, runs through all the important domains: curriculum, facilities, personnel, and financing. And so it was in Milford. Eliot's final generalization is: '. . . the realization that public policy in education is the product of discernible professional/lay interaction (sometimes conflict) at different governmental levels, may serve as a unifying conception.' (1959, p. 1051) To those who want prescriptions, this may seem too general and too vague. It fits our general view. The lesson for the Board member, the Superintendent, the teacher, the patron, is simple — a contest is always in the background, if not front and center. Some years it is hotter and more painful than others. And in some years it's not just 'professional/lay interaction' but multiple individual and subgroups within each category. That's what 'interaction/conflict' is about.

Along the way, Eliot makes a point about difficulties in generalizing from research in schooling: 'There are too many school districts, no two of them exactly alike.' (p. 1045) We believe this is an instance of one of our more general epistemological concerns, our accent on the case study vehicle, and our concerns for multiple kinds of results — facts, stories, concepts, hypotheses, models and metaphors. In our view, the concept of politics is highly generalizable, a sensitizing concept as Bruyn (1966) would label it, and one that the student or practitioner of innovation and change cannot do without.

On several occasions, over the years we have found the work of Professor Neal Gross compellingly clear, a characteristic which has helped us make our own work clearer by comparing and contrasting it with his.[2] This time we work off of his provocative little book, *Who Runs Our Schools* (1958). He states an initial premise with which we are in strong agreement: "A basic premise of this book is that superintendents and school board members, because they run our schools, are at the heart of any educational problem and its solution.' (1958, p. 2)

Our first line of analysis concerns the implicit theoretical model underlying the point of view. To do this, with a slight rewording of titles, we have organized the chapters in Gross' book into the outline presented as Figure 50. In our view, Gross presents essentially an organizational, technological, social engineering perspective on the schools.[3] If Eliot's perspective on politics is correct, and our positions is essentially congruent with his, then we have major questions about the limitations of Gross' position particularly as it deals with the question, 'Who runs our schools?' The language of obstacles — what holds school super-intendents back? (Chapter 2), who blocks the schools? (Chapter 3), who supports the schools? (Chapter 4), and who applies what kind of pressure? (Chapter 5) and to whom? (Chapter 6), assumes that the goals, subgoals, and means are in basic agreement. In Milford — the high school as college prep versus the high school as preparatory for a job, the curriculum as individualized versus the curriculum as text

Figure 50: A Partial Reinterpretation of Gross' 'Who Runs Our Schools?'

---

1 *Obstacles as a Perspective*

Chapter 2	What holds school superintendents back?
Chapter 3	Who blocks?
Chapter 4	Who supports?
Chapters 5 and 6	Who applies pressures to whom?

2 *The Evaluative Perspective*

Chapter 8	How good a job are school board members doing?
Chapter 9	How good a job are school superintendents doing?
Chapter 10	Agreements and disagreements
Chapter 11	Differing views of school board members
Chapter 12	What can be done?

---

books and basics; pupil freedom or pupil conformity to social standards in dress, attendance, smoking; and teacher militancy, activism and professionalism; and local neighborhood schools were all highly controversial. Various individuals and groups saw themselves as improving the public schools when each took a stand in contradiction to the stand of another. 'Obstacles,' and 'opportunities' depend on where one is and where one is going.

In what we have called 'the evaluative perspective,' we are arguing that Gross remains with his technical, organizational, social engineering perspective. After presenting a number of key items in which Boards and Superintendents disagree (for example, giving numerical grades on report cards in elementary schools), the final generalization is this:

> These data strongly suggest that in many school systems superintendents and school boards do not agree on the crucial problem of who is supposed to do what, on what is policy making and what is administration. It seems a reasonable prediction that a *corporation* will be headed for trouble if its president and board of directors disagree over the basic ground rules for their relationships and over policies and programs. A similar prediction may be made for school systems in which these conditions hold. (Our italics) (p.125)

But a school district is not just (or mainly?) a business corporation, rather, it is a political educational entity, and political entities are supposed to mediate the political interests of its citizenry regarding educational interests, goals and purposes.

In conclusion, when we say that 'politics' is an important sensitizing concept in thinking about innovation and change in schooling we are saying that analyses and interpretations which leave it out, which construe the 'who runs the schools?' question alternatively have a different map or template than ours. To judge one template as better than another asks for evaluative criteria. In our view, the most important criterion for educational theory is potency — which perspective will speak to more of the more important problems.[4]

In one of our preliminary analyses of our data, after describing the episode of change in Superintendents from McBride to Spanman to George in our chronicle of the Milford School District, we concluded with the question: 'One might ask, is our episode one of school chaos, vulnerability, or political democracy?' Implicitly we were challenging (at least in rural and suburban Milford) the 'vulnerability theme' raised by Callahan in his book, *Education and the Cult of Efficiency*. As he says in his preface:

> What was unexpected was the extent, not only of the power of the business-industrial groups, but the strength of the business ideology in the American culture on the one hand and the extreme weakness and vulnerability of school men, especially school administrators, on the other. (1962, Preface)

Later, in the same paragraph he uses words such as 'capitulation,' 'appeasing their critics,' and 'maintain their positions.' The theoretical position he seemed to be presenting we diagrammed in a form presented as Figure 51.

Figure 51: Our View of Callahan's (1962) Vulnerability Thesis

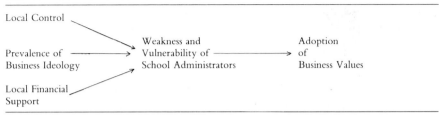

Our analysis, to this point, has suggested that 'vulnerability' might be too strong a term. Politics, political interests, and conflict seem closer to the mark in our school district. McBride's twenty-seven years, Spanman's controversial four years, and George's now more than fifteen year tenure seem apart from Callahan's more 'national view.'

Further, our view of 'business' business' in education has been less an ideological one as Callahan (1962) saw it or as some of the more recent critical theorists, for example, Sharp (1981) and Kallos (1981) might phrase it. Rather we have been persuaded more by overwhelming everpresence and mundaneness of 'business' business.' Perhaps we are more accepting and/or less perceptive. Or perhaps as the local people might say, 'We have had other fish to fry.' In the 1979–80 year a number of items arose which continued to illustrate a portion of our position.

We present just a few additional illustrations of our point. First, the Board hassled with bidders on blacktopping a parking area and on daily milk deliveries. Low bidders sometimes want to change arrangements and negotiate savings with the Board. These business events never end. Second, a long discussion (9/79) occurred over a new piece of accounting equipment. The company had indicated it would do the high school scheduling and save the District $8000 paid to a local computer firm. The $8000 saving would cost the Board $11,180.00 and Board members weren't happy. The company wouldn't budge. The Board voted to table the item and contact the school attorney. The debate on the accounting office equipment returned in January 1980. A series of split votes on buying and leasing occurred. Finally after some guarantees regarding the equipment by a company representative, the Board voted for a lease with option to buy contract. Third, late in September, 1979, bills were considered and paid, and the Board borrowed $100,000 for the operating fund. Leaking roofs continued to receive attention and the local roofing company negotiated to pay one third of the costs for damages occurring in their earlier work. A local dance studio received permission to use the Junior High cafeteria. Additional teachers' contracts were altered by steps and scales, and for Tax Sheltered Annuity programs. And finally, later in the month of November 1979, the Board received the financial statement for October and held it for regular auditing. The November bills to be paid were received. Contracts were awarded for senior diplomas ($1.91/unit) for three years, and for printing elementary diplomas ($1004.98) The siege of problems over leaking roofs, plaster and floor damage, and surveillance of repairs from the Board's long term architectural consultants received another round of attention. A Junior High pupil's semester suspension for possession of a controlled substance was upheld. Two teachers resigned, one returned from maternity leave, and several additional contract changes were made. The Board approved an early retirement incentive program for 1980–81. This is what we mean by mundane 'business' business.'

In part, it seems to us that we are 'trying to have our cake and eat it, too.' The work of Eliot, Gross, and Callahan represents some of the best research and thinking in education and the social sciences. The Milford case suggests different emphases and accents around the concept of 'politics.' We believe this altered emphasis is one of our most important findings.

Localism

The Position

The roots of localism reach deep in Suburban County as well as Milford. And they were there long before Suburban County became suburban. In the metropolitan complexity of the late twentieth century it is difficult to recall, for many of us, and difficult to realize, for most of us, how recent the rural localist tradition is. While we do not know the history of rural school consolidation across the country, we found documents, histories and stories that reported events similar to those in Milford. We cite two of those to illustrate several aspects of the general interpretive pattern we are developing:

> In 1933 a county school districting board met 16 times and emerged with a plan to merge the 90 little three-director districts in the county down to 16. . . . Wanting no part of this, the board members campaigned against it and the measures failed all over the county. (PD, 1977, p. 34)

Milford, at that time, was a 'big' school district. The high school had graduated two classes, a first through eighth grade elementary school was in operation in a new brick building, and a small two teacher school for Black youngsters had been built over ten years before.

In a situation very similar to Milford's in Suburban County, a project document reports on consolidation about the same time in the early fifties:

> The Midwest State legislature, mindful of the fact that the state of public education in Midwest was pitifully disorganized in the postwar years, enacted legislation enabling massive consolidations to take place. Such proposals originated with the county boards of education, subject to approval by the State Board of Education. *The county school board* literally lumped all of North Suburban County into one district, including old town Gentle Valley and all of Gardenville, and sent the plan in to the state board for approval. Such approval eventually was granted, and the matter was put on the ballot for *October 29, 1949.*
>
> Dr. Stanley H. Synder, county superintendent from 1916 through 1952, was against such a move as it would tend to destroy the voice those

people had exercised so many years in public school education. The farmers knew Dr. Synder objected to it, and he was their wise counselor on educational matters — if he was against it then automatically it was no good. The Forrest Hills board had hired Dr. Synder's son, Earl P. Synder, to represent them in legal matters, including the bond issue that produced the funds for their new building, and Earl Synder was against the proposal too.

'We were able to get the word to all the little three-director districts up here, and they came to the polls and voted. The Gardenville people were sound asleep, and didn't vote at all. As a result, *the proposal failed by a two-to-one majority.*' (Our italics)

Synder realized there was a provision in the law for resubmission and he knew he had to act fast. 'If we could just build ourselves the point where we had considerable area, we felt the county board would leave us alone.'

And that's what the *December 10, 1949* election was all about. They had to grow, as a means of self-defense. They couldn't take advantage of annexation statutes unless they formed themselves into a so-called 'six-director town school district.' (Our italics) (PD, 1977, pp. 98–100)

In two sentences, localism as a point of view and as a mechanism of innovation and change are clearly indicated:

All this time, Martha Walters, the clerk of the board, ran from one little district to another, encouraging the directors to come with Ingelford *rather than allow themselves to be gobbled up by an 'outsider' district.* 'It seemed like I was going all the time. Everybody else was working. Somebody had to do it, so I did,' Mrs. Walters said. (Our italics) (p. 104)

The fear of being 'gobbled up by an "outsider"' meant then, just thirty years ago, that the outsider was a small city of several thousand individuals. (Recall also at that time, Midwest State had *de jure* segregated schools.) Within a year and a half, really in two separate thrusts, a northside and a southside, over a dozen of these three-director, one-room schoolhouse school districts became the Ingelford School District, in what is perhaps a prototypic illustration of both the idea and the actualization of localism or local autonomy, in schooling and school community relationships. Images of populism, ragamuffins, and a rag tag army float through the larger account. That side of the story is awesome, when the current lament concerns the impotence of any kind of community social action regarding district and cross district action.

Earlier we cited an interview with a now elderly citizen, Mr. F. K. Tholozan, who had been on the Milford School Board as a young man, indicated how local, 'local' could be defined. Debates occurred between the two sides of the Milford District, which seemed to differ in socioeconomic status. Attempts were made to have one director representing each of those older parts of the community and one representing the newer suburban development of the 1920s.

Related to localism, we believe, is the easier consensus of the community toward defining and actualizing the common good. Mr. Tholozan, as a young man with a family, had moved to one of Milford's post World War I suburban developments. He soon was active in the local neighborhood improvement association. It was this group which had nominated and supported him for his successful election to the school board. In addition, he helped found the Milford Volunteer Fire Department and served as its captain for a number of years. He spent Sunday mornings down at the building they had built, 'drinking beer and polishing the fire engine,' according to his wife. They worked hard for roads, water, sewers, electricity, and telephone services.

The general point we are making reveals a common cause around achievement of simple material benefits for a relatively small isolated community in still a very rural county. The improvement of schools was one part of this.

Into this localist tradition, as our later discussion showed, arise issues of desegregation, integration, equality and justice, policies and practices of neighborhood schools, bussing, cross district transfers of pupils, and perhaps one large metropolitan school district. While issues of racism, prejudice and discrimination, and integration are clearly central to our latent story, analysis, and interpretation, the contention we would make is that a strong parallel strand of localism and autonomy is equally a part of the story, analysis, and interpretation.

Responsiveness to Local Needs

Without being maudlin, one part of the record on innovation and change in Milford seems intellectually simple — responsiveness to the wishes of local citizens as individuals and subgroups. The 'will of the people,' a cliché from Social Studies 101, kept appearing and reappearing. Such is the special education story. We haven't highlighted it but it weaves as a mini theme throughout our narrative from the earliest years. The Board implemented multiple alternative policies over the years: exclusion, homebound teaching, payments to other districts or private schools, special classes, and special schools. Eventually a regional program was enacted by a number of school districts. Most recently, PL 94–142, a national initiative, came to Kensington and Milford.

Vocational education and secondary school guidance are similar stories of local demands and school district response. The Board wrestled with this by expanding offerings in the secondary school, by paying tuition for a few students at a neighboring vocational high school, and, eventually, supporting a regional vocational-technical secondary program.

A smaller, but more dramatic, story was recounted in detail of the hassles over elementary school boundaries when a new school was built and parents attempted to change decisions of the Board.[5] In that mix of professional problem solving and proposals by the school administrators, oversight in the form of review, discussion and debate by elected community representatives, that is, the Board, and finally in a series of parental community action appeals, the Board changed its mind. In small and large ways, the educational lives of some of individual children were changed because of these processes. We have called it responsiveness to local needs. It seems an important part of Milford's history, its traditions, and its way of doing things. Innovators, whether professional educators or politicians, who want to do things differently or who ignore this kind of 'social reality' will find themselves 'swimming against the current,' 'batting their head against a stone wall,' or 'deviating from a strongly held normative structure.' Such actions will have some reasonably predictable consequences.

In the same vein, we have talked of naming and renaming of schools and providing signs displaying these names. Small groups of citizens came up with an idea, presented it to the Board, the Board considered it and generalized it to the other schools in the District as a whole and took action which met the initial request and maintained equity across the community. Simple but potent.

The Broader Community

National Purposes

Anyone growing up in America in the 1930s knows first hand the problems created by a great economic depression, the Rooseveltian political revolution, and the fifty years debate which was precipitated. Similarly, anyone in education living through the 1960s cannot help but perceive the momentous importance of the Elementary and Secondary Education Act of 1965 in the long argument about federal aid to education. Nor in the late 1970s and early 1980s can one help but sense that Nixon's silent majority and Reagan's new coalition represent another major watershed in politics and education.

As one reads the Milford School Board minutes, one of the incredible strengths of Mr. McBride's early tenure was his understanding of the economic and political changes in Washington, as well as locally, and his ability to obtain resources in the form of grants and loans for new school buildings and additions to old ones. The Board eagerly supported and went along with these efforts. The 1980s ogre of 'federal regulations' was present early on, caused a few problems, but did not deter anyone for very long. The WPA and PWA floated in and out of the minutes and our story. School lunches, transportation monies, and aid to defense impacted areas appeared. The Board seemed caught in that anomalous position of soliciting all kinds of Federal Funds on the one hand and on occasion taking vivid moral stands on the sins and evils of Federal Aid to Education, a potential destroyer of 'initiative and moral fiber of the American people.' This love/hate relationship, the conflict in local and national purposes, recall images of Alexander Hamilton and Thomas Jefferson. The dilemma has existed in America in one form or another for several centuries. Milford's story is probably not atypical. The longevity suggests the issue will not go away soon, but will be transformed by other particular agenda items.

Today, in the 1980s, the Depression, World War II, and the postwar population explosion, as national problems are gone. The national agenda in the 1960s and 1970s shifted to equality among races, women and the handicapped. The passing of the baby boom has left us with too many buildings and too many teachers and administrators. Socioeconomic and racial population shifts have continued particularly in the suburbs such as Milford. Inflation has intensified the economics of all the issues in the agenda. In the eyes of many citizens and professionals in Milford, federal regulations seem to now outweigh the benefits of federal dollars.

State Law

State laws seemed more than anything else to provide a set of rules, a context if not constraints in which choices about local schooling could be made. Occasionally more specific actions of helping occurred and frequently, but almost always in the background, were monitoring and judging activities. The appearance of Milford High School was in a context of accrediting of staff and accrediting of courses and opening the possibilities of graduates being readied, credentialed for higher education or jobs. State laws framed three or six director districts and the annual school elections. Foundation programs provide some continuing financial resources.

Partly because of what is to be a later concern at Kensington, the racial change in the population of students, the State law which appeared throughout our discussion was the separate but equal prohibition in educating Black and White children together. Grounded in the Supreme Court decision of 1878, Midwest State law, until 1954 prohibited the joint education of the races. As we read the minutes of 1920 through 1960, the tone is not one of hostility or maliciousness but rather of people operating with *blinders*, legally supported institutional racism, the state law. The law was there, it was to be obeyed, no one questioned it. The 1954 Supreme Court decision changed all that. The Board, the Black parents, and the NAACP, amicably so it seems, made the transitions. No doubt exists in our eyes as to who was dominant. The Attucks School was closed, later to reopen as a center for the handicapped, and still later to be a district storage facility, The Black teacher became a district attendance officer. Not fired, but also not a teacher. The high school pupils were integrated immediately — on an appeal by the parents and NAACP to eliminate long bus rides to Green City High School. The elementary pupils were integrated a year later, in the context of crowded schools and temporary housing in church educational buildings. Black parents expressed concern over losing their neighborhood school.

Finally, state law and court interpretation provided the framework for personnel changes. Nussbaum took the district to court, as did Superintendent McBride in his several major conflicts over the years. In these controversies, it is important to recall that the rules were never fixed in any ultimate sense. Even after local issues were settled, the case continued in the courts, at the behest of various groups, for a ruling to be made. They, too, wanted the clarity which comes from recent judicial interpretations of the evolving rules. In a sense these rules become important determinants of human action. Ironically, we might call them 'the man-made laws of human nature.' They provide a context for almost every action, change, and proposed innovation in the Milford District.

320

Voting

Reading Board minutes makes one a believer in the omnipresence, omnipotence, and omniscience of voting in community social action — innovative or supporting the *status quo*. The recurrent 'moved, seconded, and passed' flavor of Board decision and action, among other consequences, left us as readers and analysts with renewed faith that individuals, small groups of people, and perhaps communities of people were in control of their lives. Event after event, problem after problem, decision after decision, action after action arose. Programs — high schools and kindergartens — were started. Buildings were built. Superintendents, principals, and teachers were elected, hired or fired. All these events were mediated by Board votes.

Every year the annual school elections occurred. Incumbents were returned or ousted, remained or lost; challengers arrived or were denied. Voting by the community mediated the changes or preserved the *status quo*. At other times, and sometimes to the chagrin of professional staff or the 'right minded' Board members, the community supported or defeated tax levies and bond issues.

Words like omnipresence, omnipotence, and omniscience are not too strong.

The Constitution and Bill of Rights

Our eulogy for 'voting' as one of the fundamentals in democracy and schooling is tempered, or checked and balanced, by what was once called 'inalienable' if not 'natural rights.' This sent us back to discussions of the Constitution and the Bill of Rights and the limits in the power of the majority to control the behavior and destiny of the minority — even if that minority is a single individual. That, too, is a continuous national debate of two hundred years, with a millennium of antecedents. Tocqueville's *Democracy in America* became a necessary 'next round' of reading.

As he comments:

All the general principles on which modern constitutions rest, principles which most Europeans in the seventeenth century scarcely understood and whose dominance in Great Britain was then far from complete, are recognized and given authority by the laws of New England; the participation of the people in public affairs, the free voting of taxes, the responsibility of government officials, individual freedom, and trial by jury — all these things were established without question and with practical effect. (p. 43)

A few pages later Tocqueville continued his statement:

Everywhere on the Continent at the beginning of the seventeenth century absolute monarchies stood triumphantly on the ruins of the feudal or oligarchic freedom of the Middle Ages. Amid the brilliance and the literary achievements of Europe, then, the conception of right was perhaps more completely misunderstood that at any other time; the people had never taken less part in political life; notions of true liberty had never been less in men's minds. And just at that time these very principles, unknown to or scorned by the nations of Europe, were proclaimed in the wildernesses of the New World, where they were to become the watchwords of a great people. (pp. 45–46)

As we said, the next round of effort on 'innovation and change in schooling' must start with Tocqueville.

Power: Redistribution, Stabilization, and 'Iron Laws' in Milford

Power, the ability to influence and control people and events, is another of those concepts about which teachers as professionals and patrons as parents tend to underemphasize in their theories and ideologies of schooling. In those schemes which accent 'what is good for the boys and girls of Milford' or 'the nature of basic skills or college prep curriculum' the concept of power jars or strikes a discordant note.[6] In a sense we belong to that group. One of the most jarring views from the Board minutes was what we called 'the potent Board member.' Messrs. Lewis, Tompkins, Wilkerson, and Reeves, over the years all fit that label. The minutes that reflected their ideas, activities and interactions took on what might be called a 'look out' flavor. Their ability to gather, consolidate and use power made major differences in the day to day and long term conduct of the schools. Their stories remain both fascinating and provocative for innovation and change.

But it is not only educational theory and ideology as raised by actors in the schools that concern us but the need for more careful, fine grained accounts by our colleagues in the world of educational research and theory. For instance, we have several quarrels with Wirt and Kirst's (1982) *Schools in Conflict*. The substantive concern hinges on the initial paragraph of the preface and their comments about the 'administrative chief' and the larger losses in 'discretion,' what we would call power.[7]

> 1) The politics of education has changed dramatically since we closed our first edition in 1970. 2) It is surprising how quickly the political structures, actors, and processes of education have become so fundamentally re-organized. 3) The era of the local superintendent as 'administrative chief' was then dawning.[8] 4) We did not, however, anticipate the multitude of actors and the complexity of the governmental patterns nor 5) the large amount of discretion the chief executive would lose. 6) The 1970s will be remembered as an era when the previous hallmark of American education — local control — became fully a myth. 7) The political web surrounding the school district tightened and included many more participants. (1982, p. V)

We do not believe we are nit-picking, and we may only be echoing Eliot's (1959) concern about generalizing across school districts, or perhaps, we have a fundamental bias regarding case studies and other kinds of data. Or perhaps it's the use to which scientific accounts are put. Or perhaps generalizations between larger urban systems and smaller suburban systems are particularly tenuous. Or perhaps it's a concern over a shifting unit of analysis; national, state, and local. Or perhaps it's generalizations over time which are troublesome. But very briefly we would counter. In Milford, to follow our enumeration of Wirt and Kirst:

1   Any theme you take — desegregation, demography, teacher activism, special education, etc. has a long and vital history with major changes at several points; 1927, 1954, 1961, etc.
2   The actors and the structures are evolving but have been there, usually for years.
3   The Superintendent as administrative chief 'dawned' in the mid 1930s. His/her 'dawning' or 'decaying' was more idiosyncratic to his/her personality and interaction with the Board as with Mrs. Briggs, 1928–30, and Dr. Spanman, 1962–66.
4   In recent years the actor most dramatically involved in the government web and everything else has been the school lawyer. The legal web has increased amazingly.
5   In Milford, the real loss in discretion has been the curbing of the Board's originally near total power, (except for state laws and the will of the electorate) in the early years, pre-World War II. It was not the Superintendent's total power.
6   The Board's 'local control' may be a myth elsewhere. Even though declining over the years, the battles in the late 1970s indicates the Board's power 'local control' remains 'really real.'
7   The political web remains.

Their paragraph and the key statement or two regarding power have a curious fit and lack of fit with our stories and conceptualizations of Milford. For the theme of innovation and change, power follows easily from our concerns with nested systems, with politics, and with ill defined and entangled problems. More specifically, we extend the discussion with concerns for the redistribution of power, the increasing complexity in the exercise of power, and its current stabilization. Intertwined with these processes are images of Michel's iron law of oligarchy.

In the course of our research, we have both told stories and accumulated generalizations. One of the stories involved a high school teacher, Mr. Nussbaum, who was not rehired after seven years on the staff, for a series of reasons generally coalescing into a judgment of incompetence. He argued, that the real reasons were his activities and favorable attitudes toward teacher unionization.[9] He lost several appeals. Then several years later, in the Spanman era, he reappeared in our story as he made a further appeal to the then new Superintendent, Dr. Spanman, and also to NEA. His letter appears as Figure 52. The Superintendent's letter, drafted in consultation with the school attorney and approved by the Board, is Figure 53. Several months later a copy of a letter appears from NEA's Commission on Professional Rights and Responsibilities. It is included as Figure 54.

October 9, 1962

Dear Dr. Spanman:

My teaching contract with Milford was not renewed in 1959, after seven years of successful teaching in the district.

No doubt personnel records will indicate the reason for the abrupt termination of my services. I would appreciate professional enumeration of whatever causes led to the decision.

Yours very truly,

N. E. Nussbaum

October 17, 1962

Dear Mr. Nussbaum:

I have your letter of October 9, 1962, requesting a professional enumeration of whatever causes led to your separation from your former teaching position with the Milford School District. As you know, I was not associated with the School District during your tenure and I accordingly have no personal knowledge of the matter.

The personnel records are silent on the subject of your request. I have discussed your letter with the attorney for the School District and have been advised that no dismissal nor proceeding in which a cause for dismissal had to be established was involved in the circumstances surrounding your case, but that the Board simply notified you as required by law of its decision not to renew your contract. The attorney advises me that such decision is a matter peculiarly within the discretion of the Board and that no reason need be given or established for such decision.

You are, of course, thoroughly familiar with the decision of the courts which ruled upon the circumstances in your suit against the School District.

Very truly yours,

Steven Spanman

As we reflected on this story, juxtaposed to items such as the Superintendent's new (in 1962) personnel policy of exclusive nomination power, we are left with these generalizations:

1 Over the years, the control over school affairs has shifted from an almost absolute power of the Board to a distribution of power among the several subgroups — Superintendent, central office administration, principals, and teachers, and professional organizations. One of the more recent of these is a state tenure law which came too late to protect Nussbaum.

2 This distribution of power has become increasingly institution-alized/stabilized and makes it considerably more difficult for any one group to make arbitrary changes or to make very large changes.

Figure 54: Norman to Nussbaum

January 14, 1963

Dear Mr. Nussbaum:

Thank you for keeping us current on the status of your request for written reasons for the non renewal of your contract in Milford.

A unique situation has developed in this case. The administrator (Mr. McBride) whom the NEA Ethics Committee might have declared to be in violation of the code of ethics is no longer in a position to speak for the school district. The current Superintendent, Dr. Spanman, by your own admission, is in complete agreement that a teacher should be given reasons for non renewal but is precluded by the Board from commenting about your case.

I do not believe the Ethics Committee, in fairness to any member of the Association, can cite as unethical the former superintendent for his failure to act at this time when he is without authority. Nor could it, fairly, cite Dr. Spanman who, because of his recent employment, is not personally familiar with the case and is, therefore restrained from acting.

The NEA had no part in the sanctioning of Blue Springs School District. This was strictly a concern of Far West State Teachers' Association and I am not in a position to judge whether or not the measure was successful. Some examples of formal sanctions are enclosed. You will note that in each case where formal sanctions were used that the local or state affiliate concurred. This policy of the Association remains in force and would automatically bar considerations of sanctions against Milford until such time as the Community or State Teachers Association would be in accord.

In view of all of the circumstances outlined above, including the fact that you brought suit (without our counsel) and thereby delayed consideration of your request for two years and cut off any assistance the NEA might have rendered at that time, I do not see how the Association can proceed further in this case.

Tenure for Midwest State teachers is an imperative. The Association will continue to make every effort to alert Midwest teachers to fair dismissal practices and to tenure laws existing in other states to the end that they will secure similar statutes in Midwest State. This is the only real and permanent solution to problems like your own in Midwest State.

Very truly yours.

S. M. Norman
Associate Legal Counsel

3 Typically, the Board, which has had the largest share of the power, has fought the changes. Sometimes, as in the 3–3 Board split in the late 1970s, internal conflicts appeared. Eventually, the 'old guard' won back its power. One of the key issues in the split Board concerned the power of teachers to negotiate. As we indicated, the teachers were split into two factions at that time. Also at that later date the once fiery social studies teacher and CTA President now was aligned with the Board, as Superintendent of schools.

4 Other parts of our data suggest that local and state powers have been distributed in part to a third party, the Federal Government.

5 That third party divides into three sometimes contending groups — legislative, executive, and judicial. Harmony is not always present here.

6 Through all this, the electorate exerts a variety of forms of 'ultimate' control. We have vivid examples of bond and tax votes passing and failing,

of board incumbents supported and turned out of office, and more recently of attempts for state referenda and constitutional amendments regarding what many patrons call 'forced busing,' the two-thirds tax levy requirements, and aid to parochial schools.

For the student of innovation and change, for the appreciator of irony, and for the searcher of heroes and villains, several interesting images occur here. The NEA official who wrote the letter to Nussbaum was active in the controversy between McBride, the Superintendent, when the Board was trying to fire him in 1961–62. The Professional Rights Committee was brought into the controversy by the local CTA and its then President, Ron George. Later, Ron George would become Superintendent. Superintendent McBride and several of his Central Office staff had intimidated an earlier President of the CTA, when Nussbaum was not rehired. The exercise of power is quite complex in Milford.

Late in the day, now, as we read and think our way back through the 'Nussbaum story,' in the context of the issues of power and educational innovation, a number of implications appear for innovators and reformers. The long play of issues over the years suggests that one should anticipate long struggles in accomplishing the improvements one is working toward. Some of those struggles will not be successful. That suggests that one should be selective in one's targets. Most of us perceive a number of aspects of schooling that might be improved. Having some sense of personal and general priorities seems very important. During this long period it seems important also to develop a niche in the school organization — a position or role as teacher, principal, or central office administrator — which provides, if not maximizes, day to day satisfactions during the battles. That seems related to maintaining one's mental health or sanity in the topsy-turvy world of innovation and change. Similarly, for a variety of reasons, developing, maintaining, and supporting one's major or highest priority reference group seems very important. Finally, with the increasing litigatious nature of schooling, being congruent with the various legal statutes, unless those are what one is trying to change, seems important as well. Whether Nussbaum saw himself as an innovator we do not know. For us, his story was influential in our thinking.

Michels' 'iron law of oligarchy' and its more recent interpretation by Selznick (1950) essentially involved the politics of power. The expansion of the idea into the internal functioning of the school organization arose as we were reading and analyzing Board minutes from the Spring of 1974, regarding the possible closing of schools. Several items came together: 1) The Housing Committee was made up of Principals, the majority of whom had been in the District for years and who had survived the McBride and Spanman eras and were now into the Georgian period. 2) That group had to know 'the lay of the land' regarding the Superintendent's point of view and the current Board's position, whose key members' tenure now overlapped George's tenure. 3) On the Housing Committee, among others, was Gillespie, a teacher with George years before, and one of his first principal appointments. He was just recently appointed Director of Elementary Education (March 1974). Dr. Wales, who would come on the Kensington scene later, had just become a principal. 4) These selections, our other data would argue, were of men who shared the general perspective of the Superintendent and the Central Office staff and the group of principals they were joining. There was no coercion, no soul searching for their 'natural' proclivities tended to run in the same directions. Selection can be as powerful, if not more so, than socialization. Or socialization runs easily when one's predilections are similar. 5) The phenomenon seems 'all of a piece,' not a one shot event. Rather it is a continuous process. Presumably it begins with initial hiring of young teachers and continues with decisions as to which probationary teachers are kept and which ones are let go.

The critical point we are reaching for is the linked inference that: the very framing of the problems; the kind of concepts used in the construal; the unexplored taken-for-granted assumptions on which the discussion rests; the kind of alternatives considered; the kind of data buttressing the argument at the several critical points; and finally, the specific recommendations made are all enveloped in the prior social and organizational events.

All along the way, this process is constrained by rules, regulations and norms. Board members are elected or not. Administrative contracts are reviewed each year. Public organizations such as schools have regular open meetings and time for 'patron participation.' Individual consciences, and generalized norms of 'fair play,' the importance of democracy, and individual responsibility are not empty slogans in Milford.

But the 'natural drift' of the organization seems toward oligarchy. Individuals who are outside formal and informal structures and processes and who want to change a particular item, or even more consequently, want to alter the 'natural drift' have a huge and near intractable problem. We put 'natural drift' in quotes because it is perceived that way in common sense, but we would hold that it is socially constructed. But, as we have said, being socially constructed is not synonymous with being highly malleable. Our earlier stories of the 'potent Board President' and the 'proactive Superintendent' suggest ways and means, and, perhaps also, a more complex web of pros and cons in decisions and evaluations. But our central point is that not only the day to day decisions, actions and interactions, but also those of a more eventful kind, as was the Housing Committee, are the very bread and butter of the District running smoothly, the iron law of oligarchy.

For those who want a conception of power encased in an historically longer and a contemporaneously broader context, we might mention again that Midwest State law requires that each April, two of the six members on the Board of Education will have their status contested in a local election. When we reflected on that item, we were continually amazed at the potency of its commentary on power. Secondly, and linked with stability and oligarchies of power, Midwest State law states that upon the resignation of a member of a school board, the remaining incumbents elect the new member to finish the term. The importance of that occurred several times in Milford's history with the late 1970s 3–3 split quickly changing to 4–2 when one of the 'ladies' moved and resigned. Two elections later, the Board was 6–0. These are powerful socially constructed mechanisms surrounding 'power' in schooling in Milford.

Innovation and Ways of Schooling and Living: A Move to a General Conclusion

A Problem in Several Guises

Even in an endeavor that tried to stay close to the day to day actions, events, and episodes in the lives of the people who took part in the Milford drama, we found that broader, more abstract terms kept creeping into our discussions, commentary, and reporting. Reactive, cosmopolitan, traditional, conservative and so forth arose with one or another individual or subgroup. The ideas seemed to go to the heart of any discussion of innovation and change in the Milford District and the Kensington School. We didn't know what to do with those. In a sense we still do not, but we present them as ideas for others to consider. For the moment, the ideas have crystallized in the structural model in Figure 55.

The ideas are the dimensions or continua of conservative/liberal, traditional/modern, localist/cosmopolitan, and reactive/proactive. In its usual usage, the conservative to liberal dimension suggests the degree to which one is open to change, an accent on conserving versus an accent on changing. Other connotations suggest the liberating or freeing of someone from the restrictive state of affairs the just individual finds comfortable and worth conserving. This dimension shades easily into a more substantive dimension, an accent on the 'traditional' or the 'modern.' Traditions are social items handed down from the past. Modern, has to do with the more recent or new. Presumably one's beliefs could be contemporary, and one could want to hold them, conserve them, at least for the moment. The localist/ cosmopolitan dimension again seems to correlate, although not perfectly, with the prior dimensions. Presumably the 'citizens of the world,' could hold traditional or modern views and could conserve or accent change. Although in Milford, with its

Figure 55: General Dimensions in Ways of Schooling and Living

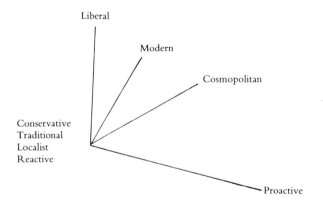

rural and small town origins and with its more post World War II lower middle working class population, the localist is more likely to be both traditional and conservative.

And finally, the proactive/reactive, again seems to relate less than perfectly with the other dimensions. The take charge, efficacious, entrepreneural Spanman became our prototype. Dr. George seemed more reactive. But even here, a better choice of polar opposites might be 'responsive,' to the wishes of the Board. Responsive seems to convery a different kinds of intentionality than reactive. Our image of McBride is less clear — but more a proactive localist.

At first we thought these dimensions might be applicable just to the superintendency and the various incumbents who have held the post, for example George is a localist and Spanman was a cosmopolitan. Then we found that each individual and group in the Superintendent's 'role set,' the Board, the Central Office staff, the patrons could be similarly classified as we thought about them. For example, the potent Board Presidents — Lewis, Tompkins, Wilkerson, Reeves — all could be categorized on the dimensions. The congruence or incongruence in orientation between these men, their Board, and the Superintendent would make an alternative way to specify stability and conflict.

As we used the labels and observed others using them, we found the terms evolving into a shorthand for 'evaluations' of the various actors. It seemed as though actions were being generalized both into larger abstract categories and these larger categories were also parts of implicit and only sometimes explicit value systems. That is, if Spanman was off to a national meeting and presenting his ideas he was becoming 'too cosmopolitan' for some, who thought he would be better off staying home and taking care of the local Milford problems. That merging of the abstract-descriptive labels with evaluative overtones occurs readily and easily with most individuals in Milford as they talk about McBride, Spanman, and George. This raises concerns for the complicated issues in conceptualizing, evaluating, and eventually measuring the nature and quality of a Superintendent's (or other's) performance.

To make one of our interpretations one more time, we are struck with the impossibility of separating out easily what we once thought might be the multiple levels of language — data, narrative, theory, and evaluation. The very labels themselves, for example, liberal, modern, cosmopolitan, and proactive or conservative, traditional, localist, and reactive seem to reflect a much more complicated picture in the philosophy of science than we had earlier imagined. These are further complicated when we introduce the particularity of Briggs, Grey, McBride, Spanman, and George and the context of the 1920s, 1930s, 1940s and on through the 1980s, all with a focus on innovation and change. And it, the people, the events, and the accounts of the people and the events, all occurred in one school district, Milford. The language of schooling in a democracy seems much more complicated than that suggested by most social science and educational theories.

Alternative Schemes and Issues

More casually than intensively we began looking for other classification schemes of key actors in schools and the implications of those schemes. Callahan and Button, in a series of publications, present a fourfold typology linked to a historical time line. Figure 56 contains their ideas. The categories do not wear easily with our five Superintendents.

Perhaps their ideal types are more a reflection of the dominant ideas under discussion at particular points in time. For instance, the last two decades in educational administration have been dominated by the 'theory movement,' which reached its high water point in the Sixty-Third NSSE Yearbook, *Behavioral Science and Educational Administration* (Griffiths, 1964).[10] From this vantage point we may better construe the dominant ideas as paradigms and turn this discussion back to our earlier account of the Griffiths-Greenfield debate. The more positivist administrative theory is under attack by a more phenomenological/social interactional/critical theorist wave of interpretation. The applied social scientist or educational realist category may be dissolving.

The other categories seem to capture different pieces of the totality. The first and third, scholarly educational leader and educational statesmen seem to share a kind of charisma but accent different substantive goals and values — the first educational, the other democratic. In our terminology, both would be proactive, probably more cosmopolitan than local but either conservative or liberal and either traditional or modern. The business manager/school executive label, while capturing an economic set of values probably also fits a more traditional and conservative image, but could well be proactive or reactive.

Once again, the descriptive, analytical, conceptual categories seem to' carry considerable implicit value components as well. Patrons and citizens on different ends of our continua might well evaluate Superintendents in each of the categories

Figure 56: An Historical Perspective on the Changing Role of the School Superintendent (from Callahan and Button, 1964; Callahan, 1964; Button, 1961)

1	Scholarly Educational Leader/	(1865–1910)
	Philosopher Educator	(1865–1900)
2	Business Manager/	(1910–1929)
	School Executive	(1915–1939)
3	Educational Statesman in	
	a Democratic School	(1930–1954)
4	Educational Realist/	(1954–1965)
	Applied Social Scientist	

differently from Callahan and Button. For instance, in Milford being a conservative, localist, business manager Superintendent is an accolade of the highest order.

Extrapolating A Step Too Far?

Imagination, courage, and speculation seem to blend in our intellectual activity toward the end of our projects. Our model in Figure 55 which clustered conservative, traditional, localist, and reactive dimensions seemed to capture the Milford patrons, Board, and superintendency circa 1980. We believe that stance can be described from a contextualist epistemology or world view (following Pepper, 1942 and Sarbin, 1977). We believe there exists a broad gap between that view and what we have seen as Hare's (1952) decision of principle. But we also believe that gap has to be narrowed in a perspective on innovation and change in schooling. Perhaps it is appropriate to quote from Hare's key paragraph, to make our point explicitly:

> Thus, if pressed to justify a decision completely, we have to give a complete specification of the way of life of which it is a part. This complete specification it is impossible in practice to give; the nearest attempts are those given by great religions, especially those which can point to historical persons who carried out the way of life in practice, Suppose, however, that we can give it. If the inquirer still goes on asking 'But why *should* I live like that?' then there is no further answer to give him, because we have already, *ex hypothesi*, said everything that could be included in this further answer. We can only ask him to make up his own mind which way he ought to live; for in the end everything rests upon such a decision of principle. He has to decide whether to accept that way of life or not; if he accepts it then we can proceed to justify the decisions that are based upon it; if he does not accept it, then let him accept some other, and try to live by it. The sting is in the last clause. To describe such ultimate decisions as arbitrary, because *ex hypothesi* everything which could be used to justify them has already been included in the decision, would be like saying that a complete description of the universe was utterly unfounded, because no further fact could be called upon in corroboration of it. This is not how we use the words 'arbitrary' and 'unfounded.' Far from being arbitrary, such a decision would be the most well-founded of decisions, because it would be based upon a consideration of everything upon which it could possibly be founded. (Hare, 1952, p. 69)

What we are saying is that students of innovation and change in schooling, as they move from the 'simple' descriptive accounts of actors and events in a district like Milford and schools like Kensington are irrevocably caught in more abstract and general concepts, theories, and interpretations. These perspectives carry major implicit and explicit value components and overtones. To deal with them one has to develop increasingly complex, comprehensive, and coherent discussions. Finally, as citizens, as professional educators, and as researchers and theorists we must take a stand, make a 'decision of principle' about schooling.

In these accounts of Milford, we believe the value issues were particularly troublesome for educationists. We believe also that educational research and theory must deal with the questions of values and both learn from and assist practitioners through their quandaries. We see some of that begun in Fein (1971), Gittel *et al.* (1973), and Rokeach (1975). The imperative in this area stems from wrenching issues in conflict today, to wit: the inherent conflict between such stances as 'fraternity/community/neighborhood school,' 'equality/justice/affirmative action/ desegregation.' or 'liberty/freedom/individualism/local control.' We have seen such divergent values in conflict at Kensington School and the Milford District. We know they are at issue elsewhere too. Whether the values and issues actually cluster in these ways more generally is an important analytical empirical problem in its own right. For our purposes here they suggest a next level of ideas with which one must contend.

Peshkin (1978) in his study of Mansfield High School and its rural and small town community puts Mansfield on the horns of a series of value dilemmas: personal identity versus intellectuality, intergenerational stability versus maximizing academic achievement, school-community harmony versus national ideals, and a balance of academics, athletics, and extracurricular activities versus school consolidation. Localism and sense of community are writ large. Finally, he poses similar dilemmas for all American communities — fundamentalist Kanawha County, White South Boston, Black and Hispanic New York City, and Amish Wisconsin— and for the larger population surrounding these communities. What kind of society does America want? What kind of schools should serve the 'communities' of America? These are questions he is implicitly asking his readers.

The ideas in these pieces of research suggest how broad the expanse is before one reaches the position explicated by Hare. This gap, it seems, needs to be filled with broader maps of values similar to the ones raised by scholars such as Kluckhohn and Strodtbeck (1961) and Morris (1956), anthropologist, social psychologist, and philosopher. In Figures 57 and 58 we suggest their positions. Rather than comment at any length, we merely try to pose some next steps in the problem.

As we read the Kluckhohn and Strodtbeck (1961) position, they begin with the comment, 'From philosophy, history, and cultural anthropology the fact has been demonstrated ever more convincingly that there is a definite variability in the ways of life human beings build for themselves' (p. 1). One does not have to go beyond the boundaries of the Milford School System to find the beginnings of such variability. But variability is not infinite, so Kluckhohn and Strodtbeck argue. Their analysis suggests a limited number of 'common human problems' exist for all peoples to solve. In addition they argue that the possible solutions exist in some form in all societies. Further they believe that some of the patterns are more highly preferred in one society or another. These beliefs constrain the most extreme or rampant forms of relativity. The half dozen 'problems' are the foundation of the

Figure 57: After Kluckhohn and Strodtbeck's Conception of Value Orientations (1961, p. 12)

Common Human Problems	Alternative Resolutions					
	Evil		Neutral	Mixture of Good and Evil	Good	
human nature	mutable	immutable	mutable	immutable	mutable	immutable
man–nature	Subjugation-to-Nature		Harmony-with-Nature		Mastery-over-Nature	
time	Past		Present		Future	
activity	Being		Being-in-Becoming		Doing	
relational	Lineality		Collaterality		Individualism	
spatial	Local		Mixed		Cosmopolitan	

Figure 58: Morris' Ways to Live (1956, p. 1)

Way 1: preserve the best that man has attained
Way 2: cultivate independence of persons and things
Way 3: show sympathetic concern for others
Way 4: experience festivity and solitude in alternation
Way 5: act and enjoy life through group participation
Way 6: constantly master changing conditions
Way 7: integrate action, enjoyment, and contemplation
Way 8: live with wholesome, carefree enjoyment
Way 9: wait in quiet receptivity
Way 10: control the self stoically
Way 11: meditate on the inner life
Way 12: chance adventuresome deeds
Way 13: obey the cosmic purposes

table we have excerpted. The first is the character of 'innate human nature.' Are human beings good, evil, neutral, or mixed? Further, is the condition mutable or immutable, or is there some in between degree of malleability if not perfectibility? Spanman and his colleagues seemed more on the mutable, perfectible end of the continuum compared to McBride or George. The data posed no easy judgment on the inherent goodness or badness of human nature in their views.

The problem of the 'man–nature' relationship offers alternatives in such well known variations of the person being subjugated to nature, in harmony with nature, or mastering nature. They argue that the latter is the characteristic American value orientation. Our proactive/reactive dimension suggests that Briggs and Spanman, and perhaps Grey, leaned to the mastery of nature and the George position was much more reactive, if not fatalistic. McBride seemed to fall less easily here, more toward the proactive mode. As we apply the labels to the individual superintendents the idea of dimensions and general labels seems less adequate than our contextualized descriptions.

Our traditional/modern dimension seems similar in content and intent to Kluckhohn and Strodtbeck's problem of time orientation. Their alternatives are a focus and priority on the past, the present, or the future. If our accounts and interpretations are correct, McBride, in his later years, seems to be caught in conflict with potent board members who wanted to bring him toward their more modern present day view. Spanman, in contrast, wanted to propel Milford into the twenty-first century, or at least his view of that time. George and the current Board seem in agreement about the values if not virtues of a more traditional past.

The 'activity' problem faced by individuals and cultures involves the value put on being, doing, or being in becoming. Other labels have been suggested, and Kluckhohn and Strodtbeck appeal to *Paths of Life*, the earlier work of the philosopher Morris (1942). 'Dionysian' is a partial synonym for being, that is, the indulgence of existing desires. 'Apollonian' replaces 'being in becoming' and refers to cultures which stress the control of desires and impulses through a detached meditation. Finally, the 'doing' alternative, with some mix of 'mastery' in the man-nature relation, becomes 'Promethean,' the active, striving orientation. If one's position stresses or values 'being' over 'doing' then the very nature of 'innovation as improvement' becomes very different. We believe that such thinking forces 'innovators' to make more aspects of their thinking problematic than is usually done. From our view that would be a gain.

Their treatment of the 'relational' problem seems different than the way our thinking has gone with the Milford data. The alternatives they suggest are individualism, a kind of autonomy; collaterality, a kind of contemporaneous sociality; and lineality, a kind of sociality extended through time and generations. An individualistic ethic seemed to run through most of the social relations of the people in Milford. Yet, the Spanman position seemed to stress the needs to be a part of a larger social enterprise — consultants, research and development centers, and school university cooperative relationships. In the later Georgian period the individualism was expressed much more in the form of self sufficiency, going it alone.

Perhaps what we are saying is that the relational becomes combined with the spatial, a category less developed by Kluckhohn and Strodtbeck. They comment: 'A sixth common human problem . . . is that of man's conception of *space* and his place in it. Unfortunately, this problem and the ranges of variability in it have not been worked out sufficiently well to be included at the present time' (p. 10). In our view, the localist/cosmopolitan distinction has been one of the most important distinctions in value orientation between Spanman and his predecessor McBride and between him and his successor, George. We believe that this is our most important addition to the Kluckhohn and Strodtbeck position.

The significance of all this for our concerns for innovation and change in schooling seems, at first blush, straightforward. A number of scholars, especially the anthropologists, have been arguing that cultures, as ways of life, have built-in meanings and values. These are useful ways to look at and think about any one culture or society. As their work has entered into descriptions, analyses, and interpretations of contemporary American culture (as well as more general contemporary Western culture), one sees the broader aspects of the choices that we as individuals make. These choices are responsive to the kinds of communities from which we spring, and, in turn, they determine the kind of individuals and communities which will follow from those choices. We believe that the conceptualization and actualization of innovation and change in schooling is irrevocably linked to the kind of ideas raised by Kluckhohn and Strodtbeck. Educators, in the universities and in the local school districts, as well as parents and citizens, must look to that level of discussion as they think about reforming the schools. For us, 'thinking about reforming the schools' includes both value oriented theorizing in the most ivy covered settings and the most pragmatic practical action contemplated by teachers, administrators, or Board members.

The Morris position captures our problem at a more individual and personal level. For our purposes, the labels are fairly self-explanatory. In his book, he presents a questionnaire with paragraph-long descriptions which can be rated. The empirical part of his work results in five factors derived from a number of samples tested. We believe that his perspective will further close the gap to the Hare position and allow us and others to make judgments about actors, issues, and events in innovation and change in Milford and other school districts, both in ways of schooling and ways to live.

Factor A he calls 'social restraint and self control.' It blends 'preserving the best that man has attained' (Way 1) and 'control the self stoically' (Way 10). This seems close to our traditional and conservative. A further sentence from Morris almost ties our entire thesis to this value cluster — 'the accent is upon the appreciation and conservation of what man has attained rather than upon the initiation of change' (p. 33).

Factor B, 'enjoyment and progress in action' loads on 'chance adventuresome deeds' (Way 12), 'act and enjoy life through groups participation' (Way 5), and 'constantly master changing conditions' (Way 6). This seems most related to our proactive stance. A further sentence or two captures this similarity. 'The stress is upon delight in vigorous action for the overcoming of obstacles. The emphasis is upon the initiation of change rather than upon the preservation of what has already been attained' (p. 33).

Factor C, 'withdrawal and self-sufficiency' with high loadings on Way 11, 'meditate on the inner life' and Way 2, 'cultivate independence of persons and things' seems not a part of the Milford scence. The mystic life seems foreign to our data and our accounts of educators and board members. As Morris says, 'The stress is upon a rich inner life of heightened self-awareness ... the simplification and purification of the self in order to attain a high level of insight and awareness' (p. 33).

Factor D is labeled 'receptivity and sympathetic concern.' Its main loadings are Way 13, 'obey the cosmic purposes' and Way 9, 'wait in quiet receptivity.' A kind of submissiveness is implied. It seemed not to appear in our data, except perhaps in the kind of responsiveness of Superintendent George to the Board. But that equation doesn't feel right.

Factor E, 'self indulgence or sensuous enjoyment' combines 'live with wholesome, carefree enjoyment' (Way 8) and 'experience festivity and solitude in alternation' (Way 4). Most of the Milford School District, at least in the data we had, seemed far too serious for this. The various faculty groups at the Kensington School seemed to reflect this more than the Board or the central administration. Perhaps this is in part a reflection of the 'live-in' data we had from our two ethnographies of the school. Humor and camaraderie were present to a high degree on each occasion. But this view seems not quite to the point of 'The stress is upon sensuous enjoyment, whether this enjoyment be found in the simple pleasures of life or in abandonment to the moment' (p. 34).

In his usual provocative style, Bruner (1983) makes a similar plea, after a brief reference to Morris' work. He comments: 'I suppose my hopes for a clarification (or even a taxonomy) of the nature of human values grew from a conviction that psychology could not live healthily in isolation from the normative or policy disciplines — jurisprudence, literary criticism, legal and moral philosophy, political science. Like many anthropologists and like 'conceptual pragmatists' generally, I believe that we constitute and negotiate our own social reality and that meaning is finally 'settled' by these constitutive and negotiatory processes' (1983, p. 281). He seems to be arguing for psychology what we have been arguing for education in general and for educational innovation in particular.[11] As we have indicated these issues run much deeper in philosophy and the social sciences. Bernstein (1978) speaks of 'the restructuring of social and political theory' and Fay (1975) speaks of the reconceptualization of 'social theory and political practice.' Their positions seem important for 'the many faces of democracy in innovation and schooling.'

Finally, this volume began as an 'historical and contemporary context' for the changes occurring in the innovative Kensington School. But it grew well beyond its initial purpose. As we began to see the theme of innovation and change in schooling, it raised intellectual questions of wide scope. Some of these have troubled us for years. Others are relative newcomers. We believe we have moved with varying depth on individual items and with varying degrees of integration and synthesis on the totality. Tentatively, we feel and believe these to be important steps.

Innovation: A Final Definition?

We are continually amazed as we work our way through data collecting, analysis, reading relevant literature, initial writing, and later editing and rewriting, how slowly come some of the essential conceptual ingredients. Innovation is a word we adopted early and somehow seemed to be stuck with, in spite of excursions into change, reform, and utopia. And we might add, in spite of parts of the educational community that treats innovation stereotypically as somehow 'all good' or 'all bad.' The all good group tend to be true believers with the one right way which they are currently advocating. The all bad group tends to be those with minimal power, frequently teachers, who are having the innovation done to or on them, with or without their consent.

Now when we think about innovation and the definition we have tried to use pretty consistently throughout our work, 'specific planned improved change' we believe we have finally gotten a broader context for the term. For us the label implies three domains of ideas. The 'planned' aspect implies intentional behavior, that is, action. Concretely, for example, when the School Board discusses, moves, seconds, and votes it is engaging in intentional action. The image of meeting after meeting, of minute after minute, moving through that same pocess, month after month and year after year was very humbling, dramatic and potent. The men and women of Milford created and recreated their schools.

The concept, 'improved,' implies a theory of value, a notion of what is important. In Milford what was important and of value was sometimes taken for granted, understood by everyone, a part of the small town ambience. At other times what was important, what was valued, was in stark conflict and highly contested. People debated, argued, played politics, lost their jobs, left the community, and sometimes came back to fight another day, and sometimes won in those later days. An educational theory worthy of those important educational life events must be able to deal with such value issues.

Finally, 'specific' seemed to imply the idea of limited scope. Within a totality, there were specific elements that were interrelated and there were specific elements that could be changed, if one put one's mind to it. Thinking one's way through issues, focusing on specific items invokes the possibilities and power of rationality.

Now when we hear 'innovation' we hear these three large bodies of interrelated ideas lurking in specific, planned, improved change. And that, we try to bring to bear on particular discussions of particular innovations in particular settings at particular times. In a sense these concluding thoughts take us back to the vignette, 'the tangle of administrative succession,' which opened this volume. That was a time of high drama in Milford, for Superintendents McBride, Spanman, and George and for what would be the innovative Kensington Elementary School. Intuitively it seemed to say much about the phenomenon of educational innovation. Those intuitions led us into the issues of 'history, politics, and agency,' which came to be the subtitle of this book. These issues captured three guiding ideas that have run throughout our attempt at thinking about 'innovation and change in schooling.' For us, all this is a major gain in understanding the 'anatomy of educational innovation.' And, perhaps that is a proper conclusion of this conclusion.

Notes

1   Among others, Wirt and Krist (1982, p. VI) accent an explosion of the kind of intellectual effort Eliot (1959) was calling for.
2   For example, see our treatment of Gross (1977) in Smith and Dwyer, *Federal Policy in Action* (1980).
3   Our view here is a particular application and interpretation of the more general position of Brian Fay's *Social Theory and Political Practice* (1975).
4   Lest we hoist ourselves on one of our own petards, recall that the mid and late 1950s was the beginning the 'theory movement in educational administration,' with its implicit

logical positivist epistemology and its substantive roots in such theorists as Barnard (1938) and Simon (1942). The Greenfields (1975 and 1978) of the world are a recent phenomenon in educational administration. And even today some scholars ignore the whole enterprise (Wirt and Kirst, 1982, p. 26).

5　Our description and analysis of 'neighborhood schools' appears in Book II, *The Fate of an Innovative School* (1987).

6　Partly here we call upon our teaching experience with teachers who are MA students in our program and the discomfort many feel when introduced to Cartwright and Zanders (1968) analysis of power and influence and French and Ravens (1959), 'Bases of Social Power.'

7　We have added the enumeration for clarity in later commentary.

8　This seems a typographical error — dying?, decaying?

9　Our analysis of the evidence concluded in agreement with his judgment of the reasons. Particularly convincing were triangulated comments from a teacher who taught with the then CTA President.

10　Others saw the mark a little less high (Halpin, 1965), and still others, (Wirt and Kirst, 1982, p. 26), ignored it altogether.

11　Bruner builds a much fuller and more general picture of his position in his recent *Actual Minds, Possible Worlds* (1986).

References

ALLISON, G. T. (1971) *Essence of Decision: Explaining the Cuban Missile Crisis*, Boston, Little Brown.

ANDERSON, H. H. and BREWER, H. M. (1945) 'Studies of teachers' classroom personalities, I: dominative and socially integrative behavior of kindergarten teachers,' *Applied Psychological Monographs*, 6.

BARKER, R. G. and GUMP, P. V. (1964) *Big School, Small School*, Stanford, Calif., Stanford University Press.

BATES, R. 'The new sociology of education: directions for theory and research,' *New Zealand Journal of Educational Studies* (in press).

BEITTEL, K. R. (1973) *Alternatives for Art Education Research*, Dubuque. Ia., Wm. C. Brown, Inc.

BERNSTEIN, R. (1978) *The Restructuring of Social and Political Theory*. Philadelphia, University of Pennsylvania Press.

BLAU, P. M. (1956) *Bureaucracy in Modern Society*, New York, Random House.

BLOOM, B. S. and BRODER, L. J. (1950) 'Problem-solving processes of college students,' *Supplementary Educational Monographs*, 73.

BOORSTIN, D. J. (1973) *The Americans: The Democratic Experience*, New York, Random House.

BRUNER, J. (1966) *Toward a Theory of Instruction*, Cambridge, Mass, Harvard University Press.

BRUNER, J. (1983) *In Search of Mind*, New York, Harper and Row.

BRUNER, J. (1986) *Actual Minds, Possible Worlds*, New York, Harper and Row.

BRUYN, S. T. (1966) *The Human Perspective in Sociology: The Methodology of Participant Observation*, Englewood Cliffs, NJ, Prentice Hall.

BURKE, K. (1967) *A Grammar of Motives*, Berkeley, University of California Press, (originally published by Prentice Hall, 1945).

BUTTON, H. W. (1961) 'A history of supervision in the public schools 1870–1950,' Unpublished PhD dissertation, Washington University, St. Louis, Mo.

BUTTS, R. F. (1978) *Public Education in the United States*, New York, Holt, Rinehart and Winston.

CALLAHAN, R. (1962) *Education and the Cult of Efficiency*, Chicago, University of Chicago Press.

CALLAHAN, R. E. (1964) *Changing Conceptions of the Superintendency of Public Education 1865–1964*, Cambridge, Mass., New England School Development Council.

CALLAHAN, R. E. and BUTTON, H. W. (1964) 'Historical change of the role of the man in the organization,' in GRIFFITHS, D. (Ed.) *Behavioral Science and Educational Administration*, Chicago, National Society for the Study of Education.

CAMPBELL, D. T. (1974) *Qualitative Knowing in Action Research*, Kurt Lewin Award Address SPSSI.

CAMPBELL, D. T. and STANLEY, J. C. (1963) 'Experimental and quasi-experimental designs for research in teaching,' in GAGE, N. (Ed.), *Handbook of Research in Teaching, Chicago*, Rand McNally.

CHAPPLE, E. and ARENSBERG, C. (1940) 'Measuring human relations: an introduction to the study of interaction of individuals,' *Genetic Psychological Monographs, 22*, pp. 1–147.

CORNELL, F. G. *et al.* (1953) *An Exploratory Measurement of Individualities of Schools and Classrooms*, Urbana, Ill., University of Illinois Press.

CREMIN, L. A. (1980) *American Education: The National Experiences 1783–1876*, New York, Harper and Row.

DAVIES, D. R. and HOSLER, F. W. (1949) *The Challenge of School Board Membership*, New York, Chartwell House.

DAVIES, D. R. and PRESTWOOD, E. L. (1951) *Practical School Board Procedures*, New York, Chartwell House.

DENZIN, N. (1970) *The Research Act: A Theoretical Introduction to Sociological Methods*, Chicago, Aldine.

DIESING, P. (1971) *Patterns of Discovery in the Social Sciences*, Chicago, Aldine-Atherton.

DRAY, W. (1957) *Laws and Explanation in History*, Oxford, Oxford University Press.

DWYER, D. (1981) *The Effects of Ideology on Organizational Evolution: A Comparative Study of Two Innovative Educational Organizations*, Washington University, St. Louis, Mo.

DWYER, D. (1984) 'The search for instructional leadership: routines and subtleties in the principal's role,' *Educational Leadership, 41* 5, pp. 32–8.

EASLEY, J. and TATSUOKA, M. (1968) *Scientific Thought: Cases from Classical Physics*, Boston, Allyn and Bacon.

ELIOT, T. E. (1959) 'Toward an understanding of public school politics,' *American Political Science Review, 53*, pp. 1032–51.

EMERY, F. and TRIST, E. (1975) *Towards a Social Ecology*, London, Plenum.

FAY, B. (1975) *Social Theory and Political Practice*, London, George Allen and Unwin.

FEIN, L. J. (1971) *The Ecology of the Public Schools: An Inquiry into Community Control*, New York, Bobbs-Merrill.

GARDINER, P. (1952) *The Nature of Historical Explanation*, London, Oxford University Press.

GEERTZ, C. (1973) *The Interpretation of Cultures*, New York, Basic Books.

GEERTZ, C. (1983) *Local Knowledge*, New York, Basic Books.

GERGEN, K. J. (1973) 'Social psychology as history,' *Journal of Personality and Social Psychology, 26*, pp. 309–20.

GITTELL, M. *et al.* (1973) *School Boards and School Policy — An Evaluation of Decentralization in New York City*, New York, Praeger.

GLASER, B. and STRAUSS, A. (1967) *The Discovery of Grounded Theory*. Chicago, Aldine.

GOFFMAN, E. (1949) *The Presentation of Self in Everyday Life*, New York, Anchor.

GOLDHAMMER, K. (1964) *The School Board*, New York, Center for Applied Research in Education, Inc.

GOTTSCHALK, L. (1947) 'The historian and the historical document,' in GOTTSCHALK, L. *et al.*, *The Use of Personal Documents in History, Anthropology, and Sociology #53*, New York, Social Science Research Council.

GREENFIELD, T. B. (1973) 'Organization and social inventions: rethinking assumptions about change,' *Journal of Applied Behavioral Science, 9*, pp. 551–74.

GREENFIELD, T. B. (1978) 'Reflections on organization theory and the truths of irreconcilable realities,' *Educational Administration Quarterly, 14* 2, pp. 43–65.

GRIFFITHS, D. (Ed.) (1964) *Behavorial Science and Educational Administration*, Chicago, University of Chicago Press.

GRIFFITHS, D. E. (1977) 'The individual in organization: a theoretical perspective,' *Educational Administration Quarterly, 13* 2, pp. 1–18.

GRIFFITHS, D. (1979) 'Intellectual turmoil in educational administration,' *Educational Administration Quarterly, 15* 3, pp. 43–65.

HARE, R. M. (1964) *The Language of Morals*, London, Oxford University Press, (orig. 1952).

HEMPEL, C. G. (1942) 'The function of general laws in history,' *Journal of Philosophy, 39*, pp. 35–48.

HEMPEL, C. G. (1965) *Aspects of Scientific Explanation*, New York, Free Press.

HEXTER, J. (1971) *The History Primer*, New York, Basic Books.

HIRST, P. (1983) 'Educational theory,' in HIRST, P. (Ed.), *Educational Theory and Its Foundational Disciplines*, London, Routledge and Kegan Paul.

HOMANS, G. C. (1941) *English Villagers of the Thirteenth Century*, Cambridge, Mass., Harvard University Press.

HOMANS, G. C. (1950) *The Human Group*, New York, Harcourt Press.

HOUSE, E. (1979) 'Technology versus craft: a ten year perspective on innovation,' *Journal of Curriculum Studies, 11*, pp. 1–15.

IANNACCONE, L. (1958) 'The social system of an elementary school staff,' unpublished EdD dissertation, Teachers College, Columbia University.

IANNACCONE, L. (1967) *Politics in Education*, New York, Center for Applied Research in Education.

IANNACCONE, L. and LUTZ, F. (1970) *Politics, Power and Policy: The Governing of Local School Districts*, Columbus, Ohio, Charles E. Merrill.

JOERGENSEN, J. (1951) *The Development of Logical Empiricism*, Chicago, University of Chicago Press.

KAPLAN, A. (1964) *The Conduct of Inquiry*, San Francisco, Chandler.

KELLY, G. A. (1955) *The Psychology of Personal Constructs*, New York, Norton.

KLUCKHOHN, F. R. and STRODTBECK, F. L. (1961) *Variations in Value Orientations*, Evanston, Ill., Row, Peterson and Co.

KUHN, T. S. (1970) *The Structure of Scientific Revolutions* (2nd ed.) Chicago, University of Chicago press.

KUPER, A. (1973) *Anthropologists and Anthropology: The British School 1922–1972*, London, Allen Lane.

LINDBLOM, C. E. (1968) (2nd ed. 1980) *The Policy Making Process*, Englewood Cliffs, NJ, Prentice Hall.

LINDBLOM, C. E. (1969) 'The science of muddling through,' in CARVER, F. and SERGIOVANNI, T. (Eds.). *Organizations and Human Behavior: Focus on Schools*, New York, McGraw-Hill.

MAIER, N. R. F. (1963) *Problem Solving Discussions and Conferences: Leadership Methods and Skills*, New York, McGraw-Hill.

MAIER, N., SOLEM, A., and MAIER, A. (1957) *Supervisory and Executive Development*, New York, Wiley.

MALINOWSKI, B. (1922) *The Argonauts of the Western Pacific*, London, Routledge.

MEEHL, P. E. (1954) *Clinical vs. Statistical Prediction*, Minneapolis, Minn., University of Minnesota Press.

MEEHL, P. E. (1971) 'Law and the fireside inductions: some reflections of a clinical psychologist,' *Journal of Social Issues, 127*, pp. 65–100.

MERTON, R. K. (1957) *Social Theory and Social Structure* (Rev.) Glencoe, Ill., Free Press.

MILLS, C. W. (1959) *The Sociological Imagination*, London, Oxford University press.

MORRIS, C. (1956) *Varieties of Human Value*, Chicago, University of Chicago Press.

MYRDAL, G. (1944) *An American Dilemma: The Negro Problem and Modern Democracy*, Vol. 1 and 2. New York, Harper and Row.

O'CONNOR, D. J. (1973) 'The nature and scope of educational theory,' in LANGFELD, G. and O'CONNOR, D. J. (Eds)., *New Essays in the Philosophy of Education*, London, Routledge and Kegan Paul.

OLSON, E. (1961) *Tragedy and the Theory of Drama*, Detroit, Wayne State University Press.

PEPPER, S. (1942) *World Hypotheses: A Study in Evidence*, Berkeley, University of California Press.

PESHKIN, A. (1978) *Growing Up American: Schooling and the Survival of Community*, Chicago, University of Chicago Press.

PRUNTY, J. (1981) *A Participant Observation Study of a Public Alternative High School: An Analysis of Factors Influencing Organizational Effectiveness*, St. Louis, Washington University.

PRUNTY, J. (1984) *A Critical Reformulation of Educational Policy Analysis*, Victoria, Australia, Deakin University Press.

REID, W. (1978) *Thinking about Curriculum*, London, Routledge and Kegan Paul.

REITMAN, W. R. (1965) *Cognition and Thought*, New York, Wiley.

REMMERS, H. H. and GAGE, N. (1955) *Educational Measurement and Evaluation* (Rev.) New York, Harpers.

ROKEACH, M. (1975) *Beliefs, Attitudes, and Values*, San Francisco, Jossey-Bass.

RYLE, G. (1949) *The Concept of Mind*, London, Hutchinson.

SANDAY, P. R. (1974) 'The ethnographic paradigm(s),' *Administrative Science Quarterly, 24*, pp. 527–38.

SARBIN, T. R. (1977) 'Contextualism: a world view for modern psychology,' in COLE, J. (Ed.), *Personal Construct Psychology. Nebraska Symposium on Motivation, 1976*, Lincoln, Nebraska, University of Nebraska Press.

SCHWAB, J. (1969) 'The practical: a language for curriculum,' *School Review, 78*, pp. 1–23.

SCRIVEN, M. (1959) 'Truisms as the grounds for historical explanations,' in GARDINER, P. (Ed.), *Theories of History*, New York, Free Press.

SELZNICK, P. (1950) 'The iron law of bureaucracy: Michels' warning to the left.' *Modern Review, 3*, pp. 157–65.

SMITH, L. M. (1978) 'Science education in the Alte Schools: a kind of case study,' in STAKE, R. and EASLEY, J. (Eds.), *Case Studies in Science Education*, Washington, DC, NSF.

SMITH, L. M. (1979) 'An evolving logic of participant observation, educational ethnography and other case studies,' in SHULMAN, L. (Ed.), *Review of Research in Education*, Chicago, Peacock Press.

SMITH, L. M. (1981) 'Accidents, serendipity, and making the commonplace problematic: the origin and evolution of the field study problem,' in POPKEWITZ, T. and TABACHNICK, B. R., *The Study of Schooling*, New York, Praeger.

SMITH, L. M. (1982) 'Ethnography,' in MITZEL, H. (Ed.). *Encyclopedia of Educational Research*, Chicago, Rand McNally.

SMITH, L. M. (1987) 'Process of curriculum change: an historial sketch of science education in the Alte Schools,' in GOODSON, I. (Ed.), *International Perspectives in Curriculum History*, London, Croom Helm.

SMITH, L. M. and DWYER, D. C. (1980) *Federal Policy in Action: A Case Study of an Urban Education Project*, Washington, DC, NIE.

SMITH, L. M. and DWYER, D. C. and PRUNTY, J. J. (1981) 'Observer role and field study knowledge, an essay review of *Usable Knowledge* and *SAFARI I*,' *Educational Evaluation and Policy Analyses, 3*, pp. 83–90.

SMITH, L. M., DWYER, D. C., PRUNTY, J. J., and KLEINE, P. F. (1987) *The Fate of an Innovative School: Kensington's First Fifteen Years*, London, The Falmer Press.

SMITH, L. M. and GEOFFREY, W. (1968) *The Complexities of an Urban Classroom*, New York, Holt.

SMITH, L. M. and HUDGINS, B. B. (1964) *Educational Psychology*, New York, Knopf.

SMITH, L. M. and KEITH, P. (1971) *Anatomy of Educational Innovation*, New York, Wiley.

SMITH, L. M. and KLEINE, P. F. (1986) 'Qualitative research and evaluation: triangulation and multi-methods reconsidered,' in WILLIAMS, D. (Ed.), *New Directions for Program Evaluation*, San Francisco, Jossey-Bass.

SMITH, L. M., KLEINE, P., PRUNTY, J. J., and DWYER, D. (1986) *Educational Innovators: Then and Now*, London, The Falmer Press.

SMITH, L. M. and POHLAND, P. A. (1974) 'Education, technology and the rural highlands,' in SJOGREN, D. (Ed.), *Four Evaluation Examples: Anthropological, Economic, Narrative, and Portrayal*, Chicago, Rand McNally.

SMITH, L. M., PRUNTY, J. J., DWYER, D. C., and KLEINE, P. F. (1984) 'Reconstruing educational innovation.' *Teachers College Record, 86*, pp. 20–33.

STAKE, R. (1977) 'Description versus analysis,' in HAMILTON, D. *et al.* (Eds.), *Beyond the Numbers Game*, London, MacMillan.

STONE, L. (1981) *The Past and the Present*, Boston, Routledge and Kegan Paul.

TOCQUEVILLE, A. DE. (1969) *Democracy in America*, New York, Anchor Books.

TYACK, D. and HANSOT, E. (1982) *Managers of Virtue — Public School Leadership in America, 1820–1980*, New York, Basic Books.

WHITE, M. (1963) 'The logic of historical narration,' in HOOK, S. (Ed.), *Philosophy and History*, New York, New York University Press.

WIRT, F. and KIRST, M. (1982) *Schools in Conflict*, Berkeley, McCutcheon.

WITHALL, J. (1948) 'The development of a technique for the measurement of social-emotional climate in classrooms,' unpublished PhD dissertation, University of Chicago.

ZETTERBERG, H. (1965) *On Theory and Verification in Sociology*, (3rd ed.) Totowa, NJ, Bedminster press.

Index

Index

White, M., 34
Who Runs Our Schools: perspectives, 313
Whyte, W. Foote, 34
Wilkerson, Mr, 13, 14, 199, 206, 207, 210,
  'strong board member', 174, 187, 189,
  190
Wirt, F. and Kirst, M., 291–3, 322–3

Wirth, 25, 26
Withall, J., 39

Zeigler and Goldhammer: contrasts,
  304–10
Ziegler, Kehoe and Reisman, 304